MULTINATIONALS AND THE RESTRUCTURING OF THE WORLD ECONOMY

VAN MILDERT COLLEGE LIBRARY

CROOM HELM SERIES IN GEOGRAPHY AND ENVIRONMENT
Edited by Alan Wilson, Nigel Thrift, Michael Bradford and Edward W. Soja

URBAN HOUSING PROVISION
AND THE DEVELOPMENT
PROCESS
David Drakakis-Smith

DAVID HARVEY'S GEOGRAPHY
John L. Paterson

PLANNING IN THE SOVIET
UNION
Judith Pallot and Denis J.B. Shaw

CATASTROPHE THEORY AND
BIFURCATION
A.G. Wilson

REGIONAL LANDSCAPES AND
HUMANISTIC GEOGRAPHY
Edward Relph

CRIME AND ENVIRONMENT
R.N. Davidson

HUMAN MIGRATION
G.J. Lewis

THE GEOGRAPHY OF
MULTINATIONALS
Edited by Michael Taylor and
Nigel Thrift

URBANISATION AND PLANNING
IN THE THIRD WORLD SPATIAL
PERCEPTIONS AND PUBLIC
PARTICIPATION
Robert B. Potter

OFFICE DEVELOPMENT: A
GEOGRAPHICAL ANALYSIS
Michael Bateman

URBAN GEOGRAPHY
David Clark

RETAIL AND COMMERCIAL
PLANNING
R.L. Davies

INSTITUTIONS AND
GEOGRAPHICAL PATTERNS
Edited by Robin Flowerdew

MATHEMATICAL
PROGRAMMING METHODS FOR
GEOGRAPHERS AND PLANNERS
James Killen

THE LAND PROBLEM IN THE
DEVELOPED ECONOMY
Andrew H. Dawson

GEOGRAPHY SINCE THE
SECOND WORLD WAR
Edited by R.J. Johnston
and P. Claval

THE GEOGRAPHY OF
WESTERN EUROPE
Paul L. Knox

THE GEOGRAPHY OF
UNDERDEVELOPMENT
Dean Forbes

REGIONAL RESTRUCTURING
UNDER ADVANCED CAPITALISM
Edited by Phil O'Keefe

THE SPATIAL ORGANISATION
OF CORPORATIONS
Ian M. Clarke

THE GEOGRAPHY OF ENGLISH
POLITICS
R.J. Johnston

WOMEN ATTACHED: THE DAILY
LIVES OF WOMEN WITH YOUNG
CHILDREN
Jacqueline Tivers

THE GEOGRAPHY OF HEALTH
SERVICES IN BRITAIN
Robin Haynes

POLITICS, GEOGRAPHY AND
SOCIAL STRATIFICATION
Edited by Keith Hoggart and
Eleonore Kofman

PLANNING IN EASTERN EUROPE
Andrew H. Dawson

PLANNING CONTROL:
PHILOSOPHIES, PROSPECTS AND
PRACTICE
Edited by M.L. Harrison and
R. Murdey

UNEVEN DEVELOPMENT AND
REGIONALISM
Costis Hadjimichalis

MANAGING THE CITY: THE AIMS AND
IMPACTS OF URBAN POLICY
Edited by Brian Robson

INTERNATIONAL GEOPOLITICAL
ANALYSIS
Edited and translated by
Pascal Girot and Eleonore Kofman

ANALYTICAL BEHAVIOURAL
GEOGRAPHY
R.G. Golledge and R.J. Stimson

MONEY AND VOTES: Constituency
Campaign Spending and Election
Results
R.J. Johnston

THE UNCERTAIN FUTURE OF THE UR-
BAN CORE
Edited by Christopher M. Law

Multinationals and the Restructuring of the World Economy

THE GEOGRAPHY OF MULTINATIONALS,
VOLUME 2

Edited by Michael Taylor and Nigel Thrift

CROOM HELM
London ● New York ● Sydney

© Michael Taylor and Nigel Thrift 1986
Croom Helm Ltd, Provident House, Burrell Row,
Beckenham, Kent, BR3 1AT
Croom Helm Australia, 44-50 Waterloo Road,
North Ryde, 2113, New South Wales
Reprint 1987

British Library Cataloguing in Publication Data

The Geography of multinationals. — (Croom Helm
  series in geography and environment)
  Vol. 2: Multinationals and the restructuring of
  the world economy.
  1. International business enterprises 2. Geography,
  Commercial
  I. Taylor, Michael, *1946 Feb 28* — II. Thrift, Nigel
  338.8'8   HD2755.5
  ISBN 0-7099-2457-7

Published in the USA by
Croom Helm
in association with Methuen, Inc.
29 West 35th Street
New York, NY 10001

Library of Congress Cataloging in Publication Data
Main Entry under Title:

Multinationals and the restructuring of the world
economy.

  (Croom Helm Series in geography and environment) bibliography: P.
  Includes indexes.
  1. International Business enterprises — addresses,
essays, lectures. 2. International economic relations,
addresses, essays, lectures. I. Taylor, Michael,
1946– II. Thrift, N.J. III. Series.
HD2755.5.M8442 1986   338.8'81   85-29081
ISBN 0-7099-2457-7

Typeset in Times Roman by Leaper & Gard Ltd, Bristol, England
Printed in Great Britain by
Antony Rowe Ltd, Chippenham, Wiltshire

CONTENTS

Preface

1 Introduction: New Theories of Multinational Corporations
Michael Taylor and Nigel Thrift   1

2 Labour Dynamics and Plant Centrality in Multinational
Corporations
Ian M. Clarke   21

3 Multinationals, Business Organisations and the
Development of the Fiji Economy
Michael Taylor   49

4 The International Expansion of an Enterprise of the
Semi-periphery: South African Breweries Limited
Barbara Tucker   86

5 Spatial Aspects of Third World Multinational
Corporations' Direct Investment in Indonesia
Dean Forbes   105

6 The Internationalisation of Producer Services and
the Integration of the Pacific Basin Property Market
Nigel Thrift   142

7 The Internationalisation of Japanese Commercial Banking
Masahiro Fujita and Kenichi Ishigaki   193

8 The Global Investments of a British International
Development Agency
C.M. Rogerson   228

9 Fruits of Independence? Philippine Capitalists and the
Banana Export Industry
Peter Krinks   256

10 The Role of Foreign Manufacturing in Britain's
Great Recession
Alan R. Townsend and Francis W. Peck   282

11 Economic Crisis and Corporate Restructuring: Multi-
national Corporations and The Paper, Printing and
Packaging Sector in Bristol
Keith Bassett   311

12 One Perspective on the Enterprise Perspective
      Bob McNee   344

References   360
Author Index   379
Subject Index   382

PREFACE

'Something fundamental happened.' This is the judgement of the International Labour Organisation (1984, p. 36) on the changes in the world economy that took place in the 1970s and into the 1980s. And it is a judgement that it is difficult to dispute. The restructuring of the world economy that was both the cause and effect of these changes touched every national economy in some degree, all the way from the great economic Leviathan, the United States, down to the lowliest developing country (Thrift, 1985). One of the chief vehicles of this restructuring of both national economies and the international economy that links them all together was the multinational corporation (MNC). This volume is an attempt to chart some of the ways in which multinational corporations contributed to the restructuring of the world economy, paying particular attention to the spatial consequences of, and responses to, their operations at a number of scales. However, in contrast to a previous volume (Taylor and Thrift, 1982), which explored the spatial consequences and responses in a very general way, this volume is more focused. It takes as its theme the *differential spatial outcomes of the restructuring of different types of multinational corporation.*

The justification for this choice of theme comes from two different and quite distinct sources. First, in economics the study of the multinational corporation has been through a period of theoretical turmoil, based in part on the rediscovery of Coase's (1937) concept of internalisation, and is now entering a period of elaboration and diversification of the new theories that have resulted (see for example Dunning, 1981; Rugman, 1982; Casson, 1983; Caves, 1983). Second, industrial geography has also been through a period of theoretical retooling, based on the integration of the geography of enterprise with quasi-Marxist perspectives, and is now entering a similar period of elaboration and diversification (see Taylor and Thrift, 1983). The challenge is to link these two areas of work, for they are, of course, potentially complementary. Thus, the new theory of multinational enterprise still lacks an integrated location theory (see Buckley, 1983, p.49), while industrial geography still lacks much appreciation of the way in which a particular internal organisation of a multinational corporation, for example, conditions its locational behaviour (see Taylor and Thrift, 1983).

As an outcome of the decision to focus this volume on the different spatial consequences of, and responses to, the restructuring of particular, different types of multinational corporation we have adopted a fourfold demarcation of the chapters. This demarcation corresponds to the *chief* characteristics of the multinationals being studied in each chapter, namely size, nationality, industrial sector and impact. In addition, the volume includes an envoi on the geography of the multinational corporation by McNee, the founder of the geography of enterprise. As with any demarcation, ours is open to dispute; for example, a number of chapters address more than one characteristic. What is not open to dispute is the increasing importance of understanding the locational behaviour of multinational corporations in a period in which they enjoy unprecedented economic dominance over the international economy and many national economies.

1 INTRODUCTION: NEW THEORIES OF MULTINATIONAL CORPORATIONS

Michael Taylor and Nigel Thrift

Introduction

The last 15 years have seen fundamental changes in the *stock* of multinational corporations as a result of the rigours of a worldwide recession and the consequent bout of corporate restructuring (Thrift, 1985a). These changes constitute a major challenge to researchers striving to understand the workings of national, regional and urban economies around the world, not least because these economies, almost without exception, are becoming more open to 'international pressures' of which the plants and offices of multinational corporations are the most important concrete manifestation. Six changes — all interrelated — are of particular importance.

First, multinational corporations have grown in number. There are no exact figures but certainly there are now many more multinationals than formerly. Many of the new multinationals are the so-called 'small multinationals' — smaller firms which have responded more rapidly to foreign production opportunities than might once have been the case (Newbould, Buckley and Thirwell, 1978).

Second, the size of multinational corporations has increased substantially. Many of the largest multinationals are now much larger, at least in terms of assets and sales, than they were 15 years ago.[1] Some of the largest multinational corporations have gone 'global' (Taylor and Thrift, 1982; Hout, Porter and Rudden, 1982), evolving integrated production and marketing strategies to enhance their share of profits. In the process they have taken on new organisational forms. The process of going global is now well advanced. Already by 1980, 32 per cent of the 180 multinational corporations covered in the Harvard Multinational Enterprise Project had switched to global production structures (Davidson and Haspeslagh, 1982).

Third, and in line with the changes in the number and size of

1

Table 1.1: The Average Foreign Content of the World's 350 Largest Industrial Corporations (in millions of US dollars and per cent)

Item and Year	Total ($)	Foreign ($)	Foreign Share (per cent)
Sales			
1971	1,769	527	30
1980	7,084	2,822	40
Net assets			
1971	956	300	31
1980	2,417	803	33
Net earnings			
1971	83	41	49
1980	266	140	53
Employment			
1971	61,318	23,958	39
1980	68,669	31,914	46

Source: United Nations Centre on Transnational Corporations (1983), p. 48.

Table 1.2: The Average Foreign Content of 50 of the Largest British-based Industrial Corporations (in millions of £ and per cent)

Item and Year	Total (£ million)		Foreign Share (per cent)
Total sales 1981/82	1,440		
		Overseas production as per cent of sales	44
Overseas production 1981/82	639		
		Exports as per cent of sales	15
Exports 1981/82[a]	209		
Total Employment	43,119		—
Foreign Employment[b]	17,851		41

Notes: a. Only 42 corporations provided export figures.
b. Only 45 corporations provided foreign employment figures.
Source: Labour Research (1983a), pp. 98-9; Labour Research (1983b), pp. 124-5.

multinational corporations, much more of the foreign production of multinational corporations is likely to be abroad, compared with domestic operations. This tendency shows up in data on assets, sales, employment, and so on (Tables 1.1 and 1.2). Even Swiss corporations, already recognised as some of the most international of multinational corporations, have continued to expand overseas, with the consequent stagnation of home-based employment. (Table 1.3).

Fourth, multinational corporations have extended into every kind of industrial sector, partly as a function of increasing multinational corporation diversification,[2] partly as a function of increasing rates of multinational merger and acquisition (see Andreff, 1984) and partly as a function of the growth of nationally-based firms into multinational corporations in industrial sectors not formerly noted for their degree of multinational penetration. For example, firms in producer service industries, such as management consultancy, real estate consultancy and accounting, have all grown into large multinational corporations quite recently.

Fifth, the mix of the nationality of multinational corporations has changed (Table 1.4). United States-based multinational

Table 1.3: Changes in the Location of Employment of Switzerland's Largest Industrial Multinational Corporations, 1970 to 1980

	The Largest 6 Firms		The 7th-15th Largest Firms		The Largest 15 Firms	
	Employment	%	Employment	%	Employment	%
In Switzerland	7,270	10.0	−4,200	−5.0	3,070	1.9
In industrialised countries	74,420	33.4	23,790	38.4	98,210	34.5
In developing countries	33,600	63.7	6,610	89.1	40,210	66.8
Total abroad	108,020	39.2	30,400	43.8	138,420	40.1
Total employment	115,290	33.1	26,200	17.0	141,490	28.2

Source: Borner *et al.* (1984).

Table 1.4: Accumulated Direct Investment Overseas by Country ($ US billions)

	1970	% Share	1978	% Share	Increase 1970-78 %
USA	78	52	168	42	115
UK	20	13	35	9	75
West Germany	7	5	29	7	314
Japan	4	3	27	7	575
Switzerland	8	5	25	6	213
Others	33	22	116	29	252

Source: Kirby (1983), p. 23.

Table 1.5: Indicators of Australian Direct Investment Abroad: Number of Firms and Level of Investment, 1975-76 and 1981-82

	No. of Australian Enterprises Investing Abroad			Foreign Enterprises in which Investment is Held			Level of Investment A$ m		
	1975-76	1981-82	Annual growth rate (%)	1975-76	1981-82	Annual growth rate (%)	1975-76	1981-82	Annual growth rate (%)
USA	51	92	10	57	105	11	88	476	32.5
Canada	15	21	18	15	21	6	23	49	13.4
United Kingdom	99	102	0	116	128	2	99	336	22.6
Other Europe (except UK)	—	—	0	53	52	0	73	166	14.7
Malaysia	45	48	1	49	58	3	24	54	14.5
Singapore	77	91	3	81	108	5	29	140	30.0
Other ASEAN	—	—	0	70	69	0	66	107	8.4
Hong Kong and Japan	—	—	0	130	174	5	43	112	17.3
Papua New Guinea	109	100	—1	140	131	—1	255	480	11.1
New Zealand	283	295	1	334	352	1	205	380	10.8
Other	—	—	0	144	180	4	105	290	18.4
Total	586	604	1	1188	1377	2	1012	2589	16.9

Source: Bureau of Industry Economics (1984), p. 6.

corporations have declined in importance relatively, while multi-nationals based in Japan, in various 'semi-peripheral' countries like Australia (Table 1.5) or South Africa, and in a few of the countries of the Third World (especially the newly-industrialising countries) have all increased in relative importance.[3]

Sixth, many multinational corporations have taken on a more explicitly *fiscal* character (Taylor and Thrift, 1982), even when they are not in the banking and finance sectors. This new level of involvement with financial matters has arisen partly from the inter-nationalisation of finance that took place in the 1970s, with the result that multinational corporations have come to rely increasingly on the international financial system to raise capital *and* generate profits, and partly through the increasing centralisa-tion of all types of multinational corporation which has been stimulated by new links between multinational banking corpor-ations and all other types of multinational corporation (see Fennema, 1982; Grou, 1983; Andreff, 1984).

What these six changes amount to is something of a paradox. There is a much greater *diversity* in the stock of multinational corpor-ations than formerly (Figure 1.1). At the same time multinational corporations have become more *integrated.* Thus, although in many ways multinational corporations now represent a larger, more coherent economic bloc, it is a bloc which is cross-cut by many more fractures and fissures.[4] The explanation of how multi-national corporations and national, regional and urban economies interact has, therefore, become correspondingly more difficult to achieve. The task of the researcher trying to characterise the operations of the multinational corporations in a country, region or city is made even more problematic because other areas of research which might provide potential guidance are themselves in a state of flux as a result of this set of changes. They can, therefore, provide only a limited source of inspiration. The three main areas of research are industrial economics, organisation theory and Marxist economic theory.

Industrial Economics

The old explanations of the multinational corporation prevailing in the 1960s in industrial economics have failed to account for many of the dimensions of the new multinational diversity (Dunning,

Figure 1.1: The Diversification of Multinational Corporations

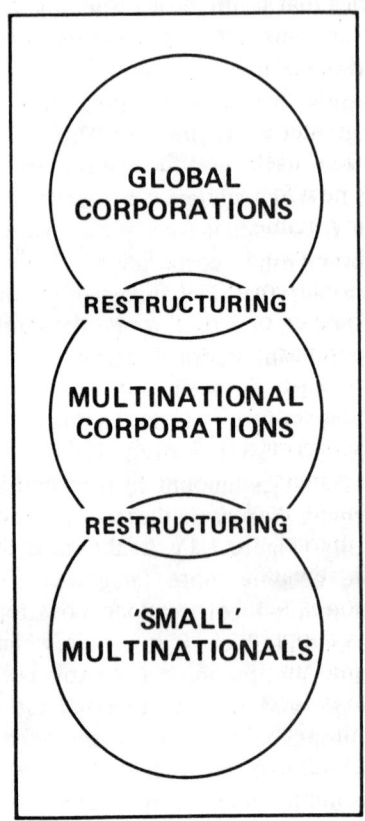

1979). For example, Hymer's approach was based upon identifying the underlying characteristics of multinational corporations which gave them a competitive edge over other firms. Another approach, usually associated with the name of Horst, was based upon the identification of factors which led multinational corporations to locate in particular countries. Finally, Vernon's work on the product-cycle theory added the question 'when' to the question 'why', posed by Hymer, and the question 'where', posed by Horst. But each explanation proved deficient in some respect,[5] partly because they relied almost exclusively on United States-based corporate activity as an archetype and partly because they concentrated upon foreign direct investment to the exclusion of all other forms of multinational activity.[6]

The new theories that have grown up in the 1970s have tended to move away from this exclusive concentration on explaining foreign direct investment to the explanation of all forms of involvement by firms outside their national borders. This has necessarily meant that much greater attention is now being given to the multinational corporation itself as the locus of all these forms of involvement. This new focus of attention clearly leads towards two main areas of study, namely the theory of the firm and organisation theory. Of these two areas of study, it is the synthesis of the study of multinational corporations and the theory of the firm, going under the banner of *internalisation theory*, that has so far proved the most popular.

Internalisation is a simple term that applies to a simple insight, namely that a whole series of *transactions* are internalised within the multinational corporation rather than taking place within the market, either to protect against or to exploit market failure. In other words, planned coordination replaces the unplanned coordination of the market. Or, as Williamson (1975; 1981) would put it, hierarchies replace markets. In this depiction the multinational corporation is seen as an island of conscious power in a sea of unconscious cooperation whose form is the result of a long history of weighing up the administrative and other costs of allowing transactions to take place within the corporation against the benefits (and the risks) of allowing the market to do the work (Rugman, 1981; 1982; Caves, 1982). The problems in this kind of depiction lie in deciding exactly how, when and where the costs of internalisation are outweighed by the benefits, for otherwise the argument becomes perilously close to tautology — corporations internalise markets until it is no longer worth doing so. The problem of making such a decision on the bounds of corporations are compounded because many of the assets of modern multinational corporations (and especially the assets of corporations operating in the service industries producing intermediate goods) cannot be reduced to something concrete and tangible. They can muster a whole series of intangible assets such as technological know-how and marketing skills which are just as important as more tangible assets but much more difficult to measure (Caves, 1983).

Certainly the concept of internalisation has stimulated new

thinking on the behaviour of multinational corporations. For example, vertical integration in multinational corporations used to be explained as arising from technological economies, a patently inadequate explanation in many cases. But, with the advent of the concept of internalisation, vertical integration is now explained as the outcome of a whole series of new factors operating in tandem to produce this particular form of internalisation — factors such as risk-reducing economies associated with long-term contracts, monopolisation in order to make it possible to enhance prices, the avoidance of government regulation (via transfer pricing, and the like), the desire to protect patents, and so on.

However, as this list of factors shows, internalisation theory is open to criticism on the grounds of its seemingly all-encompassing nature. Much of the recent work on internalisation in multinational corporations consists of precisely the addition of these new factors. Admittedly, acknowledgement of the existence of these new factors has been stimulated by the concept of internalisation. However, it is possible to question how far all these new factors can be tied together in one broad, overarching theory with internalisation as its core. As Buckley (1983, p. 42) puts it, internalisation theory is not so much a theory 'as a concept in search of a theory'. Thus,

> The search for a general theory of the multinational enterprise has led to the 'stretching' of partial concepts or to an increasingly cumbersome taxonomy. Challenges to the new orthodoxy have been met by redefinition of central concepts or increasingly long inventories of classification.

Dunning (1979; 1981; 1983) has tried to surmount the problems imposed by internalisation theory by proposing an 'eclectic' theory of the multinational corporation, increasingly referred to as the 'OLI [organisation, location, internalisation] paradigm'. As the acronym suggests, this is an attempt to add to the competitive advantage of internalisation that the multinational corporation enjoys the other determinants of foreign direct investment, namely the competitive advantages associated with ownership and location (Table 1.6). The worth of the OLI approach lies in its recognition of the fact that as well as a mushrooming 'in all types of transactions, notably of intermediate products, which are best undertaken by hierarchies rather than markets, and/or an improvement in the efficiency of hierarchies, particularly MNE

Table 1.6: The OLI Theory of International Production

Ownership advantages (of enterprises of one nationality (or affiliates of same) over those of another)

(a) *Which need not arise due to multinationality* — Those due mainly to size and established position, product or process diversification, ability to take advantage of division of labour and specialisation: monopoly power, better resource capacity and usage.

Proprietary technology, trademarks (protected by patent *et al.* legislation). Production management, organisational, marketing systems; R & D capacity; 'bank' of human capital and experience.

Exclusive and favoured access to inputs, e.g. labour, natural resources, finance, information.

Ability to obtain inputs on favoured terms (due e.g. to size or monopsonistic influence).

Exclusive or favoured access to product markets.

Government protection (e.g. control on market entry).

(b) *Which those branch plants of established enterprises may enjoy over new firms.* Access to capacity (administrative, managerial, R & D, marketing etc.) of parent company at favoured prices.

Economies of joint supply (not only in production, but in purchasing, marketing, finance etc. arrangements).

(c) *Which specifically arise because of multinationality.* Multinationality enhances above advantages by offering wider opportunities. More favoured access to and/or better knowledge about information, inputs, markets.

Ability to take advantage of international differences in factor endowments, markets.

Ability to diversify risks (e.g. in different currency areas).

Location advantages (these may favour home or host countries)

Spatial distribution of inputs and markets.

Input prices, quality and productivity (e.g. labour, energy, materials, components, semi-finished goods).

Transport and communications costs.

Government intervention.

Control on imports (including tariff barriers), tax rates, incentives, climate for investment, political stability, etc.

Infrastructure (commercial, legal, transportation).

Psychic distance (language, cultural, business, customs, etc. differences).

Economies of R & D, production and marketing (e.g. extent to which sales economies make for centralisation of production).

Internalisation advantages (i.e. to protect against or exploit market failure)

Avoidance of transaction and negotiating costs.

To avoid costs of enforcing property rights.

Buyer certainty (about nature and value of inputs (e.g. technology) being sold).

Where market does not permit price discrimination.

Need of seller to protect quality of products.

Continued on p. 10

Table 1.6 continued

To capture economies of interdependent activities.
To compensate for absence of future markets.
To avoid or exploit government intervention (e.g. quotas, tariffs, price controls, tax differences etc.).
To control supplies and conditions of sale of inputs (including technology).
To control market outlets (including those which might be used by competitors).
To be able to engage in practices (e.g. cross-subsidisation, predatory pricing etc. as a competitive or anti-competitive strategy).

Source: Dunning (1979), p. 276.

hierarchies relative to other forms of governance, to organise these and other transactions' (internalisation advantages), there has been a proliferation in, 'the demand for the types of goods, services and rights which MNCs are particularly well-equipped to supply, and/ or an enhanced ability on their part to supply and market these relative to their competitors' ownership advantages'. At the same time, 'the inducements to enterprises to produce goods and services from a foreign location have grown; and/or the demand for the type of output which is best supplied from foreign locations has increased' location advantages (Dunning, 1983, p. 102).

Using the OLI approach, many more situations in which multi-national corporations are involved can be explained than by appealing just to the advantages of internalisation. In particular such an approach allows different weights to be placed upon different situations, according to which one or a combination of the three competitive advantages are the dominant force. Thus,

> it would be unrealistic to suppose that the OLI advantages which explain investment by Standard Fruit in the banana industry of Costa Rica are the same (or have the same value) as that by NV Philips Gloeilampenfabrieken in the electrical appliances industry of Greece, or that of Trust House Forte in the hotel industry. (Dunning, 1983, p. 103)

The OLI approach has been applied in a number of different empirical situations now, from the multinational hotel industry (Dunning and McQueen, 1981a; 1981b) to the location of the offices of different multinational business service corporations (Dunning and Norman, 1983), and has proved very successful in isolating different determinants of foreign investment (Table 1.7). However, at the same time, it still suffers from some of the same disadvantages of internalisation 'theory', and specifically it is a list of factors likely to be important in the explanation of the growth of the modern multinational corporation rather than the explanation itself. Theoretical relations between the different factors too often remain untheorised (see Sayer, 1984).

Organisation Theory

The study of the internal organisation of large business enterprises, including multinational corporations, has also seen a number of new theoretical developments over the last few years which the urban and regional researcher can take account of. Ideas on inter-

Table 1.7: An Example of the OLI Approach at Work. The Advantages to Different Multinational Business Services in Undertaking Different Types of Service Abroad

Type of Service Provided Abroad	Ownership Advantages	Location Advantages	Internalisation Advantages	Types of Service which Favour MNCs
Access to information	Capital, access to markets, managerial skills, international reputation	Resources (e.g. skilled labour, information)	Secure supply of skilled labour, protection and exploitation of specialised information	Engineering design, insurance and reinsurance, management consultancy, investment banking
Familiar customer	Capital, specialist knowledge, international reputation, access to markets	Labour and other costs, size of local market, need to protect local market	Protection and exploitation of knowledge and business contacts, buyer uncertainty, high information costs	Reinsurance, executive search and accountancy management and engineering, consultancy, branch banking
Fund of organisational and managerial expertise	General regulatory knowledge, access to supplies and market outlets	Size of market access to customers, suppliers and commodity exchanges	Secure market share, exploitation of business and market contacts	Import and export merchanting

Source: Adapted from Dunning and Norman (1983), Table 1, p. 679.

organisational relations developed in organisation theory in particular, and management science more generally, has produced a number of significant and penetrating insights into the processes shaping the internal structure of large business organisations which can be used to advantage to understand the functioning of the multinational corporation. The structural contingency model, in particular, has generated a number of significant concepts.

Central to the structural contingency model is the notion that the internal structure of a large business organisation is moulded by the pressures of its external environment. That environment, however, is not conceived as an anonymous external aggregate, as is the market in industrial economics and the internalisation literature, but as a particularised set of competing, controlling and complementary organisations and institutions with which the organisation or enterprise must interact (Aldrich, 1979). The criterion of success in this model is not judged on efficiency grounds alone (maximisation of returns and minimisation of costs) but on *effectiveness* — the ability of the enterprise to continue in business and be accepted by those with which it must interact. Indeed, while it is essential to be effective in order to be efficient, it is by no means necessary to be efficient to be effective (Pfeffer and Salancik, 1978). This is a significant departure from the internalisation approach which conflates these two ideas completely. It means that the contingency model incorporates behavioural idiosyncracies in the operations of business organisations and multinational corporations from the outset. In contrast, Williamson (1975; 1981) had to import ideas of bounded rationality, opportunism and information impactedness to soften the efficiency maximising principles that underpin the internalisation approach.

The structural contingency model envisages two processes being stimulated within the multinational corporation by the pressures of its operational environment — differentiation and integration (Thompson, 1967). Differentiation is the creation of departments (labelled boundary spanning structures)[7] to confront and deal with homogeneous segments of that external environment, while integration is the vital process of coordinating these fragments to achieve harmony and effectiveness rather than dissonance and decline.

In large national or multinational corporations operating at a number of sites, these departments and functions will be spread amongst a series of sub-units — group, regional and product division headquarters, R & D centres, branch plants, and so on — and it is here that the organisation theory concept of *plant central-ity* developed by the Aston group of researchers (Hickson *et al.*, 1971) can be usefully employed to understand the internal functioning of the multinational corporation. Within an organisa-tion, whether it is multinational or not, power, resources and authority are distributed unevenly. Thus, the charter of a sub-unit within a multinational corporation — be it an office, warehouse, laboratory or plant — is reflected in the tasks and activities it per-forms, the resources it has at its disposal, the technology it employs, the decision-making autonomy it possesses and, there-fore, its centrality within the structure of the corporation as a whole. In short, there is a core and periphery *within* the multina-tional corporation.

This concept of intra-organisational centrality is a clear improvement on the way the internal organisation of multinational corporations is treated in both industrial economics and urban and regional research. In industrial economics the tendency has been to remain largely 'outside' the corporate structure very much in the tradition of the stance adopted in the classical theory of the firm (Coase, 1937; Williamson, 1975), treating the multinational corporation as though it is internally undifferentiated despite operating at a number of functionally and geographically separate sites. The implication is that the multinational operates with equal intensity at all locations. A similar assumption is implicit in most urban and regional research. It is this recognition of inequalities within corporate structures and the implication of increasing ephemerality that is associated with increasing peripherality that is one of the more valuable concepts to be derived from organisation theory.

The concept has also been extended to the inter-organisational context by Benson (1978), building upon the power networks framework first explored by Levine (1972). Here power is once more defined in terms of money (resources) and authority, with power being the ability of one enterprise to force another to do something it would not otherwise do. Such power is seen to vary substantially between one type of business organisation or multi-national corporation and another. It links them into networks of inequality that can assume myriad forms varying from monocentric to polycentric but which frequently have financial institutions at their core. This power networks approach is a marked improve-

ment over previous conceptions. By recognising the dominated and the dominant, it makes much clearer the form, direction and extent of the internalisation of transactions that might occur amongst a group of functionally-related organisations and multinational corporations, partly redressing the near tautology of the internalisation approach. It also redresses the bland neutrality and overemphasis on space that has been the hallmark of linkage studies in urban and regional research. However, promising though this avenue of research has been, it has never been explored widely beyond studies of inter-locking directorships (Pfeffer, 1972; 1981).
(Pfeffer, 1972; 1981).

Despite the advantages which organisation theory concepts offer to the study of the internal operations of multinational corporations, there are also major limitations that must be taken into account. First, organisation theory in general and the structural contingency theory in particular, is essentially *aspatial*. Consequently, the spatial differentiation of business organisations into multi-site and multinational enterprises has never been a major topic of interest. Indeed, many of the limitations and short-comings of organisation theory could well find remedies in the spatial processes elaborated by urban and regional researchers (McDermott and Taylor, 1982). Second, organisation theory is largely *atemporal*, dealing with the internal structure of large business organisations in terms of what is rather than in terms of their becoming. This naturally leads to a third shortcoming — ambiguity. To test the ideas of the structural contingency model it is essential to specify and calibrate the important dimensions of organisational structure, organisational efficiency and effectiveness, technology and environment. This has not been achieved, and no consistency or consensus has emerged on how to measure these aspects of organisation. Here too, therefore, despite the expenditure of considerable effort, the relationships between factors which impinge upon the internal organisation of the multinational corporation remain either untheorised or ambiguous.

Marxist Economic Theory

The urban and regional researcher concerned with the operations of multinational corporations can turn, finally, to Marxist theory. Certainly there is a powerful tradition of work here, which can be traced from the early interest of Hilferding and Lenin in international finance capital through the work of Hymer, Palloix and others in the 1960s and early 1970s to the present.[8] Important offshoots have included work on the role of the multinational corporation in the underdevelopment of the countries of Latin America and Africa by Frank, Amin and others.[9] In particular, this work reminds us that, 'the extant power of the multinational corporations should not be confused with an ability to transcend the structuration of action by the existing total dynamic of the capitalist world system' (Peet, 1982, p. 276). However, until recently, it sometimes seemed that Marxist economic theorists fought shy of considering multinational corporations as individual actors as a result of this stricture. Instead, multinational corporations were seen as one moment in the circulation of capital, and the proxy for this circulation was taken to be flows of foreign direct investment. But, a view is now growing up in Marxist theory which sees the multinational corporation for what it is — more than simply a passive participant in the process of capital accumulation, more than simply a series of capitals adding up to capital in general. In this tradition such reductionism is ruled out of order. The multinational corporation is seen as a collection of human beings structured by the combination of various ways of internal organisation and by external pressures but still with the capacity to produce concerted agency in what may be unexpected directions (Thompson, 1982). Quite clearly, such a conception means that determinants that once tended to be ignored, such as how the management of the multinational corporations organise the corporations (Harvey, 1982), and the various social and institutional forms the multinational corporation can take according to its nationality (Morgan and Sayer, 1983; 1984), are now recognised as important. The result is that much interesting work is now appearing in the Marxist tradition on a number of diverse aspects of the multinational corporation, for example on the links between multinational corporations and multinational banking (e.g. Fennema, 1982; Grou, 1983; Andreff, 1984) and on the formation of classes at a world scale (e.g. Connell, 1983).

Towards a Partial Synthesis

It is striking how in each of the three areas of research examined above, considerable changes have been taking place in the form and content of the theory of multinational corporations in response to the new diversity of the stock of multinational corporations and the subsequent impossibility of any longer characterising these corporations as a single unproblematic entity. This fluid state of affairs clearly poses a problem for the urban and regional researcher but it is, at the same time, a great opportunity for these researchers to intervene directly in the debates that are currently going on because of the importance of spatial organisation in forging any new synthesis.

At present each area of research contributes most to the understanding of a particular context. Thus, Marxist economic theory still emphasises the importance of the *structural context* within which all multinational corporations must operate including shifts in the structure of the world economy as a result of crisis and various responses such as the genesis of new industries. Industrial economics provides a general appreciation of the immediate *competitive context* within which particular groups of multinational corporations must operate including the strength and nature of competition and ways of meeting this competition such as internalisation. Organisation theory is best at sketching the constraints and opportunities provided by the *corporate context* including the nature of the form of internal organisation adopted and the rate of organisational change. Finally, current urban and regional research on the multinational corporation has shown the importance of *local context*, including how the plants and offices of particular multinational corporations in particular locations are tied into urban and regional economies in a symbiotic relationship. Thus, plants and offices of multinational corporations are not simply looking inwards to the corporation, but also outwards through local linkages. Each plant or office will, to variable extents, employ local people, utilise local suppliers, conform with local employment practices (Clark and Massey, 1982). No plant or office is an island — although some do come close to it.

But what is interesting is how the interests of these areas of research have expanded in search of more complete explanations with the result that they now overlap quite considerably. For example, many Marxist economic theorists have become more interested in the dynamics of multinational corporations and their internal organisation. A number of industrial economists have become interested in organisation theory as a way of taking into account the importance of internal organisation. Organisation theorists have become, through the concept of power networks, much more interested in the competitive context of multinationals. And urban and regional researchers have increasingly realised that explaining the local context of multinational corporations requires an appreciation of the structural, competitive and corporate contexts and have looked to literature that helps to illuminate these contexts.

No new synthesis exists yet. It might be more effectively argued that, instead, four new syntheses are emerging, but syntheses which now overlap more than they did before. Whatever the case, in all this the position of urban and regional research is strategic because *it is the spatial organisation of the multinational corporation which ties all the four contexts together,* and it is only urban and regional research which has ever displayed much interest in spatial organisation. It is through spatial organisation that each context is both integrated into the multinational corporation and differentiated within it.

The research task for urban and regional researchers is therefore potentially vast. Not only must each context be taken into account in explaining how multinational corporations and urban and regional economies are linked together, but also new concepts must be developed to explain how these contexts are themselves tied together in particular situations by particular forms of spatial organisation, and all this in a situation where multinational corporations are increasingly diverse. Not all is gloom, however. The increasing diversity of multinational corporations is not just a constraint. It is also an opportunity to heighten our understanding. The differences between categories of multinational corporation provide information upon all manner of salient issues and not least their different organisations of space.

In this volume we have fixed on four basic parameters distinguishing categories of multinational corporation — size, nationality, industrial sector and impacts.

The Chapters

The remaining chapters of this book are divided into five sections, reflecting the new level of diversity of the operations and impacts of modern multinational corporations. The main concern of the first section is with *size*. Global corporations are at one end of the size spectrum of multinational corporations while small multinationals with only a few, tentative, foreign operations are at the other. The first two papers provide instances of the very different strategy and structure of these contrasting scales of operation. Clarke's paper is concerned with the importance of centrality, or lack of centrality, of individual plants within a global corporation. Measuring this centrality provides some indication of the likelihood that a plant will continue to survive within a corporation. In contrast, Taylor's paper looks at the relationship between various sizes of multinational corporations and local firms in the Pacific Islands.

The concern of the second section is with *nationality*. Nationality is an important determinant of the spatial organisation and local behaviour of multinational corporations, not only because different multinational corporations have sprung from different national economic systems which are backed up internationally by varying degrees of political power, but also because these corporations must have different cultural predilections which affect the way they are organised and run. The Japanese case has been cited here almost *ad nauseam* (see, for example, Franko, 1983) but the multinational corporations of other countries have their own predilections as well. Tucker provides an example of the operations of multinational corporations from one 'semi-peripheral' country, South Africa (see Taylor and Thrift, 1981a) while Forbes provides an insight into the operations of a set of Third World multinationals from Asia, using Indonesia as a case study of their impact. Many of these firms are operated by overseas Chinese and here a particularly strong cultural tradition exists (see Hu and Hu, 1980).

The third section is concerned with the *industrial sector* within which multinational corporations operate. Too many studies of multinational corporations in the past have been restricted to the resources and manufacturing sectors while the most rapidly growing area of multinational corporation activity at present is in the provision of services, especially producer services. Thrift provides a case study of this set of producer service multinational corporations concentrating in particular on their linked effects on cities and regions of the world through a rapidly growing market in property. Because of the operations of these service corporations world cities are now truly world cities,[10] coordinating a continuously operative world financial network. Fujita and Ishigaki provide a case study of the expansion of Japanese banks over the last 15 years, a subject of vital importance to the understanding of the new world financial system. Japanese banks now challenge the prominence of the banks of the United States and other countries which have themselves internationalised to a previously unknown degree over the same period (see Michalet, 1981; Yannopoulos, 1983; Coakley, 1984). Services are not the only under-researched area, however. Rogerson proves this point with a unique case study of the activities of a government-owned multinational corporation, the British Overseas Development Corporation.

The penultimate section is concerned with the *different impacts* of different types of multinational corporation on the economies of different cities and regions in various countries. Krinks considers the impact of multinational corporations active in the food industry on the economy of the Philippines. The two subsequent chapters provide important indications of the restructuring behaviour of multinational corporations in the UK, although such behaviour has been a common phenomenon in most countries of the world (see Van den Bulcke *et al.*, 1979; Hood and Young, 1982; 1984; Gaffikin and Nickson, 1984). Townsend and Peck consider the impact of restructuring on the British operations of foreign-based multinational corporations in the period from 1976 to 1981. Bassett provides a case study of the impacts of multinational restructuring on the city of Bristol, concentrating in particular on the activities of two multinational corporations, one British-based and one foreign-based.

The final section is in the nature of an envoi. One of the founders of the geography of enterprise, McNee, provides important background on how the subject evolved and finishes by considering a number of methodological problems that still plague the study of multinational corporations.

As an edited collection, the subjects of the papers are not discrete. A number of the papers have clear and important links to others. For example, the paper by Fujita and Ishigaki could equally have been placed in the 'nationality' section, the papers by Thrift and by Taylor could have been placed in the 'impacts' section; and so on. This overlap cannot be avoided. It is a matter of fact that perhaps the most important characteristic of the multinational corporation — that it integrates various aspects of the study of the space economy — also precludes neat categorisation.

However, there is a pressing lacuna in this volume: that is the study of the construction of realistic national, regional and urban economic policies able to deal with international economic operations. Progress on this set of issues has been very slow, partly because of a lack of understanding of the changes in the operation of multinational corporations over the last 15 years which have precluded many former policy options (Thrift, 1985). However, some realistic work is now at last beginning to appear on these issues (e.g. Bluestone, 1984; Bluestone and Harrison, 1984; Castells, 1984; Carnoy and Castells, 1984; Radice, 1984) and this and other work will form the basis of the next volume.

Notes

1. A number of multinational corporations have, over the last 15 years, reduced their worldwide workforce quite substantially, usually by cutbacks in employment in the home country.

2. According to Pearce (1983), 22 per cent of the sales of the world's 430 largest multinational corporations were outside their main sphere of operations.

3. On Japanese multinational corporations, see the recent excellent review by Franko (1983). On multinationals from semi-peripheral countries, see Taylor and Thrift (1981a), Bureau of Industry Economics (1983a; 1983b; 1984). On multinational corporations from Third World countries, see the recent volumes by Lall (1983) and Wells (1983).

4. This thesis fits well with Urry's (1984) idea of 'disorganised capitalism'.

5. For a full review of these explanations, see Taylor and Thrift (1981b).

6. In particular, multinationals operating in the service sector were excluded.

7. Boundary-spanning structures include sales, purchasing, finance, personnel, transport, marketing and market research, R & D, and so on. See Hower and Lorsch (1967).

8. For reviews of this work see Brewer (1980); McFarlane (1982).

9. Whilst dependency theory, world systems theory, and the like are not explicitly Marxist, much of their inspiration comes from Marxism.

10. A substantial body of literature is now growing up on these world cities. For example, for New York see Mollenkopf, Noyelle and Cohen (1984) and Sassen-Koob (1984); for London, see King (1985); and for Los Angeles, see Soja, Marales and Wolff (1983).

2 LABOUR DYNAMICS AND PLANT CENTRALITY IN MULTINATIONAL CORPORATIONS

Ian M. Clarke

Introduction

The changing spatial distribution of employment which has resulted from the restructuring of large business organisations at regional, national and international levels in the 1970s and 1980s has attracted a substantial amount of interest in industrial geography (e.g. Massey and Meegan, 1979; 1982; Watts, 1980; Townsend, 1982b; Taylor and Thrift, 1982a). Much of this debate has been couched within the loose framework of the 'new international division of labour' as espoused by Fröbel, Heinrichs and Kreye (1980), attributing changes in this division of labour to the geographical reorganisation of individual multinational corporations. However, a major problem frequently associated with this work is that it implies a direct causal relationship between changes in the employment fortunes of otherwise separate geographical areas. For example, the search by business organisations for cheap labour havens at a global level is often cited as a prime cause of deindustrialisation in developed economies. While such spatial comparative advantages do exist, and are utilised by multinational corporations, it is argued in this chapter that such an explanation of the emerging new international division of labour has been considerably overplayed. Anecdotal and often unrelated evidence of plant rationalisation or expansion resulting in employment change has been used to support the proposition that business organisations are responding to the spatially differentiated qualities of labour, thereby invoking a direct causal link between what are otherwise only net shifts in the geographical pattern of labour use. Rather than providing another study of the employment effects of plant dynamics at an international level, this chapter concentrates on evaluating *in situ* labour dynamics resulting from changes made inside the establishment, in an attempt to reveal the nature of processes which have otherwise gone uninvestigated. Using survey data for plants belonging to one product division of a single multi-

21

national corporation, ICI, this chapter seeks to evaluate labour dynamics within a more rigorous analytical framework.

The purpose of this chapter is, therefore, to redress some of the deficiencies inherent in other studies of employment by evaluating labour dynamics at the level of the plant rather than at the level of the larger multinational business organisation. To achieve this objective, the argument is developed in three stages. In the first section, various approaches which have been used in industrial geography and related disciplines to investigate aspects of employment and labour dynamics are compared with those which have been adopted in a broadly termed 'business organisation' perspective (McDermott and Taylor, 1982; Clarke, 1984a). This part of the discussion serves to highlight the conceptual gap which exists between the business organisation and the plant. It also emphasises the need to examine labour dynamics in relation to factors inside the plant, as well as the structural context of the business organisation and its environment. In the second section, the concept of plant centrality is introduced and described as a means of providing a framework against which processes operating at the plant level within a business organisation can be evaluated. Key attributes of labour dynamics are then described, and are used as dependent variables in a stepwise multiple regression procedure in the third section. This set of analyses of plants within the paints division of ICI is designed to pick out the main factors of the environment and organisation which can be used to understand patterns of labour use in different locations within a single, multinational business organisation.

Analysing Labour Dynamics

The business organisation approach is the most recent analytical perspective to be developed in industrial geography, and it is the purpose of this brief section to highlight its potential for evaluating labour dynamics and to point out some fundamental features of employment which need to be addressed. To facilitate discussion, a distinction is made between the four ways in which labour dynamics have been examined in geographical and related approaches. These are then compared with the characteristics of different types of business organisation.

(1) Analyses at the highest level of aggregation using regional and

sectoral data (for instance, in the work of Fothergill and Gudgin (1982) and their attempt to construct 'regional employment accounts'; Keeble's (1976) 'components of change' studies; and Massey and Meegan's (1979) 'structural' accounts of regional employment change) have a fundamental weakness which stems from the assumption they make that sectoral data can somehow be translated directly into conclusions on the labour dynamics of organisations. Many business organisations overlap these sectoral divisions to a considerable extent, and different types of organisation overlap them to different degrees. Sectoral definitions effectively apply a filter to reality, and as such a business organisations approach can be more gainfully employed to construct an explanatory background for labour dynamics at national, regional and even sub-regional levels.

(2) At the second level of aggregation, disaggregated plant data, such as those found in the work of McDermott (1976) and McDermott and Keeble (1978) on the electronics industry in the United Kingdom, produce the same problem. Plant-level data are often assigned to sectors and they are, therefore, stripped of their organisational contexts. Unless the relationships between the plant and its wider organisational context are detailed more fully, it can be suggested that conclusions on labour dynamics may well be spurious.

(3) Some of these weaknesses can be remedied by a business organisation approach, which attempts to maintain the structural integrity of corporate operations. Examination of the international operations of organisations as a whole, such as Teuling's (1984) work on the Dutch group, Philips, and Clarke's (1982) study of the changing spatial division of labour within ICI, have helped to place national employment changes, where appropriate, in a corporate context, and have also aided in overcoming a general national research myopia by using a top-down perspective. However, the sheer scale of such organisations' operations often creates its own problems. Labour dynamics are usually still treated in an aggregate way simply in order to handle the quantity of information. Even at the level of analysis of such organisations' national operations (e.g. Massey and Meegan, 1979; Dicken and Lloyd, 1979; Lloyd and Reeve, 1982; Clarke, 1984b), there has been a tendency either to approach employment by tracing the ownership of plants in a traditional bottom-up way, or to maintain the top-down perspective and to fail to translate corporate aggre-

gations to the establishment level. Even analyses of corporate redundancy data (Townsend, 1981; 1982a; 1982b) have only examined the negative aspects of labour dynamics, and where it has been possible to gauge the magnitude of an organisation's employment, there have often been difficulties in breaking these figures down to a plant level.

(4) All but divorced from these aggregate levels of analysis are a series of plant-level studies which have a reciprocal set of problems. In the detailed 'anthropological' studies of plant production (e.g. Beynon, 1975; Nichols and Beynon, 1977; Gallie, 1978; Coriot, 1980; Friedman and Meredeen, 1980), for example, there is the unresolved question of whether the labour dynamics in a plant are determined by factors specific to that plant's location or by the position of the plant within the business organisation to which it belongs. Establishment-level studies adopting a business organisation approach (e.g. Adrian and Evans, 1984; Amin, 1985; Bassett, 1984), have failed to come to grips with the same problem, apart from occasional generalisations on job mix and job stability which are only tentatively related to a plant's organisational context and environmental characteristics.

In short, a conceptual gap exists between aspects of labour dynamics viewed at an establishment level and more aggregate levels of analysis. This is the case whether traditional geographical approaches or the business organisation approach is adopted. At this stage, then, the key issue lies in relating the changing patterns of employment inside the plant to wider organisational and environmental constraints.

In addition to demonstrating the existence of this conceptual gap, the discussion in this section has also emphasised three main dimensions of labour dynamics that can be used as guidelines within the empirical analysis which follows. The first dimension is *job stability*, and critical features in this respect are the size of the establishment workforce and the rate at which employment is growing or declining in the plant. A second dimension is *job mix*, including the occupational make-up of the plant. It would be useful, for example, to address variation in the plant administrative ratio in the context of different locations and intra-organisational relations. *Production efficiency* is the third dimension which affects labour dynamics at the plant level. Criteria which are needed to compare production between plants are, for instance, the levels of total labour costs, and the capital intensity of production. Furthermore, each of these factors is likely to affect productivity levels and the rate at which the productivity of a plant is changing, so these are necessarily summary measures of plant performance.

The Concept of Centrality

If the labour dynamics to be found in the separate locations occupied by a multinational corporation are to be fully understood, it is vital to relate those issues to the position of individual plants *within* a particular business organisation, as this will provide explanatory benchmarks for understanding changes in the international division of labour. To provide such a framework, the concept of *plant centrality* can be introduced. 'Centrality' was originally developed as one of a set of measures to describe the structure of an organisation by the Aston group of researchers (Pugh *et al.*, 1968; Hickson *et al.*, 1971; Hinings *et al.*, 1974). The concept of centrality provides a means of identifying the precise position of decision-making authority in organisations and can be used to explain inequalities in power relations within their structures. Consequently, the concept provides a much fuller specification of the structure of sub-units or plants within large business organisations compared with the notions of material and information linkages and ownership structures developed in industrial geography.

As the Aston studies show, any plant (or 'sub-unit') belonging to a business organisation, is granted a 'charter' (Hickson *et al.*, 1971), so the distribution of authority is critical in evaluating centrality of a single establishment within an organisation. The *tasks* or activities performed by a plant are the most tangible representation of its centrality. As Hickson *et al.* (1971) note, centrality consists of four elements: the ability of a plant to cope with environmental uncertainties; the degree to which its function can be carried out elsewhere in the organisation; the importance attached to the work carried out in the plant by the parent organisation; and its ability to regulate and control contingencies which may arise in the plant structure.

Several factors are overlooked in this theoretical schema. Business organisations constantly remould their activities over time and through space. The mix of plants they contain will evolve in line with the particular and individual historical trajectory. This same weakness has been stressed recently by Massey and Meegan (1982). The evolution of an organisation will inevitably alter the basis of the internal distribution of power within it and, hence, the centrality of individual plants with its overall structure. A second weakness is that the concepts like centrality pay little regard to the effects of spatial variations in the environment of an organisation: these 'models' are essentially *aspatial.* Both Marshall (1982) and McDermott and Taylor (1982) have commented on this weakness in organisation theory, suggesting that geography can make a positive and constructive contribution in this respect. Spatial variations in the environmental characteristics of an organisation can, in fact, be conceptualised as a series of environmental 'domains' which surround each plant (Taylor and Thrift, 1979). A third problem of the Aston group's centrality schema relates to how historical and spatial factors interact with the structure of an organisation. Individual locations are characterised by their own mix of attributes and the development and diffusion of various practices in management is uneven (McDermott and Taylor, 1982). In short, the centrality or peripherality of a plant must be explained not only in terms of its position and function within the organisation (i.e. intra-organisational relations), but also in terms of its relationship to its local environmental domain (i.e. inter-organisational relations). The most critical components of intra-organisational relations are the history, position and task performed by a plant, while the characteristics of the domain and the nature of external linkages to a wider environment are necessary descriptors of inter-organisational relations.

Measuring Attributes of Plant Centrality in Multinational Corporations

Having briefly outlined the main aspects of plant centrality, the practical problem lies in defining and more fully specifying these attributes in empirical terms, so that labour dynamics in the plants of multinational corporations can be measured against them. Thus, an attempt is made in this chapter to construct measures of the domain and intra-organisational relations of plants. The empirical analysis is built on information from plants belonging to the paints division of a single multinational, ICI. Eighteen establishments located throughout the world were surveyed, representing 57 per cent of the plants in this division of ICI.

The rationale and methodology underlying the various attributes of plant centrality and peripherality have been described at length elsewhere (Clarke, 1984a). Thirty-one domain variables derived from published sources were used to ascertain the nature of the national environment of each establishment, including their positions in the chemicals sector, and survey data were employed to describe the intra-organisational relations of the same plants using 17 variables. As these criteria were only *a priori* measures of plant centrality, it was considered judicious to remove redundant and overlapping variables. This process was achieved through factor analysis which was used to compress sets of individual variables into new composite variables. The economy of description which these 'composite' variables provide, was used to describe the intra- and inter-organisational relations of the plants in the analysis by calculating the factor scores for each case on each composite variable.

Two indices were constructed to summarise the intra- and inter-organisational relationships of the surveyed plants. These indices were generated by adding together the factor scores for each plant after each composite variable had been weighted according to the amount of variance explained. These results were then standardised so that each case could be assigned to both the intra- and inter-organisational scales, calibrated to range from 0 to 100 (Figure 2.1). These two continua summarise the characteristics of central and peripheral plant domains and central and peripheral intra-organisational relations (Table 2.1).

Central domains are typically affluent and democratic, evolve countries with stable currencies, and are, because of the relative 'openness' of their economies, vulnerable to fluctuations in trading patterns, with their trade being oriented towards the world's developed country markets. Examples of such domains covered in the present study include Australia, Canada, West Germany, Singapore, and to a limited extent, the United Kingdom. Other variables showed that central domains are located in the established industrialised countries — the major sources of foreign investment and the centres of large-scale chemicals production. Conversely, countries offering peripheral domains tend to be poorer and less democratic, with unstable currencies. In terms of trade they are less vulnerable than central domains, but increasingly, their exports are becoming oriented towards developing

Figure 2.1: Organisational Segmentation, Restructuring and Corporate Interaction

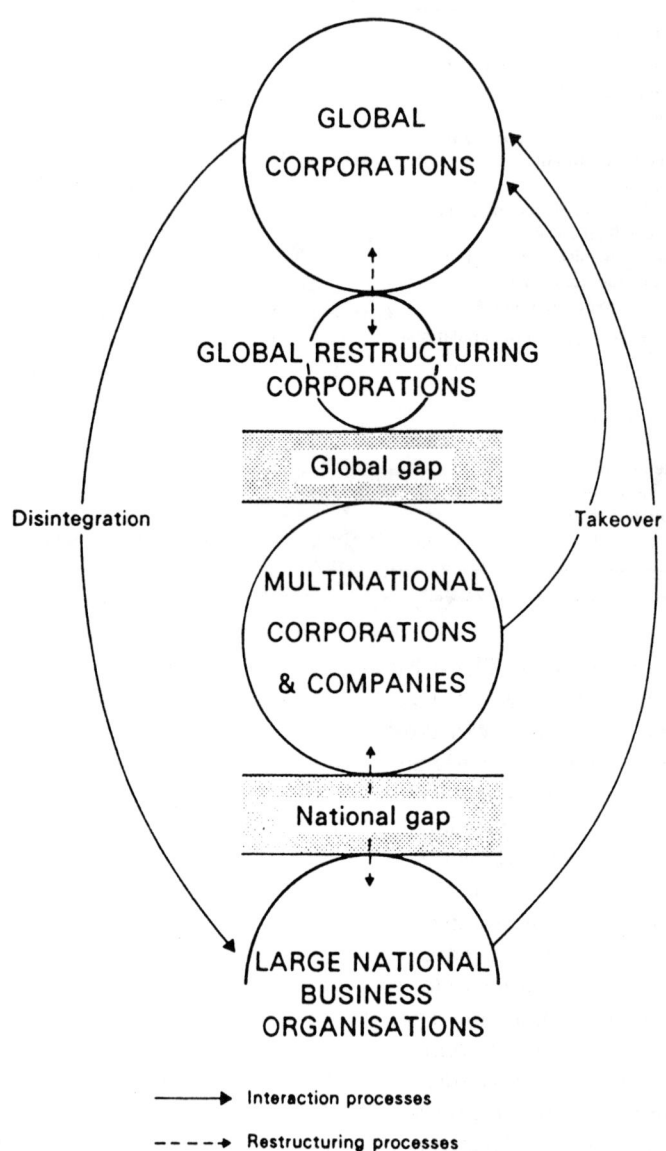

Note: Circle size is approximately equal to the market significance of each group

Table 2.1: Characteristics of Central and Peripheral Plant Domains and Intra-Organisational Relations

Plant Domain	Central	Peripheral
Index of wealth and political democracy	rich/democratic	poor/undemocratic
Currency stability	stable	unstable
Trade vulnerability	high	low
International market structure	developed markets	developing markets
Foreign investment	low	high
Aid dependency	low	high
Manufacturing productivity growth	low	high
Newly industrialising	low	high
Scale of chemicals production	large	small
Chemical sector growth	high	low
Chemical export dynamics	low growth	high growth
Plant Intra-Organisational Relations	**Central**	**Peripheral**
Plant position	high	low
Length of membership	long	short
Plant status	high (old, acquired)	low (new, branch plant)
Scale of production	large	small
Specialisation	domestic paints	industrial paints
Production technology	diverse, repetition flow-line methods	concentrated, small-batch methods

Source: Analysis of survey data.

country markets. These locations have also attracted substantial amounts of foreign investment and aid and they display high rates of productivity growth typical of newly industrialising nations. In these peripheral economies, including Pakistan, India, Thailand and Zambia, the chemical sector is of growing significance.

The intra-organisational relations of plants within ICI show a very different arrangement. Plants in the United Kingdom and Australia are most central within the organisation and, as such, they are less substitutable by ICI. These central plants had normally been acquired, and have lengthy histories of membership in the organisation. Large-scale, specialised and technologically diverse production, employing repetitive flow-line methods was also typical of central plants. In contrast, recently established plants with a low position in the corporate hierarchy, were smaller and less specialised, catering largely for a market for domestic (household) rather than industrial paints. Thus, production was concentrated on small-batch production methods, and this form of production characterised ICI's operations in Singapore, India and Zambia.

The level of association between domain centrality and the intra-organisational centrality of individual plants can be tested using rank correlation. The low value of this coefficient (r_s = 0.3849) shows that plants which are of central importance to a business organisation are not necessarily located in central domains. Similarly, peripheral domains are not always the hosts of peripheral plants. There is an important corollary to this argument. Since intra-organisational centrality relates to business organisation decision-making a plant's intra-organisational centrality will normally override considerations of domain centrality. However, in some cases the organisational and domain centrality of a plant are likely to reinforce one another. In practical terms, this means that large plants will be located in large markets, with these large markets serving to perpetuate the life of the plant. The longer a plant is able to survive, the more 'central' it becomes, because of the *power* it is able to accumulate in relation to others in the same business organisation. Central establishments are, therefore, the 'survivors', those with longstanding memberships, in part because the organisation has been willing to continue developing these sites, enlarging and carving out specialist roles for them and investing in technologically-intensive methods of production. The more peripheral plants tend to have a more precarious existence, partly because of their recent history but also because of the lesser role they play within the business organisation.

Relating Labour Dynamics to Plant Centrality

Having operationalised, in the preceding section, a centrality framework which simultaneously describes the attributes of a plant's position within both an organisational structure and a particular locational environment, it remains to ascertain the relationships between these centrality characteristics and labour dynamics inside each plant. Establishment-level data were collected for the 18 plants belonging to the paints division of ICI. These data were designed to elicit information on the three critical dimensions of job stability, job mix and production efficiency.

Workforce size (total plant employment) and *rate of employment change* (number of jobs lost or gained annually by a plant) were the two variables constructed to describe job stability. To give a broad indication of job mix, a single variable was calculated —

the *administrative ratio* — which indicates the proportion of plant employees performing non-productive functions. Four variables were used to indicate the efficiency of production: *productivity* (average output per person); *rate of change in productivity* (annual average output per person); *capital intensity of production* (ratio of total energy costs to total wage bill to run the plant); and *total labour costs*. As larger plants have larger amounts of capital invested in them, it is likely that they will have higher levels of productivity, so these final two variables indicate the baseline of production. The seven labour variables measure the state of production inside individual establishments in 1980, as well as change over time. To make the cost data from plants in different countries comparable, all currencies have been converted to United States dollars.

Stepwise Multiple Regression

Stepwise multiple regression, was used to analyse the relationship between the seven labour variables and the 17 independent variables which describe the centrality attributes of the plant's intra-organisational relations and environmental domains. This form of regression analysis models the relationship between the dependent and independent variables in a series of 'steps', gradually improving the fit of the regression line by adding variables to, and subtracting them from, the regression equation (Draper and Smith, 1960; Ferguson, 1977). The final equation accounts for a certain proportion of the variance in the data and three statistics describe the composition of the equation. First, the partial-F statistic measures the significance and direction of influence of individual variables at the final stage of the analysis. Second, the R^2 value demonstrates the percentage of unique variance in the data which is explained by each variable. Finally, the cumulative R^2 is the total variance which the final equation explains, the sum of all variables. The inclusion or removal of individual variables from the regression equation closely follows a series of pre-set criterion, in order to obtain a 'best fit'. Stepwise multiple regression tests were conducted separately on domain and intra-organisational factors to test for their effects on the attributes of labour dynamics, and the two sets of independent variables were also tested together to evaluate their relative importance. Variables which were significant in the analysis for each dependent variable are interpreted below.

Workforce size.   Several attributes of the environment domain of the plant proved to be significant determinants of the size of its workforce (Table 2.2). The first variable 'scale of chemicals production' (Factor IX, $F = 0.73885$) was the strongest indicator and shows that the size of a plant's workforce correlates with the overall size of other competing establishments and the scale and international importance of the local chemicals sector. Bound up with this explanation is a second variable, 'international market structure' (Factor IV, $F = 0.50254$) which describes the orientation of trade to centrally-planned markets and the proportion of internal trade in the domain. What is significant is that the positive association between a plant's workforce size and this variable indicates larger workforces are located in domains which are not related to trade with developed market economies. This feature might be interpreted as an effect of a large local market and trade with the more dynamic economies where the chemicals sector is growing, rather than with saturated developed markets. With regard to the paints industry, this interpretation is sensible as most plants tend to serve national rather than international markets, so that the size of a plant's workforce is proportional to the market size of the domain. Workforce size is also related to 'currency stability' (Factor II, $F = -0.45024$) in a negative fashion. This relationship suggests that plants in domains characterised by fiscal instability have smaller workforces.

The intra-organisational relations of a plant also affected the size of the workforce. The 'scale of production' (Factor IV, $F = 0.37745$) of the plant was the most influential attribute and this probably reflects the location of the plant in a domain with a large market. Also important in terms of workforce size was 'plant status' (Factor III, $F = 0.54929$), suggesting that the large-scale plants with big workforces are also the older acquired establishments, rather than the newer branch plants. This conclusion is reinforced by the negative association of workforce size with 'plant postion' (Factor I, $F = -0.41490$), indicating that more people are employed in the older acquired plants which occupy a 'high' position in the business organisation, probably because of the scale of their task, their inability to be substituted within the organisation, and their central location in large markets.

The inverse relationship which existed between the 'scale of chemicals production' of the domain and 'plant position' when domain and intra-organisational factors were tested together,

Table 2.2: Stepwise Multiple Regression: Workforce Size

Range of Variables	Significant Independent Variables	Factor Number	Partial F Coefficient	Individual R²	Cumulative R²
(A) Domain	Scale of chemicals production	IX	0.73885	0.484	0.484
	International market structure	IV	0.50252	0.095	0.579
	Currency stability	II	−0.45024	0.085	0.664
(B) Intra-organisational	Scale of production	IV	0.37745	0.304	0.479
Relations	Plant status	III	0.54929	0.175	0.479
	Plant position	I	−0.41490	0.089	0.568
(A + B)	Scale of chemicals production	IX	0.69479	0.483	0.483
	Plant position	I	−0.49967	0.129	0.612

Source: Analysis of survey data.

underlines these conclusions and shows the way in which the larger plants are located in the larger markets, thereby mutually reinforcing one another. These are the ideal conditions for large plant workforces.

Rate of employment change.   The rate of employment change inside individual plants displayed a strong negative correlation with the 'scale of chemicals production' (Factor IX, F = −0.88278) of the domain location, and was positively associated with local 'currency stability' (Factor II, F = 0.42990) (Table 2.3). These findings suggest that plants with higher employment growth rates are those which operate in domains where the sector is small but growing, with the implication that negative rates of employment change take place in domains in which the industry is already well established and possibly saturated, particularly in the developed country economies.

In terms of the effects of intra-organisational relations, the rate of employment change experienced in a plant was found to decrease with both 'plant status' (Factor III, F = −0.61429) and 'scale of production' (Factor IV, F = −0.47830). Practically, this means that the high-status plants — those which have been acquired, are older, and produce paints on a larger scale — are precisely those establishments which are shedding jobs. However, there is also the possibility that this feature simply represents the restricted scope for employment growth in large plants relative to small plants. Reasons for this tendency might be the capital intensity and economies of scale which are typical of large plants. This theme is discussed in a later section. 'Scale of chemicals production' (Factor IX, F = −0.89279) in the domain and 'length of membership' (Factor II, F = 0.51695) proved to be the most influential factors when the two sets of intra-organisational and domain attributes were tested together. The negative relationship between these two factors appears to show that employment grows more rapidly in plants which have been a part of the business organisation longer and which occupy a central position in the ownership hierarchy. Where the chemical sector of the domain is large, this tends to increase the rate of employment decline, possibly because of stiff competition between firms and an attempt to keep labour costs down in production.

Administrative ratio.   The proportion of a plant's total workforce

Table 2.3: Stepwise Multiple Regression: Rate of Employment Change

Range of Variables	Significant Independent Variables	Factor Number	Partial F Coefficient	Individual R²	Cumulative R²
(A) Domain	Scale of chemicals production	IX	−0.88278	0.730	0.730
	Currency stability	II	0.42990	0.050	0.780
(B) Intra-organisational	Plant status	III	0.61429	0.390	0.390
Relations	Scale of production	IV	−0.47830	0.139	0.529
(A + B)	Scale of chemicals production	IX	−0.89279	0.730	0.730
	Length of membership	II	0.51695	0.072	0.802

Source: Analysis of survey data.

involved in functions other than production — the 'support', 'boundary spanning' or broadly termed 'administrative' personnel — displayed little relationship with domain characteristics (Table 2.4). 'Chemicals sector growth' (Factor X, F = 0.37913) was the only attribute of any significance explaining 14.3 per cent of the variance in the data. One possible explanation for an increase in the administrative ratio in these circumstances might be the need for the plant to monitor the complex and changing business environment in order to remain competitive. The intra-organisational attributes provided a broader explanation of the reasons for changes in the administrative ratio. 'Plant status' (Factor III, F = 0.66505) was an important determinant, with the older acquired plants like Slough and Stowmarket in the United Kingdom, Clayton, Cabarita and Port Adelaide in Australia, and Hilden in West Germany having the largest proportions of administrative jobs. These are the plants most central to the organisation overall, located in the largest markets, so the reason for this pattern can be explained in historical terms. Before they were acquired by ICI, these plants were already established centres of administration and production for their previous parent organisations, and the long period since they were acquired has merely served to entrench this administrative role. For example, both Slough and Clayton are headquarters for their own regional paints divisions, a vital reason for their large component of administrative employment compared to other plants.

The negative correlation of the administrative ratio with 'length of membership' (Factor II, F = −0.37978) serves to underline this conclusion, with the newer, generally branch plants, having a smaller proportion of administrative personnel. In addition, plants which have a complex 'production technology' (Factor VI, F = −0.61019) have more administrative staff, either perhaps because of their labour-saving propensity, which causes the proportion of administrative jobs to grow, or because of the need to control and 'buffer' a much more complex production process. When the domain and intra-organisational attributes were used in a combined analysis, the two most significant factors were 'plant status' (Factor III, F = 0.70616) and 'production technology' (Factor VI, F = −0.55687), and coupled with the 'trade vulnerability' (Factor III, F = 0.45825) of the domain, helped to reinforce the need for a high administrative ratio when the operational environment is uncertain.

Table 2.4: Stepwise Multiple Regression: Administrative Ratio

Range of Variables	Significant Independent Variables	Factor Number	Partial F Coefficient	Individual R^2	Cumulative R^2
(A) Domain	Chemicals sector growth	X	0.37913	0.143	0.143
(B) Intra-organisational	Plant status	III	0.66505	0.192	0.192
Relations	Production technology	VI	−0.61019	0.310	0.502
	Length of membership	II	−0.37978	0.072	0.574
(A + B)	Plant status	III	0.70616	0.192	0.192
	Production technology	VI	−0.55687	0.310	0.502
	Trade vulnerability	III	0.45825	0.104	0.606

Source: Analysis of survey data.

Productivity. The productivity levels (output per person varied considerably between the 18 plants and, in terms of attributes of their domains, correlated negatively with 'foreign investment' (Factor V, F = −0.58604) and positively with the 'index of wealth and political democracy' (Factor I, F = 0.54344) (Table 2.5). The negative relationship with foreign investment may simply reflect the patterns of net investment in peripheral country domains, where there is less competitiveness to bolster productivity levels. The second variable measuring the wealth of a domain, simply indicates the capacity of the market for paints, promoting increases in productivity.

Three attributes of a plant's intra-organisational relations accounted for over 50 per cent of the variance in productivity between the surveyed plants. First, 'length of membership' (Factor II, F = 0.57325) was a reasonable indicator of productivity levels, suggesting that the older plants may have higher levels of productivity either, for example, because they have had time to smooth out production problems or, more likely, because their past record of performance, *ipso facto*, has enabled them to remain as part of the business organisation longer. The plants with consistently low productivity levels are precisely those which are likely to be closed or sold off. Second, 'production technology' (Factor VI, F = −0.50727) and third, 'specialisation' (Factor V, F = −0.45154), were correlated negatively with productivity. The reason for this relationship is that some plants have a number of production methods on the one site, in order to cope with a more diverse product range, and also to allow for fluctuations in demand. Thus, they have low productivity levels, as do plants which produce a range of products with a weighting to the specialised industrial end of the paints range. Alternatively, the larger plants specialise largely in producing paints for the domestic end of the market where there is a relatively high demand. Consequently, these plants are by definition mass-producers, so their productivity levels are much higher.

When the domain and intra-organisational attributes were used in a combined analysis of productivity levels, factors such as 'foreign investment', 'specialisation' and 'length of membership' were again prominent. There was, however, a negative relationship between productivity and 'chemicals sector growth' (Factor X, F = −0.66179) and 'chemical export dynamics' (Factor XI, F = −0.46748). The structure of these two factors would seem to

Table 2.5: Stepwise Multiple Regression: Productivity

Range of Variables	Significant Independent Variables	Factor Number	Partial F Coefficient	Individual R^2	Cumulative R^2
(A) Domain	Foreign investment	V	−0.58604	0.214	0.214
	Index of wealth and political democracy	I	0.54344	0.232	0.446
(B) Intra-organisational	Length of membership	II	0.57325	0.199	0.199
Relations	Production technology	VI	−0.50727	0.177	0.376
	Specialisation	V	−0.45154	0.127	0.503
(A + B)	Foreign investment	V	−0.75320	0.215	0.215
	Plant position	I	0.74916	0.308	0.523
	Scale of production	IV	0.78585	0.105	0.628
	Specialisation	V	−0.59028	0.079	0.707
	Length of membership	II	0.77168	0.073	0.780
	Chemicals sector growth	X	0.66179	0.075	0.855
	Chemical export dynamics	XI	−0.46748	0.031	0.886

Source: Analysis of survey data.

suggest that the plants with lower productivity levels are located in domains where the domestic chemicals sector is growing only slowly, if at all, and they have a limited share of the international market.

Two additional intra-organisational attributes shown to be important in the combined analysis were 'plant position' (Factor I, F = 0.74916) and 'scale of production' (Factor IV, F = 0.78585). This suggests two interesting variants. First, plants with more peripheral positions within the organisation have high productivity levels, probably because of their situation as part of a small network of branch plants, with the threat of substitution by other plants from within the subsidiary of the business organisation which owns them. Second, the largest of the central plants also have high productivity levels because of their scale of production which is energy and technology intensive. This similarity of productivity levels at the extremes of plant centrality and peripherality is for quite different reasons: the mainstay of the high productivity of central plants relying on mass production advantages, and peripheral plants performing by either virtue of their tentative peripheral position within the organisation, or perhaps, because of the recent age of their capital stock, compared to central plants. It is interesting to note that the combination of domain and organisational variables accounted for over 88 per cent of the variance in the data, making this a powerful 'model' of productivity.

Rate of change in productivity.   Compared with production levels, the rate at which productivity is changing could only be explained by one variable, 'length of membership' (Factor II, F = −0.49303) of the plant in the business organisation (Table 2.6). Nevertheless, over 24 per cent of the variance in the data was explained by this variable. The limited evidence available, therefore, suggests that the *growth rate* of productivity is lower in the older, more central plants. This situation may be due either to ageing equipment or the difficulty of maintaining high growth in productivity simply through capital investment. Overall, an asymptotic relationship (S-shaped curve) might be suggested, with the rate of productivity increasing as the plant becomes more established in the organisation and then tailing-off as production reaches a 'peak', although this sequence must remain as conjecture.

Table 2.6: Stepwise Multiple Regression: Rate of Change in Productivity

Range of Variables	Significant Independent Variables	Factor Number	Partial F Coefficient	Individual R^2	Cumulative R^2
(A) Domain	—	—	—	—	—
(B) Intra-organisational Relations	Length of membership	II	−0.49303	0.243	0.243
(A + B)	Length of membership	II	−0.49303	0.243	0.243

Source: Analysis of survey data.

Table 2.7: Stepwise Multiple Regression: Capital Intensity of Production

Range of Variables	Significant Independent Variables	Factor Number	Partial F Coefficient	Individual R^2	Cumulative R^2
(A) Domain	Foreign investment	V	−0.42743	0.183	0.183
(B) Intra-organisational Relations	—	—	—	—	—
(A + B)	Foreign investment	V	−0.42743	0.183	0.183

Source: Analysis of survey data.

Capital intensity of production.   As with the previous dependent variable, only one factor emerged to explain variations in the capital intensity of production, 'foreign investment' (Factor V, F = −0.42743) in the domain of the plant (Table 2.7). This negative relationship indicates there may be some association between the capital intensity of production and the level of external control of the economy, which may explain why productivity growth rates can be higher in these locations. In peripheral country domains, production tends to be more labour, rather than capital-intensive. Having said this, it is difficult to extrapolate conclusions from this limited finding, especially without referring to the labour costs involved in each location, which is the last attribute of labour to be examined.

Total labour costs.   The total labour costs of a plant are undoubtedly influential in terms of productivity and the capital intensity of production. There was a positive association between total labour costs and three domain attributes — 'scale of chemicals production' (Factor IX, F = 0.92302), 'chemical export dynamics' (Factor XI, F = 0.59658) and 'international market structure' (Factor IV, F = 0.58688) — and this combination of variables explained 90 per cent of the variance in the data (Table 2.8). The results emphasise the importance of the size of the domestic chemicals market and the significance of the overall scale of the chemicals sector in determining a plant's total labour costs. Also, the export dynamics of the chemicals sector are influential, as the countries with high export growth also constitute the domains where the large plants with large workforces are located. It can be contended, therefore, that total labour costs in these plants are high because they are located in markets with an established chemicals sector, geared up to the international economy.

Three attributes of intra-organisational relations were also useful in explaining total labour costs. Apart from the obvious relationship with 'scale of production' (Factor IV, F = 0.91835), total labour costs were affected by 'plant status' (Factor III, F = 0.58982) and 'production technology' (Factor VI, F = 0.38516), indicating the older acquired (high-status) plants with larger product ranges, were also those with the least technological complexity. These combined factors emphasise that such plants are those with the most up-to-date equipment producing a defined range of products on a large scale, so that new technology has been

Table 2.8: Stepwise Multiple Regression: Total Labour Costs

Range of Variables	Significant Independent Variables	Factor Number	Partial F Coefficient	Individual R^2	Cumulative R^2
(A) Domain	Scale of chemicals production	IX	0.92302	0.761	0.761
	Chemical export dynamics	XI	0.59658	0.086	0.847
	International market structure	IV	0.58688	0.053	0.900
(B) Intra-organisational Relations	Scale of production	IV	0.91835	0.768	0.768
	Plant status	III	0.58982	0.093	0.861
	Production technology	VI	0.38516	0.021	0.882
(A + B)	Scale of production	IV	0.79426	0.768	0.768
	Scale of chemicals production	IX	0.78746	0.144	0.912

Source: Analysis of survey data.

used to offset high labour costs in these locations. However, the interaction between domain and organisational forces must not be underestimated, and this seems to be particularly influential with regard to a plant's total labour costs. In the combined analysis, only two variables accounted for 91 per cent of the variance, 'scale of production' (Factor IV, $F = 0.79426$) of the plant and the 'scale of chemicals production' (Factor IX, $F = 0.78746$) of the domain.

Conclusions

The purpose of this chapter has been to investigate in the context of one division of a single, multinational corporation some of the effects of plant centrality on labour dynamics. Two principal dimensions of centrality have been recognised: an *intra-organisational* dimension reflecting the position of a plant within an MNC and an *inter-organisational* domain dimension representing the *environment* or milieu within which a particular plant must operate (here equated with the national economy of the host country). The complexity of the organisation–environment relationships revealed in this analysis show that it would be erroneous to force an explanation of labour dynamics into a simple model. In fact, the argument has stressed the interaction between locational and organisational factors which must be taken into account in explaining patterns of labour use. In wider terms, the discussion has described a method of evaluating some of the organisational forces which lie behind the creation of a new international division of labour, by describing micro scale processes within a business organisation framework.

Notwithstanding the complexity of the relationships between labour dynamics and attributes of a plant's domain and intra-organisational relations which have been demonstrated in this analysis, it is possible to form some general conclusions as to the effects of plant centrality on labour dynamics. As has been emphasised, it is rarely possible to reach the conclusion that an individual aspect of labour is determined by the position of the plant in the structure of the business organisation or, alternatively, by the environment it must operate in. In fact, based on these results, it is more common for most aspects of labour dynamics to be affected by a combination of these forces. For instance, the size of the workforce, the rate of employment change, productivity, and total labour costs incurred by a plant, seem to be related to a mixture of environmental and organisational characteristics.

In some cases, however, it is possible to discern the dominant effect of either the domain or intra-organisational forces, which impinge on a plant and determine some of its labour characteristics. Thus, although the evidence was limited, the capital intensity of production seemed to be influenced more by the environmental domain than by factors operating within the business organisation. This feature is probably contingent upon how the corporation evaluates the plant's operational environment and upon technologies being introduced which 'match' the surrounding competition, rather than being the most developed techniques which are available to the organisation. If this is the case, then it represents one concrete example of the effect of business organisations cutting across national boundaries and questions the notion of the international transfer of technology, a point also made by Newfarmer and Topik (1982).

Attributes of labour which were determined by organisational rather than domain forces, were the administrative ratio and the rate of change of productivity of individual plants. In the case of both these variables, the status and length of membership of the plant as part of the business organisation were influential, suggesting that the administrative function of selected plants has been acquired and reinforced over time. A possible explanation for the falling rate of productivity in these plants was attributed to their advanced stage of development and their level of technological sophistication, which makes it difficult to make further improvements in the efficiency of production. In the newer, more peripheral plants, the rate of increase of productivity is likely to be greater because large gains can be made by simple changes in manpower organisation and the types of technology used in production.

An appreciation of the historical development of the business organisation and the position the individual plant occupies within this framework, is necessary to make sense of a complex picture. The oldest and most established plants in ICI's paints division are generally located in central domains and, in point of fact, they reflect the broad pattern of temporal and geographical development by ICI, especially in Britain, West Germany and Australia (see Clarke, 1984b). The British plants, at Slough and Stowmarket, and their Australian counterparts at Cabarita and Clayton have, therefore, maintained their organisational centrality by virtue of their location in markets valuable to ICI. They have increased their importance simply by surviving and acquiring more power, be it in terms of their contribution to production or their administrative role, for example. Built into the structure of business organisations, therefore, is an *historical inertia* which is manifest as a network of power relations and which, it appears, has a direct bearing on the performance and operational characteristics of individual plants. Consequently, the newer branch plants are admitted or taken into the business organisation on an unequal footing from the start, and it is unlikely that they will be able to overcome the power wielded by the plants already well entrenched in the organisation.

It was pointed out in the introduction to this chapter that Fröbel, Heinrichs and Kreye's (1980) work on the new international division of labour has tended to elevate the status of labour to a primary determinant of location. The authors noted, for example, that the new international division of labour is the product of 'the relocation of production to new industrial sites, where labour power is cheap to buy, abundant and well disciplined; in short, through the transnational reorganisation of production' (Fröbel, Heinrichs and Kreye, 1980, p. 15). Although this assertion may apply to certain industries, such as the assembly of electronics components and the textiles and clothing sector, it is by no means a uniform or inviolable trend. Not all production is hyper-mobile at a global scale, most industries being tied down geographically. What this study has attempted to do, by playing down the effect of the *relocation* of production sites, is to illustrate the importance of *in situ* labour dynamics for the changing spatial division of labour within a business organisation. It is hoped that this preliminary analysis will help provide a deeper understanding of the processes promoting the emergence of a new international division of labour and, more importantly, provoke interest in the relationship between the multinational structure of business organisations and micro scale processes of production as they are played out in space.

Acknowledgements

I would like to thank the Australian National University for supporting the fieldwork on which this chapter is based, plant managers in ICI for providing the data, and Mike Taylor for helping with the analysis.

3 MULTINATIONALS, BUSINESS ORGANISATIONS AND THE DEVELOPMENT OF THE FIJI ECONOMY

Michael Taylor

This chapter seeks to explore the changing relationships between multinational capital and domestic enterprise in the context of the developing country economy of Fiji. Studies of the operations of foreign-owned multinational corporations in developing countries are notable for two major limiting characteristics. The first is the implicit assumption that all multinational enterprises are the same; effectively having the same goals and aspirations, having equivalent resource bases, and employing similar methods of operation. The assumption is not always immediately obvious in these studies, especially those in geography, but it is most readily apparent when the investment activities of multinationals are reduced to the single category 'foreign private direct investment'. The use of this simplifying device completely removes from consideration the aspirations, operations and idiosyncracies of a host of quite separate legal corporate entities. The second characteristic of these studies is the tendency for multinational corporations as a whole to be treated as isolated and discrete facets of the developing economies within which they are situated. This approach is very much a legacy of the dualistic models that have dominated development studies for more than a decade. It is also an approach which disparages indigenous activity in developing economies as something less than 'economic', reinforcing the arrogance of western industrial activity. In short, obfuscation by assumption has left the social sciences, especially geography, economics, management science and, to a lesser extent sociology, woefully ill-equipped to appreciate the dynamic relationships that underpin the functioning of developing country economies.

In a preliminary fashion, this chapter seeks to penetrate this obfuscation of the functioning of developing country economies by adopting the business organisations approach which has been elaborated in industrial geography (McDermott and Taylor, 1982; Taylor, 1984a) to explore the nature of interaction between foreign- and locally-owned enterprise in the context of the small island economy of Fiji. This approach seeks to re-establish firms and business organisations as active agents of change within economies rather than reactive cogs in some economic machine powered by external macroeconomic forces (Taylor and Thrift, 1983). Macroeconomic approaches have tended to dominate analysis to date, invoking either the overarching laws of capital in Marxist literature, the equally over-generalised neo-Ricardian models of trade, or the maximising assumptions common to both schools of thought (Thompson, 1982). More properly, the business organisation or enterprise, which should not be confused and equated with the plant and establishment as is all too often the case, should be regarded as the crucible within which macro- and micro-economic forces meet, interact and are played out. The adoption of this enterprise perspective, especially in the context of developing country economies, opens up new areas of questioning about the nature of not only multinational corporations but also about the nature of the operations of domestically-owned enterprises with which they compete, which they complement or with which they simply coexist. Only by appreciating the disparities, inequalities, inevitabilities and injustices that are involved in these interactions between organisations can the dynamics of economic change be recognised and understood in terms which do more than add a few cursory social variables to unrealistic macroeconomic logic that reduces people to average GNP per capita.

This is not to deny that a number of disciplines have shown an interest in the functioning of individual enterprises in general and multinationals in particular as they operate within national and global economies. Interest has been particularly strong in geography, economics and development studies. However, each of these disciplines approaches the study of multinationals from very different perspectives and also with different armouries of implicit and explicit assumptions. These perspectives create rigidities which seriously detract from the ability of these disciplines to appreciate the functional significance of enterprises of different types.

Geographers have tended to be preoccupied with the development paths of individual enterprises (Rees, 1972; 1978; Håkanson, 1979; Watts, 1980; Taylor and Thrift, 1982; for example) and where multinationals locate their operations in host regions and countries (Hamilton, 1976; Abumere, 1982; Blackbourn, 1982). Indeed, even the host country impacts of multinationals have been viewed in these essentially spatial terms. Some sections of geography have been willing to discard maximising assumptions about the functioning of enterprises and MNCs but have never developed a conceptualisation of the structure and functioning of those organisations which could be used in their stead. Rather, random handfuls of variables have been used to describe organisational form, and at best this approach can be described as unhelpful (see argument in McDermott and Taylor, 1982). A possible conceptualisation has been suggested by McDermott and Taylor (1982) and Taylor and Thrift (1983), building on the structural contingency model of organisation theory and concepts of business organisation segmentation. The absence of such a framework, however, leaves only space as a touchstone for geographic studies of multinationals with all the attendant dangers of spatial fetishism. It can be argued, therefore, that geography is the discipline least well equipped to deal with the role and functioning of multinational corporations in developing country economies.

Economics, however, can be said to be inappropriately equipped in this field. This discipline has been preoccupied with the internal and external pressures that encourage an enterprise to internationalise its operations and has, in consequence, developed a wide range of theories (see Taylor and Thrift, 1982; Caves, 1982). The assumption of profit-maximisation is also especially well developed in this discipline so that all enterprises, including multinationals, are treated as a homogeneous set of economic actors differentiated only to the extent of being in mining, manufacturing, trade, services or transport, and coming from a variety of home countries. Microeconomic theory of the firm has succeeded in constructing such an intricate framework of assumptions about the functioning of enterprises that variations in firm type and operation have been quite effectively assumed away. Grosse (1982, p. 108) has now gone so far as to suggest that the multinational firm is simply 'an extension of the standard firm in micro-economic theory' strapping it, too, into the straightjacket of assumptions constructed in microeconomic theory. This is essentially the stance adopted in much recent economics literature on multinationals, especially that advocating a transactions costs and internalisation approach to multinational development (Rugman, 1982; Caves, 1982).

As with microeconomic approaches, homogenisation by

assumption is evident in macroeconomic perspectives that reduce the overseas investments of individual enterprises to a single figure for private direct foreign investment. It has removed from the purview of analysis the nature of the investment decision-making organisation, the form and sophistication of the operations that are set up in host countries, the forms of relationship these overseas operations have with their larger corporate parents, and the unequal relationships these same overseas operations, in turn, are able to establish with locally-owned businesses. By ignoring these sets of relationships both micro- and macroeconomic perspectives are unable to come to grips with corporate distortions of prices and the great range of what appear to be widely practised transfer-pricing mechanisms (Plasschaert, 1979; Murray, 1980). Indeed, the World Bank (1983, p.57) still maintains that '[i]n most instances ... price distortions are introduced by government directly or indirectly in the pursuit of some social or economic objective', implicitly discounting '[p]rice distortions ... caused by monopolistic tendencies in the private sector' (p.57).

An equivalent homogenisation of business organisation types, which simultaneously eradicates the functional ramifications of those enterprises also occurs in Marxist approaches to uneven development through the adoption of the same overwhelming maximising assumptions (Thompson, 1980). Gibson and Horvath's (1983a; 1983b) sub-modes of production approach, for example, which attempts to develop a theory of transition within a mode of production, goes as far as identifying four variants of the capitalist mode ('transitional', 'competitive', 'monopoly' and 'global') which might be loosely interpreted as four types of capital or enterprise. These types, however, are seen as compartmenta-lised and isolated rather than as sets which interact on wholly unequal terms. In consequence, the four sub-modes sit uneasily with the overarching assumptions of rationality, maximisation and perfect knowledge, and if they are treated other than in isolation they could be said to be in contradiction of those assumptions. Capital, therefore, remains as homogenised capital, undifferen-tiated by the impact and idiosyncracies of human agency.

In development studies, there has been a tendency to neglect consideration of business organisations rather than homogenise them through assumption as has been the case in economics. Indeed, there has been a predisposition to assign firms, enterprises and businesses of all types to formal or informal, traditional or modern, foreign or domestic sectors, for example, in accordance with a dualistic model (e.g. Boeke, 1961). These sectors have been interpreted as working quite independently of one another, acting in parallel and yet being quite separate. The unequal relationships between one type of enterprise and another have therefore been looked at in only very generalised terms as, for example, between large and small firms. The differentiation of firm types has been minimal and that which has been attempted has been amongst small firms owing to the importance that has been attached to the informal sector in development studies literature. What is more, the equally important and asymmetric relationships *within* enterprises, between branch plants and head offices in the same firm, for example, have also been ignored. The outcome of this approach is that the differentiation of business organisations into different types has been addressed only partially and inadequately in the economic development literature. What has been brought about is a homogenisation of business organisation form equivalent to that in micro- and macroeconomics but through a process of homogenisation by compartmentalisation rather than homogenisation by assumption.

The conclusion that can be drawn from this discussion of approaches to the role and functioning of enterprises developed in geography, economics and development studies is that currently we are very ill-equipped with frameworks that enable us to appreciate the role of business organisations — either formal sector multinationals and domestic businesses or informal sector enterprises — in economic development. In geography, the organisation has for too long been underconceptualised. Macro-, micro- and Marxist economic approaches offer only visions of an homogenised world in which a firm is merely a firm and implicitly indistinguishable from its neighbour. Models of economic development, embracing dualism, modernisation, conservation and dissolution, for example, offer little more and describe only compartmentalised diversity in which sets of different types of enterprise operate in functional isolation.

To begin to penetrate the labyrinth of rigidities and assumptions erected by different disciplines in their treatment of the role of business organisations in the process of economic development, there is an urgent need to appreciate the diversity and mix of the different types of business organisation and enterprise present in such economies. In developing country economies the foreign-owned enterprise is now almost universally looked upon as the engine of growth. But not all multinationals offer the same growth potential and not all multinationals are functionally the same. Domestic enterprises are equally diversified and they, too, cannot be expected to develop uniform relationships either between themselves or with different kinds of multinational. Inequality is, in fact, the key to interaction and it is this inequality between enterprises that imparts a dynamic to developing economies. The dual economy model came closest to recognising this diversity of enterprise but oversimplified its complexity and prejudged the nature of interrelationships (especially in the conservation/dissolution literature). What is now required, therefore, to revitalise discussion is a fuller appreciation of the types of enterprise, both foreign and domestic, that interact in a developing economy.

The analysis presented in this chapter attempts such a specification in the context of the small Pacific island nation of Fiji. Tiny and isolated, Fiji has a population of 600,000 which is roughly half Fijian and half Indian (the Indians originally having been brought in as indentured labour by the British), and the country has been independent since 1970. There is a strong planning tradition, and even before independence from Britain, industrialisation had been encouraged to diversify the economy away from the production of sugar and copra. An initial emphasis on import-substitution industrialisation was reoriented in the current Eighth Development Plan (DP8) to begin to encourage export-oriented growth. Foreign capital, mainly from Australia, New Zealand and the United Kingdom, has always dominated the economy although indigenous enterprise, established principally through the efforts of Indian entrepreneurs, has grown substantially in recent years. There is, therefore, a range of types of enterprise operating within the Fiji economy; old colonial trading multinationals, peripheral branches of global corporations, the first overseas ventures of small Australian and New Zealand companies, expatriate-owned companies, large local enterprises, state-owned concerns, small, government-supported Fijian ventures, livelihood and informal sector enterprises. It is the unequal, asymmetric relationships that have developed or are developing which impart a particular dynamic into the economy and it is the nature of the types of business involved and the interrelations they develop with the rest of the economy that this chapter seeks to explore.

The discussion is divided into five sections. In the first, the types of multinational enterprise found in the Fiji economy are described. There are two dimensions to this description; the first considering the types of multinational that have invested in Fiji and the second describing the types of operation that these corporations have established. Since both these dimensions of multinational investment are in a constant state of flux, the second section addresses the dynamics of multinational business organisations in Fiji and the third section describes their role in Fiji's trading patterns. The remaining sections of the chapter discuss the locally-owned businesses operating in Fiji. In section four the various locally-owned components are elaborated, while their dynamic relationships within the economy are discussed in section five. The broad threads of the discussion are drawn together in the conclusion.

The Multinational Component of the Fiji Economy

Foreign capital in the form of foreign-owned multinationals dominates the Fiji economy (Table 3.1). Official data tend to understate the importance of these enterprises since a significant element of foreign ownership and control is also involved amongst

Table 3.1: Shares of Company Turnover (1980), Foreign and Local Companies

	Foreign Companies[a]	Local Companies[b]
Agriculture	56.2	43.8
Mining and quarrying	99.6	0.4
Manufacturing	85.6	14.4
Electricity, gas and water	100.0	0.0
Construction	28.9	71.1
Wholesale, retail, restaurants	64.8	35.2
Hotels, etc.	81.8	18.2
Transport, communication, storage	77.8	22.2
Banking and finance	93.2	6.8
Real estate, business services	34.5	65.5
Community, social, personal services	27.4	72.6
Not classified	87.6	2.4
Total	73.5	26.4

Notes: a. All companies with foreign equity.
b. Companies incorporated in Fiji treated as 100 per cent locally-owned even if they have foreign parents.

Source: Carstairs and Prasad (1981).

those companies that are classified as local simply because they are locally registered. This dominance embraces virtually all sectors of the formal economy and in 1981 in all but construction, real estate, business services, community, social and personal services, foreign-owned companies accounted for at least half and in most cases over three-quarters of each sector's turnover.

But it would be wrong to think of this foreign component of Fiji's economy as uniform and undifferentiated. It may well span all sectors of the economy and attempt to monopolise certain significant subsectors within it (Taylor, 1984a; Utrecht, 1984), but it also displays important internal diversity. This diversity has two quite distinct components; an inter-organisational component and an intra-organisational component.

At the inter-organisational level, the types of corporation investing in Fiji, as in all developing countries, are very diverse. Dealing with the international chemicals industry, for example, Clarke (1984) has shown there to be at least three broad sets of companies that can be recognised: global corporations, global restructuring corporations and multinationals. Fragmentary information for Fiji would suggest that many more types than these are involved.

Some insight into this diversity can be gained from data on a sample of 60 foreign-owned companies with operations in Fiji. These data, for 1983, concern the number of subsidiaries in each corporation, the home country of the enterprise and the proportion of those subsidiaries located outside the home country (i.e. the degree of multinationality). In diagrammatic form the data are presented in Figure 3.1. Of particular importance, the size distribution shows this sample of multinationals to be divided into at least two (and possibly more) discrete groups. The first group contains those multinationals present in Fiji that have fewer than 20 subsidiaries in total. They appear to be quite different from those with more than 20 subsidiaries. Amongst these smaller multinationals there is absolutely no relationship between enterprise, size and degree of multinationality ($R^2 = 0.269$ per cent) with multinationality ranging from 8 per cent to 96 per cent. This group does, in fact, fall into two separate sub-sets. On the one hand, there are a small number of small multinationals that are, in reality, regional components of global corporations and reflect little more than the niceties of legal definitions. In their ranks are, for example, Amatil and Commonwealth Industrial Gases which are parts of British and American Tobacco and British Oxygen, respectively. These corporations are the vehicles of 'stepping-stone' investment, recognised by Taylor and Thrift (1981) and Rogerson (1982). On the other hand, there is the sub-set of genuinely small multinationals which in this case represent the first overseas moves by expanding Australian and New Zealand companies. They include small companies that have been encouraged to invest overseas by the Australian and New Zealand governments (Bellam, 1980), and they also include a substantial group of companies from both countries that have gone multinational as contractors and subcontractors in major construction projects not infrequently financed by their own government's aid dollars.

The members of the second group of multinationals each have more than 20 subsidiaries and they demonstrate a range of relationships between corporate size and multinationality depending upon their country of origin (Figure 3.1). For New Zealand multinationals, at one extreme, multinationality barely increases with size, in part owing to the small sample involved, but also suggesting that New Zealand corporations tend to be home country-oriented no matter what their size. These are also the smallest multinationals having, on average, 86 subsidiaries. At the other extreme, multinationals, mainly from the USA and UK, which make up the 'other MNC' category, are much larger, with an average of 181 subsidiaries, and become most rapidly multinational with increased size. Intermediate to these two groups are the Australian multinationals, reinforcing the conclusion that multinationality is directly related to home country size and the extent of home country development.

To these various sets of multinationals with operations in the Fiji economy, two additional groups must be added which are far more difficult to pinpoint and which demonstrate quite closely the difficulty of dividing between foreign-owned and locally-owned companies within any economy. The first group is those that are expatriate-owned. Where the owners are not citizens their companies are considered as foreign investment in Fiji although the owners themselves may be permanent Fiji residents. A number of tourist accommodation businesses fall into this category as do some car distributorships, equipment dealerships, engineering and paint manufacturing businesses, for example. In some instances they are multinational enterprises at the most primitive scale, in

Figure 3.1: Types of Multinational with Operations in Fiji

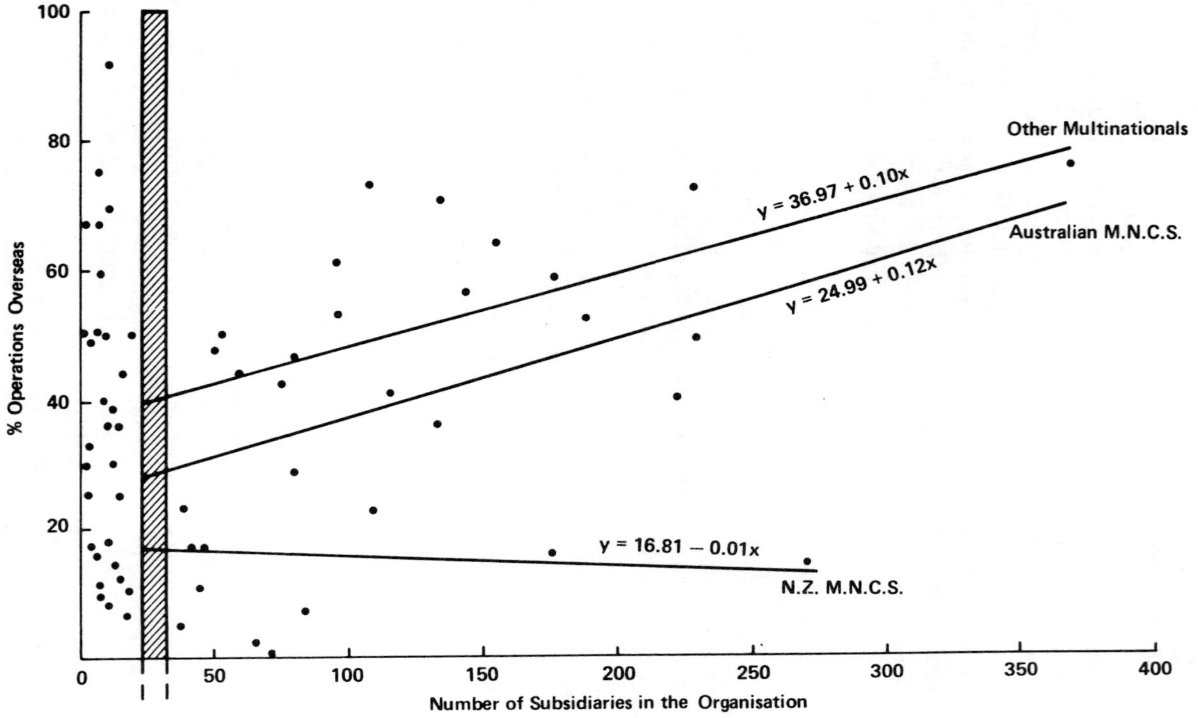
% Operations Overseas
100
80
60
40
20
0
50
100
150
200
250
300
350
400
Number of Subsidiaries in the Organisation
Other Multinationals
y = 36.97 + 0.10x
Australian M.N.C.S.
y = 24.99 + 0.12x
y = 16.81 – 0.01x
N.Z. M.N.C.S.

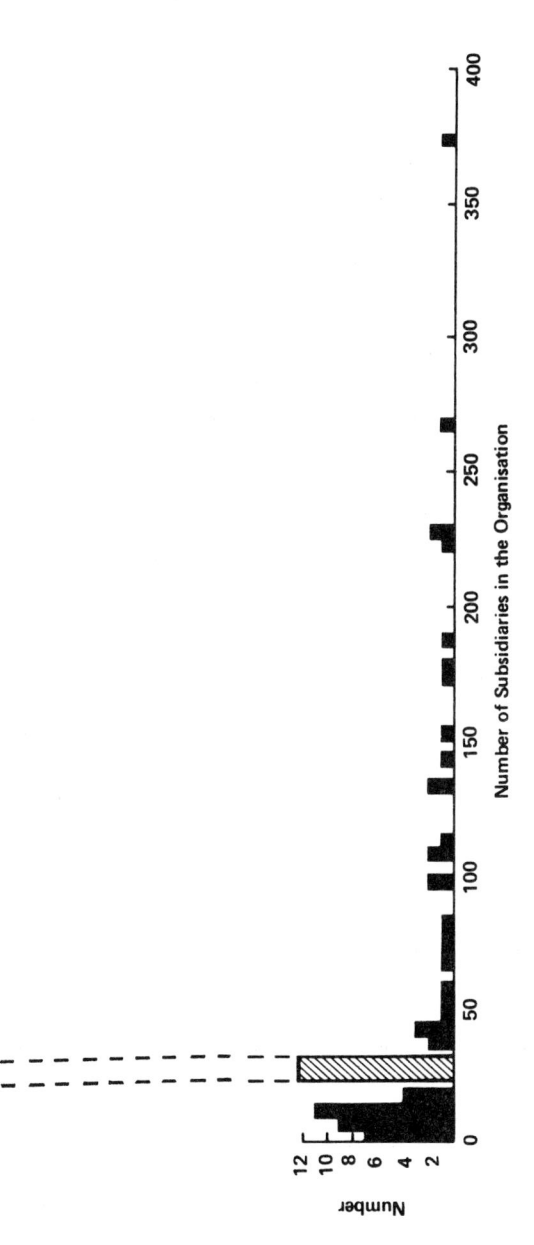

others they are not multinationals at all and simply have non-nationals as owners.

The second group of companies is equally ambiguous, and these are the franchisees. As part of a franchise agreement, a franchisor may offer a local company capital or credit and may even take a small stake in the business. Under some circumstances, therefore, franchisees become classified as foreign-owned. The nature of this foreign involvement, however, is very difficult to trace, although it is to be found in Fiji, for example, in fast-food operations, electrical goods distribution and tyre retreading. Certainly, international brand names are involved like Kentucky Fried Chicken and Pizza Hut. Deciding what multinational corporation is involved, however, is obscure when the franchise itself is held by another multinational, and deciding whether multinationals are involved or not is ambiguous when the franchisee is a locally-owned concern. Franchising that involves locally-owned enterprises can, perhaps, be more properly looked upon as a form of indirect foreign capital involvement in an economy like Fiji's — a form of multinational expansion that suits risk-averse corporations, especially in the service and retail industries.

At the intra-organisational level there is again a diversity of types of establishment present within the Fiji economy. By definition a multinational corporation is a multi-site, multi-establishment enterprise. However, not all those separate establishments perform identical functions or have the same significance within the corporation as a whole. As in relationships between organisations, the power of individual units within an organisation can be conceptualised as being a function of the money and authority wielded by any particular establishment (Benson, 1975; Pfeffer, 1981). This creates intra-organisational power networks with well-defined cores and peripheries. The branch plant is thus the most peripheral, subordinate and potentially emphemeral component of a corporation while the regional head office and the corporate headquarters are progressively more central, and obviously wield more power. The same pattern of dominance and subordination will not be repeated and replicated in all organisations and these relationships will also change over time. However, some broad schemes of interrelationship — that is, broad patterns of intra-organisational power — have been recognised in the economics literature. Stopford and Wells (1972) and Franko (1976), for example, writing in the European and North American contexts, have recognised 'mother–daughter' structures, product division and regional division structures, while more recent literature (Knight, 1976) has described complex matrix forms of organisation.

In industrial geography, a simple scheme of intra-organisational differentiation has been proposed by Taylor and Thrift (1983). This scheme envisages the multi-plant multinational corporation as comprising four main elements which will be found in different combinations in different enterprises. These elements have been labelled 'leader', 'intermediate', 'laggard' and 'support'. *Leader* elements are the innovative core of the business organisation, generating new products, processes and services. *Intermediate* elements, which may be subsidiaries or even separate divisions, are the heart of the enterprise, yielding steady and reliable profits from the production of established goods and services. *Laggard* elements mass-produce commodities which often compete in hyper-competitive markets and are fast becoming obsolete. They must, therefore, continually search for higher productivity and lower costs to off-set shrinking profit margins. Finally, *support* elements provide general services, especially managerial services, but also supply internalised inputs of commodities to the companies of multidivisional, multinational corporations. They are, therefore, fundamental to the integration of multinational and global corporations being the modes through which transfer pricing mechanisms are operated (Plassehaert, 1979; Murray, 1980; Taylor, 1984b). Within an intra-organisational power network, centrality can thus be envisaged as declining from the most central support elements, through leaders to intermediates and finally to the peripheral, laggard branch plants.

The significance of the intra-organisational centrality and peripherality of foreign-owned companies operating within the Fiji economy can be established from a survey of 36 such companies conducted in 1983 (Taylor, 1983). For the initial assignment of survey respondents to the separate segments of this notional intra-organisational scale of centrality and peripherality, rules drawn from existing segmentation literature were employed (see Taylor and Thrift, 1982; 1983 (unpublished)). However, 10 variables describing organisational structure collected as part of the survey help to clarify this structural differentiation within foreign-owned companies operating in Fiji (Table 3.2).

The highly peripheral, laggard branch plants tend to be parts of

Table 3.2: Structural Differentiation of Foreign-owned Corporate
Organisations in Fiji, 1983

	Support	Leader	Intermediate	Laggard
% Equity held by largest shareholder	73.67	—	73.92	92.57
No. of boundary spanning functions[a] used	7.67	—	9.92	9.38
No. of boundary spanning functions[a] on-site	6.67	—	6.83	6.48
No. of boundary spanning functions[a] supplied by parent	1.67	—	2.17	2.52
Index of board representation[b]	2.00	—	1.83	0.48
% Whole organisations employment controlled from site	12.27	—	11.42	1.70
Age of enterprise (years to 1983)	55.00	—	17.75	12.19
On-site employment	69.33	—	54.08	79.67
Whole organisation employment	9906.67	—	5693.25	21914.95
Administrative ratio[c]	100.0	—	47.23	42.06
No. of cases (Total — 36)	3	0	12	21

Notes: a. Twelve boundary-spanning functions were recognised: sales and marketing, purchasing, market research, research and development, advertising, transport, maintenance, personnel, accounting, data processing, legal services, management research.
b. Scored as 1 — no representation on a higher board; 2 — representation on an intermediate board; 3 — representation on the ultimate board.
c. Administrative employment as a per cent of total employment.
Source: 1983 Survey.

the largest corporations which employ the largest numbers of people and have been established in Fiji for the shortest period of time. In addition, as shown in Table 3.2, they have the weakest board representation, control little if any of the organisation as a whole outside their own premises and, as shown by the number of boundary-spanning functions supplied by their parents, have their interactions with other organisations controlled for them more than any other type of corporate segment. This pattern of sub-ordination is reinforced by a low administrative ratio and the tendency for them to be owned almost exclusively by one corporation. Intermediate corporate operations, in contrast, tend to be parts of the smallest corporations that are represented in Fiji (Table 3.2). On average, they are the smallest foreign-owned operations within the country but also exercise control over other parts of the organisation. However, while they are relatively strongly tied into the organisation as a whole through representation on higher level boards of directors, they are also subordinated within that organisation through the supply of boundary spanning functions by their parent. Finally, support companies in Fiji, of which only three were surveyed, are almost exclusively concerned with administration. They control important segments of the larger organisation to which they belong but they are also subordinated within that organisation by having some functions fulfilled by their parent companies. They employ quite large numbers of people in their own right and have been operating in Fiji for many years. Quite clearly, this type of foreign-owned operation embraces the old colonial trading companies that have played a major role in shaping the economies of Fiji and Pacific Island States (Taylor, 1984a).

Two features of this survey are particularly striking; first, the predominance of laggard corporate segments within Fiji, and second, the complete absence of any leader corporate concerns. Laggard corporate operations dominate, making up 58 per cent of the sampled businesses but accounting for over 66 per cent of the sampled jobs. The intermediate operations of the smaller corporations operating in Fiji are far less significant, providing approximately one quarter of the surveyed jobs, while the support operations, which wield considerable economic clout, generate little in the way of employment. Without leader corporate operations there is no stimulus to corporate growth in Fiji beyond that provided by government through tax holidays and other investment incentives. There is obviously no commitment by corporations to innovation in Fiji so that the country becomes a product-taker and not a product-maker. Such a conclusion bodes ill for a government seeking export-led growth, as is the case in Fiji and other developing countries. However, it is wholly consistent with the dominance of foreign-owned laggard branch plants in the economy and the fact that Australian corporations are interested in the Pacific Islands only as a market for their goods and services and not as manufacturing bases for export (Bennett *et al.*, 1981).

An equally disconcerting aspect of Fiji's branch plant economy is the fact that laggard corporate concerns are the youngest foreign-owned operations in the economy, being, on average, a little over 12 years old (Table 3.2). This feature can be interpreted in two ways. On the one hand, it may represent an innovation in corporate structure in this small island economy. This is new peripheralisation. On the other hand, it may reflect the speed with which branch plants come and go or the speed with which they are exchanged between different corporate parents. This is corporate ephemeralisation. Either way, they offer little to a country like Fiji. However, these possibilities also raise the important issue that the specification of inter- and intra-organisational differentiation attempted here has been only a static, cross-sectional description for the early 1980s of a set of patterns and relationships which are, in essence, highly volatile and dynamic. The following section, therefore, seeks to examine the dynamics of the inter- and intra-organisational differentiation of foreign-owned business organisations within the Fiji economy.

The Dynamics of Multinationals in Fiji

Business organisations, no matter what their size, are always in a state of flux; investing, disinvesting, expanding and contracting. As the conditions of global, national and regional economies change, so the resources, authority and power of different types of enterprise will also change.

The magnitude of this continuous corporate change can be gauged from information on the subsidiary structure of Burns Philp and Co. Ltd between 1972/73 and 1981/82 (Table 3.3). A major subsidiary of this company, Burns Philp (South Seas) Ltd, has long been regarded as a pillar of not only the Fiji economy but also Fiji society. The annual reports of Burns Philp give information on the numbers of subsidiaries formed and liquidated internally and also on those acquired and sold. For the acquisitions and sales, the value of the net tangible assets involved is also given. When these figures are combined and expressed as a proportion of the total assets of the company in any particular financial year they provide a crude index of the extent to which the company reconstructed itself during that year. In the 10 years covered by the data of Table 3.3, the principal activity of Burns Philp and Co. has been acquisition to effect corporate expansion. The activity has been continuous. However, major takeovers appear to be followed by a number of years of internal reorganisation when subsidiaries are liquidated rather than being sold off. Two such events are evident

Table 3.3: Changes in the Subsidiaries of Burns Philp and Co. Ltd
1972/73 to 1981/82

Financial Year	Formed No.	Liquidated No.	Acquired No.	NTA[a] $000	Sold No.	NTA[a] $000	Index of Reconstruction[b]
1972/73	3	0	35	3940	1	103	1.98
1973/74	0	10	7	365	10	10	0.14
1974/75	1	19	12	2933	19	1324	1.45
1975/76	0	2	18	6985	2	144	2.10
1976/77	0	7	5	420	7	169	0.17
1977/78	0	6	4	23308	6	464	5.44
1978/79	1	1	3	616	1	937	0.33
1979/80	7	4	106	61111	4	1	8.89
1980/81	1	17	8	2987	17	478	0.48
1981/82	9	9	68	55370	9	15875	8.30

Notes: a. NTA — net tangible assets.
b. Index of reconstruction — NTA (acquisitions) + NTA (sales)

$$\frac{\text{NTA (acquisitions)} + \text{NTA (sales)}}{\text{Total assets}}$$

Source: Company Reports (various years).

in Table 3.3, the first in 1973/74 and 1974/75 following a major takeover in 1972/73 when 35 subsidiaries were acquired; and the second most notably in 1980/81 following takeovers involving 106 subsidiaries in 1979/80. More significantly, the index of corporate reconstruction has increased strongly in the 10 years to the early 1980s. The index shows a strong biannual cycle and while it hovered at a maximum of about 2.0 per cent in the early 1970s, by the early 1980s it exceeded 8.0 per cent and approached 9.0 per cent.

It is completely spurious, therefore, to regard multinationals like Burns Philp as unchanging monoliths, as is often the case in small developing countries. Now more than ever before, the larger multi-nationals are simply capital-chasing investment opportunities changing their form at increasing speed. It is wrong to see them in the paternalistic light they liked to be seen in in the 1940s and 1950s, and in countries like Fiji this is a hard adjustment to make.

Extending this pattern for Burns Philp to a wider canvas, inter- and intra-organisational patterns of multinational business organisation differentiation will, therefore, alter through time so that the mixed enterprises in a small island economy such as Fiji, will constantly evolve. At the inter-organisational scale, some multinational companies and corporations will expand and others will contract and all will modify their goals, aspirations and investment strategies to a greater or lesser extent. In consequence, multinational enterprises, whether they are large or small, will constantly reappraise their investments in countries like Fiji bringing about changes in their intra-organisational structures. The argument has been made, however, that this process of reappraisal is by no means haphazard (Taylor, 1984a). Rather, it has been argued, the internationalisation of production and the parallel internationalisation of the world financial system has brought in its wake the synchronisation of separate corporate reappraisals so that waves of multinational investment and disinvestment now move back and forth across the fixed territorial framework of the world's nation-states. For Fiji and the Pacific Islands nations as a whole, the chronology of these changes has been seen as a wave of investment in the 1960s and early 1970s being followed by massive disinvestment in the late 1970s and early 1980s (Taylor, 1984a).

At the inter-organisational scale, dealing with corporations as a whole rather than the particular elements of a set of corporations that are found in a single country, Taylor (1984a) has demonstrated this reappraisal for Australian corporations with investments in the Pacific Islands in general and Fiji in particular. Paralleling the types of multinational described in the previous section, three types of Australian enterprise were recognised; 'Australian colonials', 'other Australians' and 'Australian foreign-owned'. The *Australian foreign-owned* are those ostensibly Australian companies that are ultimately foreign-owned with parents in the UK and USA in particular (for example, CIG, ICI and Kilpatrick Green). The *Australian colonials* are those that have been in the vanguard of commercial and economic development in the Pacific Islands especially in retailing, trade, shipping, mining and plantations. Their ranks include Burns Philp and Co., W.R. Carpenter and Emperor Goldmines. The *Other Australians* are large, truly Australian organisations like Australian Consolidated Industries, Westpac, Wormald International and Nicholas Kiwi.

To show the changing significance of broad regions of the world for the operations of those types of organisation, the contributions of subsidiaries to the consolidated group profits of 34 companies for 1974/75 and 1980/81 have been extracted from company reports (Table 3.4). This index has been used in preference to

Table 3.4: Contributions to Consolidated Group Profits of the Overseas Operations of Three Types of Australian Company

	1975		1981	
	$000	%	$000	%
Australian Colonial (N — 8)				
Australia	11,013	51.66	25,228	56.30
New Zealand	5	0.02	(7)	(0.02)
Pacific Islands	10,125	47.49	16,492	37.13
ASEAN	—	—	469	1.06
E. Asia	—	—	1,649	3.71
Europe	91	0.43	2,671	6.01
N. America	83	0.39	(2,077)	(4.68)
Rest	—	—	(8)	(0.02)
Total	21,319	99.98	144,417	100.02
Other Australian (N — 18)				
Australia	177,729	93.79	568,770	93.69
New Zealand	7,934	4.19	9,533	1.57
Pacific Islands	2,379	1.26	6,581	1.08
ASEAN	2,452	1.29	15,204	2.50
E. Asia	200	0.11	1,106	0.18
Europe	(2,291)	(1.21)	13,466	2.22
N. America	747	0.39	(6,784)	(1.12)
Rest	349	0.18	(769)	(0.13)
Total	189,499		607,107	
Foreign-owned (N — 8)				
Australia	69,452	97.85	220,550	94.66
New Zealand	736	1.04	4,982	2.14
Pacific Islands	534	0.75	3,708	1.59
ASEAN	236	0.33	430	0.18
E. Asia	17	0.02	1,999	0.86
Europe	1	0.00	606	0.26
N. America	—	0.00	726	0.31
Rest	—	0.00	(6)	0.00
Total	70,976		232,995	

Source: Taylor (1984b).

assets owing to the greater consistency with which these data are recorded in company reports.

The *Australian foreign-owned* have always derived most of their profits from Australia. In the seven years to 1980/81 New Zealand and the Pacific Islands have become slightly more prominent, but no more so than East Asia. These companies are very much regional operations of often global corporations. They have no mandate for independent action and global expansion. Indeed, their regional structures reflect the policies of their ultimate owners. So, for instance, should the New Zealand and Pacific

Islands market grow, the Australian-controlled facets of the business operating in those areas may be hived off as a new New Zealand-based regional node. These data on the *Australian foreign-owned* are, in consequence, an entirely inadequate window on a number of major global corporations.

The *Other Australians* are again mainly home-oriented in their operations and their Australian operations are stable in their contribution to group profits. Since the mid-1970s they have re-oriented their overseas operations, and there is some evidence in Table 3.4 that this involves disengagement from both New Zealand and the Pacific Islands and expansion into Europe, the USA and ASEAN.

The most dramatic changes in the reorientation of investment have occurred amongst the *Australian colonials.* As sources of profit for these companies, the islands have slumped (Table 3.4). Australia has gained a new appeal and so too has Europe, North America (again unprofitably), ASEAN and East Asia. If the *Other Australians* are in the process of disengagement from the Pacific Islands, then the *Australian colonials* are in headlong retreat. Prominent amongst these retreating companies is Burns Philp and Co. Ltd.

Redirection of this company's investment away from the Pacific Islands has involved the sale of urban real estate and retail proper-ties, the sale of plantations and the trimming of shipping operations (*Pacific Islands Monthly*, 1982; Taylor, 1984a). The outcome has been that, while at current prices the book value of this company's assets in both Papua New Guinea and Fiji rose steadily from 1973 to 1979 and 1980, since 1980 there has been an absolute decline. New investment has gone elsewhere. Thus, in 1973, 38 per cent of the book value of Burns Philp's investments was in Papua New Guinea. In 1980, this figure was 15 per cent; and in 1982 it was only 8 per cent. The equivalent figures for Fiji were 8 per cent in 1973, 10 per cent in 1979 and 4 per cent in 1982.

Retreat and disengagement from Fiji and the Pacific Island economies is not only the preserve of the large foreign-owned and multinational enterprises. Many small enterprises that have moved into the Islands to take advantage of their national government's aid programmes and other capital projects specifically associated with tourism have also withdrawn, possibly from international operations altogether. Some indication of the extent of this process can be gained from the reanalysis of data on New Zealand-owned companies operating in Fiji compiled for 1973 by Livesey (1973/74). Sixty-six New Zealand companies were recognised as operating in Fiji at that time, although a number were ultimately owned in Australia, the UK or the USA. Notwithstanding this limitation, 29 were large (having more than 20 subsidiaries at home and abroad) and 37 were small (having fewer than 20 subsidiaries). In addition, these companies could be divided into two sectoral groupings; contractors and allied enterprises (including civil engineers, air conditioning firms, electrical suppliers, and so on) and all other types of enterprise (Table 3.5).

From the reanalysis presented in Table 3.5, a number of significant points emerge. Of the 66 enterprises present in Fiji in 1973, only 40 per cent (26) were in contracting or allied activities. The majority were in manufacturing or other services. By 1983, however, 68 per cent of the 1973 population of 'small' contractors had closed and withdrawn from Fiji, and 60 per cent of the 'larger' contractors had gone the same way. These figures compare with 24 per cent and 21 per cent closure rates, respectively, for 'small' and 'larger' enterprises in all other activities. From an employment perspective this withdrawal of New Zealand-based enterprise has been even more dramatic. Combining the large and small multinational contractors, 1212 jobs have been lost in Fiji — 83 per cent

Table 3.5: Closures of New Zealand Companies in Fiji, 1973 to 1983

	No. in 1973	No. closed 1973-83	Av. 1973 employment of estabs. closed in Fiji	Total jobs lost from closure	%
Large multinationals (>20 subsidiaries)					
(i) Contractors and allied enterprises	10	6	103	618	42.3
(ii) Other enterprises	19	4	52	208	14.3
Small multinationals (<20 subsidiaries)					
(iii) Contractors and allied enterprises	16	11	54	594	40.7
(iv) Other enterprises	21	5	8	40	2.7
Total	66	26	56	1460	100

Source: Livesey (1973/74); Carstairs and Prasad (1981); *Who Owns Whom* (1983); field survey (1983).

of all the 1973 jobs lost from the withdrawal of this set of companies.

These New Zealand contracting companies were involved in the early 1970s in projects such as the building of the Nadi–Suva highway, the construction of the Nasinu Teachers College and extension of the Nadi airport. They also had a considerable stake in the building associated with the first major expansion of Fiji's tourist industry (Britton, 1982). Large multinationals are obvious contenders for major construction contracts including aid projects. However, as Livesey (1973/74) has pointed out, much of the subcontract work goes not to local enterprises but to small foreign-owned businesses who are often embarking on their first overseas venture. The local multiplier effect of major investments and aid projects is, therefore, considerably reduced when these small firms close. What is more, the spin-off employment in small building concerns is, in effect, made more vulnerable and ephemeral owing to this foreign-ownership component.

However, just as whole corporations are changing, so too is the form and nature of their representation in Fiji. This intra-organisational change occurs through the differential growth and contraction of individual establishments and the rationalisation associated with takeovers and mergers. Takeover and merger, which is often directed from outside Fiji, leads to the peripheralisation of acquired plants, establishments and companies within the enlarged corporation. The management science literature points only too frequently to the difficulty of incorporating established structures acquired by takeover into existing organisational forms. Evidence from Europe suggests that the unequal struggle is usually given up within five years when the acquired enterprise, or at least major portions of it, are liquidated (Smith and Taylor, 1983).

Thus, Emperor Goldmines is peripheralised in a corporate sense following the take-up of part of its equity by the Australian resources company, Western Mining. The goldmines that were once the sole concern of one Australian corporation are now no more than a minor part of a major mining corporation. In a similar fashion, the peripheralisation of W.R. Carpenter's Fiji operations may be accelerated following the company's takeover by the Australian investment company, Griffin Holding. The same process is illustrated by the creation of Industrial and Marine Engineering Ltd (IMEL) to consolidate the engineering and ship repairing operations of three corporations in Fiji (W.R. Carpenter,

Burns Philp (South Seas) and Inchcape) which incurred the incidental loss of 100 jobs.

The process of peripheralisation and disposal that occurs under the guise of rationalisation is particularly well illustrated by the restructuring of Kiwi United in Fiji in 1982. Having been established as a joint venture by Kiwi International, Bowater Scott and UEB, it was completely dismembered immediately before and immediately after the merger that created the major Australian multinational Nicholas Kiwi in 1982. Before the merger three operations were conducted on one site outside Nasouri; match production in a wholly-owned subsidiary (Pacific Manufacturers), container-making, and paper and plastic bag manufacture. As competition from locally-owned companies had grown dramatically, the result was inevitable. The match production business was sold in 1982 to another foreign company, Wilkinson Sword (incorporating Bryant & May), the container division was sold to a locally-owned company, Golden Manufacturers Ltd, and the paper and plastic bag operations were sold to a privately-owned New Zealand company, Caxton Paper Co. Ltd.

The employment dynamics of the Fiji-based facets of foreign-owned corporations also vary greatly. Returning to the 1983 survey of 36 foreign-owned plants in Fiji (Taylor, 1983), the average annual growth rates of different types of employment in the three segments of multinationals recognised in Fiji are reported in Table 3.6. The slowest overall growth has been in laggard segment plants. With virtually no management growth, the Fiji population can gain little experience from these enterprises. Growth of clerical and sales employment in these laggard branch plants has, however, been high. Intermediate segments of multi-

Table 3.6: Employment Growth in Foreign-owned Organisations in Fiji, Late 1970s to 1983

Average Annual Growth Rates[a]	Support	Corporate Segments Leader	Intermediate	Laggard
Employment growth on-site	6.03	—	9.80	4.96
Growth of management employment	2.16	—	6.69	0.31
Growth of clerical & sales employment	6.49	—	2.79	7.62
Growth of operative employment	0.00	—	8.98	2.87

Note: a. All respondents supplied information for 1983, but earlier data were generally for 1977, 1978 or 1979.
Source: Survey (1983).

nationals do, in contrast, show quite extensive growth of managerial jobs and also of operative employment. However, in controlling support operations managerial growth has been slow.

When these employment and job-generation trends are added to the growing peripheralisation of foreign-owned plants and the retreat of foreign corporations, exacerbated by reductions in new company registration (Taylor, 1983), the labour market implications for Fiji are disturbing. In effect, the foreign-owned sections of the economy can be expected to create fewer jobs in the future in a country already severely affected by youth unemployment. What jobs are created will only be for operatives and low level administrative personnel. The corollary is that Fiji can in future expect even less skill transfer and on-the-job training from its foreign-owned enterprises than has been the case in the past.

The Role of Multinationals in Fiji's Trading Patterns

The type of operation run in Fiji by foreign multinationals obviously has a profound impact upon the country's trading patterns. Table 3.7 reports survey findings on the trading relationships of three types of corporate concern. Support organisations, which in the survey were also regional headquarters, had very simple trading patterns buying all their material requirements within the larger organisation within Fiji. Intermediate plants and laggard branch plants, however, performed very differently. Each bought only about one-third of their imports from Fijian sources and each bought little if anything from other Pacific Island sources. What is particularly striking is the intermediate companies' dependence on New Zealand sources and the dependence of branch plants on more varied and distant sources. What is more, while branch plants depended on single orders in addition to supply through contractual ties with group affiliates, the intermediates were far more reliant on group affiliates. These differences can be attributed to the regional nature of most intermediate plants in this sample. The intermediates are most frequently members of moderately-sized New Zealand and Australian-owned groups while the laggard branch plants are usually members of much larger global organisations.

This distinction between intermediate plants and branch plants within multinationals is also evidenced in output linkage patterns.

Table 3.7: Input–Output Relationships of Foreign-owned Companies in Fiji, 1983

	Inputs			Outputs		
	Support/ Regional Offices	Inter- mediate Plants	Laggard Branch Plants	Support/ Regional Offices	Inter- mediate Plants	Laggard Branch Plants
Location						
1. Fiji	100.0	35.8	34.6	95.0	81.2	77.5
2. Australia	0.0	17.1	22.5	0.0	5.4	8.7
3. New Zealand	0.0	30.7	15.4	0.0	1.5	2.6
4. Other Pacific Islands	0.0	0.4	0.0	5.0	3.9	9.2
5. Elsewhere	0.0	16.1	26.4	0.0	8.2	2.1
Contract Type						
1. Single orders	0.0	22.5	41.7	0.0	57.4	59.9
2. Single contract & tender	0.0	5.2	8.3	0.0	13.5	16.9
3. Short-term contract, schedule & call-off	0.0	16.5	3.8	0.0	17.1	17.9
4. Long-term contract, standing orders	0.0	14.6	16.5	0.0	4.2	1.7
5. Ownership with contractual ties	100.0	40.8	28.8	100.0	7.8	3.7

Source: Survey, 1983.

Although the branch plants export most, these exports are usually to Australia, New Zealand and especially to the other Pacific Islands. What is more, 94 per cent of these sales are sold as single orders and no more than short-term contracts. Branch plants are, almost exclusively therefore, regional suppliers within global corporations exploiting the Pacific regional market. Intermediate components of multinationals export more widely with over 8 per cent of their output going outside the South Pacific region. There is a tendency, however, for these types of operation to be more dependent on long-term or stronger contractual ties (12 per cent of the value of output).

These multinational plants appear to be developing Fiji's exports. Whether this is much sought after export-led growth, however, is another matter. When a global corporation uses a Fiji-based subsidiary to serve the broad South Pacific regional market, apparent export-led growth is created. The very success of that development can, from Fiji's point of view, be its undoing. Should exports expand sufficiently the corporation may well be encouraged to set up another subsidiary in a second South Pacific country. The result for that second country is new import substitution and the fresh prospect of its own export-led growth. The result for Fiji is a blow to the balance of payments, a loss of exports and even a loss of jobs. A natural government response is to offer investment incentives. Thus, corporate rationality can be a national disaster and the corporate quest for maximum profit can create a new international game of beggar-your-neighbour.

This conflict between corporate interests and national interests can be demonstrated for Fiji in terms of the geographical transfer of value. To maximise profits and minimise global tax burdens, multinationals shift income and value created in one location to others within the organisation despite national government attempts to stop them. These intra-organisational transfers of value can be effected, for example, through royalty payments, payments for managerial services, payments of dividends and interest on loans, the giving and taking of trade credit, paying too much for inputs and receiving too little for outputs (Robbins and Stobaugh, 1973; Plasschaert, 1979). In essence, such gains and losses to national economies represent the impact of multinational corporate structure and the nature of multinational involvement in any particular economy. Using limited available data, a recent conservative estimate would set the net transfer of value out of Fiji in the early 1980s at about $F 30 million, or $F 45 to $F 50 per head of population, each year (Taylor, 1984b). This, in effect, is the hidden cost of economic growth through multinational investment — growth which is already being assisted by government aid and incentive schemes which seek to create jobs, encourage training and skills, and stimulate technology transfer.

The Locally-owned Component of the Fiji Economy

It is hardly surprising, therefore, that the government of Fiji has sought to encourage the development of local entrepreneurship to bring about economic development. The first national development plans said little or nothing about fostering locally-owned business activity. However, since 1976, the most recent plans, Development Plan Seven (DP7) (Fiji, Central Planning Office, 1975) and Development Plan Eight (DP8) (Fiji, Central Planning

Office, 1980) have sought to encourage this sort of development. DP7 was long on rhetoric but took the first positive steps and set up the Fiji Business Opportunity and Management Advisory Service (BOMAS) to train and educate Fijians to raise their level of entrepreneurship, and to make loans to Fijians (as opposed to other races); also to encourage entrepreneurship. DP8 sought to encourage local enterprises with capital requirements of less than $F100,000 in order to create jobs, stimulate entrepreneurship, and substitute for imports. To this end, the plan proposed the expenditure between 1981 and 1985 of $F888,000 on capital items and $F761,400 on operating costs in small, medium and cottage-scale industries, especially those producing handicrafts. Current government policy, as reported by the Economic Development Board (EDB), is very clearly that local enterprise takes preference where skills and abilities exist (Economic Development Board, 1982). Thus, while new foreign company registrations have fallen by almost 50 per cent in the past decade, new local company registrations have risen consistently.

In Fiji, as in other countries, however, there is not simply one type of locally-owned firm but a variety of types all of which can contribute very differently to the economy. They are not, however, autonomous in their actions but are dependent in one way or another on the operations of other organisations in the economy, including the government. Thus, different types of local firm can be envisaged as arising from different forms of dependency relationship, chiefly between themselves and foreign-owned organisations. The relative significance of different types of local firm within an economy, therefore, reflects not only existing unequal relationships but also has an important bearing upon how the economy develops in the future. In short, present inter-organisational relationships create future rigidities as these relationships channel an economy in a particular direction.

Three broad types of locally-owned firm can be recognised in Fiji in the early 1980s. The first is a small group of large multi-site national enterprises which are diversified in their activities and represent a strong challenge to the dominant foreign-owned concerns. The second is a growing group of subcontracting organisations which includes firms that are also locked into foreign-owned operations through agencies, distributorships and franchising agreements. Finally, there is a residual category of other local enterprises, most of which are very small. In the European small firms literature these are livelihood enterprises which provide their owners with incomes no better than could be achieved in formal-sector wage employment. The previously mentioned 1983 surveys of business organisations in Fiji throw considerable light on the very different roles that these three types of locally-owned enterprise play in this developing island economy.

However, a disturbing feature of the Fiji economy is that the surveys revealed no locally-owned firms that could be described alternatively as 'leaders', 'innovators' or 'high fliers'. This type of enterprise is seen very much as the key to new economic growth in the industrialised countries (Storey, 1983). They are reliant on the inventiveness of individuals who produce new processes or products, open new markets or develop new services. They are brief, shining stars prone to takeover, finding it difficult to raise capital and susceptible to business-cycle fluctuations. As a group, therefore, they tend to have high birth rates and high death rates — at least in a developed country context.

The survey conducted in Fiji was small, but there are tentative indications that the environment needed to create leader small firms has never existed in Fiji. First, there is the fact that many foreign-owned firms have internalised certain functions which under other circumstances they might buy in. Power production by Emperor Goldmines is one example, and Livesey (1973/74) has provided other examples in the context of the operations of foreign contractors engaged in major construction projects in Fiji. Second, strong home country protection, export incentives and specific home country government schemes for overseas economic expansion, such as the Pacific Islands Industrial Development Scheme (PIIDS) operated from New Zealand, have all helped to mop up business opportunities that might have spawned leader small firms in Fiji (Bellam, 1980). Finally, local society may not be in tune with the idea of creating leader small firms. As Howie (1977) has pointed out in Fiji, local people who leave industry to set up on their own do not establish skill- or technology-based enterprises, only small stores. So, the type of small firm that planners usually have in mind when they talk of small firm-based growth may be in particularly short supply in Fiji.

It can be conjectured that this current absence of leader small firms reflects the past rigidities of a colonial economy. The dominance of colonial trading and production companies like Burns Philp and Co., Morris Hedstrom, W.R. Carpenter, Emperor Goldmines, Colonial Sugar Refiners and the operations of multinational corporations in general, left little room for local initiative. Indeed, Howie (1977) has shown how large foreign-owned corporations in Fiji have actively exercised their power to deny local entrepreneurs the chances that might have spawned successful local businesses. The initiative that has been taken has been taken by a few mainly Indian entrepreneurs who have larger multi-site and national enterprises that in a few instances are themselves embryonic multi-national concerns. Their ranks include Motibhai, R.V. Patel, Punja and Sons, Gokal Ltd, Tapoo Ltd and Lees Trading, for example.

These larger local concerns have a distinctive organisational structure (Table 3.8). They are highly centralised and usually family-owned, although some have an element of foreign or expatriate ownership often related to joint venture activities. Apart from some old colonial companies, these are amongst the oldest enterprises in Fiji with an average age of 29 years. Their average establishment-level employment is also similar to that of many foreign-owned concerns (Table 3.2) and, on average, they employ twice as many people as other locally-owned concerns. The

Table 3.8: Structural Differentiation of Locally-owned Fiji Business Organisations

	Larger Multi-site and National Enterprises	Satellite Enterprises	Livelihood Enterprises
% Equity held by largest share-holder	93.56	100.00	100.00
No. of boundary-spanning functions used	9.00	8.33	6.63
No. of boundary-spanning functions on-site	6.33	6.00	5.18
No. of boundary-spanning functions supplied by parent	1.33	0.50	0.00
Index of board representation	0.22	0.00	0.00
% Whole organisation employment controlled	67.78	84.08	100.00
Age of enterprise (years to 1983)	28.89	10.83	14.64
On-site employment	47.56	17.67	28.09
Whole organisation employment	111.11	55.83	28.09
Administrative ratio	30.10	39.18	19.89
No. of cases (Total — 26)	9	6	11

Source: Survey, 1983.

administrative component of these companies is much smaller than that of any type of foreign-owned operation, and even their administrative ratio is 12 per cent lower than that of foreign-owned branch plants.

The role of these larger national companies in the Fiji economy falls midway between those of, on the one hand, foreign-owned businesses and, on the other hand, other types of local enterprise (Tables 3.7 and 3.9). They import extensively, but not as extensively as satellite local firms. They buy and sell on a wide range of contact types, and while they export more than other locally-owned firms, they are still very strongly dependent in Fiji's home market.

Table 3.9: Input–Output Relationships of Locally-owned Companies in Fiji, 1983

	Inputs			Outputs		
	Large Multi-site and National Enterprises	Satellite Enterprises	Livelihood Enterprises	Large Multi-site and National Enterprises	Satellite Enterprises	Livelihood Enterprises
Location						
1. Fiji	33.2	15.0	75.0	96.4	98.5	99.8
2. Australia	7.7	13.7	4.7	0.0	0.0	0.0
3. New Zealand	32.2	25.0	14.2	0.0	0.0	0.0
4. Other Pacific Islands	0.0	0.0	0.0	3.6	1.5	0.2
5. Elsewhere	31.8	46.3	6.2	0.0	0.0	0.0
Contract Type						
1. Single order	36.8	33.3	100.0	65.9	72.5	74.9
2. Single contract & tender	13.3	0.0	0.0	11.3	9.2	25.1
3. Short-term contract schedule & call-off	12.3	0.0	0.0	6.9	8.3	0.0
4. Long-term contract, standing orders	17.6	66.7	0.0	4.8	10.0	0.0
5. Ownership with contractual ties	20.0	0.0	0.0	11.1	0.0	0.0

Source: Survey, 1983.

The broad organisational characteristics of locally-owned satellite enterprises are also described in Table 3.8. These companies are amongst the smallest formal sector establishments in Fiji and sometimes belong to small groups. They are the youngest businesses covered by the survey, which suggests either that they are a relatively new phenomenon within the Fiji economy or that their numbers turnover quickly owing to a susceptibility to go out of business. There is probably an element of truth in both of these contentions, but which one is more important is difficult to determine. Their role in the economy is quite distinctive (Table 3.9). They import largely from outside the Pacific region on long-term contracts but sell almost exclusively to the Fiji market and mainly on single orders.

Locally-owned livelihood enterprises are shown in Table 3.8 to be very simple organisations. They are small (and smaller than the average of 28 employees would suggest), single-site businesses, often with only one administrator (an owner-manager), hence their extremely low administrative ratio. They are young and use few boundary-spanning functions showing that their relationships with their operational environments are simple and uncomplicated. Thus, three-quarters of their inputs are sourced within Fiji, meaning that they deal primarily with agents and importers and all their purchases are bought as single orders with no contracts or tenders being involved. Similarly, they export virtually nothing, and sell only single orders or single contracts (Table 3.9). In short, they are oriented towards only the local economy and even then are only lightly embedded within it.

The mix of these types of local enterprise within the Fiji economy is necessarily in a state of flux not least because of the reappraisal of their investments being undertaken by the dominant multinationals operating within the economy. The large national concerns are able to enter areas of the economy relinquished by foreign concerns. Indeed, competition from these enterprises has been cited as one cause of multinational retreat. Minimising risk, while emphemeralising and peripheralising their activities in Fiji, can also stimulate the establishment of subcontract relationships between foreign-owned and locally-owned companies. Meanwhile, government incentives can create a favourable environment for all local firms, especially livelihood enterprises. The next section, therefore, examines the dynamics of these three types of local-owned business organisation in Fiji.

The Dynamics of Locally-owned Business Organisations

The three types of locally-owned business venture recognised in the previous section have shown very different rates of development in recent years (Table 3.10). The small sample of large national concerns has shown, on average, only modest total employment growth, with the greatest increases having occurred in low-level administrative and operative positions. These figures, however, mask wide variations between enterprises which can be ascribed by and large to the idiosyncracies of family ownership. Individual satellite establishments have, during the same period, experienced virtually no growth at all, with jobs lost at the managerial and operative levels having been off-set by jobs gained at clerical and sales levels. However, these figures do not reflect the rate at which locally-owned companies are being drawn into subcontract relationships with foreign-owned multinationals that are themselves in the process of restructuring. Finally, the strongest employment growth amongst both foreign-owned and locally-owned businesses has been in livelihood enterprises. It has to be borne in mind, however, that in most cases this is growth from a very small base, but these livelihood enterprises have shown particularly strong growth in operative employment.

The success of a number of large national enterprises can be illustrated by the example of Motibhai and Company Ltd. This is one of a set of companies that have been described as 'the new breed of flourishing local companies in Fiji, the kind moving in,

Table 3.10: Employment Growth in Locally-owned Fiji Business Organisations, Late 1970s to 1983

Average Annual Growth Rates	Larger Multi-site and National Enterprises	Satellite Enterprises	Livelihood Enterprises
Employment growth on-site	2.76	0.63	9.84
Growth of managerial employment	1.24	−4.08	2.88
Growth of clerical & sales employment	5.33	7.23	4.23
Growth of operative employment	3.97	−1.11	12.99
No. of cases (Total — 26)	9	6	11

Source: Survey, 1983.

taking over and then developing where the old-timers are dying off' (*Islands Business*, April 1984, p. 40). Motibhai began as a family-owned and run business in the small town of Ba and grew rapidly in the 1960s. The company has a subsidiary in Suva (Fiji Foods Ltd) making margarine, cooking oils and other food products. It blends and packages OMO soap powder under licence from Unilever, packages Bushells tea, owns three supermarkets, and holds more than 100 agencies for fashions, perfumes, cameras, and so on. These are a major asset as Motibhai also operates the duty-free shop at Nadi international airport. The operations of the company are not, however, confined to Fiji. In 1983, Ronson Australia Ltd was bought, although the company had been oper- ating in Australia as Motibhai (Australia) Pty Ltd for a number of years making mesh bags and dealing in leather-wear, perfume and other up-market goods. The reasons for the company's growth are a matter of controversy. Outside commentators see the closeness of the managing director, Mahendra Patel, to the prime minister, Ratu Sir Kamisese Mara, and the ruling Alliance Party as a major reason for the company's success. Indeed, turnover was nearly $F 40 million in 1983, should exceed $F 40 million in 1984 and is expected to reach $F 50 to $F 60 million in 1990. The company's explanation revolves around enlightened family ownership, with family elders having stood aside to allow the young to take over, and the fact that Motibhai went public in 1977 (although not all the offered shares were taken up and the company is not listed on the Suva stock exchange). Going public was a political decision which helped to allay anti-Indian sentiment in a country where commerce is dominated by the Indian community. There is prob- ably some element of truth in both sets of explanations of this company's growth. However, the destructive potential of family disagreement is only too clearly demonstrated by the recent dis- membering of G.B. Hari Ltd, one of Fiji's longest-established Indo-Fijian businesses.

Taking Motibhai and Company Ltd as a model it can be suggested that a significant fraction of Fiji businesses are at least partially casting off family-ownership bonds, diversifying, and moving, or at least contemplating moving, off-shore. They are, in fact, rapidly assuming the guise of the small multinationals that already operate in Fiji. Any distinction that can be drawn between foreign- and locally-owned business, therefore, is rapidly becoming blurred and obsolete. It can be conjectured that the future can only bring conflict between the national goals and aspirations of government and the corporate goals of a significant section of the Fiji business community, notwithstanding the political patronage that may have aided their success.

But, an equally fast-growing facet of Fiji-owned business is subcontracting. There is now evidence that the current restructuring of foreign-owned companies operating in Fiji favours the harnessing of local enterprise through subcontracts which are often wholly informal. At present, this strategy is being adopted principally in the furniture industry, although similar developments are occurring in the clothing industry. The relationships developed by Courts (Fiji) Ltd are illustrative of this process.

A London-based corporation with operations in Europe and the Caribbean, Courts Furnishers plc set up in Fiji in 1971. Beginning in the Suva suburb of Samabula, they have expanded to 11 sites throughout Fiji, and the current structure, location and workforce of the company is listed in Table 3.11. The supply of furniture is controlled by subcontract and comes from five Indo-Fijian small firms — R.D. Mohamed, Rup Industries, De Lux Furniture, Ali's Furnishing Shop and Shiri Nath Cabinets — all of which are exclusive suppliers to Courts (Fiji) Ltd. There are no formal subcontracts involved in these transactions.

Rup Industries had been set up in Suva in 1968 as a small family firm with fewer than 12 employees. Being tied into a subcontract relationship with Courts has allowed the company to grow. The Suva plant that was set up in 1968 now employs 42, a Lautoka plant set up in 1973 now employs 21 and a Labasa plant

Table 3.11: Geographical Structure of Courts (Fiji) Ltd, 1983

Location	Function	Employment
1. Samabula (Suva)	head office/warehouse/store	55
2. Lautoka	warehouse/store	35
3. Labasa	warehouse/store	22
4. Suva town	store	5
5. Nasouri	store	4
6. Raki Raki	store	2
7. Ba	store	4
8. Nadi	store	4
9. Sigatoka	store	5
10. Navua	store	2
11. Savu Savu	store	2

Source: Survey, 1983.

opened in 1981 currently employs eight. Still 90 per cent of Rup Industries' output is absorbed by Courts and the company's expansion has been lock-step with that of Courts taking it to new locations close to the furniture retailer's warehousing operations. This pattern is far from unique and survey respondents suggested that Morris Hedstrom (part of the Carpenter Group) and H.P. Kasabia have developed similarly informal subcontract relationships. Indeed, while the *Yellow Pages* would suggest that no more than 35 furniture manufacturers are to be found in Fiji, the survey of Suva businesses alone would suggest that at least a quarter of these businesses are tied into subcontract relationships with foreign-owned corporations.

There are a number of corollaries to the development of subcontracting. First, it is needed by foreign corporations to maintain economic dominance in Fiji and the generation of group income while at the same time reducing capital involvement and minimising risk. Second, it creates new local enterprises which are highly vulnerable, which will take on and lay off labour with great speed, and which will themselves come and go very rapidly. Third, it introduces a downward pressure on wage rates in the economy. Subcontracting externalises wage-fixing processes to a large number of small firms which are free from the pressure exerted by government and the unions on the larger and foreign-owned companies involved in the tripartite agreement. As Taylor (1984c) has shown for the furniture industry, while local firms as a whole pay only half the hourly wage rate paid in foreign-owned firms, the hourly wage rates paid by known subcontractors are lower than those in other local firms by at least 10 per cent. Fourth, subcontracting transfers the burden of raising capital to the locally-owned small firms in the economy — precisely those organisations which are receiving preferential treatment in Fiji at present. Finally, it places the onus of controlling trade credit on a large number of small firms. Small firms internationally are notoriously inept at controlling trade credit and the magnitude of long-term debt revealed by a large number of small, locally-owned firms surveyed in the Suva district is alarming. Debts owed to small firms for more than 90 days were frequently more than 20 per cent of all debts, and in two cases rose to more than 70 per cent.

It would appear, therefore, that the remaining livelihood component of local Fiji-owned business, that is being encouraged by the Fiji government, has two potential roles in the economy. The first is to continue as small-scale business mainly in retailing activities but also in small-scale manufacturing, while the second is to act as a reservoir of enterprise that can be drawn into sub-contract relationships with foreign corporations and even large national concerns. In this role they will flourish briefly while being exploited although ultimately they will be discarded.

Conclusions

The argument that has been developed in this chapter is that the nature of economic development in small developing economies is predicated upon the dynamic functional relationships that are established between different types of foreign-owned and locally-owned enterprise. Not only is there a wide variety of multinationals with operations in Fiji but also the nature of those Fiji-located ventures differs widely from corporation to corporation. There would appear to be a general tendency, however, for multinationals to be pulling back from investment in the Pacific Islands in general and Fiji in particular, progressively peripheralising and ephemeralising within these corporations the establishments and subsidiaries involved. In part these multinational operations are meeting new competition from a set of local businesses with particular entre-preneurial abilities, that have been in existence since before independence, and which may also have benefited from political connections and political patronage. At the same time, multi-national concerns are locking a substantial and growing portion of the local business community into informal, dependent, subcon-tract relationships. Other local firms that remain independent may then represent no more than a reservoir of potential subcontractors waiting to be exploited.

The picture painted here, therefore, is one of direct foreign control in the Fiji economy giving way to indirect control through the creation of formal and informal subcontract relationships. This change may bring benefits to the economy in some respects through rationalisation of the intense competition that exists at present amongst local small firms; through improvement in the quality of the products produced by local industry, which have often been said to compare unfavourably with imports; and through a reduction in the over-capacity and over-capitalisation that has been identified amongst Fiji's small firms since the late 1960s. However, there are also significant costs. In particular there is a new downward pressure on the wage rate in the formal private sector bringing a reduction in domestic demand and a possible drop in living standards. Returns to foreign capital, however, remain unaffected and may even be enhanced. The commitment of these companies to the Fiji economy is, nevertheless, reduced. Peripheralised foreign investment and subordinate local enterprise combine in the final analysis only to increase the vulnerability of an already fragile economy.

There are clear development implications in this analysis. The least peripheralised multinational investments are those that have been made by the smaller New Zealand and Australian corporations operating in Fiji. Owing to their greater commitment to the country, excluding from their ranks the 'old-timers' or 'old colonials', these are perhaps the types of company that need to be encouraged rather than the highly peripheralised branch plants of global corporations. At the same time, the large national concerns that Fiji has spawned offer some hope of 'buying back the farm', but even these benefits may be transitory as they too become multinational. The message, however, is clear. Different types of foreign- and locally-owned company will produce different forms and rates of growth in an economy. Encouraging one type or another will not only stimulate that form of growth but will set important constraints on what growth can be expected in the future.

4 THE INTERNATIONAL EXPANSION OF AN ENTERPRISE OF THE SEMI-PERIPHERY: SOUTH AFRICAN BREWERIES LIMITED

Barbara Tucker

Introduction

Over the past decade, a major stream of geographical research has been devoted to interpreting the corporate growth patterns of multinational corporations that have expanded from advanced core economies into semi-peripheral and peripheral economies. The existing literature contains studies which are both theoretical (Taylor, 1975; Håkanson, 1979) and empirical (Krumme, 1981; Savey, 1981). The rise of large business enterprises based in semi-peripheral or peripheral economies is a very recent phenomenon (Wells, 1982; 1983; Lall, 1983) and so far has engendered little research. The importance of understanding this new breed of multinational corporation stems from the suggestion that their patterns of corporate growth may differ significantly from those of corporations based in advanced core economies (Taylor and Thrift, 1981; 1982).

In the semi-peripheral economy of South Africa, research concerning the geography of multinational corporations has focused on the growth and spread within South Africa of corporations based in Europe and North America. This work has examined, in particular, the spatial pattern of foreign manufacturing investment and its relationship with the state strategies of industrial decentralisation and regional 'development' (Rogerson, 1981a; 1981b; 1982a; 1982b). In recent years there has been a heightened awareness of the importance of not only foreign corporations investing within South Africa, but also the increasing tendency for South African corporations themselves to invest outside of the country. The phenomenon of the South African-based multinational corporation has resulted from high rates of capital accumulation, accompanied by increasing centralisation and concentration of capital (Innes, 1983). The internationalisation of South African-based companies over the last decade has been surveyed by Kaplan (1983) while the historical growth of the largest South African-based multinational corporation, Anglo-American Corporation, with roots in the mining industry and currently quoted as the single largest foreign investor in the USA, has been documented by Innes (1983). Although the international spread of South African capital has been led by enterprises with foundations in mining, there has also been an international expansion of South African companies whose base is in sectors such as retailing, manufacturing, tourism, insurance and banking (Kaplan, 1983). Kaplan (1983) identifies one of the major challenges facing researchers concerned with the international spread of South African capital as the need to carry out a series of microstudies such as that of the Anglo-American Corporation.

The present study seeks to further this cause by tracing the historical growth and spatial expansion of a large South African corporation which is based entirely outside mining. The South African Breweries Corporation (SAB) is an investment holding company responsible for an array of business spanning the sectors of beverages, hotels, retailing and manufacturing (Figure 4.1). From its origins as a single-plant, brewing operation, SAB has expanded into a multi-product, multinational conglomerate which from its South African base has spread into the surrounding countries of Central and Southern Africa, and more recently has begun to extend its operations into the advanced industrialised economies.

The growth, diversification and geographical spread of SAB can be split into four broad phases. First, there occurred an early period of investment in breweries and hotels within the neighbouring colonial territories of Northern and Southern Rhodesia. This initial phase in the international spread of SAB began in 1902 and continued into the late 1950s. The second phase, from the early 1960s extending into the early 1970s, is marked by the expansion and diversification of interests in Rhodesia and new investment in breweries and hotels throughout the surrounding states of Southern Africa and the Indian Ocean islands. The third phase, from the early 1970s through to the 1980s, is notable for a shift of capital southwards following the attainment of political independence of former colonial territories. In retreat from the advance of political independence in Black African states, SAB sought to concentrate its investments geographically in those territories still strongly under South Africa's political influence. This third phase is, there-

Figure 4.1: South African Breweries' Major Investment Interests, 1983

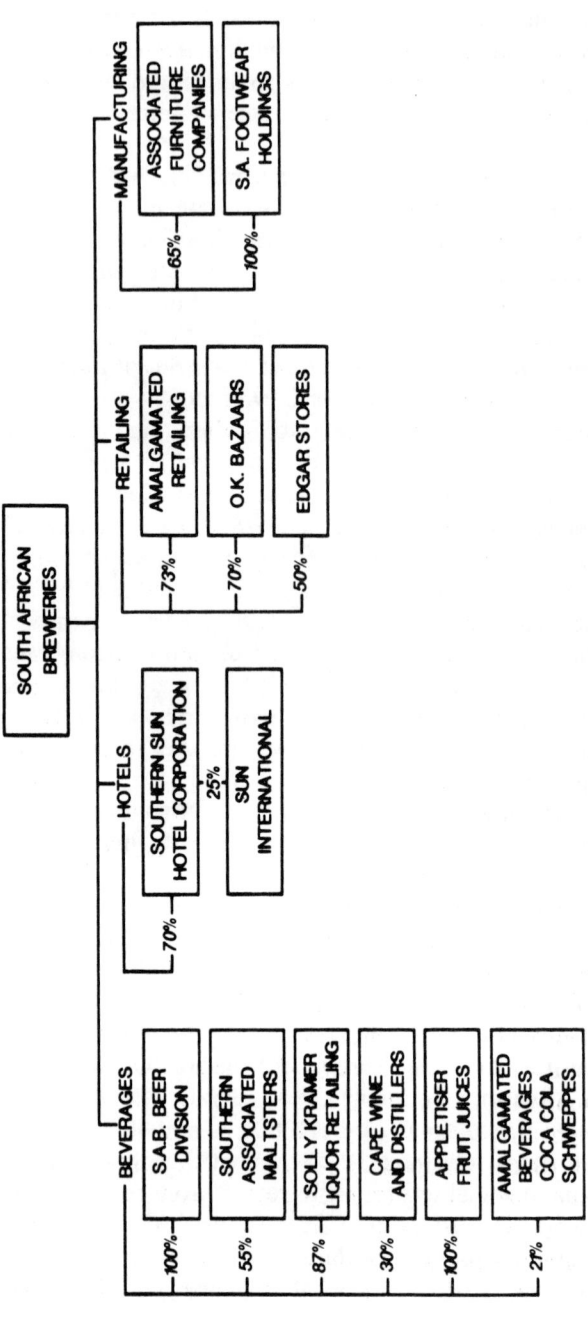

fore, characterised by the withdrawal of SAB from Mozambique and Angola, the stabilisation of existing assets in post-independence Zimbabwe, new investments in Botswana, Lesotho and Swaziland (states economically dependent on South Africa), and more recently investment into the so-called 'independent' black homelands within South Africa. In the fourth phase during the 1980s, there occurs a shift towards the true internationalisation of SAB with attempts to invest outside Africa and into the advanced core economies.

Early Growth and International Spread into Colonial Africa

In common with many South African companies the initial capital of SAB was British in origin. SAB was floated in 1895 on the London stock exchange as a British investment company with the objective of investing in or purchasing small under-capitalised breweries in Southern Africa. For the first half-century of its operations this South African-based brewing enterprise was headquartered and registered in the United Kingdom. Only in 1950 did there occur a legal transfer of the head offices to Johannesburg and registration of the company in South Africa. The first phase of the international spread of this South African multinational corporation thus took place when SAB was not formally a South African company.

Following the purchase of a series of breweries throughout the major urban centres of South Africa, SAB became established as a leader enterprise within the brewing industry of South Africa (Tucker, 1985). Expansion outside the South African base occurred very early in the history of SAB. In 1902 the company entered the brewing industry in the neighbouring colonial territory of Southern Rhodesia, acquiring a number of shares in a small Bulawayo brewery. This first northwards expansion proved unsuccessful, and the brewery was liquidated in 1905 (SAB Minutes, 22 January 1902). In 1910, SAB re-entered Southern Rhodesia and bought the entire stock in an under-capitalised brewery in Salisbury (SAB Minutes, 23 March 1910), which was renamed The Castle Brewery, Salisbury, in accordance with the branch plant network of SAB Castle Breweries throughout South Africa. This initial move northwards into other British colonial territories was a natural progression for South African-based enterprises particularly in view of the prevailing political climate which suggested that the colony of Southern Rhodesia might be incorporated within a larger South Africa. Moreover, the expansion of SAB into neighbouring territories parallels the findings of early multinational expansion from enterprises based in Argentina and Brazil (Wells, 1982; Lall, 1983).

Diversification away from brewing began in the 1930s with SAB's takeover of hotels in Bulawayo, Southern Rhodesia (*Rhodesia Herald*, 18 May 1932) and Broken Hill, Northern Rhodesia (SAB Minutes, 5 September 1934), the latter representing the first investment by SAB in that colony. This pattern of diversifying investment mirrored and extended the model of SAB's brewing and hotel investments in South Africa itself. In what was known as the 'tied-house' system, brewing companies were able to 'tie' hotels, public houses and bars to contracts whereby a guaranteed percentage of a particular brewing company's beer would be sold on their premises. The tied house system operated widely in Northern and Southern Rhodesia, and was instrumental in expanding both the brewing and hotel investments of SAB.

The economic boom which occurred after the Second World War provided the impetus for further SAB expansion into the two Rhodesian colonies. In particular, Northern Rhodesia became an attractive focus, and in 1951 a new brewery was opened at Ndola to supply not only the Northern Rhodesian market but also for export to the adjacent territories of the Belgium Congo and East Africa. The Salisbury Brewery continued to supply Southern Rhodesia as well as neighbouring Mozambique, Bechuanaland and Swaziland. While the post-war boom brought forth opportunities for SAB, it also introduced competing brewing enterprises into Southern Rhodesia. In 1948, an opposition brewing company was floated on the Rhodesian Stock Exchange (Rhodesian Breweries First Annual General Meeting, 27 August 1948) and subsequently built a brewery in Bulawayo (*Rhodesia Herald*, 1 March 1950). This brewery was purchased by SAB in 1952 to eliminate competition, but more significantly to acquire a Rhodesian registered and domiciled company (RB Minutes, 19 June 1952). The takeover of this Rhodesian enterprise was an important step in the multinational expansion of SAB, for unlike earlier takeovers, SAB did not absorb the Bulawayo brewery into the South African-based network of Castle Breweries. Instead, SAB incorporated The Castle Brewery, Salisbury, The Castle Brewery, Ndola and the recently acquired Bulawayo brewery into a new SAB subsidiary company, namely Rhodesian Breweries Ltd (RB). The new company was registered and headquartered in Salisbury and became a powerful force in the two Rhodesias accounting for 97 per cent of the total beer trade in Southern Rhodesia and 89 per cent in Northern Rhodesia (RB Minutes, 19 June 1952). Against a background of massive capital accumulation in the 1950s with rising prices for copper and tobacco, considerable opportunities were opened up for the growth of consumer-oriented industries in both Northern and Southern Rhodesia. In response to this growth, Rhodesian Breweries underwent a phase of expansion, assuming responsibility for all SAB interests in Southern and Northern Rhodesia (RB Minutes, 15 October 1952; 12 June 1957). Henceforth, Rhodesian Breweries Ltd was to become a large, self-generating and expanding organisation, the fulcrum of SAB's geographical expansion outside South Africa.

Consolidation in Rhodesia, Expansion in the Rest of Southern Africa

During the early 1960s, SAB began a wave of new expansion outside South Africa at a time when decolonisation was beginning on the continent. Two trends are of particular note for the period of the early 1960s through to the early 1970s. First, there was the major extension and deepening of SAB's interests in the Rhodesias, and second, the new hotel and brewing investments were made in a series of territories on the verge of independence. As the next section will demonstrate, the advance into decolonising Black Africa was, in many cases, to be characterised by retreat and disinvestment.

Consolidation in Rhodesia

Until the late 1960s, SAB investment outside South Africa took place through the major foreign subsidiary, Rhodesian Breweries. The extension of SAB's interests in the two Rhodesias is primarily a history of the diversification and spread of Rhodesian Breweries' operations in Southern Rhodesia and Rhodesia after UDI (Figure 4.2). With the grant of political independence to Northern Rhodesia in 1964, SAB's operations in what became Zambia underwent an enforced restructuring. Thus, the theme of consoli-

Figure 4.2: South African Breweries' Investments in Northern and Southern Rhodesia, 1960

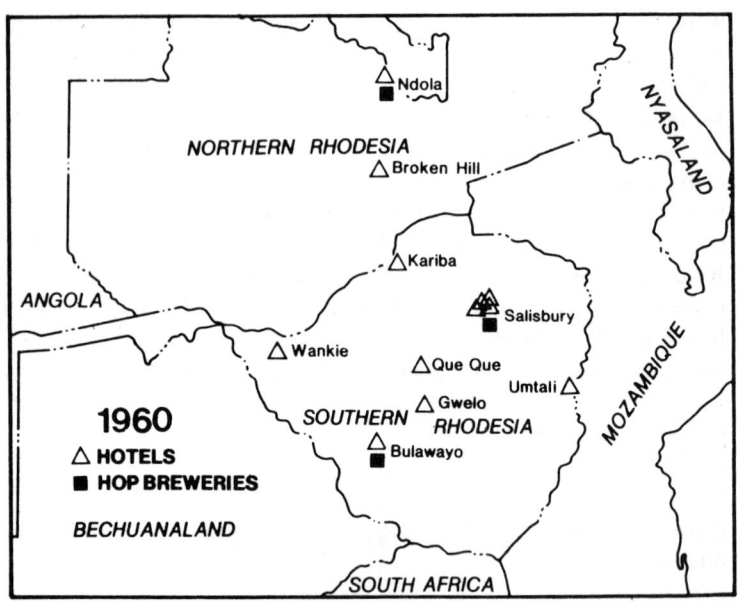

dation in the two Rhodesias must be treated separately.

Rhodesian Breweries' first investments outside breweries and hotels were in enterprises involved in the beverage industry. In 1958 Rhodesian Breweries purchased an interest in African Distillers, a local wine company (*Rhodesian Property and Finance*, September, 1958), and in 1960 bought the entire share issue of Canada Dry (Rhodesia) Ltd, a company which held the franchise to bottle and distribute *Canada Dry* and *Pepsi Cola* soft drinks in Northern and Southern Rhodesia (RB AR., 31 March 1960). Although the soft drinks division of Rhodesian Breweries Ltd was never to be a major profit-generator, African Distillers expanded rapidly. This expansion was very dependent upon the import of sugar from Portuguese East Africa and, in an attempt to find local sources, Rhodesian Breweries embarked on a joint project to build a distillery and molasses plant at Hippo Valley citrus estates (RB AR., 3 March 1962). Further diversification away from malt beer took place in 1968 with the purchase of a substantial interest in brewing sorghum beer, an industry which was based on the production of an African traditional brew. Historically, the manufacture of sorghum beer in urban areas had been the monopoly of municipal authorities. However, outside their jurisdiction there were no such restrictions and several sorghum breweries in rural areas had been established by the Heinrich Chibuku Breweries Ltd (*Sabre*, 1975). This company was absorbed into the Rhodesian Breweries network. Following this investment in sorghum brewing, substantial investments were made in the food industry through the acquisition of several small food manufacturing enterprises. These interests were placed under the management of a newly-created, wholly-owned subsidiary, Rhodesian Food Corporation (RB Press Release, 6 June 1969). The final area of diversification was concerned with the transformation of the company's commercial hotels and public houses into a chain of luxury hotels. The strategy was largely the input of the SAB group which had successfully transformed the group's South African hotel assets into a chain of luxury tourist hotels organised and managed by the South African-based SAB subsidiary, Southern Sun Hotel Corporation. In 1974, Rhodesian Breweries secured the franchise to use the name 'Southern Sun' from their parent organisation and developed a chain of luxury tourist hotels strategically located around Rhodesia (Figure 4.3).

The trajectory of SAB's brewing interests in Northern Rhodesia took on a markedly different direction from those in Southern Rhodesia. With the impending independence of Zambia in 1964, SAB undertook a far-reaching structural reorganisation of its investments in the 'two Rhodesias'. Most notably, Rhodesian Breweries sold off 50 per cent of its holdings in the Ndola brewery, placing the remaining investment into a new subsidiary, Northern Breweries Ltd. Following the Unilateral Declaration of Independence in Rhodesia in 1965, SAB adopted a group policy to distance itself from both Northern Breweries and Rhodesian Breweries. To achieve this goal, a new offshore subsidiary, International Breweries Ltd, based in Bermuda was created, and the entire shareholdings in Northern Breweries and Rhodesian Breweries sold to this SAB subsidiary (RB AR., 1967). The result of this arrangement was that effectively Northern Breweries and Rhodesian Breweries no longer had any dealings with South Africa. In reality, however, the web of indirect shareholdings ultimately led back to the SAB head office in Johannesburg. Northern Breweries experienced a period of considerable growth after Zambian independence and a new brewery opened in Lusaka in

Figure 4.3: South African Breweries' Investments in Southern Africa and Mauritius, 1974

1967. The advance of this subsidiary in Zambia was to be short-lived, however, for in 1968 the Zambian government took a controlling share of Northern Breweries as part of nationalisation policy, and in 1972 SAB finally disposed of all of its remaining Zambian assets (SABAR, 1969; 1973). Thus, at a time when SAB was extending itself for the first time into many other Black African countries, it was beginning a slow retreat from a former sphere of operations.

Breweries and hotels outside the Rhodesias

The geographical spread of SAB outside the Rhodesias hinged upon the company's two traditional strengths in brewing and hotels. The initial foray of SAB brewing expansion was into Africa's last colony, Namibia, where in 1968 SAB bought a 25 per cent share in South West African Breweries which operated two plants in the major centres of Swakopmund and Windhoek (SABAR, 1969). Expansion into the Portuguese colonial territories of Mozambique and Angola occurred almost simultaneously and was facilitated by investments channelled through a second SAB Bermudan holding company, Southern Breweries Ltd (Figure 4.4). Entry into Mozambique was secured by the purchase of a 10 per cent stake in the colony's second largest brewing enterprise, MacMahon Breweries, which had operations in Nampula and Lourenço Marques, as well as interests in soft drink bottling (Figure 4.3) (*Sunday Times*, 11 July 1971). A similar pattern of investment in Angola occurred in 1973 with a 15 per cent holding in Southern Angola Breweries, which subsequently constructed a brewery in Sal da Bandeira (Figure 4.3) (*Star*, 17 August 1972). The establishment of the Angola Brewery was a classic 'turnkey' operation with the brewery staffed entirely by Angolans, while management, technology and finance were controlled wholly by SAB (*Sabre*, 1975).

The establishment of a chain of luxury tourist hotels was the second major element in the international diffusion of SAB. Building on the foundation of the Southern Sun Hotel Corporation, which had been establishing luxury hotels in South Africa itself, a subsidiary operation, Southern Sun International, was created in 1970 (*Rand Daily Mail*, 31 January 1973) and once again registered in Bermuda. It was through this international subsidiary that new hotel projects began to be examined, initially in Madagascar, Mauritius and the Seychelles. Southern Sun's first

Figure 4.4: South African Breweries' International Investments, 1974

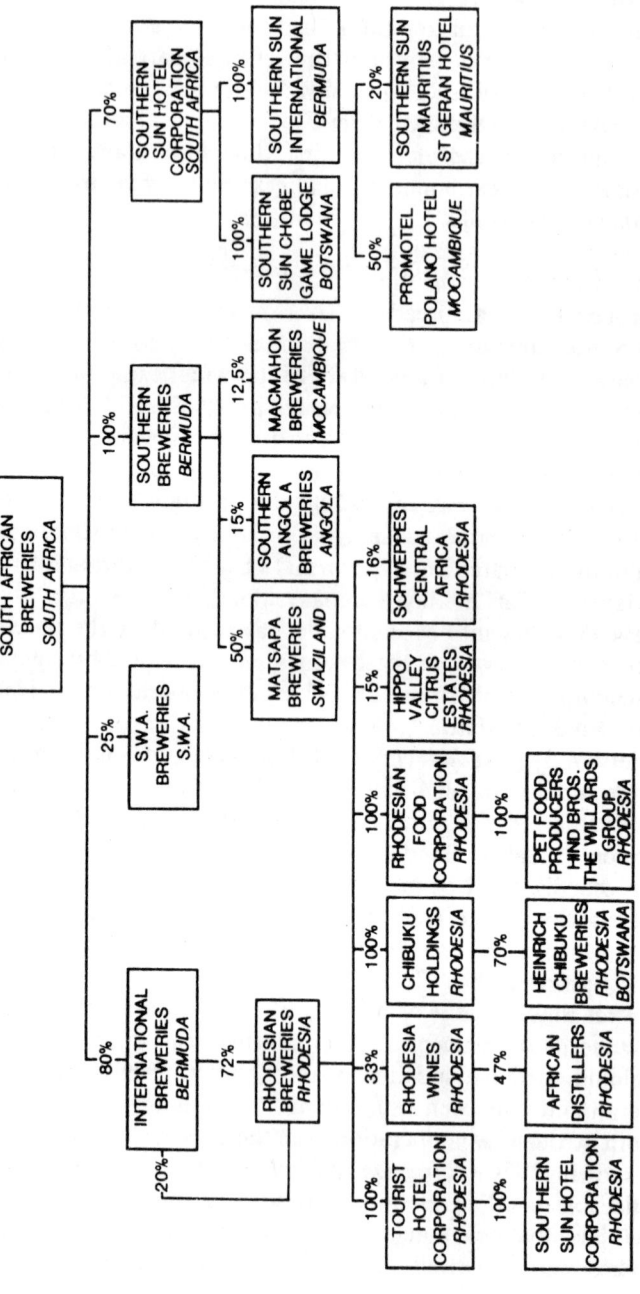

international venture in Madagascar proved to be an abortive affair. SAB planned to purchase a hotel on the island of Nossi Be with finance to be derived partly from South Africa and partly from the Madagascar government. But in 1972 it was announced that SAB was withdrawing from the deal and that the company's hotel interests were to be bought out by loans provided to the Madagascar government by China. More successful than the Madagascar episode was Southern Sun's arrangement to develop hotels in colonial Mozambique, and in particular the joint purchase and management of the famous Polano Hotel in Lourenço Marques. Other luxury hotel developments announced by Southern Sun in the early 1970s included a Game Lodge at Chobe in Botswana, and hotel developments in Mauritius, Swaziland, the Seychelles and Reunion. In the latter two cases, SAB's involvement was not welcomed by the respective governments and the proposed projects did not come to fruition. None the less, the hotel and casino developments in Botswana, Mauritius and Swaziland established the Southern Sun arm of SAB as a major force in tourism in the Southern African region (Figure 4.4) (*Rand Daily Mail*, 31 January 1973).

By 1974, a snapshot of SAB's international holdings reveals the widespread geographical (Figure 4.3) and sectoral (Figure 4.4) diffusion of the organisation. From its headquarters in Johannesburg, SAB controlled, through its several subsidiary companies, a variety of interests. However, with the exception of Rhodesia, the major thrusts of SAB internationally had been in the areas of hotels and breweries.

The Southward Retreat

It is apparent that, in the changing political circumstances of Central and Southern Africa, SAB was forced to halt its northward advance in Africa. What occurred during the mid-1970s was the beginnings of the withdrawal of SAB from former spheres of operation, particularly in those newly independent states in which South African capital was not welcome. Against this background of growing hostility in several African states, there occurred a noticeable southward retreat in the geographical spread of the SAB group's investments. Major new investments occurred only in those countries which still remained heavily under South African political influence, creating favourable economic climates for SAB activities.

The revolutionary transformations which occurred in the two former Portuguese colonial territories of Mozambique and Angola brought to power governments which were committed to socialist paths of economic development and overtly hostile to apartheid South Africa. Withdrawal of SAB from Mozambique and Angola occurred shortly after these new political developments. The three breweries of SAB subsidiaries were abandoned and the Southern Sun Group withdrew their management from the luxury hotel developments in Mozambique (SSAR, 1976). Following the earlier divestments in Zambia, by 1975 Angola and Mozambique were also no longer part of SAB's sphere of operation.

Although political circumstances in Rhodesia during the 1970s were problematic, this period was one in which the interests of the SAB subsidiary, Rhodesian Breweries, were consolidated and still further extended. Notwithstanding losses sustained by the tourist arm of the Rhodesian operations as a consequence of the mounting guerilla war, Rhodesian Breweries continued to generate large profits, and grew to such an extent that by 1978 it had become the largest profit-generating organisation in that country (*Rhodesia Herald*, 19 October 1978). By this time, Rhodesian Breweries, far from being a simple brewing enterprise was a large and diverse holding company. The company's name was changed, being restyled Delta Corporation Ltd, further extending its activities in sorghum and malt brewing, and opening up new areas of activity in retailing and furniture manufacture (Figures 4.5 and 4.6) (Delta, AR 1978; 1983). With the coming to power of a socialist government in Zimbabwe, following independence in 1980, the investment climate for Delta's activities in that country came under threat.

With growing hostility in much of Black Africa towards investment emanating from South Africa, from the mid-1970s SAB increasingly shifted the locus of its new investments to politically safer territories. Of particular significance has been a range of brewing and hotel developments in the states of Swaziland, Botswana, Lesotho, the island state of Mauritius, and new investments in the so-called 'independent' homeland states created as offspring of South Africa's separate development policy. New malt breweries were established in Swaziland in 1974, in Botswana through acquisition in 1978 (Harvey, 1981), and most recently in

Figure 4.5: Delta Corporation Group Investments in Zimbabwe, 1983

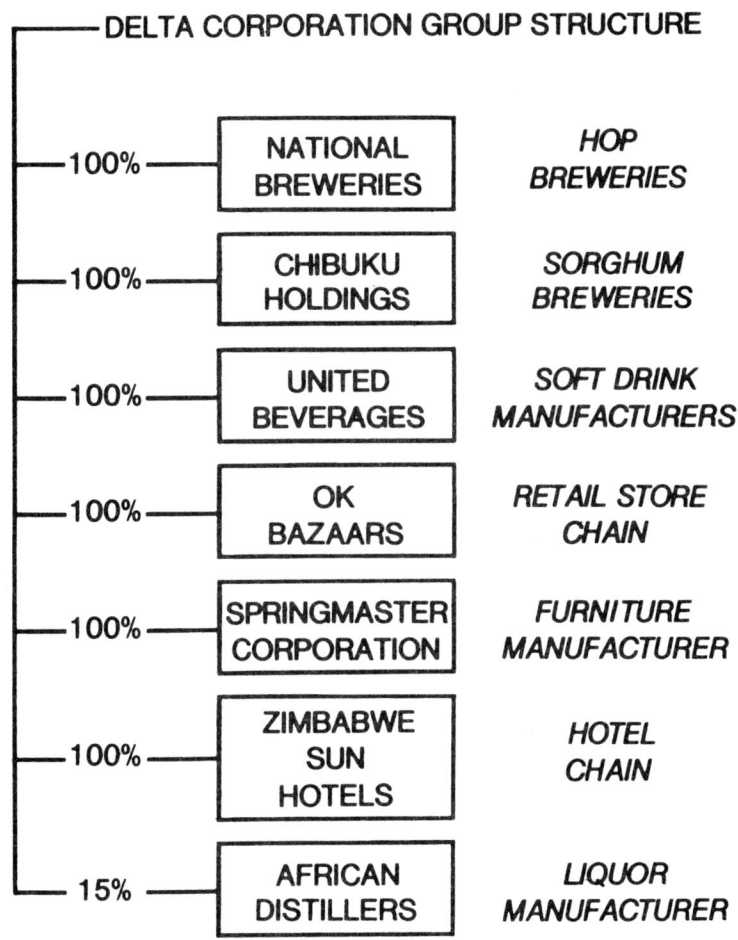

DELTA CORPORATION GROUP STRUCTURE

100%	NATIONAL BREWERIES	*HOP BREWERIES*
100%	CHIBUKU HOLDINGS	*SORGHUM BREWERIES*
100%	UNITED BEVERAGES	*SOFT DRINK MANUFACTURERS*
100%	OK BAZAARS	*RETAIL STORE CHAIN*
100%	SPRINGMASTER CORPORATION	*FURNITURE MANUFACTURER*
100%	ZIMBABWE SUN HOTELS	*HOTEL CHAIN*
15%	AFRICAN DISTILLERS	*LIQUOR MANUFACTURER*

Lesotho in 1982 (*Sunday Times*, 3 October 1982). The 'independence' of several of the black homelands of South Africa prompted new 'international' ventures by SAB in malt brewing in Transkei (*On Tap*, December 1978), Bophuthatswana (*Rand Daily Mail*, 8 December 1982) and most recently in sorghum beer production in Ciskei (*Citizen*, 14 August 1983).

Figure 4.6: The Geographical Location of Delta Group Investments in Zimbabwe, 1983

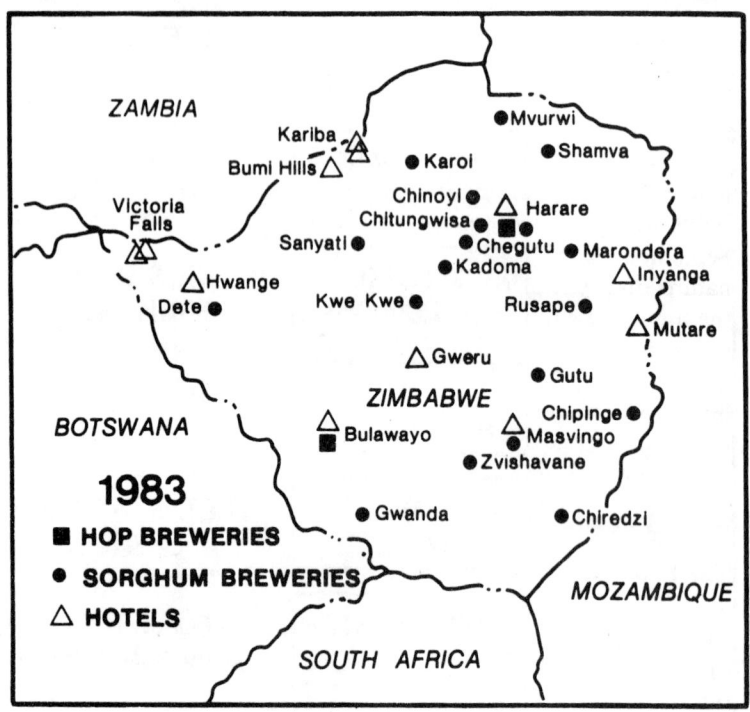

The response by SAB's hotel division, Southern Sun, to events in Southern Africa has been very similar to that of the brewing division. Withdrawal from unfavourable political environs in Madagascar and Mozambique was followed by the closure of the luxury game lodge in Botswana. Compensating for this retreat from these former spheres of operation, Southern Sun Hotels embarked upon a major investment programme to establish casinos in the 'independent' homelands of South Africa. The casino developments in these areas were prompted by the strict regulations which prohibited gambling in South Africa itself. The lucrative nature of casino development in Southern Africa led to a major scramble between Southern Sun and the rival Holiday Inn Corporation to obtain casino rights in the various homelands (Wellings and Crush, 1983). The major successes of Southern Sun were in Bophuthatswana, where the Sun City casino and entertainment complex was established. Other casino developments of Southern Sun occurred at Mmabatho close to the Botswana border, and at Bisho in Ciskei (*Rand Daily Mail,* 28 October 1981). Against the trend for socialist governments to disallow South African enterprises to operate in their countries, Southern Sun extended their operations in Mauritius after the coming to power of the Mouvement Militant Mauricien in 1982. In Mauritius, two more hotels and a casino were purchased in a joint-venture operation. However, the lease and management rights were awarded entirely to Southern Sun (*Sunday Times,* 12 September 1982). This arrangement indicates the exportable nature of South African management as a commodity. In 1983, the hotel and casino industry in Southern Africa underwent major restructuring. Southern Sun's luxury hotels and casinos geographically located outside South Africa were merged with similar interests belonging to the Holiday Inn Group, and incorporated into a new company, Sun International, in which Southern Sun now owns a 25 per cent shareholding.

The Expansion into Advanced Economies

The most recent phase in the international spread of SAB operations began in 1982 with the first halting attempts to break out of the problematic investment arena of Africa and instead to invest in Western Europe, North America and Australia. This fourth stage in the spatial spread of a South African-based corporation occurred in the context of high rates of profits, which fuelled domestic concentration and centralisation of capital within South African enterprises (Kaplan, 1983).

Three major investment projects, only one of which has come to fruition, illustrate the efforts currently being made by SAB to break out of the straightjacket of Africa. The first proposed involvement of SAB outside Africa was by the Southern Sun corporation participating in the establishment of a new large casino complex on the Queensland Gold Coast of Australia (*Star,* 13 October 1982). The proposed venture was to be modelled along the lines of the highly successful Sun City complex. However, considerable objections were raised to South African capital participating in this joint venture by the giant Australian Commonwealth Superannuation Fund. As a result of these objections, Southern Sun was not invited to participate in the venture, not because of any deficiency in terms of finance or managerial expertise, but largely on political grounds (*Star*, 19 November 1982). The experience of Southern Sun in Australia was repeated in a second proposed venture to develop a US$250 million casino hotel complex in Atlantic City, New Jersey. Management expertise in this proposed project was to be provided by Southern Sun (*Star*, 16 November 1982). Again, participation by South African capital engendered considerable opposition with anti-apartheid lobbying finally resulting in the sponsors of the project seeking more acceptable partners, free of the taint of apartheid (*Star*, 16 May 1983). Once more, political factors appear paramount in blocking the expansion of a South African enterprise into advanced economies.

In light of the controversies surrounding South African investment overseas and the particular experiences of SAB, it is not surprising that little publicity surrounded the third proposed overseas venture. Building upon the strengths of its successful fruit juice operations in South Africa, SAB proposed to extend the production of its apple-based fruit juice 'Appletiser' to the United Kingdom and the USA (*Rand Daily Mail*, 24 June 1983). Entry into the United Kingdom was secured through a joint investment project with both the Schweppes Corporation and McMullens Brewery, Hereford. The project launched South African fruit juices on the United Kingdom market by exporting the concentrate from South Africa for dilution and bottling in the United Kingdom (*South African Wine and Beer*, October 1982). It appears from the current strategy of the SAB group that this fruit juice subsidiary is 'looking towards investment in North America in the near future' (*Star*, 12 May 1983). The propensity for SAB to channel an increasing volume of its investments through its offshore companies makes it difficult to trace the penetration of South African capital into advanced capitalist societies, a problem also noted by Kaplan (1983).

Conclusion

This chapter has sought to document the expansion of a multinational corporation based in the semi-periphery as opposed to a core economy. The case study of SAB demonstrates clearly that the semi-peripheral-based multinational does exhibit certain differences which merit specific study. The expansion path of SAB was one of initial penetration into geographically contiguous peripheral economies. The advance of the international operations was severely circumscribed by political events during the 1960s and 1970s. Confronting an increasingly hostile macro environment for investment in much of Africa, a geographical retreat in the patterns of SAB's investments was observed. But perhaps more significant than the withdrawal into those states most directly under South African influence in Southern Africa, is the most recent phase of SAB's international expansion in terms of its thrust into other semi-peripheral and advanced core economies. That companies based in the semi-periphery do have capital, technology and management expertise to export to peripheral economies is not surprising. But it is increasingly apparent that major South African-based multinational corporations, including SAB, are also capable of penetrating the economies of advanced capitalist countries.

In the specific case of SAB, this process of international expansion has been accompanied by an organisational strategy which has sought to distance the internal South African holdings of the company from the international operations through the formation of offshore ventures. This strategy has been pursued in order to overcome the problems for investment emanating from the apartheid economy. It is clear that opposition to investment from apartheid South Africa has been an influential factor shaping the geography of SAB's international ventures. Yet it is still likely that South African-based multinational corporations will become a force to be reckoned with in the international economy over the next decade.

Appendix

Primary sources are referred to in the text in an abbreviated form. The full titles of these sources are as follows;

| Delta AR | Delta Corporation Annual Report (1978; 1983) |
| RB Minutes | Rhodesian Breweries Minutes (1902; 1910; 1934) |

RB AGM	Rhodesian Breweries First Annual General Meeting (1948)
RB AR	Rhodesian Breweries Annual Report (1960; 1962; 1967)
RB Press Release	Rhodesian Breweries Press Release (1969)
SAB Minutes	South African Breweries Minutes (1902; 1910; 1934)
SAB AR	South African Breweries Annual Report (1969; 1973; 1983)
SS AR	Southern Sun Hotel Corporation Annual Report (1976)

Acknowledgements

I would like to thank Chris Rogerson for his valuable comments and Wendy Job for preparing the diagrams. Access was obtained to the archives of South African Breweries and the assistance of Mr B.C. Waigel and Mrs P. Hooijer is gratefully acknowledged.

5 SPATIAL ASPECTS OF THIRD WORLD MULTINATIONAL CORPORATIONS' DIRECT INVESTMENT IN INDONESIA

Dean Forbes

It is widely accepted that, during the last decade and a half, there has been a fundamental restructuring of the world economy and with it a changing international division of labour. The growing concern with deindustrialisation within core capitalist countries has been paralleled by an appreciation of the significance of multinational corporations (MNCs), the emergence of 'new industrialising countries' (NICs) and the development of a 'multipolar world economy'. A number of generalised theories of capitalist industrial restructuring have been developed to explain the history of restructuring and its present form (e.g. Wallerstein's (1979) 'world systems theory'; Fröbel, Heinrich and Kreye's (1980) 'new international division of labour'; see also Fröbel, 1982).

Palloix (1975; 1977) terms the most recent phase of capitalist restructuring the internationalisation of production. Since the mid-1960s industry has been faced with declining rates of profit and the environmental crisis, manifest in shortages of raw materials and in pollution, while contradictions in the labour process (particularly 'Fordism'), and the development of new labour processes such as neo-Fordism, have contributed to the thrust towards restructuring. Advances in technology mean the labour process can now be better divided up and distributed over different places. In addition, the separation of control and manual execution has allowed the concentration of administration and the dispersal of manual work, meaning that it is crucial to see regional industrial structures in terms of the organisation of the MNCs themselves rather than as spatially autonomous mixes (Perrons, 1981; Forbes, 1984a).

Characteristically, discussions about MNCs, foreign private direct investment and internationalised production usually play down the spatial significance of these processes. It is assumed that the OECD nations are the sources of MNC investment, and the NICs and Third World countries the hosts. This probably was a fair assumption in the 1960s and early 1970s, but the growth of

MNCs and private direct investment from Third World countries now challenges this rather simplified international division of labour. Yet having identified the growing importance of Third World MNCs, we need to ask ourselves, what is the significance of this process? The focus of the chapter is Indonesia, a country without significant capital exports of its own (though see Habir and Rowley, 1983), but one of the principal hosts of foreign investment in the Southeast Asian region. The chapter addresses two interrelated questions. First, what empirical and theoretical importance can be attached to the growth of the Third World MNC? How large is Third World investment in Indonesia, compared with other sources, what are its distinctive characteristics, and what does this tell us about the current state of the world economy?

Second, what is the contribution of Third World investment to the shaping of the Indonesian space economy, and does it differ in any significant way from foreign investment sources in OECD countries? Typically foreign investment in Indonesia is concentrated in Western Java, and only enticed away from this core region by major resource projects. Are Third World MNCs any different in their spatial behaviour, what are the consequences of this for the host country, and what is the influence of government on this process? The argument is developed in three parts. In the first, the literature on foreign investment and industrial development is discussed, focusing particularly on the character of the so-called Third World MNCs. The second part of the paper examines the internationalisation strategies of Asian firms and the place of Indonesia within them, as well as the significance of Asian firms to foreign direct investment in Indonesia. Part three looks at the regional distribution of industry in Indonesia, concentrating on the distinctive locational strategies of Asian MNCs and the role of government influence on the location of foreign direct investment in Indonesia.

Third World Multinationals

While debates about structural shifts in the world economy have catapulted discussion of MNCs to the forefront of social (Evans, 1981), economic (Caves, 1982) and geographic (Taylor and Thrift, 1982) research, a number of aspects of restructuring have remained relatively unexplored (Forbes, 1984a). Particularly, those firms which have headquarters in Third World countries and own or maintain equity in productive or service investments in other countries — Third World MNCs — have not been widely documented or discussed. Moreover, their spatial strategies and the consequences of their investments for the natural and built environments and labour markets in general have scarcely been raised at all. There can be little doubt, however, of the potential importance of the flows of foreign direct investment within the Third World (Wells, 1981). First, it has been estimated that around 50 Third World countries are homes to MNCs, and the top 15 countries among them have around 1300 foreign manufacturing and trading subsidiaries (*The Economist,* July 23, 1983, p. 61). Second, the stock of Third World direct foreign equity is estimated to be around $US 10 billion (Lall, 1983, p. 620). To keep this in perspective, it should be noted that in 1976 developed market economies' stock of direct investment abroad totalled around $US 287 billion (Linge, 1984). Nevertheless, we might expect some Third World countries to make up some of this ground in the future. The rate of industrial growth in the NICs, from where the bulk of Third World foreign investment is coming, has been impressive of late. Between 1966 and 1975 the top 10 NICs accounted for nearly three-quarters of the entire increase in Third World manufacturing output, which in turn had grown between 1960 and 1980 from 8.2 per cent to 10 per cent of world industrial output (ARB, 13 August 1983, p. 1074).

Third World MNCs seem to share a number of distinctive characteristics, which suggest they are a worthy object of theoretical analysis in themselves (Giddy and Young, 1982), though it has also been put forward that these differences are overdrawn and that Third World MNCs are not all that different from those originating in the developed world (Lall, 1983, p.625). Third World MNCs tend to be small, adopt a relatively low profile, are often labour-intensive, and use locally made materials, and deal in mature low technologies which nevertheless allows innovation in order to tailor output to the particular needs of Third World societies. Competition with domestic firms and developed economy MNCs is based on lower costs of production and cheaper prices; output is often undifferentiated; brand names are not as common; and there is less investment in advertising and marketing. Joint ventures are more common than for developed economy MNCs, because, it is argued, Third World MNCs have poor financial resources and fewer secrets (e.g. technology) to protect (Lecraw, 1977; Wells, 1977; Streeten, 1979; Heenan and Keegan, 1979; O'Brien, 1980; Linge and Hamilton, 1981, pp. 85-6).

However, not all Third World MNCs are the same. Broadly speaking, two methods have been used to differentiate between Third World MNCs. The first method is based on the characteristics of the country of origin. Lall (1983, p. 624) argues that 'small open economies basically export production know-how and efficient management and marketing. Larger, more closed economies export some basic technology and capital goods as well as production know-how, but their technologies may be somewhat outdated and their marketing skills relatively less developed.' Another means of separating firms is based on the nature of, and the access to, the capital market in the country concerned (Agmon and Lessard, 1977, pp. 208-12), while yet another distinction is between firms from resource-rich developing countries (e.g. OPEC), labour-rich, rapidly industrialising countries (Hong Kong, Singapore), and market-rich, rapidly industrialising countries (Brazil, Mexico, the Philippines) (Heenan and Keegan, 1979, pp. 102-3).

A second means of differentiation is based on the characteristics of the firms themselves (Table 5.1). Distinctions vary between writers, partly depending on the places considered, as in the case of O'Brien whose category of 'genuine multination firms' are only to be found in Latin America where specific multination firms are formed to develop a particular resource. A number of distinctions are common to more than one writer. For instance, the distinction

Table 5.1: Types of Third World MNC

	O'Brien Model	Panglaykim Model
Locally-owned Private Firms	Locally-owned private firms Genuine multination firms	Private firms (commenced pre-war) Private firms (commenced post-war)
Colonial Trading Firms		Colonial trading companies
Parastatal Firms	Public-sector companies	Parastatal enterprises Joint government/private corporations
Affiliates of OECD MNCs	Affiliates of OECD MNCs	

Source: O'Brien (1980); Panglaykim (1979).

between state and private corporations is an important one (Linge, 1984), as are the distinctions between affiliates and subsidiaries of OECD MNCs, colonial trading companies, and the indigenous firms of the Third World.

The Geographic Origins of Third World MNCs

Hong Kong MNCs are considered the source of most Third World direct investment, controlling stock valued at around $US 2 billion, the bulk held by colonial trading companies but with $US 600-800 million in the hands of Chinese enterprises. Brazilian companies are also important, followed by MNCs from Singapore. The remaining key countries include South Korea, Taiwan, Argentina, Mexico, Venezuela and India, each with MNCs holding direct overseas investment valued between $US 50-100 million. The focus of capital exports reflect the type of industrial development within the country. Around 95 per cent of Brazilian investment is in exploration, construction and agriculture, while 70 per cent of Korean investment is in trading and natural resources. There are four main investors in manufacturing: Hong Kong, Singapore, Argentina and India. Hong Kong firms specialise in the manufacture of simple exportable products such as textiles, garments, plastic goods and simple consumer electronics. Their comparative advantage derives from shifting standardised products to new locations in order to keep production costs down, and there is little technology transfer. Singapore firms, on the other hand, specialise in import-substituting commodities and ethnic Chinese consumer goods, as well as investing heavily in services (Lall, 1983).

The motivation for Third World firms to internationalise is widely canvassed, and the list of possible causes very long. Demand limitations in the domestic market, import barriers in the industrialised countries, risk diversification, the search for raw materials, to make use of comparative advantage in competition against OECD MNCs, to seek foreign technology not available at home, servicing ethnic minorities abroad, government incentives or requirements for importers to earn foreign exchange, restrictions on domestic growth and many more reasons for internationalisation have been offered.

The Geographic Focus of Third World MNCs

The consensus is that Third World MNCs on the whole invest more in developing than developed countries. Moreover, geographical proximity and cultural affiliations, superficially at least, seem determinant. It has been noticed that 'the Asian countries invest in Asia and the Latin Americans in Latin America' (O'Brien, 1980, p.304), with some exceptions such as Indian, Hong Kong and Brazilian investment in parts of Africa. The Chinese and Indian MNCs invest in countries where their respective communities are well established, for as O'Brien (1980, p.304) has noted, around 46 per cent of the approved agreements for joint ventures from India are lodged in countries where important positions in the economy are held by Indian migrants. Third World MNCs 'do not have the wherewithal to compete with developed country firms on their home ground' according to Lall (1983, p.620). Nevertheless, Linge (1984, p.185) has pointed out that the South Korean corporation, Hyundai, has set up a subsidiary in Silicon Valley, California 'responsible for research and development, pilot production, transfer of technology and marketing in the US'. Moreover, Australia's Foreign Investment Review Board noted that around 16 per cent ($A856 million) of total investment expenditure in 1983 would be made by Southeast Asian investors, $A469 million of which would be in real estate, accounting for 45 per cent of spending in that sector (*The Canberra Times*, 10 November 1982).

The sub-national regional impacts of Third World investment are poorly investigated. There is a small but growing literature on the regional consequences of internationalised production in the Third World (see selected essays in Hamilton and Linge, 1981; Taylor and Thrift, 1982; Moulaert and Salinas, 1983) but virtually nothing directly on the peculiarities of Third World investment. However, Daly (1982) and Thrift (Chapter 6, this volume) have analysed the impact of Asian investment on Sydney's land market, while Thee Kian Wie (1981) has noted the concentration of Indian manufacturing investment in Indonesia in Surabaya. Wells and Warren (1979, p.77) believe that Third World MNCs are less inclined to invest in buildings than their counterparts from developed economies, which is 'consistent with the fact that developing country investors are somewhat more likely to be in Jakarta (two-thirds of their projects) than are industrialised country investors (less than one-half of their projects), who seem to gravitate toward the less crowded areas.' On the whole, the lack of understanding about the spatial distribution of Third World MNCs, and their regional impact, is symptomatic of a focus in the literature on the origins of capital investment, macroeconomic interpretations of industrial restructuring, and microeconomic concerns with theories of the firm.

Asian MNCs Investment in Indonesia

Western Pacific Basin countries have been at the forefront of industrial restructuring, yet world-scale changes have been differentially distributed through the region (Forbes and Rimmer, 1983). In the *Economic and Social Atlas of the Pacific Basin* five main sub-regions were distinguished, arranged in a 'Pacific Cross' (Forbes *et al.*, 1985). Lying at *the core* is the main regional industrial power — Japan — and the newly industrialising countries (NICs), Hong Kong, South Korea, Singapore and Taiwan, surrounded by a group of countries with good recent rates of growth and some promise of following in the footsteps of the NICs, namely Malaysia, Sri Lanka, the Philippines, Thailand and Indonesia. To the north is the *communist bloc*, to the east the *Pacific Islands*, to the west *South Asia* and to the south *Australia and New Zealand*. For different reasons each of these groups of national economies share slow rates of growth, although industrial restructuring within the slow-moving, relatively heavily protected Indian economy, and within the 'mature' industrial economy of Australia, has resulted in some private transfers to the core of economic growth.

A shift-share analysis of industrial production within the region between 1975 and 1979 highlights some of the details of industrial restructuring and particularly the place of Indonesia within this process. Broadly speaking, Japan and Australia shared relative declines in crude steel production, radio receivers and TV receivers (though Japan's automobile industry boomed while Australia's fell behind). Indonesia, partly due to starting from a low base, recorded strong gains in output of fabrics and a modest increase in the production of crude steel, cars and commercial vehicles, and TV receivers, though it experienced a strong negative shift in radio receiver production. South Korea's strong overall performance in the indicators selected is worthy of note (Forbes *et al.*, 1985). It is clear from these data that there are fairly substantial changes taking place in the Pacific Basin, and these changes are closely related to the internationalisation of production which

Palloix has identified. The question is, however, where does Indonesia fit into this schema?

Foreign Direct Investment in Indonesia

The coup that ousted President Sukarno and prepared the way for President Suharto to assume office in Indonesia in 1968 effectively marked the beginning of the 'New Order' in Indonesia. Foreign investment was to play a large part in the new administration's economic strategy, but it took several years to establish a suitable climate for foreign investors.

Figure 5.1: Foreign Investment Implementations in Indonesia, 1970-1980

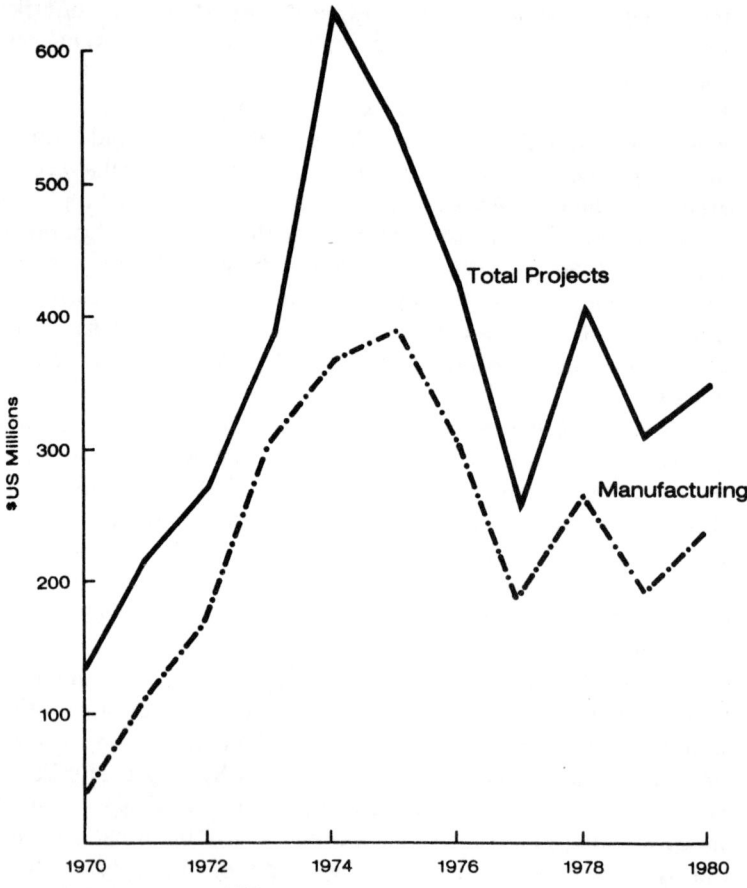

Source: Bank Indonesia, 1982.

There was steady growth in foreign investment in Indonesia from 1970 to 1974, but then, due to the impact of the word recession and unfavourable publicity given to new tax arrangements for foreign oil companies operating in the region, a sharp fall-off took place (McCawley, 1979, p.66). However, in the following years the desirability of foreign investment seems to have been reaffirmed (Figure 5.1). The Investment Coordinating Board (Badan Koordinasi Penanaman Modal or BKPM) after 1977 began to publish its Daftar Skala Prioritas (Investment Priorities List, BKPM, 1981) and although commentators note an ambiguity in attitudes to, and the reality of, Indonesia's openness to foreign investment, official policy apparently favours increased investment. Doubts persist about the value of foreign investment, however, for it is not clear that it has brought about an improvement in management and marketing skills, nor has it produced lower-priced goods (Anwar, 1980, p.218). Since 1977 it seems as though foreign investment has again been on the increase, but by comparison with neighbouring countries like Singapore, and in view of the size of Indonesia, investment has not been excessively large (McCawley, 1979, p.66).

Excluding the oil and gas sectors, which do not fall within the control of BKPM, foreign investment is predominantly in manufacturing industries, particularly textiles and leather production and metal products (Table 5.2). In 1980, manufacturing soaked up 67.9 per cent of investment implemented in that year. However, we need to qualify the significance of manufacturing to the Indonesian economy. First, manufacturing contributes only 9 per cent of Indonesia's GDP, compared to 25 per cent in the Philippines, 18 per cent in Thailand, and 15 per cent in Malaysia. Moreover, manufacturing is largely directed towards import substitution, rather than export. In 1975, manufactured goods contributed a little over 2 per cent to Indonesian exports, compared to 32 per cent in India. Second, despite its relative smallness, manufacturing output as a whole has grown quite strongly in the last few years, between 1971 and 1977 for instance growing at an annual average of 13.3 per cent, and in some areas (chemical industries, metals and machinery) probably higher (McCawley, 1981, p.65; Anwar, 1980, p.209; Soehoed, 1982; BPS, various issues). Third, foreign investment has played a significant role in the growth of manufacturing. Between 1967 and 1977 BKPM approved manufacturing investments of $US8.1 billion, split

Table 5.2: Implementation of Foreign Investment Projects by Sector, 1967 to 1980 ($US millions)

Sector	1967-75	1976	1977	1978	1979	1980	Total Investment Plan	Number of Projects
Agriculture, forestry and fishery	*329.1*	*39.2*	*37.4*	*38.6*	*34.0*	*48.6*	*526.9*	*132*
Agriculture	32.2	8.0	12.5	10.1	4.3	14.5	81.6	51
Forestry	237.6	22.7	22.1	15.0	19.2	26.2	342.8	68
Fishery	59.3	8.5	2.8	13.5	10.5	7.9	102.5	13
Mining	*256.8*	*42.4*	*20.1*	*57.3*	*47.5*	*49.4*	*473.5*	*9*
Manufacturing industry	*1,425.4*	*301.2*	*186.2*	*267.0*	*192.0*	*235.4*	*2,607.2*	*391*
Food	125.6	10.8	11.9	14.9	7.1	7.4	177.7	45
Textiles and leather	625.1	91.8	27.9	31.4	41.7	78.7	896.6	59
Wood and wood products	16.1	4.6	1.4	0.4	0.1	3.3	25.9	7
Paper and paper products	14.6	3.3	9.6	11.8	1.4	6.1	46.8	11
Chemicals and rubber	192.2	45.7	28.0	71.7	44.8	32.0	414.4	117
Non-metallic minerals	139.5	71.3	42.9	9.0	3.2	30.0	295.9	24
Basic metal	81.1	30.7	27.8	37.8	47.5	23.9	248.8	19
Metal products	221.0	42.4	35.4	89.9	36.0	52.0	476.7	102
Others	10.2	0.6	1.3	0.1	10.2	2.0	24.4	7
Construction	*30.0*	*4.5*	*3.0*	*1.4*	*12.0*	*0.8*	*51.7*	*51*
Trade and hotels	*62.2*	*17.6*	*6.2*	*17.2*	*3.2*	*0.4*	*107.9*	*13*
Trade	9.9	0.2	—	0.7	—	—	10.8	3
Hotels	52.3	17.4	6.2	16.5	4.3	0.4	97.1	10
Transportation and communication	*11.9*	*4.4*	*2.0*	*4.7*	*21.9*	*3.8*	*49.7*	*18*
Transportation	5.5	4.2	1.8	1.3	0.1	2.1	15.0	17
Communication	6.4	0.2	0.2	3.4	21.8	2.7	34.7	1
Services	*64.2*	*12.3*	*3.8*	*14.0*	*6.9*	*7.2*	*108.4*	*31*
Trade services	55.4	12.3	3.5	5.1	6.9	7.2	90.4	24
Personal services	8.8	—	0.3	8.9	—	—	18.0	7
Others	*105.6*	*3.9*	*0.1*	*5.0*	—	—	*114.6*	—
Total	2,285.2	425.5	258.8	405.2	318.6	346.6	4,039.9	645

Source: Bank Indonesia (1982), p. 97.

almost equally between foreign and private investment. However, it should be added that, in total, foreign investment contributed 53.4 per cent of all approvals, and that the ratio of approved investments since the mid-1970s has switched in favour of domestic investment (McCawley, 1981, Table 3.3).

Asian Direct Investment

The origins of foreign investment approvals issued by BKPM between 1967 and 1982 are listed in Table 5.3. Japan is the dominant investor, accounting for 35 per cent of the total, and together with other OECD investment contributes 63 per cent of the total (Forbes, 1982). Nevertheless Hong Kong is the second largest investor in Indonesia, its 11.4 per cent share of non-oil investments exceeding investment from countries like the USA and the Netherlands. Altogether Asian Third World MNCs accounted for 20.4 per cent of Indonesian investment approvals, totalling $US 2134.7 million. Figure 5.2 shows the changing origins of foreign investment approvals, accumulated for 1967-75, and annually to 1980 since then. The fluctuations from year to year cloud the picture, but it does illustrate the fact that Asian investment in Indonesia has remained fairly consistent, after peaking in 1976/77, at between one-quarter and one-fifth of total investment approvals. Investment implementations may reveal a different pattern, but data are not published by country of origin.

Figure 5.3 shows the recorded home offices of MNCs with investments in Indonesia between 1978 and 1981. By these calculations there were 393 MNCs operating through 571 subsidiaries in Indonesia in 1980/81. Japan again is dominant, but the USA and the UK appear rather more important by this measure,

Table 5.3: Foreign Investment Approvals, 1967-1982 ($US millions)

	$US millions	Per cent
Hong Kong	1,190.7	11.4
Philippines	303.0	2.9
India	156.2	1.5
Singapore	152.9	1.5
South Korea	130.7	1.2
Taiwan	129.6	1.2
Malaysia	50.0	0.5
Thailand	21.6	0.2
Japan	3,660.1	35.0
North America[a]	1,507.7	14.4
Europe	1,205.7	11.5
Australia	220.9	2.1
Other/joint	1,735.8	16.6
Total	10,464.9	100.0

Note: a. Includes Panama.
Source: IDN, May 1982.

Figure 5.2: Origins of Foreign Investment Approvals, 1967-1980

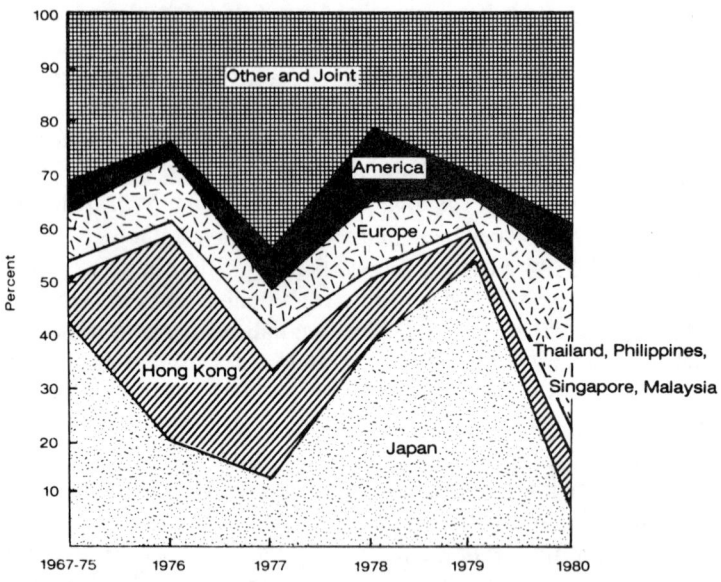

Source: Bank Indonesia, 1982.

followed by the Netherlands, Australia and West Germany. Some
51 of the 393 MNCs recorded were Asian firms (13 per cent),
mainly from Singapore (21), Hong Kong (17) and Malaysia (7). A
number of factors will affect the differences between the numbers
of firms involved and the money value of foreign direct investment
in Indonesia. For instance, the latter figures for Australian involvement in Indonesia are swollen by the preponderance of Australian
companies with small investments in Indonesia (Forbes, 1984b), in
contrast to the large projects of the big Japanese investors.
Furthermore, documentation problems plague this sort of work. It
has been noted that there is significant unrecorded Asian investment in Indonesia, many projects passing as domestic (Wells and
Warren, 1979, p. 70; Thee Kian Wie, 1981, p. 136).

Nevertheless, there are a number of characteristics of Asian
investment in Indonesia worth documenting. Table 5.4 is
compiled from investment applications processed and approved in
Indonesia in 1979. A total of 52 projects were handled, 22 from
Hong Kong, Singapore, India and South Korea, and 28 from the
rest of the world (including Japan). Manufacturing industry

Figure 5.3: Home of Multinational Corporations with Investments in Indonesia, 1980/81

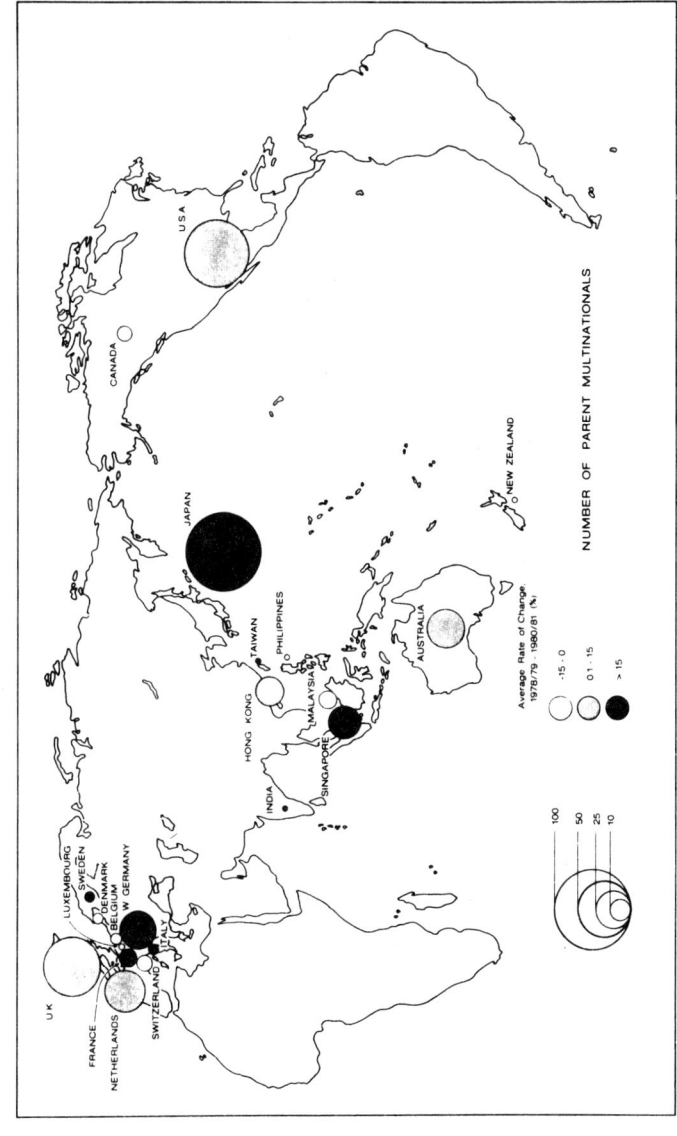

Source: *Who Owns Whom*, various editions.

Table 5.4: New Investments Processed, 1979

Place of Origin	Number	Expected Total ($US 000)	Investment Average ($US 000)	Expected Average Indonesian	Employment Average Expatriate	Agriculture, Fishing and Forestry	Mining and Quarrying	Manufacturing	Restaurants and Hotels	Construction, Real Estate and Business Services
Hong Kong	13	161,237	12,403	708	25	4	—	7	—	2
Singapore	4	38,258	9,565	1,160	8	1	—	2	1	—
India	3	50,715	16,905	294	25	—	—	3	—	—
South Korea	2	6,142	3,071	228	44	—	—	2	1	2
Sub-total	22	256,352	11,652	711	23	5	—	14	—	1
Japan	7	27,246	3,892	171	9	1	—	5	—	3
USA	7	61,150	8,736	1,539	17	2	—	2	—	—
Europe	11	110,718	10,065	296	17	—	—	11	—	—
Australia	3	12,450	4,150	204	5	1	—	2	—	4
Sub-total	28	211,554	7,556	577	13	4	—	20	—	—
Other/joint	2	313,468	156,734	359	5	—	1	1	—	—
Total	52	781,374	15,026	637	17	9	1	35	1	6

Source: BKPM, 1979.

comprised the majority of the Asian and non-Asian projects, particularly chemicals and chemical products (13), machinery and fabricated metal products (7), wood products (4) and textiles (3). Of the non-manufacturing industries, fisheries (6) were the most important, followed by real estate and business services (5). The sample was too small to distinguish meaningfully between Asian and non-Asian projects at this (ISIC two-digit) level of disaggregation. However, Chen (1981) has noted that Hong Kong firms first shifted into Indonesia soon after the proclamation of the Foreign Direct Investment Law of 1967. Between 1967 and 1976 the bulk of investment (51.9 per cent) was directed into manufacturing, and much less into services (29.9 per cent) and the primary sector (18.2 per cent). Early in this period, Hong Kong investors concentrated on the textile industry in order to circumvent developed country quotas, as well as to find a use for outdated machinery. However, during the 1970s Indonesia turned down many applications because it wished to develop its own textile industry, with the result that Hong Kong manufacturing investment shifted into chemicals, while non-manufacturing investment concentrated on hotels, trade services, recreational services and timber. Most of this investment has been directed to the domestic market, and not for export.

The average size of Asian projects approved in 1979 was $US 11.7 million, exceeding the average $US 7.6 planned by non-Asian investors (Table 5.4). Wells and Warren (1979, p. 78) believe a dual-firm structure exists. They noted that, on the one hand, developing country projects in Indonesia were characterised by large investments in the food industry, but that, on the other hand, small investments predominated. Official investment information is strongly skewed in favour of the large projects. Thee Kian Wie (1981) found that BKPM held records of only four investments by Indian firms, but by using Embassy and industry groups was able to find a total of 24 Indian projects in Indonesia. The poor quality of the data, then, is a severe restriction on conclusions about the size range of Asian investments in Indonesia, although the evidence suggests that it would be quite wrong to dismiss all Asian investments as small-scale.

On average, Asian firms planned in 1979 to employ 711 Indonesians per project, compared to 577 by non-Asian firms. However, this is not a sign of the labour-intensive technology which Wells and Warren (1979, pp. 74-7) believe developing

Table 5.5: Selected Asian Firms' Interests in Indonesia, 1982

	Location of Head Office	Turnover $US million	Principal Subsidiaries & Associates	Country of Incorporation of Principal Subsidiaries and Associates						Indonesian Investments		
				Hong Kong	Singapore	Malaysia	Australia	USA	Indonesia	Company	Equity	Activity
Haw Par Brothers International Ltd	Singapore	130.91	63	17	27	11	1	–	1	P.T. Sanyo Industries Indonesia	32	Distribution of consumer goods
Hongkong Land Company Ltd	Hong Kong	994.46	58ᵃ	30	1	1	10	1	1	P.T. Jaya Mandarin Agung	50	Hotel
Inchcape Berhad	Singapore	392.7	92	7	30	46	–	–	2	P.T. National Assemblers	25	Motor vehicle assembly
										P.T. Wisma Kosgoro	43	Property development and management

Table 5.5 continued

Jardine Matheson Hong Kong and Co Ltd[c]	1,658.49	173[b]	59	8	8	12	9	1	P.T. Jakarta Land	25	Property development and management
Jardine Fleming Hong Kong Holdings Ltd	—		29	17	3	1	1	1	1	P.T. Multinational Finance Corp.	10	Finance

Notes: a. Excludes subsidiaries and associates of Jardine Matheson.
b. Excludes subsidiaries and associates of Hongkong Land.
c. Figures for 1981.
Source: Company reports.

country firms bring to Indonesia, for Asian firms were intending investing $US 16,400 per job compared to the figure of $US 13,100 for the remainder. Moreover, if the ASEAN fertiliser project, included under other/joint in Table 5.4, had been included in the Asian firms figure, investment per job would have been much higher. The under-enumeration of the smaller projects which could reasonably be expected to be labour-intensive is again a factor to be taken into account, yet there are still questions that can be raised about the supposed technology of Asian firms. From the information available Asian firms expect to employ 23 non-Indonesians per project, compared to 13 for the other firms (cf. Wells and Warren, 1979, p. 80).

All the planned projects in 1979 were to be joint ventures, in line with Indonesian policy, which aims towards 51 per cent Indonesian equity within 10 years of establishment. One project provided an exception to this rule. This was a project planned by National Semiconductor Corporation of the USA, which intended manufacturing semiconductors at a plant in Bandung. The American company retained 100 per cent ownership, due to the desire of the Indonesians to promote high-technology industrial development. Asian firms had on average 72.5 per cent equity, while non-Asian firms controlled on average 64.2 per cent. This corresponds closely to the findings of Wells and Warren (1979, p. 81) and Thee Kian Wie (1981, p. 139).

Asian MNCs Spatial Strategies

Shifting from the general picture to the specific, what evidence is there of changing interest in Indonesia by Third World MNCs based in Asia? At present, Indonesia figures in two different capacities for Asian firms moving off-shore. First, the corporate structure and spatial extent of investment by the large Hong Kong- and Singapore-based general trading houses suggests investments in Indonesia are somewhat peripheral to the core of corporate activity. The spatial extent of five such companies is documented in Table 5.5.

Haw Par, Hongkong Land, Jardine Matheson, Jardine Fleming and Inchcape Berhad between them control some 415 subsidiary and associate companies, yet only six (1.5 per cent) are located in Indonesia, compared to 45 (16.1 per cent) in Malaysia. Moreover, their equity holdings in Indonesian associates ranges between 10 and 50 per cent, averaging only 30.8 per cent and hence well below the figure quoted earlier of 72.5 per cent. Figures 5.2 and 5.3, discussed above, were ambiguous about the changing significance of Asian investment in Indonesia. Investment approvals (Figure 5.2) fluctuated from year to year, while the measurement of Asian investment based on the number of corporations involved (Figure 5.3) depended on a small sample and small time-period, and differed significantly from country to country. At the level of individual companies, there is some evidence of withdrawals from Indonesia. Hongkong Land, for instance, has, since 1973, been involved in four projects in Indonesia. By 1982 it only retained a major interest in one of them, the Hotel Jakarta Mandarin, owned by P.T. Jaya Mandarin Agung (Table 5.6). In itself this evidence is inconclusive, but it does reinforce a belief in the peripherality of Indonesia to the large trading companies.

In contrast, a number of smaller, more specialised Asian companies appear, from the limited evidence available, to depend more heavily on investments in Indonesia. The Tai Ping Insurance Company Ltd was founded in Shanghai in 1929, and by 1934 had branches spread through the main ports of China, as well as in Southeast Asia. In 1948 it shifted operations to Taipei, and gradually phased out its overseas branches, the last in Saigon closing in 1974. Its current focus is underwriting all forms of non-life assurance, and it had a combined income from insurance, co-insurance and reinsurance of $US 24.33 million in 1982. Apart from its two domestic branches, Tai Ping Insurance now has an

Table 5.6: Major Hongkong Land Company Ltd Investments in Indonesia

	Activity	Location	Company Equity %	Years of operation
P.T. Aero Garuda Dairy Farm	Food distribution	Halim Airport Jakarta	40	1972-78
P.T. Halim Park	Residential estate development	Halim Park Jakarta	42	1973-75
P.T. Manning Development	Rental property Wisma Hayam Wuruk	Jalan Hayam Wuruk Jakarta	30	1975-82
P.T. Jaya Mandarin Agung	Hotel Jakarta Mandarin	Jalan Thamrin Jakarta	50	1973-

Source: Company reports.

affiliate in Taiwan, as well as one in Hong Kong and Indonesia, P.T. Asuransi Artapala, which has its head office in Surabaya and branch office in Jakarta.

Another specialised Asian firm with investments in Indonesia is Prima Ltd, a Singapore flour milling company (Table 5.7). It built a major flour mill in Ujung Pandang, Indonesia, which came into production in 1972. The mill cost Prima over $S 25 million, but for that Prima retained 100 per cent ownership of the company until January 1980, when it sold off 25 per cent of the shares. Between 1974 and 1978, P.T. Prima Indonesia and Prima Lines Private Ltd, owner of the Motor Vessel Prima King, contributed between 43.4 per cent and 56.0 per cent of the gross profit of Prima Ltd. In 1981, when more detailed information was available, this had dropped to 21.0 per cent, while P.T. Prima Indonesia's contribution stood at 8.7 per cent. In part this drop was brought about by Prima Ceylon Ltd's very profitable flour mill in Trincomalee, Sri Lanka, coming into production in 1980, providing 65.8 per cent and 74.7 per cent of Prima Ltd's profits in 1981 and 1982, respectively. Nevertheless, Prima Ltd sold the Ujung Pandang flour mill in March 1982 to an Indonesian company, PTPP Berdikari, for $US 21.5 million, although it has retained an office (P.T. Prima Pantas) in Jakarta.

ASEAN Industrial Cooperation

The Indonesian government has tried particularly to promote joint investments among the ASEAN countries. Three forms of ASEAN industrial cooperation are encouraged. First, there are the ASEAN industrial projects, whereby each country undertakes a large-scale project. Though launched in 1977, the programme has not proved successful, although Indonesia has built a urea plant (see Staab, 1980). Second, the ASEAN industrial complementation scheme was also launched in 1977. Component parts were to be manufactured in ASEAN countries and exchanged with others on preferential trading terms, yet though some progress was made on an automotive project, the scheme is not operating well (*AF*, December 1982, pp. 181-2).

The third form of cooperation is the private sector ASEAN industrial joint venture, an agreement initialled by ASEAN ministers in 1982. It was an Indonesian initiative for stimulating joint-venture projects among private sector companies within the ASEAN region, and emerged in part from the failure of the indus-

Table 5.7: Principal Subsidiaries of Prima Ltd, Singapore

| | Activity | Location | Company Equity | Years of Operation | Contributions to Group Profit | | | | | |
					$S'000 1980	%	$S'000 1981	%	$S'000 1982	%
P.T. Prima Indonesia	Flour mill	Ujung Pandang Indonesia	75ᵃ	1972			1,514	8.7	—	
Prima Lines Private Ltd	Shipping	Singapore	100	—	10,404	56.2	2,136	12.3	2,400	11.6
Prima Tower Private Ltd	Real estate	Singapore	100	1980			108	0.6	8	0.0
Prima Ceylon Ltd	Flour mill	Trincomalee Sri Lanka	40	1980	—		11,543	65.8	15,441	74.7
Supra Private Ltd	Housing project	Amokiah	60	1982	—		—		—309	—

Note: a. 1970-1980, 100%.
Source: Company reports.

trial complementation scheme. Joint-venture projects are to be approved by the ASEAN economic ministers, who are charged with responsibility for ensuring a long-run equitable distribution of benefits among the partners. The ASEAN Finance Corporation, formed in 1981, will aid in finance, while a proposed ASEAN Trading and Investment Corporation is intended to assist in the promotion of investment, trading and marketing activities. It is hoped that the new joint ventures will concentrate on inter-mediate-level products, aimed particularly at regional import substitution, and hence at promoting inter-regional trade. If the agreement is ratified, 'the accord could go into force in early 1984, when it will clear the way for some 21 industrial joint-venture projects which have been stalled on the drawing board for quite some time' (Sricharatchanya, 1983, pp. 76-7).

Third World MNCs, and private direct investment from the Third World, needs to be taken more seriously than it has in the past, yet its significance should not be overstated. Less than 3 per cent of the stock of foreign investment is controlled from the Third World, while in Indonesia investments originating in and routed through Third World countries have never comprised more than about one-quarter of investment approvals. Its theoretical significance is not so easily quantified, however. These flows are relatively recent, and there is every prospect of them increasing with the result that, as capital mobility speeds up, the distinctions between source and host countries of foreign investment is increasingly blurred. The geographical consequences will grow proportionately. To explore these we need to look at the pattern of regional distribution of current investment.

The Regional Distribution of Asian Investment in Indonesia

The growth of Third World MNCs and a tendency towards a new international division of labour has substantial implications for the spatial economy of Indonesia, yet this is an issue about which we know relatively little. The major studies of Indonesian industrial structure (Donges, Stecher and Wolter, 1974; 1980; McCawley, 1979; 1981; World Bank, 1981) deal only marginally with the spatial distribution of industry, although work is in progress on major reviews of the industrial space economy for the National Urban Development Strategy Project (1983) and the World

Bank's project on Selected Issues in Spatial Development (Rice, 1983). The main tension to be focused on in this section is, inevitably, the centralisation and decentralisation of industry. A highly centralised money economy and a primate urban system (Jakarta in 1980 was 3.2 times as large as the second ranking city, Surabaya) has led to a disproportionate concentration of resources in Jakarta which the government has tried to off-set through a variety of regional programmes. This section will be restricted to a consideration of three aspects of Indonesia's industrial geography and the impact of Third World MNCs upon it: first, a brief description of the regional distribution of industry highlighting the location of foreign investment projects; second, an examination of the distribution of Asian MNCs investment in Indonesia; and third, a discussion of some of the attempts by government to influence the location of industry, and especially industry supported by foreign investment.

The Geographical Distribution of Indonesian Industry

Industry is concentrated in Java. Around 78 per cent of medium and large-scale firms are located on Java, along with 86 per cent of total manufacturing employment (Forbes, 1984c). In fact some 50 per cent of employees in the large and medium sector are concentrated in 20 *kabupaten*. Overall, there is a pronounced concentration in Jakarta (where it is noted the social diseconomies of agglomeration are approaching a very high level) and in the large provincial cities in the rest of the country (Tamba, 1976; Donges, Stecher and Wolter, 1980, p. 369). Much of this concentration can be explained in terms of history and proximity to markets. Tea processing, sugar refining, rubber milling, etc. are, of course, resource-based industries dependent on the agricultural estates, while the weaving and *kretek* cigarette industry are the product, according to McCawley (1979, p. 63), of historical accident. There is a higher proportion of large and medium firms in Jakarta and West Java than anywhere else in the country. In 1974/75, 31 per cent of registered firms in Jakarta, and 21 per cent in West Java, were either large or medium firms (i.e. employing 20 or more), involved in plastic products, printing, knitting and weaving, among others. There are also significant concentrations of large and medium firms in Central Java (weaving, batik, tobacco), East Java (tobacco, weaving, *kretek*), and lesser concentrations in East Kalimantan (timber) and North Sumatra (rubber mills, saw mills).

Most firms, however, employ fewer than 20 people. These rice mills, saw mills and brick-makers account for much of the employment in industry in places like South Sulawesi and South Sumatra (McCawley, 1979, Table 13).

Figure 5.4 looks at the pattern of non-oil foreign investment implementation between 1967 and 1979. (A number of small investments were omitted from this data.) The geographical concentration on Jakarta and West Java is strikingly evident, with Java as a whole capturing 73 per cent of the total invested. Less significant investments have gone to North Sumatra, East Kalimantan and Irian Jaya. Broadly speaking the Java–Outer Islands distinction corresponds to a manufacturing–resource extraction distinction (see World Bank, 1981, Annex 1:8). The net gains from foreign investment, it follows from this, have flowed disproportionately to the Jakarta and West Java core, compounding the spatial unevenness of Indonesian economic development. Following this up with Figure 5.5, which looks at foreign investment approvals between March 1980 and March 1982, it is apparent that Jakarta and West Java still feature as major poles attracting industry, though the share of Java as a whole drops back to 43 per cent. Certainly, it should be noted that these are approvals and only cover two years, and that there are only two investments in Aceh, one very substantial (a cement works). Nevertheless, it does suggest a possible shift in foreign direct investment away from the core. This is particularly the case for the investment figures for Riau, which include those destined for the Batam Island Export Processing Zone.

Economists have offered a number of reasons why there has been a concentration of industry in Jakarta, selected parts of Java, and some of the large provincial cities. The close link between bureaucrats and industrial development and the need for access to senior government officials, the amenities of Jakarta (and to a lesser extent the other major cities), and a close link between industrialisation and urbanisation (markets, availability of a workforce, credit, material supplies, etc.) have been mentioned. There has been no attempt to 'unpack' the industry/location nexus, except by sector, and the question of differences between types of firms has not been raised at all in this context. It is also a little surprising that the availability and quality of labour supply does not feature more strongly in these sorts of explanations, as there is evidence within industrial geography to suggest labour to be

Figure 5.4: Regional Distribution of Foreign Investment Implementation, 1967-79

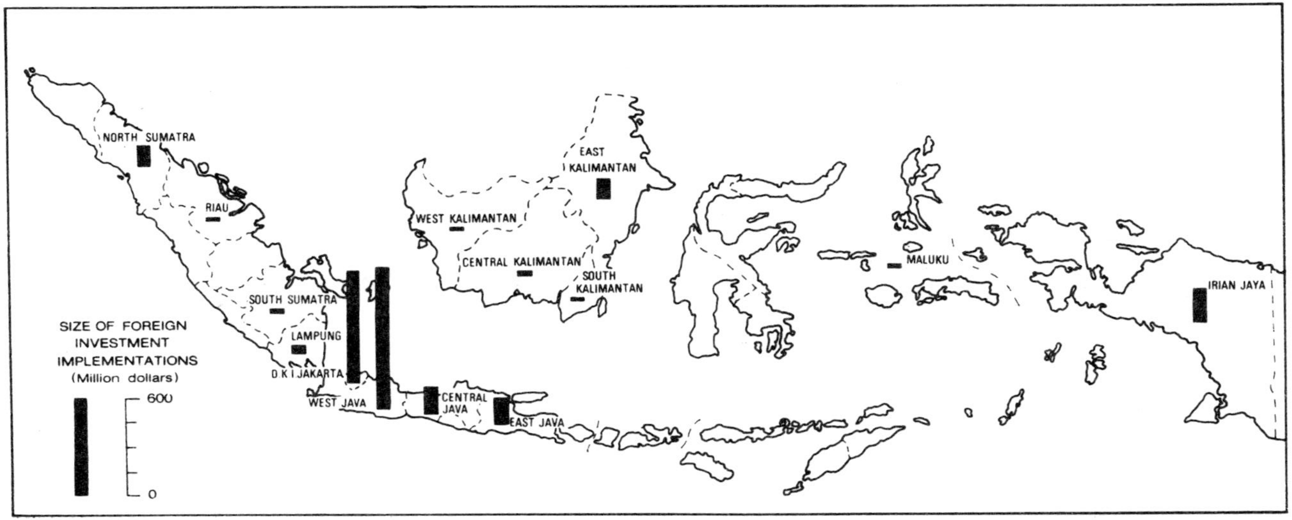

Source: IDN, April 1980.

Figure 5.5: Regional Distribution of Foreign Investment Approvals, March 1980-March 1982

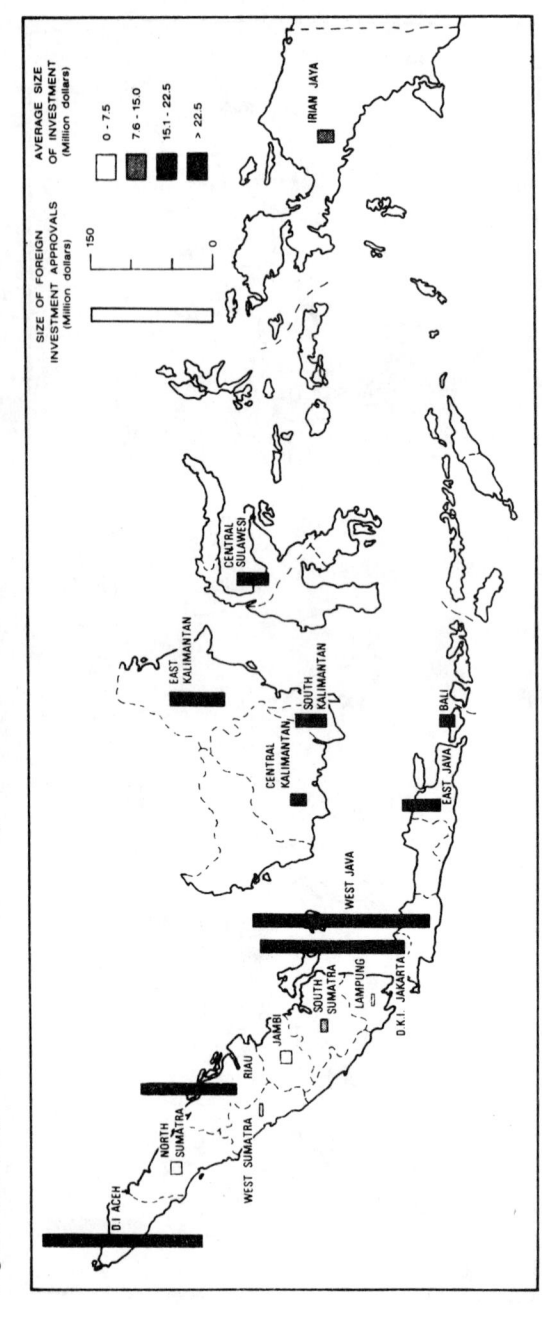

Source: IDN, various issues.

crucial in industrial location and relocation. Moreover, the fact that these are MNCs in which control and execution is separated would tend to play down the importance of local executive amenity in the location decision-making process. However, while there has been some discussion of wages and working conditions (Manning, 1978) and the development of management skills in foreign enterprise (cf. McCawley, 1979, p.67; Anwar, 1980, p.218), the locational dimensions of labour supply for foreign firms have not been discussed in any depth.

Asian Firm Location

Looking at Asian firm location in Indonesia can potentially tell us two things: first, to what extent Asian firms in Indonesia are different from other foreign firms; second, how they are likely to contribute to the Indonesian space economy. On the available evidence, the distribution of Asian firms corresponds fairly closely to the overall distribution of foreign investment in Indonesia (Figures 5.3, 5.4, 5.5). Investment approvals in 1979 (Table 5.8) were concentrated in Java and West Java, with a few firms planning to locate in Sumatra, Sulawesi, Kalimantan and East Java. The Java–West Java firms accounted for 59.0 per cent of the planned total investment, and Java as a whole 69.4 of the total. This tendency corresponds with the findings of Wells and Warren (1979) and Chen (1981) and the corporate information discussed earlier (e.g. Tables 5.5, 5.6, 5.7). Thee Kian Wie (1981, p.142) noted that 13 Indian investments out of 24 were located in Jakarta or West Java, and another six in Surabaya, which has the next best infrastructure and urban amenities in Indonesia after Jakarta.

The spatial distinction between Java and the Outer Islands also holds for Asian investment, much as it does for foreign investment as a whole. Enterprises on Java are involved in food manufacturing, textiles and apparel, chemicals production, real estate and business services. Thus, the Hong Kong and Indian companies tend to be in Java and not the Outer Islands (see also Wen-Lee Ting and Chi Schive, 1981). With the exception of some centres of manufacturing, such as North Sumatra, Asian interests in the Outer Islands concentrate on resources projects and resource-related manufacturing. South Koreans have shown extensive interest in forestry and timber products (Richardson, 1979), while Singapore has sought direct access to Indonesia's outlying regions as a means of securing supplies of natural gas and petroleum gas,

Table 5.8: Location of Project Approvals, 1979

	Jakarta	West Java	East Java	Sumatra	Sulawesi	Kalimantan
Origins						
Hong Kong	5	4	—	1	2	1
Singapore	1	—	—	2	1	—
India	—	2	1	—	—	—
South Korea	—	—	—	1	—	1
Total	6	6	1	4	3	2
Activities	Textiles and apparel (3) Food manufacturing Construction Real estate and business services	Manufacture chemicals (4) Agriculture Food manufacturing	Manufacture fibre glass	Forestry Manufacture wood products Fabricated metal products Hotels	Fishing (3)	Wood products (2)
Investment ($US 000) Total	54,813.0	96,443.0	26,700.0	44,848.0	21,458.0	12,098.7
Average	9,135.5	15,073.8	26,700.0	11,212.0	7,152.7	6,049.4
Indonesian employment Average	1,073.8	183.5	487.0	830.4	253.0	448.5

Source: BKPM (1979).

as well as wanting to establish direct links to Yogyakarta and Bali for tourists passing through Singapore (Awanohara, 1982). Tourist interests have met with some success. In March 1983 five new gateway airports, at Batam Island, Padang, Menado, Ambon and Biak, were opened to facilitate tourism (IDN, March 1983).

Asian MNCs do not appear to differ markedly in site location from other foreign investors in Indonesia, at least at the general level discussed here. However, the poor quality of the available data and the small numbers of firms involved lend a qualification to this conclusion. It follows that Asian investment has tended to compound the contrast between core and periphery in Indonesia, contributing further to the concentration of industrial investment (outside of the major natural resource sectors) in Western Java. However, industrial location in Indonesia is subject to a variety of government regulations and is not simply the product of market forces. Since the early 1970s one of the goals of industrial policy has been to redistribute industry and break down the regional concentration, and it is this which the next section focuses upon.

Government Influence on the Location of Industry

The role of government in industrial development in Indonesia has been criticised strongly in recent years, not least in an unpublished World Bank Report (World Bank, 1981). The Report recognises the goals of 'the extensive system of regulations' which control the industrial sector — 'employment creation and income distribution; the development of the indigenous entrepreneurs and the control of the non-indigenous business class; "orderly" industrialisation; development of a strong industrial base; and regional dispersion' — but argues the net result is 'a substantial disincentive effect ... which restricts the expansion of industrial output' (World Bank, 1981, p.iv). The constantly changing complex of licences, regulations and permits, combined with the existence of 'irregular payments', the Report argues, contributes to a general air of uncertainty within both the domestic and foreign business communities (see also Hiemenz, 1982). In general, this growing bureaucratic maze is thought to explain in part the drop-off in foreign investment in Indonesia after the mid-1970s.

Until the middle of the last decade 'there were no conscious policies with respect to the regional pattern of industrial development: no attempt was made to spread industry throughout the country nor to promote concentration of industries in major cities'

(Donges, Stecher and Wolter, 1980, p. 368). Since then the goal of industrial policy has been to alter the concentration of industry, encouraging new investment to locate in rural areas and providing incentives to invest outside Java. Three different sorts of centrally directed strategies seeking to affect the location of foreign investment can be distinguished: first, the BKPM 'Investment Priorities List'; second, the various industrial zones policies; third, the bonded warehouses and export processing zones policy. Understanding the distribution of Third World MNC investment in Indonesia requires an appreciation of the details of each of these policies.

Each year BKPM publishes an 'Investment Priorities List' which formally declares the patterns of incentives and prohibitions upon locations for foreign investments. Figure 5.6 shows the locational priorities for manufacturing and hotel investment in 1981. Hotel investment is directed towards the key tourist destinations — North Sumatra, Jakarta, Yogyakarta and Bali. Food processing industries are strongly encouraged to locate almost anywhere outside Java, while the main forested areas (Aceh, North and South Sumatra, Central, South and East Kalimantan, and Western Java) are priorities for timber processing. North Sumatra and East Java are a prime focus for metal products. In contrast, various aspects of glass and non-metallic product manufacturing are specifically excluded from Java. Locational decisions are based on the potential supply of raw materials and the economic potential of the region concerned, although it is added that new investment projects should 'not compete with existing traditional enterprises or with enterprises reserved for weak economic groups' (BKPM, 1981, p. xii). There are three main tax incentives concerned with location. Location outside Java earns for an investment an extra year's tax holiday, white-washing of capital is permitted for investments outside Java, and there are additional tax incentives for industry 'absorbing a large number of labour or earning a big amount of export earning or locating and opening with infrastructural facilities in remote areas' (BKPM, 1981, p. xv).

Complementing the BKPM proposals are the formation of industrial zones and estates, and the recently announced 'special development areas'. According to the then Minister for Industry, A.R. Suhud, a special development area is 'a region possessing the right geographic and resource parameters where therefore the setting up of a cluster (or zone) of basic industries would generate

Figure 5.6: Priority Provinces for Investment in the 1981 *Investment Priority List*

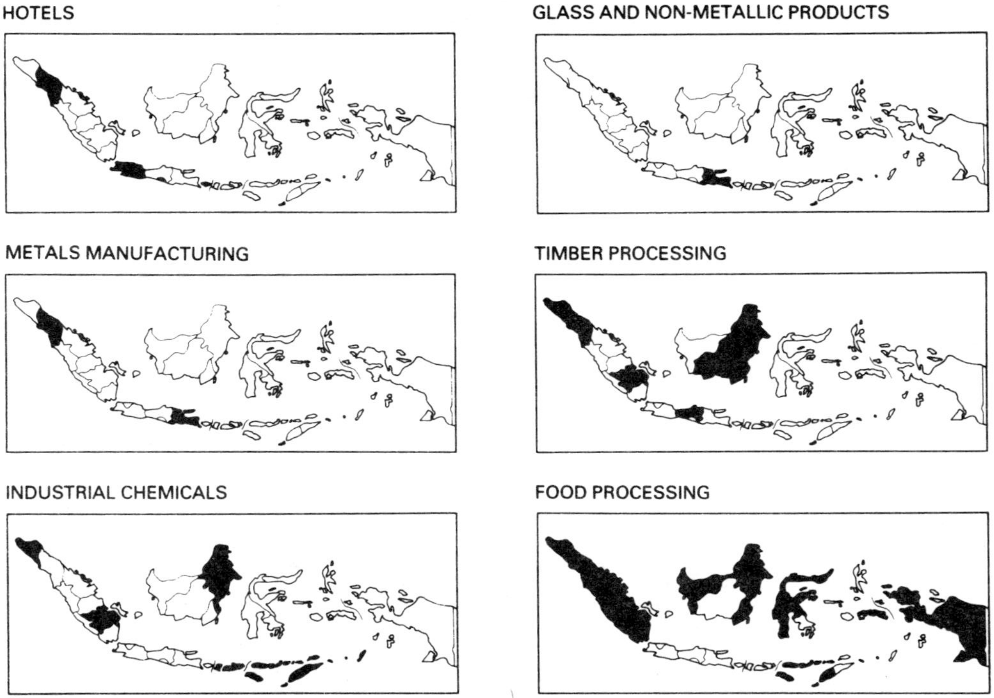

HOTELS

GLASS AND NON-METALLIC PRODUCTS

METALS MANUFACTURING

TIMBER PROCESSING

INDUSTRIAL CHEMICALS

FOOD PROCESSING

Source: BKPM, 1981.

the growth of other manufacturing and related activities within the area' (Awanohara, 1983, p.45). Five such regions have been identified (Figure 5.7), though it is the industrial zone (a more geographically specific region) around Lhokseumawe in Aceh that is the most developed. With investments of the order of $US95 billion, including a gas liquification plant (P.T. Arun) and an almost completed urea plant (P.T. Asean Aceh Fertiliser) (see the analysis of location in Staab, 1980), and another urea plant and pulp and paper factory under way, the Lhokseumawe industrial zone has been labelled 'the heaviest concentration of investments in Indonesia' (Awanohara, 1983, p.44). The purpose of the industrial zones is to concentrate on processing raw materials, producing intermediate goods for later processing by manufacturers. In other words, the aim of the zones is to develop intermediate industries to complement the relatively well-developed resource extraction and light manufacturing industries.

Industrial estates, seldom successful in the past in Southeast Asia, except in Singapore (Lefeber and Datta-Chaudhuri, 1971), are features of a number of the industrial zones. P.T. Surabaya Industrial Estate Rungkut, a company established in 1974, opened its 246 hectare estate in Surabaya in 1980, with 115 approved projects from 10 countries, covering 65 per cent of the available area (IIF, March 1980, p.9). Another industrial estate is being developed at Cilegon in West Java. This 550 hectare estate is owned by P.T. Krakatau Steel, and consists of plots of from 4 to 20 hectares, intended for steel-related industrial ventures (IDN, December 1981, p.7). Other major estates are at Pulogadung (Jakarta) and a rather less successful one at Lomanis (Cilicap) (Budiono, 1984), while further estates are planned in a number of centres.

Finally, Indonesia has formed an Export Processing Zone (EPZ), based on the model of similar zones in Asia's NICs (Ho Kwon Ping, 1979; UNIDO, 1980; Kawahara, 1981). The only operational EPZ is in Jakarta, close to the port of Tanjung Priok. Established in 1973, it is a customs restricted zone that combines the characteristics of a free trade zone and an industrial estate, and is administered by a state company, P.T. (Persero) Bonded Warehouse Indonesia (BWI). It is only small in size — 10.5 hectares — and contains 18 companies. All of these are Asian, giving some insight into the activities of one group of Third World MNCs. Twelve are owned by Hong Kong, Singapore, Taiwanese or Indian

Figure 5.7: Special Development Areas

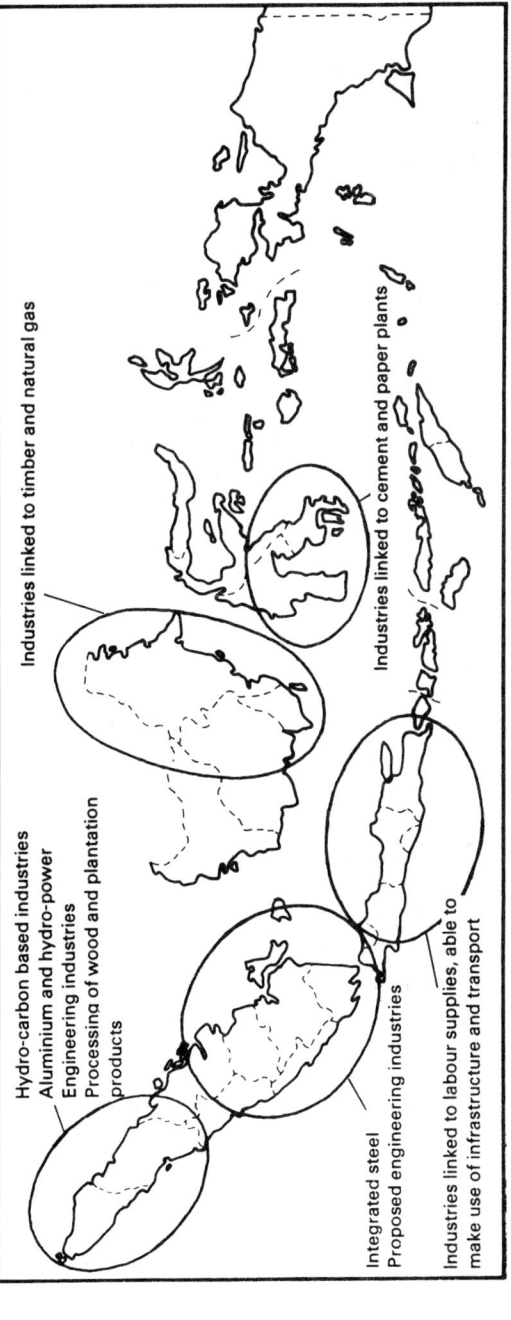

Hydro-carbon based industries
Aluminium and hydro-power
Engineering industries
Processing of wood and plantation
products

Industries linked to timber and natural gas

Industries linked to cement and paper plants

Integrated steel
Proposed engineering industries

Industries linked to labour supplies, able to
make use of infrastructure and transport

Source: Awanohara et al., 1983.

interests, three joint ventures with Indian and foreign Chinese, and three were nominally Indonesian-owned. While it is evident that ultimate ownership of some of these companies lies outside Asia, the management of these firms is in the hands of Indians, Chinese and Indonesians.

Interestingly, three of the first four Asian MNCs to enter the zone after it opened in 1977 were garment manufacturers whose primary function was to re-label clothing produced in Hong Kong and Singapore, allowing it to be re-exported as Indonesian-produced, thus avoiding EEC quotas on garment imports. Re-labelling activities appear to have ended between 1978 and 1980. By the end of 1981, there were 16 garment firms in the zone employing 7038 people, and two other firms employing a further 482, producing exports for that year of $US 28.7 million (Warr, 1983). The significance of the Jakarta zone is as a model for further EPZ development in Indonesia. Plans have been made to establish a further eight EPZs, developing the industrial estate of Pulogadung and the government warehouse at Cakung (both in Jakarta), and establishing new zones in Surabaya, Cilacap, Banjarmasin, Palembang, Medan, and Ujung Pandang. However, government initiatives in this area have been slow by Asian standards, and many of these zones may never operate.

The other major, much heralded EPZ of this type is on Batam Island (IIF, October 1979; December 1979; March 1980). Being sited a short ferry-ride of just 20 kilometres south-east of Singapore, Batam has long been viewed by Indonesia as a potential rival for the entrepot trade of the region. In the early 1970s, Pertamina, the state oil company, began work on developing an EPZ on Batam, in conjunction with a planned oil refinery, but with Pertamina's collapse in 1975 the programme lapsed. Initiatives were revived later in the 1970s, and a Batam Industrial Development Authority formed under the chairmanship of Dr B.J. Habibie (Jenkins and Awanohara, 1979). Declared a priority industrial area 10 years ago, Batam officially became a bonded free-trade zone in 1978. Forty manufacturing and service industries, producing both for export and the domestic market, have been given priority and a variety of incentives to locate on the island have been formulated (IDN, August 1982, pp. 3-7). Apart from tariff-free imports and exports, the airport has been recently upgraded, infrastructure is being developed, and a harbour and town (Batam Centre) are being planned. A few foreign projects are already located on Batam, including P.T. McDermott Indonesia, which designs and constructs off-shore oil facilities, P.T. Patra Vickers, a machine shop venture, and two companies involved in petroleum services, P.T. Dresser Magcobar and P.T. Milchem Indonesia. Singapore signed a 'Batam Cooperation Agreement' in 1980, suggesting Batam is increasingly being seen as a complement to Singapore rather than a rival. As Singapore shifts into high-technology and high value-added manufacturing, plans are that Batam will become a focus for the sort of labour-intensive industries that once located in Singapore (IDN, June 1983, pp. 6-7). With its potentially ample supplies of land and good access to Singapore, Batam's location gives it certain advantages in attracting industry, but whether these can be realised is another matter. Nor is it just the problem of providing adequate infrastructure, labour and sufficient incentives, as one not untypical response suggests:

> when people talk about investing in Indonesia they are usually talking about Jakarta or West Java. No one really wants to go to the outer islands unless they have to in order to dig up minerals. (Jenkins and Awanohara, 1979, p. 45)

It is too early to assess the effectiveness of these policies in shifting the concentration of foreign investment away from Western Java, with the exception of the Lhokseumawe initiatives, and it is impossible to distinguish the specific impact on Asian investment. Although the concentration of Asian firms in the Jakarta EPZ is notable, the industrial estates and EPZs are insufficiently developed to decide accurately their potential contribution to industrial geographical redistribution. As was shown in Figure 5.5, there is a suggestion that Aceh (Lhokseumawe) and Riau (Batam Island) have grown as a focus of foreign investment approvals in the period between 1980 and 1982, but Western Java remains dominant. Finally, a number of studies have considered the local impact of these concentrations, and raised questions about the extent to which they have brought benefits to local populations. Wong and Saigol (1983) question the income generation and multiplier effects of growth centre development in Surabaya, P.T. Indoconsult suggest greater attention needs to be paid to extending the impact of industrial development around Lhokseumawe to the Aceh economy (Awanohara, 1983, p. 46), while only by including 'unofficial levies' is Warr's (1983) cost-benefit analysis of the Jakarta EPZ able to end up in the black. Once again, however, it is not possible from the available information to separate out Asian firms from other foreign investors. The exception is the case of the Jakarta EPZ, which suggests the net effects of Asian firms are unlikely to be any better, if at all, than other foreign investors, but this could only be tested by a controlled evaluation of their relative linkages with the surrounding economy.

Conclusion

The growth of the NICs, with their strong focus on export-oriented industrialisation, promoted a rate of domestic capital accumulation which could only ultimately be sustained by capital exports. Yet when Asian firms moved off-shore from Hong Kong and Singapore, while the majority moved to other developing countries in the Asian region, they were selective in their targets. Asian investment in Indonesia has been quite substantial, yet the large companies in the region, particularly the Hong Kong and Singapore-based general trading companies, seem to have developed peripheral investments there. The signing of the various ASEAN agreements promoting internal investment, and on-going attempts to relax some of the more excessive bureaucratic impediments to foreign investment in Indonesia, along with the continued growth in NIC economies might well lead to the growth of Asian firm investment *vis-à-vis* OECD multinationals.

However, the internationalisation framework is stretched to account directly for the growth of Asian investment in Indonesia. Asian firms, in line with most industrial development in Indonesia, are more strongly oriented to domestic production and import substitution industries than to export goods. In other words what is occurring is not internationalised production, in the strict sense outlined by Palloix, but rather a (new) phase of internationalised capital investment. Asian capital has been attracted to Indonesia by generous government incentives and prospects of a monopoly in a potentially large domestic market. It is rather difficult to distinguish anything very distinctive about Asian MNCs on these grounds.

Nevertheless, although Indonesia is host to relatively small amounts of Asian MNC investment, and is peripheral to the internationalisation of production, these changes in the economic structure of the Pacific Basin are having an impact on the spatial structure of the Indonesian economy. The major concentration of industrial investment in Jakarta and West Java (and to a lesser extent Surabaya) reinforces the core—periphery structure, although the Asian investment in various resources in the outer islands (fishing and forestry in particular) provides a small, but perhaps countervailing trend. More importantly, the growth of the Lhokseumawe region and the potential growth of Batam Island, although not a particular foci of Asian investment, might provide a more attractive alternative to Western Java. However, such developments are well into the future. Current examples of real decentralisation of foreign investment are much harder to find, and even then, the flow (or trickle-down) of benefits to local and regional communities is by no means ensured.

There can be no doubt that Asian investment in Indonesia, and the growth of Third World MNCs in general, have become of particular importance in the last decade. The theoretical significance of the growth of this fraction of capital is more difficult to pinpoint. For the home country it is an important demonstration of the growth of a domestic bourgeoisie, while the growth of capital exports within the western arc of the Pacific Basin is evidence of the growing economic integration of this region. However, the significance for the host country — as discussed in this chapter — is more difficult to disentangle from other foreign investment.

Acknowledgements

Suzie Jeffcoat drew the figures for this chapter. Mike Taylor, Nigel Thrift and Vikram Nehru made useful comments on the first draft and I benefited from discussions on the topic with Godfrey Linge. The chapter was prepared for a Workshop on Indigenous Multinationals and the Role of the Family Firm in the Pacific Basin, held at the Australian National University in 1983.

6 THE INTERNATIONALISATION OF PRODUCER SERVICES AND THE INTEGRATION OF THE PACIFIC BASIN PROPERTY MARKET

Nigel Thrift

Introduction

A considerable amount of attention has been given in the geographic literature to the internationalisation of production, howsoever defined (see, for example, Taylor and Thrift, 1981; 1982a). Some attention has also been given to the parallel internationalisation of finance, although not as much attention as the importance of the subject warrants (see Taylor and Thrift, 1982b). Much less attention has been given to the internationalisation of producer services other than finance. This chapter sets out to begin to remedy this deficiency.

The reasons for attempting to right this balance are twofold. The first reason is a more general one concerned with understanding how the internationalisation of production and producer services intertwine. The emphasis on the internationalisation of producer services forms a necessary complement to the internationalisation of production. The two form a synergic whole wherein producer service firms do not just slavishly follow on in the wake of large multinational corporations but can also direct these corporations' activity or even create the opportunities for such activity to exist. The second reason is more geographical. The emphasis on the internationalisation of producer services draws attention to the peculiarly geographical aspects of the current form of internationalisation. In particular, in certain *world cities* (Heenan, 1977; Cohen, 1981; Friedmann and Wolff, 1982; Noyelle, Ross and Trachte, 1983; Thrift, 1983), the role of producer service firms in providing sites and other services for the headquarters, regional headquarters and other associated offices of large multinational corporations is crucial. So is the subsequent location of the offices of producer service firms near to these corporate offices so that producer service firms can provide services locally for their corporate clients. Also important is the

142

subsequent movement of these firms into servicing locally-based producers — as well as their original clients — with the effect of providing considerable foreign penetration of local producer service markets. In other words, producer service firms themselves provide much of the growth in demand for offices and other employment that takes place around the original corporate nuclei.

In particular, the formation of world cities seems to have come about in part because of the arrival of swarms of international producer services following their corporate clients, with the consequent demands on office and residential space. In order to highlight this geographical aspect of the internationalisation of producer services the major part of this chapter is devoted to consideration of producer service firms specialising in real estate (and particularly office) development and management, and especially the activity of these firms in two major world cities, Hong Kong and Sydney.

The paper is therefore divided into four parts. The first part considers the nature of the internationalisation of producer services, concentrating on producer service firms specialising in real estate development and management. The second part of the paper is concerned with how these services have built up in Hong Kong. The third part of the paper concerns where these international producer services are likely to go given the possible demise of Hong Kong as a world city. Data limitations mean that the inferences have to be drawn from a more general study of Southeast Asian investment in property in the Pacific Basin, and especially in Sydney. Finally, a more specific study of the likely direction of investment by producer service firms specialising in property development and management that currently own or manage sites in Hong Kong is made through the example of the Hongkong Land Company.

The Internationalisation of Producer Services

Before it is possible to consider the internationalisation of producer services it is important to be clear about which services are producer services. Conventionally, producer services are regarded as those that provide services to other industries (which may themselves produce goods or provide services) which are of the 'intermediate type', that is they are intermediate inputs into a final product (see Greenfield, 1966; Singelmann, 1978; Gershuny and Miles, 1983). The most useful classification of these kind of services is probably that of Browning and Singelmann (1978). In this classification producer services span the following seven industries:

(1) Banking, credit and other financial services.
(2) Insurance.
(3) Real estate.
(4) Engineering and architectural services.
(5) Accounting and bookkeeping.
(6) Miscellaneous business services.
(7) Legal services.

No classification is perfect and the Browning and Singelmann classification is no exception to this rule. For example, 'hotels' are not included under 'personal services', yet many large international hotel chains specifically cater for businessmen and have internationalised along with the large multinational corporations (see Dunning and McQueen, 1982a; 1982b). Be that as it may, the classification is probably the nearest approximation so far to what activities can legitimately be regarded as producer services.

Producer services have a number of important characteristics, of which two stand out. First, they provide a large proportion of service sector output — 22 per cent for the UK, 38 per cent for the USA. Second, they have provided a consistent growth in tertiary employment over the last 30 years in most countries of the world, although this growth has never matched the growth in their share of output. Whereas, however, in many of other service categories there has been a fall in employment, often both relatively and absolutely, growth in employment has been consistent in producer services. Further, the evidence is that this is now one of the only employment growth areas in some economies, such as the UK, especially as one of the other major sources of services employment growth — government — is cut back. Indeed, there is every reason to believe that output from and employment in producer services will continue to increase. For example, Gershuny and Miles (1983) found evidence of a clear growth in demand for such services in the EEC in the 1970s. If growth in output and employment in producer services does continue some of the cause must be the internationalisation of producer services in response to the current form of the internationalisation of production. Already, a quarter of world trade consists of services but there is no precise method for measuring how much of this trade is in producer services.

The Internationalisation of Real Estate Producer Services

Within the general orbit of producer services this chapter concentrates on the set of producer service firms that provide real estate (and especially offices) for large corporations. The reason for this choice is fairly obvious. Real estate services provide the most concrete link between the current form of the internationalisation of production and producer services and built form. But, of course, as a category 'real estate' covers a multitude of actors. Feagin (1982) has listed the actors in development decisions (see Table 6.1). Of course, these actors do not have to be separated out into particular functional types of firm. Thus, a large corporation may well 'include within it a development subdivision ... a real estate brokerage, and an architectural department. Or a major insurance company may have a financial department as well as its own urban land development subsidiary' (Feagin, 1982, p. 41). Even

Table 6.1: The Actors in Development Decisions

---

1. Industrial and commercial location decisions:
   Industrial companies
   Commercial companies

2. Development decisions:
   Development companies
   Land speculators
   Landlords and landowners

3. Financial decisions:
   Commercial banks
   Insurance companies
   Pension Funds
   Property Trusts

4. Construction decisions:
   Architectural firms
   Engineering firms
   Construction companies
   Building materials companies

5. Support decisions:
   Real estate brokers
   Leasing companies

Source: Feagin (1982).

companies which specialise in the development of real estate have often diversified into other allied areas, such as hotels and retailing, as in the case of the Hongkong Land Company which is investigated below.

What is certain is that real estate producer service firms have internationalised strongly in the last 10 to 15 years and it seems that most of the activity of the companies involved has been concentrated on a few cities, namely the world cities and a number of 'second tier' (Noyelle, 1983) cities that have the same concentration of services as these world cities but on a generally smaller scale and serving more localised regions. The extent of activity is reflected, to some extent at least, in office rental levels (Table 6.2).

The fact of internationalisation of real estate producer services can be shown by the example of the two British-based international real estate consultancies, Jones Lang Wootton and Richard Ellis. Both of these firms consist of a set of interlocking

Table 6.2: Rental Levels in Selected Cities for a 10,000 sq.ft Air-conditioned Suite of Offices in a Central Location, January 1984.

	Equivlent Net Rent in $m² p.a.	Total Occupation Cost in $m² p.a.
London (City)	482	819
London (West End)	342	540
Manchester	101	191
Glasgow	105	215
Brussels	76	107
Paris	240	312
Amsterdam	106	128
Frankfurt	160	202
Madrid	111	144
Barcelona	69	88
New York	584	724
Chicago	277	396
Los Angeles	315	391
San Francisco	358	458
São Paulo	114	156
Singapore	287	436
Hong Kong	314	393
Tokyo	543	657
Johannesburg	123	148
Melbourne	180	245
Sydney	287	350
Perth	127	182

Notes: a. Total occupation cost − net rent + service charge + rates/property taxes.
Source: Richard Ellis (1984), *World Rental Levels.*

partnerships and they provide a wide range of real estate services — mainly but not exclusively to the corporate sector — including advice on development (which sites and how to acquire them), valuation, the management and administration of properties, rent reviews, as well as the more basic real estate agency functions. They both stress their international dimension. For example, Jones Lang Wootton has 'global dimensions — now so relevant to the increasing internationalisation of business in general and institutional investment and property marketing in particular' (Jones Lang Wootton, 1982, p. 6).

The pattern of internationalisation of Jones Lang Wootton and of Richard Ellis is shown in Tables 6.3 and 6.4. From these tables it is possible to see how in the 1970s and 1980s the two firms have moved out from the old Commonwealth country of Australia, in which their international activities had been concentrated (and in which considerable activity still takes place),[1] to the other areas of the world. Jones Lang Wootton now has offices in Europe, the Far East, and the United States. Richard Ellis now has offices in Europe, the Far East, Africa, South America and the United States. Quite clearly, the opening of these offices has corresponded with the activities of particular clients in the manufacturing and financial spheres coupled with the attractions of serving particular real estate markets. For example, in Europe:

The nature of the firm's business dealings in the various European countries has tended to vary from market to market. In some the emphasis was more on providing a service to British companies — perhaps associated with one of the major pension funds — that had overseas interests and were seeking suitable property for investment purposes in a country where they were operating, although the firm has always aimed to build up a local clientele as quickly as possible. In others the firm has found itself more consistently involved with local clients engaged in property investment or development, or who simply required in a local context the agency, appraisal or management services that Richard Ellis specialises in. (Richard Ellis, 1982, p. 27)

Sometimes the movement into Europe has had effects on the UK market. Thus, 'occasionally, the firm has been able to assist EEC clients with an eye on expanding in Britain to acquire either

Table 6.3: The Pattern of Internationalisation of Jones Lang Wootton

Number of Offices in:		Opening of Office in:	Number of Partners in:
London	4	1939	42
Glasgow	1	1962	5
Edinburgh	1	1970	3
Jersey	1	1970	1
U.K.	7		51
Dublin	1	1965	6
Paris	1	1971	7
Amsterdam	1	1972	7
Rotterdam	1	1970 ⎫	
The Hague	1	— ⎬	5
Frankfurt	1	1973 ⎫	
Hamburg	1	1974 ⎬	3
Dusseldorf	1	1974 ⎭	
Brussels	1	1965 ⎫	
Antwerp	1	1973 ⎬	5
Europe	10		26
Sydney	3	1958	18
Melbourne	1	1958	6
Perth	1	1958	6
Brisbane	1	1958	5
Adelaide	1	1958	3
Canberra	1	1958	1
Australia	8		39
Hong Kong	2	1973	9
Singapore	1	1973	6
Kuala Lumpur	1	1973 ⎫	
Penang	1	1973 ⎬	4
Jakarta	1	1980	1
Far East	6		20
New York	2	1975	13
Los Angeles	1	1978	1
Houston	1	1980	3
Chicago	1	1981	1
Greenwich, Conn.	1	1981	2
San Francisco	1	1982	1
Washington, D.C.	1	1982	—
USA	8		21
Total	39		157

Table 6.4: The Pattern of Internationalisation of Richard Ellis

Number of Offices in:		Opening of Office in:
London	3	
Manchester	1	1978
Glasgow	1	1965
UK	5	
Paris	1	1969
Amsterdam	1	1973
Brussels	1	1965
Geneva	1	
Madrid	1	1974
Barcelona	1	
Europe	6	
Sydney	1	1965
Melbourne	1	
Perth	1	1966
Brisbane	1	
Adelaide	1	1969
Australia	5	
Hong Kong	2	1978
Singapore	1	1976
Jakarta	1	1982
Far East	4	
Johannesburg	1	1969
Cape Town	1	1969
Durban	1	1969
Pretoria	1	1969
Harare	1	1973
Africa	5	
Rio de Janeiro	1	1979
São Paulo	1	1980
South America	2	
New York	1	1982
Chicago	1	1976
Atlanta	1	1978
Houston	1	1981
Dallas	1	1982
San Francisco	1	1980
United States	6	
Total	33	

property or property investments in the UK' (Richard Ellis, 1982, p. 27).

In South America, in contrast, the emphasis has been very much on serving British corporate interests, like Unilever:

> Here, the firm has moved in mainly as advisers to the many long-established British trading houses that have built up strong business connections in the South American markets, and in the process have acquired substantial property holdings through the subcontinent. Now many of the firms, in line with current practice in the UK, feel the time is ripe to ensure that these holdings represent a positive asset to their organisation or, if they do not, to obtain professional advice on the steps that need to be taken to make the most of their value. (Richard Ellis, 1982, p. 28)

The very recent expansion of both firms into the United States is particularly interesting because it is so clearly a long-term strategic move, planned in advance. The expansion coincides with the increased activity by British international corporations in the United States in the 1970s and 1980s but also stems from a careful study of the United States real estate market investment possibilities with an eye to the internationalisation of the investment portfolios of British pension funds and insurance companies (current practice being that 33 per cent of such portfolios should be in property). Take, for example, the case of Richard Ellis:

> It was in January 1975 that the firm, attracted by the potential of the vast American real estate market, but as yet quite unversed in the intricacies of operating within it, undertook an extensive study of the possibilities, concentrating special attention on investment opportunities. The results of the research operation were sufficiently encouraging to justify the opening of the first Richard Ellis office in the United States — in Chicago, Illinois in October 1976. The firm decided from the start on judiciously combining the traditional expertise of the British chartered surveyor with local real estate know-how, and the staff were consequently drawn partly from the firm's London investment department and partly from Americans knowledgeable in real estate operations. (Richard Ellis, 1982, p. 28)

As a result of this expansion, Richard Ellis placed $US 500 million of property investments in its first five years of operation in the United States, mainly, but not exclusively, into office developments. The firm is now the property adviser to the American Property Trust, a unit trust designed to enable UK pension funds to invest in commercial property outside the UK (about 300 British pension funds now subscribe to the Trust, which in 1981 had a worth of $US 165 million).

There seems little doubt that producer services firms internationalised extensively in the 1970s and 1980s in response to the current form of the internationalisation of production and as part of the parallel internationalisation of finance. The internationalisation of the real estate industry has been a particularly noticeable part of the whole process. What are the geographical consequences of this internationalisation of the real estate industry? Some of these consequences may be illustrated from the example of the Crown Colony of Hong Kong.

The Rise of Producer Services in Hong Kong

Hong Kong has taken on world city status in the last 10-15 years, mainly because of the colony's emergence as the leading financial centre in the Asia–Pacific region. This emergence of Hong Kong as a financial node has been very rapid (see Lethbridge, 1980; Jao, 1982; Youngson, 1982). One of the most important aggregate indicators of this emergence as a financial centre is the value of international financial flows or transactions emanating from the colony. At the end of 1969 offshore loans from Hong Kong stood at $HK 34 million. By the end of 1982 they had increased nearly 500 times to $HK 16,946 million (Economist Intelligence Unit, 1983). Most of the borrowers tend to be the developing countries of the Asia–Pacific region but developed countries in the region, especially Japan, Australia and New Zealand, are also net borrowers. Another aggregate indicator of Hong Kong's increasing financial status is the amount of assets and liabilities held in foreign currencies (i.e. Eurocurrency). At the end of 1982, 59.7 per cent of total assets and 61.7 per cent of total liabilities were held in such currencies (Economist Intelligence Unit, 1983).

In all this the lack of government regulation has been important and has helped the colony to stave off potential challenges from

Singapore and Sydney to become the Asia–Pacific region's leading financial centre. It is generally agreed that while Singapore has the edge on Hong Kong in terms of inter-bank funding, Hong Kong leads Singapore in almost every other financial market, including the syndication of foreign loans, insurance, fund management and gold. (Hong Kong's gold market is the fourth largest in the world.)

Not surprisingly the contribution of producer services to the colony's economy has increased markedly over the last 10-15 years and Hong Kong now has the largest pool of legal, accounting and other expertise in the Asia–Pacific region. As in other countries the increase in share of output in these services (at least as measured by GDP; see Table 6.5) has been more rapid than the rise in employment, but even so the gains registered in employment have been important (see Table 6.6). By 1980 producer services accounted for 27 per cent of GDP and nearly 5 per cent of employment.

How rapid the rise in producer services has actually been can be seen from the example of the banking, insurance and finance sectors. At the end of 1969 Hong Kong still had a monolithic banking structure, dominated by commercial (or as they are known in Hong Kong 'licensed') banks, with few representative offices of foreign banks (see Table 6.7). But then in 1970 two merchant banks intruded into the local banking scene and spawned a host of local imitators in the form of finance companies. In 1976, in order to bring the proliferation of such companies under control, merchant banks were given the official title of 'deposit-taking companies' (DTCs) and they were required to register with the authorities and satisfy a minimum paid-up capital requirement. The number of these deposit-taking companies has multiplied rapidly (see Table 6.7). Then in 1978 the requirements for becoming a licensed bank were liberalised resulting in an influx of international banks eager to establish branches and provide full banking services (see Table 6.7). By the end of 1982 there were no less than 131 licensed banks with 1474 branches or sub-branches. There were 115 representative offices of foreign banks and there were 361 deposit-taking companies. Altogether over 300 foreign banks and depositary institutions were represented in one form or another in Hong Kong. In addition, at the end of 1982 there were 294 insurance companies, of which 163 were of foreign origin, and numerous foreign brokerage houses along with many foreign exchange dealers, mutual funds, unit trusts, pension funds and

Table 6.5: Proportion of GDP ($HK millions at current market prices) derived from Finance, Insurance, Real Estate and Business Services, 1970-80

	1970	1971	1972	1973	1974	1975	1976	1977	1978	1979	1980
Total GDP	19,214	21,873	25,854	33,796	38,786	40,574	51,973	59,615	69,557	89,473	112,981
GDP derived from finance, insurance, real estate and business services	2,855	4,004	5,682	6,519	6,221	6,283	8,319	10,877	13,576	20,248	30,283
% Total	14.86	18.30	21.97	19.28	16.03	15.48	16.00	18.24	19.52	22.63	26.80

Source: Economist Intelligence Unit (1983).

Table 6.6: Employment in Finance, Insurance, Real Estate and Business Services in Hong Kong

	1971	1976	1979	1980	1981	1982
Total employment	1,582,849	1,867,480	2,119,900	2,268,000	2,404,067	2,405,000
Employment in finance, insurance, real estate and business services	—a	62,090	91,100	110,100	115,870	125,400
% Total	—	3.32	4.29	4.85	4.82	5.21

Note: a. Different classification used in Census.
Source: Hong Kong Yearbook, various years.

Table 6.7: Number of Banks in Hong Kong

	1970	1971	1972	1973	1974	1975	1976	1977	1978	1979	1980	1981	1982
Number of licensed[a] banks	70	70	74	74	74	74	74	74	101	115	113	123	131
Number of branches of licensed banks	399	431	478	593	331	703	759	803	878	1011	1146	1301	1474
Number of representative offices of foreign banks	32	40	44	50	66	80	93	100	106	114	108	121	115
Number of deposit[b]-taking companies (DTCs)	–	–	–	–	–	–	179	201	241	269	302	350	343

Notes: a. Licensed banks are normal commercial banks.
b. Companies licensed to take deposits. These were first set up in 1976.
Source: *Hong Kong Yearbook*, various years.

other financial institutions. According to the Economist Intelligence Unit (1983, p. 12), 'in terms of the sheer number of foreign financial intermediaries, Hong Kong probably ranks third in the world, next only to London and New York'.

The Hong Kong Real Estate Market

Without a doubt, the influx of producer service firms helped to fuel the rapid rise in land prices and office rents that took place in Hong Kong in the 1970s and 1980s. With the exception of the 1974-75 period and 1981 onwards land prices and office rents exhibited a general upward trend (see Figure 6.1). As the colony became the centre of numerous regional headquarters and as it became a major financial centre (the two being interconnected), the increased level of corporate activity, coupled with generally favourable real estate conditions, tempted many international real estate service companies to open offices in Hong Kong. Jones Lang Wootton opened their first office in 1973. Richard Ellis opened their first office in 1978 and now manages Hongkong Land's Central property portfolio (see below). But the major beneficiaries of the real estate boom (especially in offices) were the local property companies and most especially the giant companies specialising in real estate like Hongkong Land and the rapidly growing Chinese-owned companies like Cheung Kong. Other large Hong Kong corporations with interests in Hong Kong property, such as Jardine Matheson, Swire Pacific and Hutchinson Whampoa also did very well out of the boom.

However, the Hong Kong economy — and the Hong Kong real estate market — has always been sensitive to conditions in China. In 1967, when the Cultural Revolution spilled over into Hong Kong in the form of riots, the economy was put under pressure and land prices and rents plummeted. And since 1982, the Hong Kong economy has again been under pressure as the lease on the colony has been 'renegotiated'. From 1973 to 1981 Hong Kong's annual rate of growth in real terms averaged a remarkable 9.8 per cent. But in 1982 the real growth rate plunged to only 2.4 per cent. Land prices and rents fell as well (see Figure 6.1), 'a situation aggravated by over-supply, dating from the time of the property boom. 21 per cent of Hong Kong's office space now stands empty' (*The Economist*, 1984). The economic downturn was partly due to the world economic recession finally catching up with Hong Kong but it was also to do with political uncertainty. The year 1997

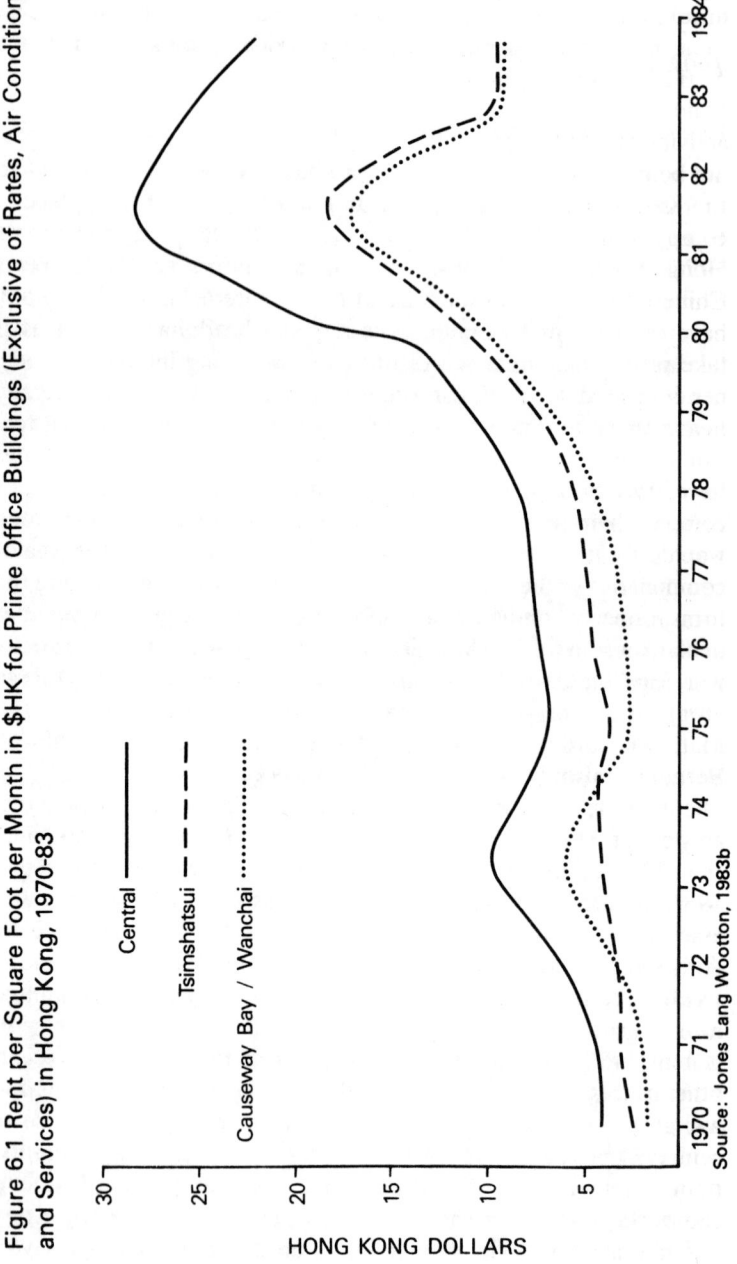

Figure 6.1 Rent per Square Foot per Month in $HK for Prime Office Buildings (Exclusive of Rates, Air Conditioning and Services) in Hong Kong, 1970-83

Central ——————
Tsimshatsui — — — —
Causeway Bay / Wanchai ·············

Source: Jones Lang Wootton, 1983b

bulks large now and can no longer be seen as part of some remote future.

1997

It now seems possible that there will be an exodus of economic activity out of Hong Kong as 1997 approaches. This exodus will not be general. Certain large Chinese-owned corporations, such as Li Ka-Shing's Cheung Kong properties (the second largest company in Hong Kong) seem to have decided to retain their Hong Kong base when China takes over, while many small Chinese firms, especially those engaged in manufacturing, do not have the resources to get out. But, a substantial exodus may still take place. This exodus, if it occurs, will have four main components. The first of these will be the withdrawal of the regional headquarters of large foreign-based multinational corporations from the colony. Indeed some corporations, such as Dow Corning, have already made the move (see Uckey, 1983) and 'most foreign companies in Hong Kong are at least considering where else they would move to' (*The Economist*, 1983a, p.72). The second component will be the withdrawal of some of the larger indigenous firms, especially those that have diversified internationally. In particular those British–Chinese *hongs* still domiciled in Hong Kong will leave. Of course, Swire Pacific's ultimate head office has always been in London. But the announcement by Jardine Matheson in March 1984 that it would move its legal domicile to Bermuda may only be a sign of things to come for the other *hongs*. The departure of the Hong Kong and Shanghai Bank would probably be the greatest blow, 'although it has been slowly shifting its asset base outside the colony for several years' (*The Economist*, 1984, p.65). The third component will be the withdrawal of the assets of the many large and small Chinese-owned firms overseas. Although Chinese businessmen remain noncommital (see *Asiaweek*, 1983a) the fact remains that many Chinese entrepreneurs have been salting capital away overseas for some time now in order to build up a nest egg and qualify for citizenship requirements in other countries. Along with this generalised (if not general) exodus will go much of Hong Kong's *raison d'être* as a regional financial centre. Thus there will be a fourth and final component of withdrawal, one closely intertwined with the other three. This final component will be the withdrawal of many producer services, both international and indigenous, from the colony. These producer services will range all the way from the representative offices of the largest foreign banks through insurance and finance companies to legal, accounting and real estate firms. These four components of withdrawal might be expected to feed off one another, stimulating an ever faster rate of withdrawal. For example, as more regional headquarters of large foreign-based multinational corporations leave, so will more producer service firms.

This exodus has already begun, at least in so far as this can be inferred from the sparse data that are available on capital outflow. There has been a massive outflow of capital from Hong Kong in the last 5 to 10 years. This outlow of capital has been initiated by both the large corporations and the smaller Chinese-owned firms. For example, Hutchinson Whampoa's decision in March 1984 to pay a special $HK 4 share dividend has been interpreted by some 'as a way of pumping cash out of the colony' (Shearlock, 1984). In 1983 over $2 billion flowed out of the colony to Canada and Australia alone. A considerable amount of this money is undoubtedly going into property.

> Whatever big foreign companies are doing, Southeast Asia businessmen are definitely hedging their bets by withdrawing some of their investments from Hong Kong, where they can easily be liquidated. The favourite haven for this money is property on the west coast of America and Australia. Money that is leaving Hong Kong but staying in the region is going into property rather than into stock and bond markets. Thailand's residential property market has picked up noticeably. Singapore's has not fallen as far as its property experts were predicting. (*The Economist,* 1983a)

The Economist (1983a) sums up the situation even more concisely: 'every Hong Kong Chinese who can afford it is looking to buy property overseas.'

Hong Kong Eclipsed and the Pacific Basin Real Estate Market

The direction of the capital outflow from Hong Kong which is going into property, and more particularly into the offices in which are housed corporate regional headquarters, the financial community, and other producer service firms, provides one indirect indicator of which city or cities is likely to assume Hong Kong's role of major regional centre, because the movement of large corporate headquarters, the financial community and other producer service firms out of Hong Kong is bound to produce increased demand for new office space in other cities. This 'movement' may involve just the shutting down of a particular office in Hong Kong and the strengthening of offices in the other cities in the Asia–Pacific region or it may involve the actual opening of new offices in these other cities. When this movement is added to these other cities' increasing success in competing with Hong Kong, which in itself fuels a demand for more office space, the overall effect is an office property boom in particular cities, to which Hong Kong investors are bound to be attracted. Inevitably, such a boom will be affected by local circumstances such as the existing supply of office space, the supply of development land, the restrictions on foreign investment, and the like, but the relation between the direction of capital outflow from Hong Kong into office property and the likely success of a city as a competitor to Hong Kong can still be expected to hold in general.

However, the exact amount and direction of the outflow of Hong Kong capital into office property (and related developments such as expatriate housing and specialised retailing) is not easy to gauge. There are no specific figures on the amount, let alone the duration, of capital outflow from Hong Kong. We must therefore turn to figures from the countries of the Pacific Basin on the origin of investment. Once again, however, such figures are difficult to find and even when, as in the case of Australia, they are available they are restricted to Southeast Asian investment. Therefore in what follows much of the evidence is anecdotal, drawn from newspaper accounts and the like, and consequently very general. In many cases it is not possible to consider Hong Kong investment in office property but only Southeast Asian investment in property. However, given that this Southeast Asian investment will always include a substantial Hong Kong component this is not too much of a constraint. It is also usually possible to indicate whether the investment is being made by larger corporate concerns (the major focus of this paper) or the many thousands of smaller Southeast Asian property investors.

Southeast Asian Investment in Pacific Basin Real Estate

Most Southeast Asian investment in property is concentrated on the larger cities of North America and Australia, and the city state of Singapore, one of Hong Kong's main rivals as a regional financial centre. However, there is also considerable interest in some of the smaller second tier cities of the region, such as Denver, Melbourne and Jakarta.

North America.   In Canada, Vancouver is the major recipient of Southeast Asian property investment (Cutler, 1975; Fraser, 1981). Table 6.8, although rather outdated, still provides a useful breakdown of foreign property investment in the city. In the past Hong Kong companies such as Sea Chant Ltd and Kingsville Realty Corp. have been the major Southeast Asian investors in Vancouver but now investors from Singapore, Malaysia and the Philippines are also active (for example, Delta Investments (BC) Ltd, a Malaysian/Singapore controlled company). Purchases in the commercial and retail sector range from $C 500,000 up to $C 10 million, usually on a 50 per cent cash, 50 per cent mortgage basis. But, although Vancouver office rents are now the third highest in Canada (after Toronto and Calgary), investment by Southeast Asian companies and smaller investors in the office sector is still low especially when compared with purchases of large hotels (for example, the Georgia Hotel, the Georgian Towers Hotel and the Mandarin are all owned by Southeast Asian concerns) and residential real estate. Purchases in the residential sector are mainly by the smaller Southeast Asian investors:

> Southeast Asians often buy only single-family houses to be used by their children when they come to university here or when the parents retire. They mainly zero in on three prime residential areas of the city — Kerrisdale, Shaughnessy and West Vancouver, all three of which have the highest property prices in North America. (Fraser, 1981, p.62)

In the United States, Los Angeles, San Francisco and Honolulu are the largest recipients of Southeast Asian property investment (see Stewart, 1981; Hobson, 1981) although in each of these cities Southeast Asian investment is still overshadowed by Japanese, Canadian and European property investments. The office sector of Los Angeles and San Francisco is particularly attractive to Southeast Asian investors although the residential property market is also affected, especially in San Francisco. In Honolulu, luxury

Table 6.8: Identified Foreign Investment Flowing into Vancouver Real Estate in 1973 ($C million)

	Equity	%	Debt	%	Total	%	Office Building	%	Shopping Centres	%	Apartment and Row Housing	%	Other[a]	%
Southeast Asia	39.3	(68)	61.5	(73)	100.8	(71)	9.3	(31)	3.0	(100)	84.0	(83)	4.5	(53)
Germany	9.1	(16)	14.3	(17)	23.4	(16)	2.4	(8)	—	(0)	17.0	(17)	4.0	(47)
United Kingdom	7.5	(13)	2.5	(3)	10.0	(7)	10.0	(34)	—	(0)	—	(0)	—	(0)
United States	2.0	(3)	6.0	(7)	8.0	(6)	8.0	(27)	—	(0)	—	(0)	—	(0)
Total	57.9		84.5		142.2		29.7		3.0		101.0		8.5	

Note: a. Small commercial buildings and land.
Source: Cutler (1975), p. 36.

apartments are popular with Southeast Asians. On average, at least $US30 million is paid into this sector each year from Southeast Asia although the actual amount fluctuates — when the Hong Kong stockmarket goes up property investment by Southeast Asian interests in Honolulu goes down, and vice versa (Hobson, 1981). (The hotels of Honolulu are very much the province of the Japanese; see Zagaris (1981).)

Singapore and Australia.   The Southeast Asian interest in property is not confined to the major cities of the West Coast of North America. It is also attracted to the other major cities of the region and specifically Singapore and the cities of Australia. Although currently suffering something of a slump in the real estate market owing to over-supply, Singapore is still a major site for Southeast Asian property investment. Until recently large Southeast Asian investors were absent from Singapore but this is most definitely no longer the case. Major Southeast Asian-owned buildings in Singapore in 1982 included: the 12,350 m^2 Octagon office building in the CBD owned by an Indonesian Chinese, Jauw Tung Sin and associates; the Marina City project in Orchard Road, again owned by Indonesian Chinese interests; the Wisma Indonesia site on Orchard Road (which includes a 10,000 m^2 department store, 12,000 m^2 of speciality shops and 11,000 m^2 of offices) owned by Asia Goldland (International) Ltd; Horizon Towers, a residential tower with 212 apartments; the part Hong Kong-owned Oriental Hotel and the Promenade, a 10,700 m^2 Hong Kong-owned retail and commercial development (Jones Lang Wootton, 1980-83a). Australian cities are now a major focus of Southeast Asia property interest but they will be dealt with below in a separate section.

The Second-tier Cities.   It is important to point out that the Pacific Basin world cities are not the only cities in the region being invested in by Southeast Asian property interests. A number of the second-tier cities of the region are now receiving investor interest, partly because so much money is available and partly because these cities approximate the economic structure of world cities (although on a smaller scale). The list would include Denver in the United States, Melbourne and Perth in Australia (see below), Auckland in New Zealand,[2] Kuala Lumpur in Malaysia (although its property market is currently in a slump, see *Asiaweek*, 1983b), Macau (see Jolliffe, 1983), and Jakarta in Indonesia. Jakarta is a good example of how property investor interest is attracted by corporate expansion. In this case, growth by both local and, more particularly, foreign-owned companies (especially those companies associated with the oil industry) has put pressure on both office and residential space in Jakarta. Thus, in the 10-year period from 1971 to 1981 the approximate source of office space take-up in the city was: oil companies, 35 per cent; foreign equity companies, 32 per cent; financial organisations (most of whom were foreign-owned), 14 per cent and local Indonesian companies, 19 per cent (Jones Lang Wootton, 1982a). In addition to the pressure on office space, pressure was also put on expatriate housing. This is not so surprising. In 1981 there were only 9 apartment buildings in Jakarta suitable for expatriate housing, yet there were at least 40,000 expatriates.

The pattern of foreign property investment in the cities of the Pacific Basin region is not, of course, just a matter of decisions by property investors. It also depends upon the different foreign investment regulations of the countries involved. These range from the relatively harsh, such as those of Australia (which, however, has no capital gains tax), to the relatively easy-going, such as those of Canada and the United States. In Canada most foreign investment in real estate does not come under the auspices of the Foreign Investment Review Act (although some provinces now have their own laws and regulations) (Government of Canada, n.d.). In the United States there are very few regulations governing foreign investment in real estate (see Zagaris, 1980). Further, any foreign national who invests $US40,000 is entitled to a permanent resident's visa, a boon to small Asian investors, especially those from Hong Kong (Hobson, 1981). In many of the poorer Southeast Asian countries actual attempts are now being made to woo Hong Kong property investors. For example, both Thailand and the Philippines offer permanent residence to those who invest over a certain amount (*Asia Research Bulletin*, 1983).

Southeast Asian Investment in Australian Urban Real Estate[3]

Australia is a useful case study of recent patterns of Southeast Asian urban real estate investment for three reasons. First, the Australian cities form a buoyant real estate market, with over-supply diminishing in most cities and rents on the rise (see Figure 6.2). This increased level of activity arises, in particular, because of the genesis of Property Unit Trusts which have supplanted institu-

Figure 6.2 Rent per Square Metre in $ Australian for Prime Office Buildings in Five Australian Cities, 1973-83

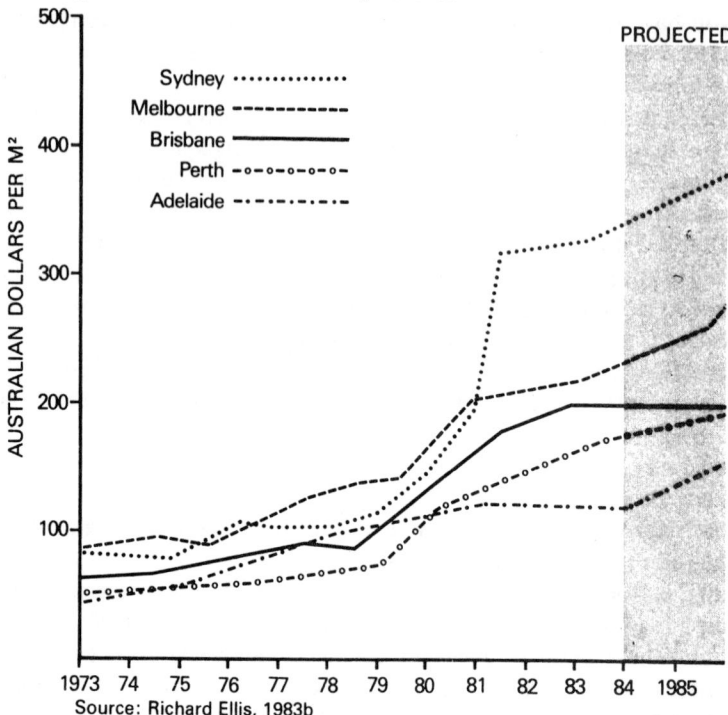

Source: Richard Ellis, 1983b

tions and pension funds as the major buyers of property. Thirty-six prospectuses were issued in 1983 and another 20 are in the pipeline (Richard Ellis, 1983a). Second, unlike for example the United States, reasonably accurate and up-to-date data have been available since 1976 on proposals over $A 250,000 to April 1981 and thereafter for proposals over $A 350,000.[4] This is because of the establishment of the Foreign Investment Review Board (FIRB) in 1976. Finally, there is little doubt that Australia is currently one of the major nodes for Southeast Asian investment in the Pacific Basin region.

Southeast Asian investment in Australian urban real estate can be split into two main types. First, there is a large amount of smaller overseas Chinese (mainly Hong Kong) investment which does not show up in the FIRB figures because it comes in below the $A 350,000 limit. Of course, this limit can be surmounted, by nominee companies or by aggregated purchases. As one Sydney

real estate agent explained, 'most Chinese families prefer to do business with each other, and with ten relatives bringing $A350,000 each,
you have quite a lot to invest in property' (cited in Spiers, 1983,
p.59). Another way to avoid the limit is to work through an
Australian-Chinese partner. And, if all else fails, there is always
the suitcase. The exact amount of investment by the smaller
Southeast investor in Australian real estate is, of course, very hard
to gauge. The current FIRB estimates (Foreign Investment Review
Board, 1982) show a dramatic increase from $A19.8 million in
1978/79 to $A85.9 million in 1980/81 and $A133.2 million in
1981/82. If these figures are correct and they are almost certainly
underestimates, then the small Chinese investor accounted for an
extra 31 per cent of Southeast Asian investment in real estate in
1980/81 and 28 per cent of Southeast Asian investment in real
estate in 1981/82 on top of the official FIRB figures. The effects
of these smaller investors, especially on the more select residential
markets, the small office and the retail sector may therefore be
quite strong.

The second type of investment is by the larger corporate investor. Such investors range from the smaller property companies to
the giant Hong Kong corporations such as Hongkong Land or the
property division of Swire Pacific. These investors have concentrated in the office and hotel sectors and have also shown some
interest in large apartment blocks and, more recently, expensive
town house developments. Since most investments made by this
kind of investor will exceed the $A350,000 FIRB limit this kind of
investment registers in the FIRB figures and so can be enumerated
in some detail.

The FIRB data[5] show that Southeast Asian expected investment
in Australia by this kind of investor has more than doubled in the
period from 1976 to 1982 (Table 6.9). It now constitutes some 15
per cent of all foreign expected investment. Somewhere between
25 and 75 per cent of Southeast Asian expected investment in any
one year is in real estate (which includes rural property as well as
urban real estate) and another 30 to 60 per cent is in services
(which includes parts of the real estate market such as hotels and
other tourist accommodation as well as wholesale and retail
business, aviation, private hospitals and services to the mining
industry) (Figure 6.3). Thus, expected Southeast Asian investment
is heavily concentrated in these two sectors unlike, for example,
Japanese foreign investment which is just as heavily concentrated

Table 6.9: Total Expected Investment in Australian Real Estate and Services ($A million) by Fiscal Year by Country of Origin

	1976/77	1977/78	1978/79	1979/80	1980/81	1981/82
Total investment in all sectors	2603.0	2990.8	3521.0	5807.8	6618.2	5446.9
Total investment in all sectors: Southeast Asia	80.0	90.5	—	—	1041.5	855.5
Total investment in all sectors: Japan	—	185.2	436.0	360.3	367.9	388.3
Investment in real estate	258.0	225.3	225.0[a]	269.0	555.9	1040.2
Investment in real estate: Southeast Asia	23.0[b]	64.9[c]	—	—	275.8	469.1
Investment in real estate: Japan	—	2.2	—	—	4.8	3.5
Investment in services	—	—	646.0	385.09	1291.5	1175.8
Investment in services: Southeast Asia	—	—	—	—	626.1	274.5
Investment in services: Japan	—	—	76.0	47.0	6.3	53.8

Notes: a. Three different figures are given for this year according to different definitions. These are 90.0, 225.0 and 274.6. Accordingly, I have taken the middle figure.
b. Far East and Oceania.
c. Pacific Basin (excluding Japan).
Source: Foreign Investment Review Board (1977-82).

but in the mining and manufacturing sectors. The bulk of this expected investment in real estate is in *urban real estate* and Table 6.9 gives a more direct indication of investment in urban real estate. Table 6.10 gives an indication of the types of proposal received for investment in urban real estate as a whole, although data by region of origin are not available. The table suggests that development for own use (that is, purchase of residences and offices by foreign companies) is on the increase, as is development for sale. Development for retention has, however, decreased relatively in terms of number of proposals although not in terms of development expenditure or total expected investment. Data on *hotels* and other tourist accommodation are difficult to separate from data on services. However, as Table 6.11 shows, in 1980/81 nine proposals were approved by the FIRB. Payments made for assets totalled $A159 million and new investment was expected to be $A261 million. By contrast, in 1981/82 only two proposals were approved and no payments of assets had been made over for these proposals by the end of the year. Thus it can be seen that hotels can be a major part of investment in urban real estate (compare Table 6.9) but that this is a highly variable inflow. Once

Figure 6.3 Total Expected Foreign Investment in Australia ($A million) 1976-82

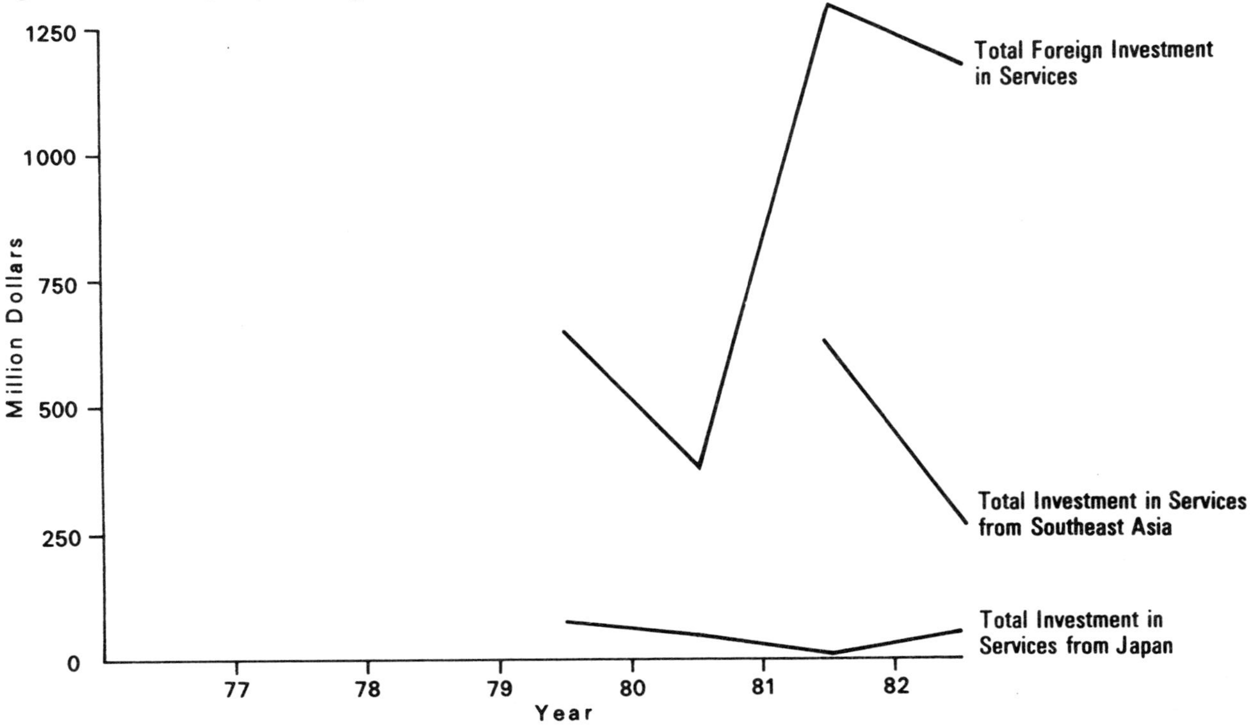

Total Foreign Investment in Services

Total Investment in Services from Southeast Asia

Total Investment in Services from Japan

Million Dollars

1250
1000
750
500
250
0

77   78   79   80   81   82

Year

Source: Foreign Investment Review Board, 1976-82

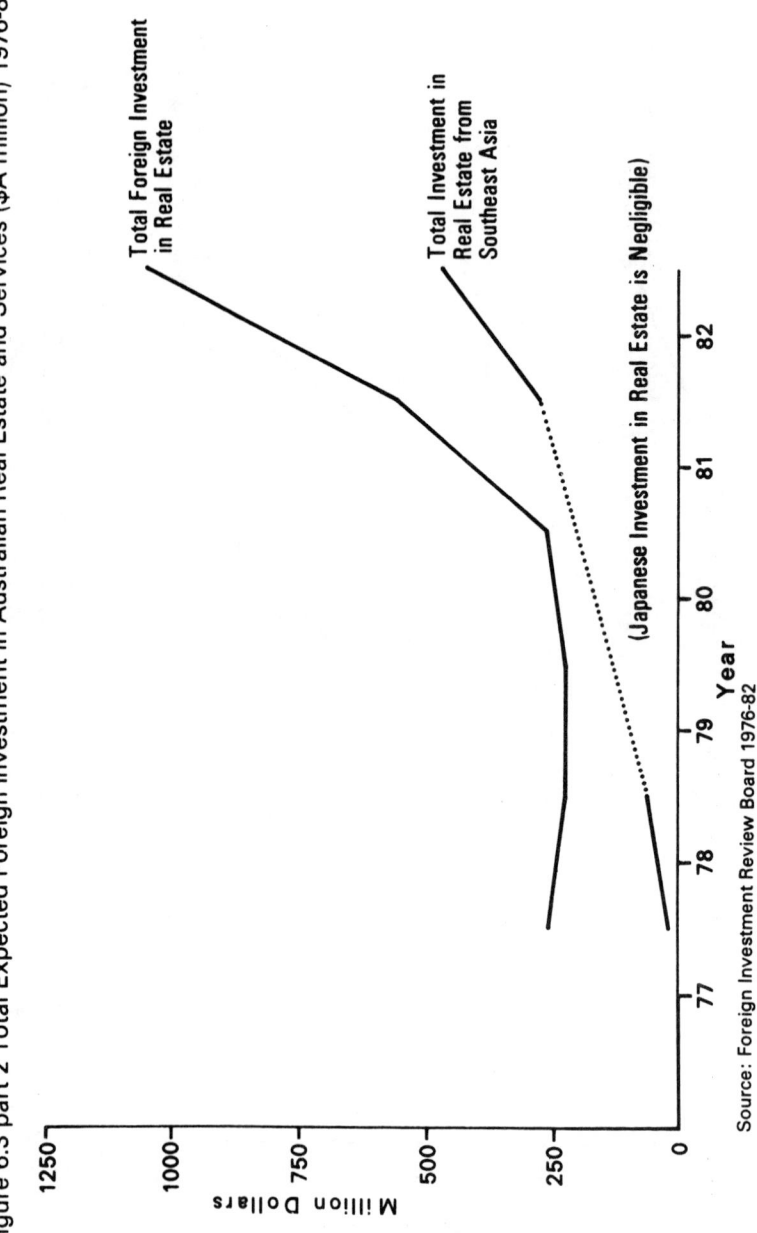

Figure 6.3 part 2 Total Expected Foreign Investment in Australian Real Estate and Services ($A million) 1976-82

Total Foreign Investment
in Real Estate

Total Investment in
Real Estate from
Southeast Asia

(Japanese Investment in Real Estate is Negligible)

Year

Million Dollars

Source: Foreign Investment Review Board 1976-82

Table 6.10: Foreign Investment in Urban Real Estate by Type of Proposal

Type of Proposal[a]	1978/79				1979/80				1980/81				1981/82			
	A	B	C	D	A	B	C	D	A	B	C	D	A	B	C	D
Development for Sale	24	22.9	61.2	—	37	93.8	81.2	—	49	113.4	439.4	552.8	76	170.8	631.9	802.7
Development for Retention	4	4.3	58.4	—	14	24.0	52.7	—	16	29.1	113.0	142.1	17	33.3	387.6	421.0
Own Use	10	14.8	4.2	—	9	10.2	0.6	—	34	48.6	8.7	57.3	35	40.4	0.2	40.6
Australian Citizens																
Resident Abroad	1	0.4	0	—	8	1.9	0	—	7	2.4	0.1	2.5	18	12.5	0.3	12.8
Intending Migrants	6	2.1	0.9	—	18	7.5	5.7	—	53	20.8	10.6	31.4	36	17.4	9.4	26.8
Other	18	34.1	0	—	16	13.0	0	—	10	25.9	0	25.9	13	20.5	0	20.5
Total[b]	63	78.5	124.7	—	102	93.8	140.2	—	169	240.3	571.9	812.2	195	295.1	1029.3	1324.4

Notes: a. A — number of proposals: B — consideration ($m), payments for shares and assets; C — estimated development expenditure ($m); D — total expected investment ($m).

b. Totals are not exact owing to rounding error.

Table 6.11: Foreign Investment in Tourist Accommodation and Tourist Facilities

	1978/79	1979/80	1980/81	1981/82
Number of proposals	8	11	9	2
Consideration[a] ($m)	58.4	27.4	158.7	—
Estimated development expenditure ($m)	116.2	64.8	261.0	—

Note: a. Payments of shares and assets.
Source: Foreign Investment Review Board (1981).

again data by region of origin are not available but in recent years most of the significant foreign purchases of Australian hotels have been Southeast Asian.

The Spatial Pattern of Southeast Asian Investment in Australia

Where, then, does Southeast Asian investment in real estate go? The FIRB estimates that some 40 to 50 per cent of all foreign investment in any one year in real estate goes to New South Wales (and especially to Sydney) with the remainder being equally spread between Western Australia, Victoria and Queensland. Very little of such investment goes to South Australia, Tasmania or the Northern Territory. There is little reason to think that the Southeast Asian pattern of investment in real estate is any different from this overall pattern.

Not too much should be made of the overall importance of foreign investment in real estate, of course. For example, it forms only a small part of the overall transactions in real estate in New South Wales each year, probably in the order of 1-2 per cent (Foreign Investment Review Board, 1982), and there is little reason to believe that this figure is any greater in any other state. However, foreign real estate obtains its potency from its *concentration* — both sectorally in offices, hotels and expensive residences, and spatially in CBDs and particular, high-class, residential areas. There is some reason to believe that, if anything, Southeast Asian investment is even more spatially concentrated than foreign investment overall. It is to the topic of spatial concentration of this investment that attention is now turned.

The pattern of Southeast Asian investment in urban real estate is strongly spatially concentrated in the larger urban areas and most especially in Sydney, Melbourne, Perth and Brisbane. The origin of investment is differentiated by city. Thus Perth tends to attract more Singapore and Malaysian interest because of its relative proximity to Singapore and Malaysia. Sydney and Melbourne attract more interest from Hong Kong.

In Perth, millions of dollars from Singapore, Malaysian and Hong Kong Chinese investors are going into housing and apartment blocks in Perth's better suburbs.

> Maurice Owen at Jones Lang Wootton in Perth points out that a very pleasant home in Perth can be bought at ... around $200,000 which is below the ... FIRB's upper limit and many Malaysian and Singaporean Chinese are buying. Kevin Sullivan, President of the Real Estate Institute of Western Australia, says there is a particular interest by Asian buyers in Swan River-front homes in Perth. (Rowley, 1981, p. 57)

Commercial property is also being taken up as the Perth CBD increases its office space. A recent example is the hotel, office and retail complex in Adelaide Terrace being developed by the Australian Multiplex Group in conjunction with the Merlin Malaysia Bhd company. However, as one local Chinese-Australian property magnate, Stephen Chew, points out, 'the proportion of overseas money in local property is insignificant compared with the position in Vancouver, Honolulu, London, Toronto or many parts of California' (*Asiaweek*, 1983a, p. 51).

Adelaide does not as yet seem to have been a major focus of Southeast Asian investor attention. What attention there has been has concentrated on the office sector. An example is Adelaide House, a large office block bought in late 1982 by Charlick Operations Pty Ltd, an Australian company associated with Singapore developers, for over $A5 million (Jones Lang Wootton, 1983). The situation in Adelaide is in marked contrast to that in Melbourne. Melbourne has received considerable attention from small Southeast Asian investors in the residential housing market ('We are serving up property on a plate to Asians [at current prices]', commented L.J. Hooker's investment sales manager (cited in Rowley, 1981, p. 58)) and from larger Southeast Asian investors more interested in the office and hotel sectors. The CBD now has a considerable Southeast Asian component (Table 6.12). The major Southeast Asian real estate operation in Melbourne has undoubtedly been that of the Singapore-based Jack Chia-MPH

Table 6.12: Examples of Major Southeast Asian Office Property
Interests in Central Melbourne, 1982

David Wang Chinese Emporium, Bourke St
103-110 Little Bourke St
471 Little Bourke St (Jack Chia International Ltd, Hong Kong)
1-9 Collins St (Jack Chia International Ltd, Hong Kong)
Singapore Airlines House, Collins St
384 Elizabeth St
Presgrave Building, Flinders Lane
43-61 King St
117-121 Lonsdale St
280-286 Little Lonsdale St
20-26 Queen St
178-182 Queen St
195-197 Russell St
196-222 Russell St

Source: Spiers (1983).

Group. The Jack Chia Group now has seven large properties
under its control in the city which, when development is complete,
will represent an investment of nearly $A 500 million. This invest-
ment includes a 12.3 acre site comprising retail, residential and
commercial space in South Yarra, a prime inner suburb (which is
likely to cost $A 400 million to develop over eight years), as well
as downtown office properties. Other major Southeast Asian
interests include the Melbourne Regent Hotel and a proposed
$A 100 million hotel in Collins Street with which the Singapore
Hyatt chain is associated (*Asiaweek*, 1983a).

In Brisbane and on the Gold Coast, Southeast Asian investors
have also been busy. In the boom period a lot of money was able
to be made; 'using typical Hong Kong tactics, investors in Surfer's
Paradise high-rise apartments buy in on 10 per cent deposit, then
sell out before completion. Something like 30 per cent of apartments change hands in this way' (Rowley, 1981, p.61). Although
the Gold Coast property market is currently in something of a
slump, Southeast Asian investors are still to be found. For
example, the new Gold Coast casinos in Surfer's Paradise and
Townsville are being developed by a syndicate which included
until May 1983 (see Chapman, 1983) the Malaysian property
company, Genting Bhd through its subsidiary World Resorts Ltd.
The Hong Kong company Jardine Matheson is also involved in a
number of Surfer's Paradise property developments including the

$A 80 million Bayview Harbour scheme consisting of four residential towers and two marinas (in which it has a 60 per cent share) and residential developments at Main Beach (Way, 1983).

Southeast Asian Investment in Sydney

However, as has been shown, it is Australia's world city, Sydney, that has attracted the bulk of Southeast Asian investment. Sydney has all the major characteristics of a major regional world city. First, the city is undoubtedly the focus of numerous corporate head offices. In 1978, for example, 52 of the top 100 Australian listed companies were headquartered in the city. It also has its share of foreign-owned regional headquarters offices as well as a swarm of foreign and domestically-owned regional branch offices (see Taylor and Thrift, 1980; 1981). Second, and as both cause and consequence of the first characteristic, Sydney is now a major international business and financial centre, with a swarm of producer services. For example, in 1982 95 foreign banks were represented in the city. Already, in 1976 the city was listed ninth in a list of world financial centres. (In contrast, Melbourne was only 23rd; see Daly (1982a; 1982b; 1984).) The extent of Sydney's dominance of international business in Australia is indicated by the pattern of outgoing international telex traffic from Australia in March 1981. Over 50 per cent of such traffic originated in Sydney, compared with 30 per cent for Melbourne and 14 per cent for all other capital cities together (Langdale, 1982). Third, much of Sydney's employment is in the office sector. Office-type jobs comprised 36 per cent of the city's workforce in 1976 and accounted for 67 per cent of metropolitan employment growth between 1971 and 1976 (Alexander, 1982). Over time, relatively more of the professional and executive office-type jobs have come to be concentrated in the CBD at the expense of clerical jobs (see Table 6.13). By 1976, 56 per cent of the Sydney CBD's total floor space was given over to offices. Within office employment, employment in finance and business services now predominates, as would be expected in a world city. Probably as much as 50 per cent of the office workforce is now concentrated in finance and other producer services.

Sydney is now vying with Singapore to become the major financial centre of the Asia-Pacific region. The general freeing-up of the Australian financial system in the wake of the Martin report will help Sydney to compete with Singapore. There are even plans to

Table 6.13: The Changing Number of Office-type Jobs in the
Sydney Central Area, 1961-76 (thousands)

	1961	1971	1976
Professional and executive	74	86	88
Clerical	116	136	129
Total	190	222	217
% Sydney office-type jobs	58	47	41

Source: Alexander (1982), p. 58.

make Sydney into an offshore banking centre, complete with a 10
per cent tax on the profits of offshore banking units (the current
corporate tax level is 46 per cent). It comes as no surprise, then,
that Sydney has a buoyant office property market, particularly
because there is no over-supply of office space. Rents are climbing,
especially in comparison with other Australian cities (see Figure
6.2). The value of Sydney's prime commercial properties has more
than doubled in the last two years.

Southeast Asian investment in urban real estate is drawn to a
city so obviously a part of the world property market like iron
filings to a magnet. Most of this investment is from Hong Kong
and Singapore Chinese although there is also some investment
from Malaysian, Philippines and now Vancouver Chinese (see
Rowley, 1981). Although there is considerable investment by
small investors in residential and small commercial real estate, the
rest of this account focuses on the larger Southeast Asian corporate investors' interests in Sydney office, apartment block and hotel
space. Table 6.14 shows the current extent of the larger Southeast
Asian investors' investment in real estate in Sydney's CBD. This
investment is both recent (mainly post-1978) and considerable. In
1980, for example, Southeast Asian investors purchased about
$A 100 million of property in central Sydney representing about
half of all the property purchased in central Sydney in that year
(Daly, 1982a). Major purchases since 1980 include the 400-room
Hyatt Kingsgate Hotel and shopping complex which cost $A 25.5
million in December 1980 and the Birkenhead Point tourist
complex which cost $A 21 million in 1981. Both of these pur-
chases were made by the Singapore Chinese, Ho Whyechung and
Ho Sim Guan. Another major purchase was made by Yap Lim
Sen's Malaysian Ipoh Gardens Group which bought the Anthony
Hordern's store complex in 1981 for $A 14.5 million and plans to

Table 6.14: Examples of Major Southeast Asian Property Interests in Sydney, 1982

1. Offices

Site	Ownership
Old Government House, Boomerang St	Hongkong Land (Hong Kong) with NSW Superannuation Board
124-128 Castlereagh St	—
National Mutual Life Building, George St	—
58-66 King St	—
135 King St (formerly Chandris House)	—
Macquarie House, Macquarie St	Hongkong Land (Hong Kong)
Anthony Hordern Building, Pitt St	Ipoh Gardens Sdn Bdh (Malaysia)
Phoenix House, Pitt St	C Y Tung (Hong Kong)
Orient Overseas Building, Pitt St	Chee Hwa Tung (Hong Kong) Chia Nien Loh (Hong Kong) and two Australian investors
140-144 Sussex St	—
146 Sussex St	—
General Credits House, York St	—
Queen Victoria Building, York St	Ipoh Gardens Sdn Bdh (Malaysia)
36-42 Young St	—
Northpoint House, North Sydney	Hongkong Land (Hong Kong)

2. Hotels

Site	Ownership
Boulevard, William St	Southern Pacific Hotel Corp Ltd (Tan Sri Khoo, Singapore)
Carlton Hotel	—
Intercontinental Hotel, Macquarie Place	Aspley Park Hotel Co Ltd (Hong Kong)
New Chevron Hotel, 81 Macleay St	James Wu (Hong Kong)

Table 6.14 continued

2. Site	Ownership
Regent Hotel, George St	Robert Kwok Group (Singapore, Malaysia) with Australia Civil and Civic Pty Ltd
Shangri La Hotel and Convention Centre —	
Trades Hall Hotel	Sally Aw Sian (Hong Kong)
3. Mixed Developments	
Site	Ownership
Hyatt Kingsgate Hotel and shopping complex, Kings Cross	Kingsgate Investments — Ho Whyechung, Ho Sim Guan (Singapore)
Birkenhead Point Shopping and Tourist Centre, Sydney Harbour	Ho Whyechung (Singapore)
Waltons Department Store	(Hong Kong) with Walton Bond
4. Residential	
Site	Ownership
The Connaught, Hyde Park	Hongkong Land (Hong Kong)
Park Lane Towers	Hongkong Land (Hong Kong)
5. Other	
Site	Ownership
Chequers Night Club, Pitt St	—
Chinatown, Dixon St	—
Fortune Court Restaurant	Sally Aw Sian (Hong Kong)
Mandarin Club, Pitt St	—

Source: Spiers, (1983); Jones Lang Wootton (1980-83a); Sydney Cityscope.

redevelop it into a hotel, apartment block and retail complex at a cost of another $A 300 million. Developments recently completed include the $A 45 million, 620-room Regent Hotel which was financed by a Southeast Asian syndicate, Austintel Holdings (Australia) Ltd, in association with local construction experts in Australia, Civil and Civic Pty Ltd. Regent Hotels International of Hong Kong owns 25 per cent of Ausintel and a consortium of property investors from all five ASEAN nations owns the remainder. Developments nearing completion include: the $A 100 million redevelopment of Waltons Department Store in Park Street (as a 28-storey office tower and four-level retail complex) by the Australian Walton Bond Group in conjunction with Hong Kong interests including Carrian; Hongkong Land and the New South Wales State Superannuation Board's redevelopment of Old Government House and the Malaysian Ipoh Garden Group's restoration of the Queen Victoria Building.

Hotels

The mention of hotels brings up to a recent phenomenon in Southeast Asian urban real estate investment, the takeover of Australia's largest hotels, especially in Sydney and Melbourne. This has had significant effects on the stocks of Australian real estate in Southeast Asian ownership. Southeast Asian groupings now active include: the aforementioned Whyechung-Sim Group with its hotels in Sydney (the group also has matching interests in New Zealand); the Hong Kong-based Regent International Group (with hotels in Sydney and Melbourne); the Hong Kong-owned Intercontinental Group building a hotel in Macquarie Place, Sydney, for completion in 1987; the Malaysian Merlin Group with a hotel in Perth and the Southern Pacific Hotels Corporation. This latter corporation which is part of the Singapore-based Goodwood Hotels group owned by Tan Sri Koo Tech Phuat, bought control of the Southern Pacific Hotels chain from the Saudi Arabian investor Adnan Kashoggi in 1981 for $A 110 million. The chain operates 55 hotels and motels with 7000 rooms in Australia, New Zealand, Fiji, Tahiti, Papua New Guinea and New Caledonia although currently it only has one top-line hotel, the Sydney Boulevard (others are under consideration) (Haselhurst, 1982). But mention of the Southern Pacific Hotels Corporation brings us to one final point about Southeast Asian investment in Australia. That is the influence of the FIRB.

The Influence of the State: the Foreign Investment Review Board

The FIRB can and does turn down real estate investment proposals on a number of grounds. First, proposals which are purely for capital gain or investment income will be rejected. Second, for proposals to be accepted, there has to be evidence that real estate has been made available to Australian buyers. Third, there must be substantial Australian equity. Indeed, since 1982 the policy that has been followed has been to promote at least 50 per cent Australian equity in both the hotel sector and the rest of the urban real estate sector, although a specified amount of time may be given to reach this figure. An example is the Southern Pacific Hotel organisation. This acquisition (which was 100 per cent foreign-owned before its recent acquisition by Goodwood Hotels) was approved partly because Tan Sri Khoo was an intending migrant.

The acquisition was approved by the Government on the basis of the business becoming owned by Australian residents. The approval was subject to the condition that Tan Sri Khoo and his family arrange their affairs so as to satisfy the Government, on a continuing basis, that at least 50 per cent of the income distributed from SPHC would be taxable in the hands of Australian residents. Moreover, if at any time the Government is not satisfied in respect of the abovementioned arrangements, it would be incumbent upon Tan Sri Khoo and his family to introduce, within two years, Australian equity to meet the 50 per cent equity requirement. (Foreign Investment Review Board, 1981, p. 15)

(Tan Sri Khoo is expected to move to Sydney soon. His two daughters already live in Australia.)

Similarly, approval was given for the Sydney Birkenhead Point tourist complex acquired by Singapore interests only on the condition that the purchasers introduced 49 per cent local equity within a five-year-period.

The decision to allow the purchasers to hold a controlling interest in the business reflected the contributions the purchasers propose to make to the upgrading and development of the tourist aspects of the business plus a recognition that Australians were not interested in acquiring the property which had been providing its former owner with a non-commercial rate of return. (Foreign Investment Review Board, 1981, p. 15)

Again, the Sydney Regent Hotel was allowed to slip through the FIRB requirements because it promised 'significant economic benefits' to tourism. However, 49 per cent of the equity must be offered to the Australian public within 10 years (*Asiaweek*, 1983a).

The FIRB conditions have caused problems for a number of Southeast Asian property interests. The Jack Chia Group is having major problems in finding local equity because of the scope of its projects in Melbourne. For example, the FIRB wants the South Yarra project to be half Australian-owned within three years but this is proving difficult to arrange (Spiers, 1983). Similarly, the Ipoh Gardens Group has had problems in meeting the equity criteria.

Ipoh has considered both flotation of its Australian operations and also local quotation of its parent's shares in Australia. However neither proposition appealed. Barrett (executive director of Ipoh) said this was because 'in Malaysia, as in most of Asia, property companies sell at a premium, whereas in Australia they often sell below asset backing'. (McPhee, 1983, p. 36)

Another major property company having problems with the FIRB is Hongkong Land. And it is to this company that we now turn.

The Hongkong Land Company

Although there has been considerable investment by smaller Chinese investors and the smaller Chinese property companies in the Pacific Basin city property market over the last 10 or 15 years, much of the inflow of investment into world city property is still the preserve of a few major property companies. Many of these companies are British (such as the Metropolitan Estates and Property Company (MEPC)) or, more recently, Arab-owned (such as the Kuwait Government's St Martins Property Company) but a substantial number are also from Hong Kong and Singapore. Prominent amongst this latter group of companies is the Hongkong Land Company, the largest property company in the world and, indeed, the largest company in Hong Kong.[6] The worth of property companies like Hongkong Land should never be underestimated. Such companies are as large as the largest industrial companies and their assets — office blocks, hotels, apartment blocks and the like — are substantial.

For example, early in 1974, the 280,000 sq. ft Commercial Union Building in the City of London was worth over £100 million, which at the time, was twice as much as the capitalized value of British Leyland and was worth more than other industrial firms such as Pilkington Glass and Plessey. (Ambrose and Colenutt, 1975, p. 41)

Therefore, these companies are important in their own right.

The case study of Hongkong Land that follows illustrates a number of related themes. First, it shows how these large property companies concentrate almost exclusively on the world city property market. Second, it shows how one Southeast Asian property company has invested in the Pacific Basin world city property market and, particularly, in Australia. Third, it gives some indication of what will happen to the large Hong Kong-based property companies as 1997 approaches. And, finally, it shows the problems of over-acquisitive property investment.

The Hongkong Land Company 1889–1982

The Hongkong Land Company was originally established on 2 March 1889. The Hongkong Land Investment and Agency Co. Ltd, as it was then called, was the result of an association between Catchick Paul Chater (1846-1926), a businessman of Armenian extraction with interests in brokerage, bullion and land, and James Johnston Keswick (1845-1914), Jardine Matheson's[7] senior representative in the colony and part of the strong Scottish link that still exists with the company. Indeed, the Keswick family still own between 8 and 10 per cent of the company's shares and 6 Keswicks have, since the company's birth, filled the positions of chairman of the board or managing director, in that dynastic fashion so beloved of writers of novels on Hong Kong.[8] The original board of the company were all non-Chinese but at the first board meeting in 1889 two prominent Chinese businessmen were invited to join the board (mainly in order to ward off competition from a rival Chinese real estate company). Chinese capital and interests were brought into the company on a 50-50 basis, half the new shares going to existing shareholders and half to Chinese investors. Here, then, was the beginning of a classical British–Chinese-owned *hong.*

The newly-formed company proceeded to do what it has done ever since — buy and sell Hong Kong property. Even the Second World War only brought a temporary halt to this activity. The company suspended business for 3 years and 8 months but at the end of the war:

> Mr Field [the company secretary] was able to muster virtually the complete local staff when he reopened the offices in early September [1945]. At the executive level, the Company had lost Mr Oscar Eager, Secretary, in an air raid on Stanley Cin Lian POW camp; and Mr Field, formerly Assistant Secretary, had been appointed in his place while still in the Shamshuipo POW

Table 6.15: Location of Principal Subsidiary and Associate
Companies of Hongkong Land, 1972-82

1. Country	1972	1973	1974	1975	1976	1977	1978	1979	1980	1981	1982
Hong Kong	17	17	21	23	26	27	30	28	26	29	30
Australia	10	11	11	11	10	11	11	12	12	13	10
Bermuda	0	1	1	1	1	1	1	1	1	1	1
Brunei	0	0	0	1	1	1	1	1	1	2	2
Canada	0	0	0	0	0	0	0	0	0	1	1
China	0	0	0	0	0	0	0	0	0	1	1
Guam	1	1	2	2	2	2	2	2	2	1	1
Indonesia	1	1	3	3	3	3	3	3	2	2	1
Japan	0	0	0	1	1	0	0	0	0	0	0
Macau	0	0	0	0	0	0	0	0	0	1	1
Malaysia	0	1	4	3	3	3	3	3	3	2	1
Netherlands Antilles	0	0	0	0	0	0	0	0	0	1	1
New Zealand	1	1	1	1	1	1	1	1	0	0	0
Philippines	0	0	0	1	1	1	1	1	0	0	0
Saipan	0	0	0	1	1	1	1	1	1	0	0
Singapore	0	1	1	2	2	2	1	1	1	1	1
Thailand	3	2	3	3	3	3	2	2	2	2	2
USA	0	0	0	0	0	1	1	1	1	1	1
Total	33	36	47	53	55	57	58	57	52	58	54
% Overseas	48.5	52.7	55.3	56.6	52.7	52.6	48.3	50.8	50.0	50.0	44.9

Source: Annual reports, various years.

camp by the then Chairman, Major J.J. Patterson who was also
a prisoner of war with him. The Accountant, Mr Francis Reid,
had also been killed during the war and Mr R.O. Baker, who
was in the same camp as Mr Field, was appointed accountant.
Mr Field, in fact, had passed many an otherwise unprofitable
and tedious hour while in prison camp during the occupation in
writing up the duties, procedures, and forms of the company
from memory — invaluable material on the reopening of the
offices. (Cameron, 1979, p. 34)

The major activity of the company in the pre-war years has
undoubtedly been the building up of its Hong Kong property base,
especially offices. Indeed, until the early 1960s this was the only
activity the company engaged in. But, since that date, the
company's activities have also been characterised by a certain
amount of *diversification* and *internationalisation* (Table 6.15).
The rationale for diversification, mainly into the hotel and food
trades, is clearly set out in the company history.

It has become ever more apparent that the company should indulge in activities that complement each other. Office accommodation implies that the office tenants need flats to live in. People need food, want to entertain and to be able to accommodate their business contacts both in Hong Kong and from overseas. Hence the need to be in the hotel trade, which in itself generates food requirements, as do the tenants of the flats and offices. The logical step, therefore, was the acquisition of a food chain to satisfy these requirements. (Cameron, 1979, p.61)

The rationale for internationalisation was partly a natural result of this process of diversification, partly a response to the internationalisation of producer services and partly a response to worries about Hong Kong's future. For example, it is by no means a coincidence that the company's first hesitant step into the international property market took place in 1967 at a time of riots in Hong Kong set against the background of the Cultural Revolution in China. Indeed, with the benefit of hindsight, the company has probably been too conservative in its programme of internationalisation, something for which it is now paying the price.

The result of the company's activities in the Hong Kong real estate market and the limited programmes of diversification and internationalisation have been very profitable. Hongkong Land's net profit (profit after taxation and minorities) has risen consistently, increasing tenfold in the 10-year period between 1972 and 1980. Dividends increased nearly eightfold in the same period. Profits from property development and more particularly from property rentals increased steadily (while profits from food, hotels and restaurants also became a major component in the balance sheet). The expansion of the company that is reflected in these profits has also lead to an expansion in its workforce. In 1972, the workforce was about 3000. By 1982 it had increased to 12,843. As a consequence of the programmes of diversification and internationalisation, the workforce has also become progressively more international. The non-Hong Kong component of the workforce has increased from 2662 or nearly 36 per cent of the workforce in 1976 to 6445 or just over 50 per cent of the workforce in 1982.

Overseas Investment in Real Estate by the Hongkong Land Company

What have been the overseas investment policies followed by the

Hongkong Land Company in the post-war years? The immediate post-war years saw the company inward-looking, preoccupied with the redevelopment of its prime properties in Central (see Cameron, 1979). But in the late 1960s it began to take an interest in overseas property. This subsequent history of internationalisation can be split into three main areas — offices and apartment blocks, hotels and retail outlets.

Offices and Apartment Blocks. The first signs of company interest in overseas office property were directed at Australia. In 1966, an in-depth study of real estate prospects in Australia was carried out resulting, in 1967, in the incorporation of the Land Company Pty Ltd in New South Wales. In 1969 this new company entered into an agreement with the Australian Club in Sydney to take over the 75-year lease on the Club's site and build on the site what was later known as Macquarie House. This 20-level office building was finally completed in 1972. Office properties in other parts of the world followed. These included the 23-level Davies Pacific Centre in Honolulu, acquired in 1978, the Wisma Hayam Wuruk in Jakarta, a 30 per cent joint venture developed with the Hong Kong and Shanghai Banking Corporation in 1975, and a 21-level office building in Kuala Lumpur, another 30 per cent venture with the Hong Kong and Shanghai Banking Corporation (and also the Malaysian government's Urban Development Authority) completed in 1979.

Since 1980, the Hongkong Land Company has also been involved in building and managing apartment blocks and other residential developments overseas, especially in Australia, Singapore and Hawaii, which parallel its interest in such property in Hong Kong.

Hotels. Even before the Second World War, the company had owned the Gloucester Hotel in Hong Kong. In 1961 it formed a company, City Hotels Ltd, which was put in charge of taking over an old Hong Kong office site belonging to Hongkong Land and transforming it into the Mandarin Hotel which opened in 1963. It was not long before the company turned to the international hotel business, initially through a joint venture with Italthai to redevelop the Oriental in Bangkok (completed in 1974) and then through other hotels in Manila (the Mandarin completed in 1976 and transferred to the company in 1980), Jakarta (the Mandarin completed in 1979 and transferred to the company in 1980), another hotel in Bangkok (the Royal Orchid, completed in 1982), a hotel in Vancouver (the Mandarin, completed in 1983) and hotels in Macau and Singapore (the Excelsior and the Oriental, to be completed in 1984 and 1985 respectively). All these hotels are managed by a wholly-owned subsidiary of City Hotels, Mandarin International Hotels Ltd. (see Dunning and McQueen, 1982a; 1982b).

Retail Business. The company's move into international retail business came about almost entirely through acquisition (Table 6.16). For example, in 1972 the company acquired the Dairy Farm Ice and Cold Storage Group of companies with its considerable range of supermarkets, food processing plants, caterers, cold storage facilities and supermarkets operating in a number of Pacific Basin countries, including Australia, Brunei, China, Guam, Singapore and Thailand. In 1973 the Fitzpatrick group of companies was integrated into Dairy Farm. In 1979 the company acquired the Franklins supermarket chain in Australia, a Sydney-based group which is now the third largest grocery retailer in Australia. Again this group was integrated into Dairy Farm. Although this group was concentrated in Sydney at the time of acquisition, it is now expanding into Queensland and Victoria.

The Recent History of the Hongkong Land Company

In early 1981 the horizon could not have looked brighter for Hongkong Land. Its portfolio of prime Hong Kong Central real estate like The Landmark, Alexandra House, Swire House, the Connaught Centre and the Mandarin Hotel and a list of continuing developments in Hong Kong, Kowloon and the New Territories

Table 6.16: Retail Outlets Owned by Dairy Farm, 1979-82

	1979	1980	1981	1982
Hong Kong	43	59	85	101
Australia	89	94	102	110
(of which Franklins)	(76)	(81)	(89)	(97)
Singapore	7	8	8	9
Other (Malaysia, Brunei)	4	10	10	8
Total	143	171	205	228

Source: Annual Reports, various years.

seemed to be a veritable gold mine. Its overseas property portfolio looked fairly impressive. And after a 36 per cent/42 per cent share swap with its sister company Jardine Matheson (which, incidentally, through payment in kind for shares brought the company control of a number of Jardine's overseas properties such as Northpoint in Sydney) it looked able to withstand the share raids of aggressive Chinese entrepreneurs like Li Ka Shing of Cheung Kong Holdings (see Bartholomew and Rowley, 1980; Shroff, 1980). Even in early 1982 the company was still acquiring shares from other companies.[9]

But events would now show that Hongkong Land had not internationalised enough. When the Hong Kong property market started to subside in the summer of 1981, so too did Hongkong Land. This subsidence became a number of serious cracks in the company's fabric because the company had entered into a number of unwise joint ventures to develop Hong Kong property, principally with the notorious Carrian Group but also with EDA-related investors, notably Aik San Realty and E. Wah Realty, in the Vermillion Land project. These ventures now came badly unstuck when each partner became insolvent. The need to continue to support other ventures, especially the gigantic Exchange Square project, but now with no prospect of cash flow from the joint ventures, the need to provide heavily against the joint ventures themselves and the plummeting property market all showed up swiftly in the balance sheets. Net profits decreased from $HK 1429 million in 1981/82 to $HK 814 million in 1982/83 to $HK 168 million in 1983/84. This decline was nearly all able to be traced to property trading. In October 1983 the Company announced a half-year *loss* of $HK 107 million, and for the first time in the company's history it was forced to waive its dividend (*The Economist*, 1983d). By March 1983 that loss had increased to $HK 500 million and in March 1984 a loss of $HK 1282 million was declared.[10] Although Hongkong Land had, for a property company, a fairly modest gearing (debt to equity) ratio of 76 per cent in early 1983, debt now became a problem in the absence of cash flow. By October 1983, the company's debts had reached $HK 15 billion (and they are expected to peak at $HK 17 billion) (Shrof, 1983). This debt problem was further compounded when the company's shares fell in the general Hong Kong stockmarket downturn. In May 1983, for example, its shares fell 45 cents to $HK 3.58 in just two days, as did the shares of most other property houses (*The Economist* 1983b). To add to this blow the company's Hong Kong properties had to be revalued downwards as land prices and rents fell.

In the light of this performance it is no surprise that there has been a change at the top. In March 1982 it was announced that Simon Keswick would become chairman-designate of Hongkong Land (and, by tradition, of its sister company Jardine Matheson as well) replacing D.T. Newbigging from June 1984 (see Wood, 1983).[11] Keswick, in turn, replaced the managing director of Hongkong Land, Trevor Bedford, with the vice-president and financial director of the British property company, MEPC, David Davies. Davies took up his appointment in mid-October, 1983. Certain short-term holding operations were immediately put into operation. For example, the company's 34.8 per cent interest in Hong Kong Telephone was sold in March 1983 for $HK 1400 million (it should be noted that this gave a profit of $HK400 million) and 10 of the company's 50 outstanding projects were cancelled (*The Economist*, 1983d). These short-term measures cut back the Company's borrowing requirements by $HK 3 billion (Rowley, 1982), but obviously more severe measures were called for. There was even rumour of a merger between Hongkong Land and its sister company, Jardine Matheson, allowing the rationalisation of both Group's interests (and permitting Jardine, which is in even worse trouble than Hongkong Land, to borrow against Hongkong Land's property assets). A more likely outcome is that Jardine Matheson will get rid of its shares in Hongkong Land which continue to drag its profits down. One likely buyer of these shares is Cheung Kong properties (*The Economist*, 1984, p.66).

Assuming this latter move does not take place, what is likely to be the long-term strategy followed by Hongkong Land in the years to come? First, core companies like Dairy Farm and Mandarin International are likely to be retained because they continue to produce steady and reliable profits. Second, all the indications point to a fairly rapid internationalisation of property investments on a much greater scale than before. It is known that, even before the crisis, the Keswicks were becoming concerned about the company's Hong Kong focus (see Davies, Lee and Rowley, 1983). The present crisis can only have confirmed their fears. Secondly, the new managing director's history must have strengthened the expectations of rapid internationalisation. Davies joined MEPC in 1974/75 when it was in a similar situation to the one now facing

Hongkong Land. The London property market had slumped and the company was in further trouble because an Australian associate, the Mainline Corporation, had been declared bankrupt (see Daly, 1982a).

MEPC gradually got itself back into shape by rescheduling loans, making sales, contracting operations and shelving a housebuilding subsidiary. By 1979-80 the results showed an almost 50 per cent leap in pre-tax profits to £21 million, with Benson and Davies said to be in an expansionary mood and preparing to steer the company into an era of 'conservative prosperity'.

At the end of 1982, MEPC — with about a third of its current development portfolio geared to foreign developments — announced a pre-tax profit of £33.4 million. Pre-tax profits to March 1983 rose again to £19.1 million, largely as a result of an increase in gross rental incomes following acquisition in the United States. MEPC's property portfolio is currently worth more than £1 billion. (Nelson, 1983)

In contrast to MEPC, Hongkong Land has only 8 per cent of its current development portfolio geared to foreign developments and income from overseas property rentals contributed 7 per cent of profit after tax in 1981 and only 1.8 per cent of profit after tax in 1983. This, it must be emphasised, is in a company with its headquarters and its main sources of profit based in a location with an uncertain future. As if this were not sufficient indication of impending internationalisation Simon Keswick is not only chairman of Hongkong Land but also of Jardine Matheson, a company which has just quit Hong Kong.

Where, then, is the new overseas property investment likely to go? Figure 6.4 shows Hongkong Land's overseas property portfolio in 1982. The concentrations of property in world city locations are quite clear. The first such location was Sydney and the company has continued to expand there. For example, in November 1982 it was awarded the site of the Old Government House on which it will develop, by 1986, an office block in a joint venture with the New South Wales Superannuation Board. In 1980, it was estimated that the company had a projected million dollars' worth of real estate in Sydney alone (Daly, 1982a). By the beginning of 1983 the company had five major properties plus

Figure 6.4: The Spatial Distribution of Hongkong Land's Overseas
Property Portfolio, 1982

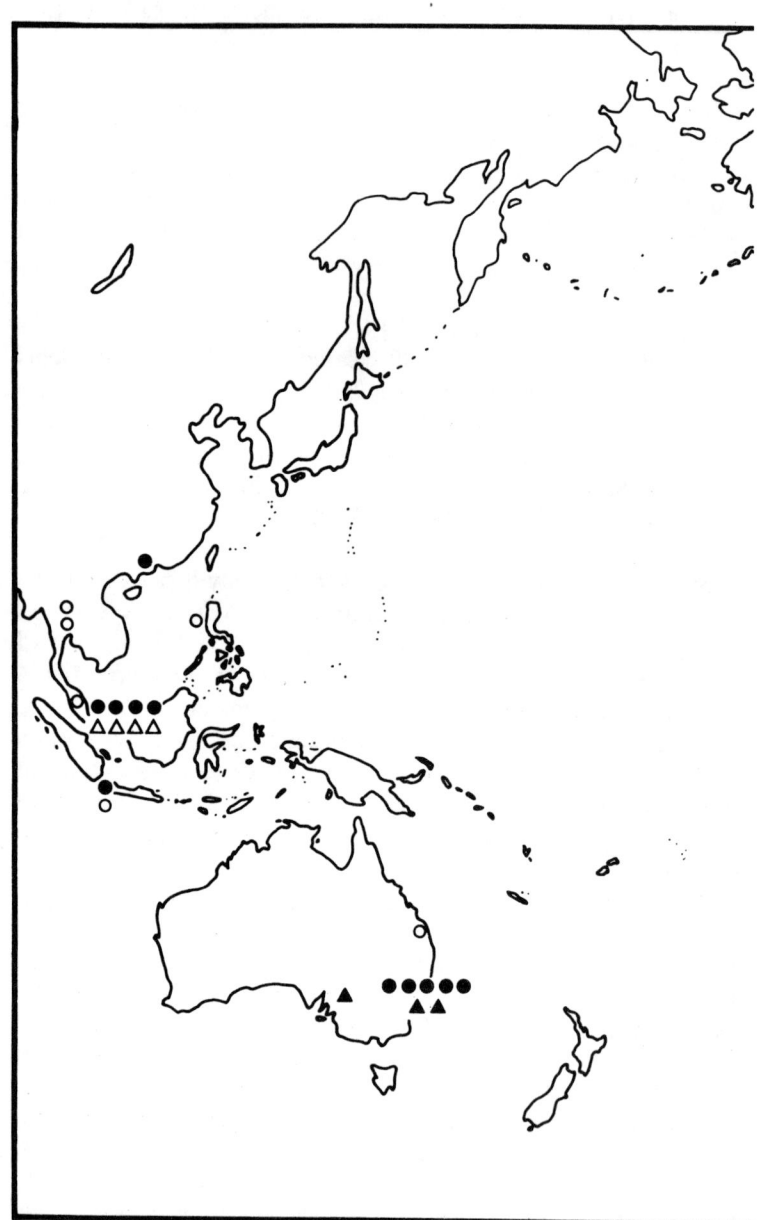

Source: Annual Reports

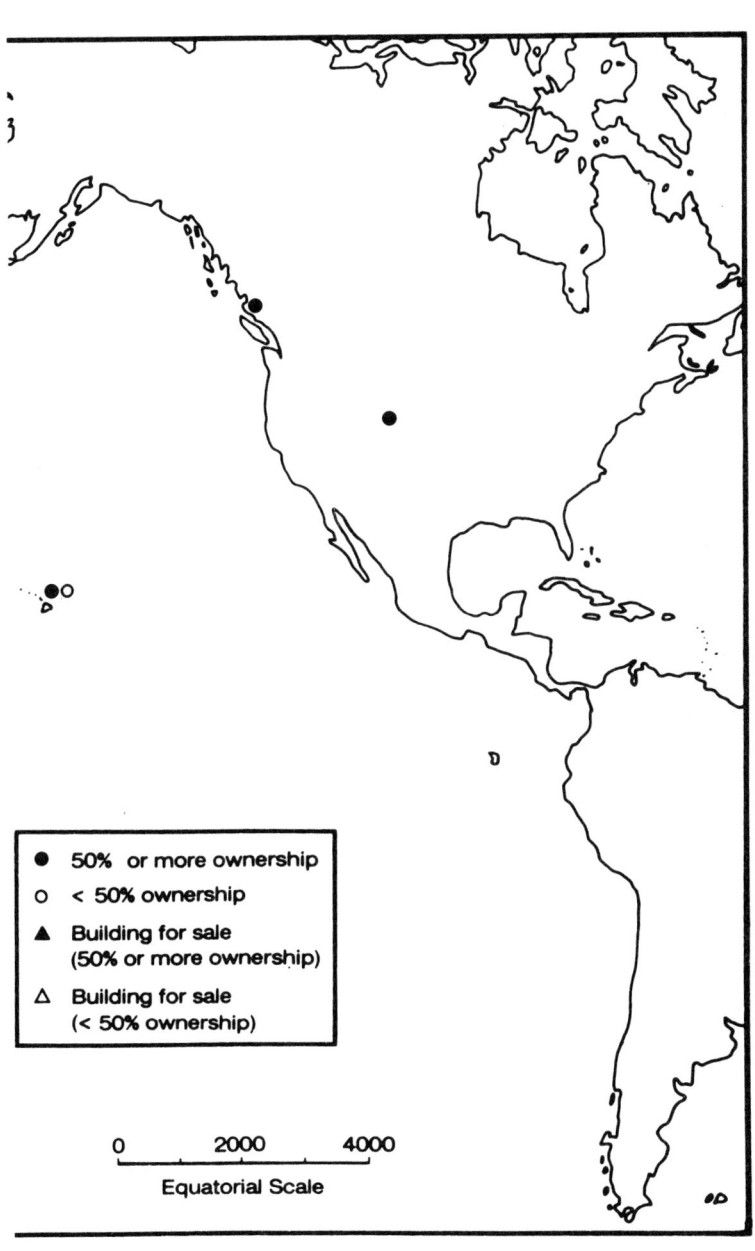

●	50% or more ownership
○	< 50% ownership
▲	Building for sale (50% or more ownership)
△	Building for sale (< 50% ownership)

0   2000   4000

Equatorial Scale

supermarkets and duty-free stores in the city. The second world city location was Singapore. Here the company had five major properties, supermarkets and a hotel. The third location was Honolulu. The company had two major properties here. The other non-world city locations were still quite small and often represented by just one hotel outpost.

It seems likely that this world city focus will remain. Property investment will go to Australia, to Singapore and, more and more, to the United States. Within these countries, Sydney will remain the main target in Australia and in the United States the West Coast is likely to see more and more investment (a joint venture to build an office in Denver may be a sign of things to come).

This does not, of course, mean that there will be no decisions made to sell property or shares of property overseas. The current debt crisis has enforced some such disposals in the short term.[12] Most of these sales are likely to be amongst residential and industrial property developments in Australia and Singapore which have not produced the expected rates of return. In Australia, for example, the sale of 15 per cent of the equity in the Connaught residential development in Sydney is likely to be followed by more. The company has also been sitting on a Marochydore town house development waiting for the market to improve. This development is almost certain to be sold (Way, 1983). And the Simarloo Fruit and Nut Farm (part of the Dairy Farm Group) has also been placed on the market (*Australian Property News*, September, 1983). Further office properties have not been immune when sufficient profit can be realised on their sale. In October 1983, for example, the Davies Pacific Center in Honolulu was sold for $US 59.9 million (Shroff, 1983). In Australia FIRB requirements have added to the pressure to sell. For example, FIRB requirements to sell 50 per cent of the company's stake in Northpoint and 35 per cent of its stake in Macquarie House, which had been resisted because Hongkong Land 'could not find a buyer at the right price' (Way, 1983, p. 11) have now ceased. The 63-year leasehold interest in Macquarie House was sold in late 1983 for a price rumoured to be $A 30 million. What seems certain, however, is that after such rationalisation the company's property investment overseas will, as a matter of urgency, be on a much greater scale and its main targets will be the world cities and the second tier cities that are scattered around the Pacific Basin.

Conclusions

This chapter represents a first attempt to weave together a number of themes and, in particular, the internationalisation of production, the internationalisation of producer services and the growth of an international market in real estate. The importance of making the connections between the new international geography of multi-national corporations (whether their main activities are in manufacturing industry or services) and urban form and function seem self-evident whether justified in theoretical or policy terms. But clearly the existence and importance of particular connections requires considerable further research. For the fact remains that we still lack fundamental information about the recent bout of global economic restructuring and how this restructuring has affected urban form and function. This lack of knowledge is the result of two inadequacies. The first of these is theoretical. For example, there is a need to link into the analysis the influence of the financial institutions that provide the funds that enable large property companies to function (see Lamarche, 1976; Massey and Catalano, 1978; Feagin, 1982; Daly, 1982a), the role of the state (the influence of the Australian FIRB is only one instance of this) and the social consequences of corporate property investment such as unsatisfied demand for housing and increases in housing prices (see Ambrose and Colenutt, 1975; Feagin, 1982; Daly, 1982a). The second inadequacy is empirical. There is a striking lack of data about so many of the issues, actual or potential, that are raised in this chapter. This chapter is therefore a *very* preliminary statement.

Notes

1. JLW still has 300 staff in Australia.
2. Recent Southeast Asian investments in Auckland include the International and Arundel hotels, the Princes Court Office Building and the Eden Hall apartment block, all owned by the Singapore investors Ho Whyechung and Hoan Sim) (see below) (Jones Lang Wootton, 1982a).
3. I am taking a broad definition of urban real estate that includes not only offices, retail developments and housing but also hotels.
4. This limit was cumulative so that only $A 350,000 can be spent in total. Since 1983, second and subsequent acquisitions of all real estate by foreigners, other than urban and rural business, will be subject to approval even where the cumulative total invested is within the $A 350,000 limit.

5. The Foreign Investment Review Board data require some comment. First, and most generally, the data do not cover purchases made with funds in Australia. Second, some of the investment (generally a very small amount) is by intending migrants and citizens resident abroad. Third, some of the investment, especially that where real estate is being acquired as part of a business (such as hotels, for example) requires Australian participation. Fourth, with respect to '*expected investment*', not all such investment is always made, although most is. Fifth, with respect to the category '*real estate*', this category includes a rural land component. However most expected investment goes on urban real estate. Sixth, with respect to the category '*services*', this category is inclusive of some urban real estate such as hotels and retail business (see text).

6. The company headed the list of the 20 largest companies in Hong Kong in 1982 in both *The Times* (*The Times*, 1982) and *Asia Corporate Profile* (*Asia Corporate Profile*, 1983) lists; followed by the Hong Kong and Shanghai Bank Jardine Matheson and Swire Pacific.

7. Jardine Matheson was founded in 1841.

8. The Keswicks also currently own between 10 and 20 per cent of Jardine Matheson, Hongkong Land's sister company. According to the nineteenth century articles of incorporation, Jardines is the pre-eminent *hong* and the chairman and managing director of Jardines must also be the chairman and managing director of Hongkong Land. There have been accusations that the Keswicks run both companies as their own personal fiefdom, and, certainly, the share-swap between Hongkong Land and Jardine Matheson protected their interests but it is now, of course, causing great problems as debt in one company rebounds on the debt of the other (see Shroff, 1980). The Keswicks are able to retain greater control than their shareholding represents mainly because of the wide spread of shares held by other shareholders in both companies. Hongkong Land currently has some 40,000 shareholders.

9. In February 1982 it acquired approximately one-third of the share capital of the Hong Kong Telephone Company and in April 1982 approximately one-third of the capital in Hong Kong Electric Holdings. In both cases one of the reasons for acquisition was to gain control of potential sites for property development *in Hong Kong*. In the current crisis the Hong Kong Electric Shares cannot be sold at a profit because of the stockmarket crash.

10. Although it cannot continue to do this without losing trustee status for its shares among pension funds, something it will want to avoid.

11. Newbigging has since vacated his position as chairman.

12. As it forced Jardine Matheson to sell off a profitable South African subsidiary, Rennies.

7 THE INTERNATIONALISATION OF JAPANESE COMMERCIAL BANKING

Masahiro Fujita and Kenichi Ishigaki

Introduction

This chapter examines the nature and extent of the internationalisation of Japanese commercial banking during the 1970s. Generally speaking, the internationalisation of finance has three aspects. First, it involves the internationalisation of domestic currency — that is, domestic currency becomes also an international vehicle currency and reserve currency. Secondly, it involves the internationalisation of banks and other financial institutions — financial institutions transact either with non-residents through both domestic and foreign currency, or with residents through foreign currency. Thirdly, it involves the internationalisation of the money and capital market — that is, both short-term and long-term funds move freely in to and out of the markets, and market interest rates are determined by market forces.

These three aspects are closely interrelated. The internationalisation of a currency and of the money and capital markets promotes the internationalisation of banking business. Conversely, the development of the latter may contribute to the promotion of the former. It would therefore seem to be necessary to approach the issue of the internationalisation of banking in the light of these considerations. However, as will be discussed in more detail later, one of the features of the internationalisation of Japanese banking is that it has developed without significant corresponding developments of the currency or the money and capital markets. This chapter will concentrate on the examination of the internationalisation of Japanese banking, with the other aspects being noted for their effects on the internationalisation.

During 1977 and 1978, our research group[1] conducted a survey on the internationalisation of Japanese banking. Bankers were asked to respond to a questionnaire and be interviewed. Ten of the 12 city banks, all three of the long-term credit banks, one specialised foreign exchange bank and one regional bank participated in the survey.[2] Although some other banks, such as trust banks, are also internationalising their business, we limited our concern to city banks, long-term credit banks and specialised foreign exchange banks, since they represent virtually all the Japanese banks which are currently international. They account for 90 per cent of the foreign exchange asset balance, 94 per cent of all overseas branches of Japanese banks, 95 per cent of overseas representative offices, and 92 per cent of local finance company subsidiaries of banks. It thus seems reasonable that this survey will provide a fairly accurate assessment of the internationalisation of Japanese banking.

With the objective of clarifying the current situation as regards the internationalisation of Japanese banking and examining the points at issue, the questionnaire was divided into seven sections:

(1) The purpose and motives of the internationalisation of banking.
(2) The establishing of branches, offices and local banks.
(3) International banking operations.
(4) The present situation and performance of the internationalisation.
(5) The difficulties and limitations in the promotion of internationalisation of Japanese banking.
(6) The administration and regulation of internationalisation of banking.
(7) Present and future problems.

The chapter is not intended to be merely a report of the results of the survey. It will depict the internationalisation of Japanese banks against the background of the Japanese economy and discuss the problems and limitations of internationalisation as revealed by the data collected through our research and from other sources[3] (Hayden, 1980; Horne, 1980). The subsequent sections deal with the internationalisation of the Japanese economy and Japanese banking, the aims and motives of internationalisation, the present situation in overseas bases and the performance of internationalisation. The chapter will also draw out the major issues and note the limitations of internationalisation as they emerge from the data collected in the survey.

The Development of the Internationalisation of the Japanese Economy and of Japanese Banking

Since the Second World War, Japan has gradually shifted from a closed to an open economy. GHQ (General Headquarters) controlled Japanese foreign trade immediately after the war, but some private foreign trade eventually resumed, and in 1949 the single exchange rate of 1 dollar = 360 yen was determined. In 1960, the Program of Liberalisation of Trade and Foreign Exchange was initiated to promote liberalisation of trade transactions and increase the percentage of liberalised trade categories to some 80 or 90 per cent. The programme resulted in an increase from 42 per cent in 1960 to 93 per cent in 1964. In 1960 the National Income Doubling Plan was introduced, coinciding with the period of high economic growth in Japan. In 1964 Japan accepted the obligations of Article VIII of the IMF Agreement and became a member of the OECD. This meant that Japan accepted the prohibition of exchange controls on both visible and invisible trade without the approval of the IMF, and agreed in principle not to restrict invisible trade transactions and long-term capital movement. This shift from a closed to an open system indicates that a certain degree of liberalisation of foreign trade had been reached by 1964. In that year Japan's share of world trade was 4.1 per cent.

Liberalisation of capital transactions, especially direct investment in Japan, followed the liberalisation of foreign trade. The fundamental policy for the liberalisation of direct investment in Japan was determined in 1967, and proceeded in four stages. Owing to the policy, the number of liberalised business categories increased to 527. Still, in 1969, the level of liberalisation of Japanese capital movements was not as high as that of other advanced countries. However, at the beginning of the 1970s the Japanese balance of payments surplus, especially the current balance, increased. It remained at a high level so the Japanese authorities actively promoted the liberalisation of trade and capital transactions. The proportion of import trade categories which had been liberalised reached 97 per cent with only 32 goods, such as beef, flour, leather and computers, remaining unliberalised. During this same period an across-the-board reduction of 20 per cent on tariffs on mining and manufactured products and processed agricultural products was implemented. With this reduction, Japan's tariff levels reached the international level. The liberalisation of capital transactions also proceeded during this period, with four stages finally leading to 100 per cent liberalisation in principle by 1973. Japanese direct investment overseas was automatically permitted in principle from 1972.

The process of the liberalisation of trade and capital trans-actions is really also the process of the internationalisation of the Japanese economy. Table 7.1 shows Japan's share of world foreign trade. Japanese exports and imports accounted for 3.2 per cent to 3.3 per cent in 1960, reaching 6.4 per cent in 1975. Table 7.2 shows the level of flow and stock of direct overseas investment by Japan, USA and West Germany. It indicates that Japanese over-seas investment increased rapidly during the late 1960s and the 1970s, especially in 1972. It also shows that, although the level of both the stock and flow of Japanese overseas investment in the late 1970s was considerably lower than that of the USA, Japan's stock levels were about the same as those of West Germany while its flow level was higher.

The internationalisation of the Japanese economy, that is the development of an interdependent relationship between the Japanese and world economies together with the increasing importance of Japan's position in the world economy, obviously has affected the activities of various large banks, such as city banks, which have played a major role in the financial activities of Japan. However, it should be noted that the internationalisation of the Japanese economy has not been accompanied by a sufficient internationalisation of the currency (yen) and of the money and capital market. Table 7.3 and Table 7.4 show the relative positions of currencies such as the US dollar, the mark and the yen in inter-

Table 7.1: The Position of Japan in World Trade ($US millions)

		1960	1965	1970	1975	1979
World	Exports[a]	127,700	186,400	311,800	873,779	16,270,302
	Imports[b]	134,800	197,400	327,300	905,906	16,792,250
Japan	Exports[a]	4,055	8,452	19,319	55,754	103,045
	Imports[b]	4,491	8,170	18,883	57,865	110,672
Share of Japan (%)	Exports[a]	3.2	4.5	6.2	6.4	6.3
	Imports[b]	3.3	4.1	5.8	6.4	6.6

Notes: a. FOB.
b. CIF.
Source: *UN Yearbook of International Trade Statistics* (1979).

Table 7.2: Direct Investment Overseas by Japan, USA and West Germany ($US millions)

	Japan		USA		West Germany	
	Total	Ratio to Domestic Private Investment	Total	Ratio to Domestic Private Investment	Total	Ratio to Domestic Private Investment
1967	275	1.2	4,791	5.8	516	3.5
1968	557	2.0	5,372	6.0	573	3.7
1969	665	1.9	6,246	6.3	886	4.2
1970	904	2.2	7,255	7.2	958	3.6
1971	858	2.0	7,577	7.3	816	2.4
1972	2,338	4.3	7,434	6.4	880	2.5
1973	3,494	4.3	11,435	8.4	2,086	4.8
1974	2,396	3.1	8,859	5.9	1,880	4.1
1975	3,280	4.7	14,040	9.4	1,993	4.5
1976	3,462	4.5	13,032	8.0	2,140	4.0
1977	2,806	3.2	11,538	6.1	2,420	3.7
Cumulative total	22,211		148,782		22,458	

Source: Kinyu Mondai Kenkyukai (1979), *Kokusaika no shinten ni tomonau wagakuni kinyukikan no arikata.*

Table 7.3: Percentage of International Trade Transactions in Domestic Currency[a]

	Export	Import
Japan	18.8%	1.2%
West Germany	86.9	42.0
England	73.0	40.0
France	68.3	31.5
Netherlands	50.2	31.4
Austria	54.7	24.7
Belgium	47.7	25.4
Denmark	54.0	23.0
Sweden	66.1	25.8

Note: a. Figures for Japan are for 1977; others are for 1976.
Source: Kinyu Mondai Kenkyukai (1979).

national trade and financial transactions. Clearly, the position of the yen is extremely low in comparison with the US dollar and is lower than the mark in both transaction categories. With regard to the internationalisation of the money and capital market, there has been little improvement in the internationalisation of the short-

Table 7.4: The Percentage of Money-Capital Transactions in Each Currency

	(1) Syndicate Loan		(2) Issue of Securities		(1)+(2)	
	1977	1978	1977	1978	1977	1978
US dollar	93.7%	89.6%	51.1%	38.6%	76.0%	75.2%
D. mark	3.8	2.8	20.3	24.6	10.7	9.0
Japan yen	0.9	3.2	5.1	12.4	2.7	5.8
Swiss franc	0.4	0.3	15.5	16.0	6.7	4.7
Netherlands guilder florin	—	1.1	2.2	2.8	0.9	1.6
Saudi Arabia riyal	0.3	1.3	0.2	0.3	0.3	1.0
British pound	0.4	0.9	0.7	0.9	0.5	0.9
Kuwait dinar	—	0.2	0.5	1.7	0.2	0.6
French franc	—	0.2	—	0.5	—	0.3
Luxembourg franc	—	—	0.4	0.7	0.2	0.2
Others	0.3	0.3	3.8	1.3	1.8	0.6
Total	100	100	100	100	100	100

Source: Kinyu Mondai Kenkyukai (1979).

term money market, although there has been a recent improvement in long-term capital transactions such as the issue of foreign yen-denominated bonds in the Japanese market.

In contrast, the internationalisation of the Japanese economy does seem to have promoted the internationalisation of some Japanese banks. Generally speaking, this means the increase of transactions with non-residents in yen or foreign currencies and of transactions with residents in foreign currency as a ratio of trans-actions with residents in yen. More concretely, these operations include dealing in foreign exchange and trade credit, loans made to non-residents, merchant-banking activities and dollar fund-raising. It is natural, therefore, that dealing in foreign exchange and trade credit and loans to Japanese companies overseas increases with the increase in the volume of Japanese trade and the greater inroads made by banks' customers into overseas markets.

It follows from the discussion so far that one of the features of the internationalisation of Japanese banking is that it has been promoted by the internationalisation of the Japanese economy, but has not been accompanied by the internationalisation of the yen or the Japanese money and capital market. It should be noted, however, that Japanese banks have themselves initiated internationalisation of some aspects of their operations against the background of the development of international finance markets, such as the Eurodollar market. These factors will be explored in the next section.

The Purpose and Motives of the Internationalisation of Japanese Banking

The main long-term purpose of the internationalisation of Japanese banking must be the acquisition of profit, although various shorter-term objectives are subsumed within this. This section will first discuss the target proportion for total bank profits which might come from international business, and then consider other short-term objectives apart from the making of profits.

The survey research indicates that the long-term target for the proportion of profits to be derived from international business which city banks and long-term credit banks consider feasible is between 11 per cent and 30 per cent. The upper-rank group of city banks gives a figure of 20-30 per cent, while the middle and lower ranks, except the specialised foreign bank and the long-term credit banks, give figures of between 11 per cent and 20 per cent. The specialised foreign exchange bank has a very high target.[4] It is interesting that the higher target figure of the upper-ranking banks (30 per cent) is similar to the actual figure of three internationalised German banks (Deutsche Bank, Dresdner Bank, Commerzbank) whose internationalisation is a little more advanced than Japan's banks. These banks' figures were 35 per cent, 30 per cent and 30 per cent, respectively in 1977.

Besides profit-earning, Japanese banks consider enlarging the number of customers (12 banks) and accumulating techniques and 'know-how' in international banking (nine banks) to be important long-term objectives. Other objectives include the collection of overseas information and the maintenance of banks' prestige in the face of competition. The upper-rank group tends to emphasise as important the enlargement of numbers of customers and the accumulation of knowledge, while some middle and lower groups give more weight to the maintaining of prestige.

We now turn attention to the motives and methods for the internationalisation of Japanese banking in the past. There are two main ways in which internationalisation of banking can develop. First, banks may internationalise in accordance with the internationalisation of their customers. Secondly, they may initiate the internationalisation themselves. The survey reported here suggests that more than half the banks (7 of 13) thought that customer-led internationalisation was most significant, three thought that bank-led internationalisation was most significant, while the remaining three stated that their internationalisation had paralleled that of their customers. It would seem, therefore, that internationalisation in Japanese banking has been primarily motivated by, and has proceeded together with, the internationalisation of their Japanese customers. That is, the liberalisation of trade and capital transactions and the increased overseas activities of Japanese companies have resulted in an increased demand for various foreign exchange and finance dealings on behalf of the banks. Figure 7.1, which shows the relationship between Japanese companies' direct overseas investment and the increase in the number of overseas branches and local banks, confirms this. It indicates that this branch and local bank expansion increased with the increase of direct overseas investment.

However, this is not to say that self-initiated internationalisation is an insignificant aspect of the internationalisation of banking. For example, the specialised foreign exchange bank proceeded on its own initiative, competing with foreign banks in various aspects of banking business well before the internationalisation of Japanese companies. In the case of other banks, too, there are examples of this type of internationalisation. For instance, Japanese banks often help customers with their internationalisation, especially where the customer is a small or medium-sized enterprise without enough knowledge of overseas conditions to proceed alone. In addition, in the early 1970s, when finance market conditions eased due to excessive domestic liquidity and it seemed that the demand for investment funds was going to slacken in the long term, banks actively sought new business in the international finance market. Similarly, the easing of the regulation of foreign exchange transactions after 1972 by Japanese monetary authorities helped Japanese banks develop international business.

In summary, then, the fundamental reason for the Japanese banks' promotion of internationalisation has been the quest for larger profits. They have been assisted in this by the background of liberalisation of trade and capital transactions against which it has

Figure 7.1 Movement of Japanese Direct Investment Overseas and the Establishment of New Branches and Local Banks

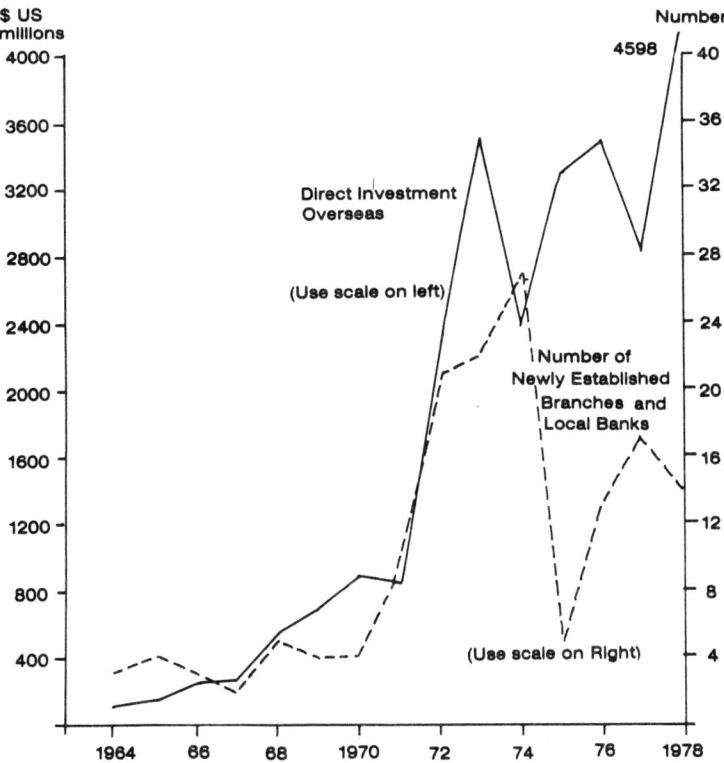

been carried out. However, self-initiated internationalisation has also been a feature, although a secondary one, of Japanese banking and, as will be discussed later, indications are that it will become increasingly important.

Establishing Branches, Offices and Local Banks[5]

To begin international banking business from Japan, banks need to obtain an authorisation from the monetary authorities to deal in foreign exchange. They then need to establish foreign exchange sections within domestic banks and enter into correspondent bank contracts with foreign banks overseas. At the end of March 1979, there were 119 authorised foreign exchange banks in Japan. However, the establishing of overseas branches, representative offices and local banks is the main way international banking is advanced. The overseas operations of Japanese banks, especially fund-raising and accommodation of funds, are conducted in foreign currency, usually US dollars, so the internationalisation of the yen and of the Japanese money and capital market has not progressed far. In these circumstances, the establishing of overseas branches and affiliates is critically important for banks. At the end of March 1979, the situation as regards overseas branches, representative offices and local banks was as follows. Twenty-three banks had a total of 123 overseas branches, 25 banks had a total of 150 representative offices, and 20 banks had a total of 66 local banks (i.e. more than 50 per cent ownership).

Table 7.5 and Figure 7.2 show the number and geographical distribution of overseas branches, offices, local banks and Japanese staff. In terms of the geographical distribution of overseas branches, North America has 38 per cent, Europe 33 per cent and Asia 25 per cent. In total, these three areas account for over 95 per cent of branches. Forty-three per cent of Japanese staff are located in North America, 38 per cent in Europe and 16 per cent in Asia. Representative offices are more scattered, with 22 per cent in America, 22 per cent in Asia, 14 per cent in Central and South America, 13 per cent in Europe, 12 per cent in Oceania, 12 per cent in the Middle and Near East and 3 per cent in Africa. The distribution in terms of staff is similar to the above. Thirty per cent of local banks are in Europe, 30 per cent in Asia, 17 per cent in North America, 11 per cent in Central and South America, 4 per cent in the Middle and Near East and 4 per cent in Oceania. The distribution of Japanese staff, however, is very different — 55 per cent in North America, 20 per cent in Europe and 14 per cent in Asia. This indicates that local banks in North America are considerably larger than those in other countries.

The geographical distribution of overseas branches, representative offices and local banks differ considerably from each other and, as will be discussed later, they have different but complementary functions in advancing the internationalisation of Japanese banks. The local distribution of Japanese staff through these three kinds of overseas bases is very uneven. Table 7.5 (final column) shows that North America, Europe and Asia have over 90 per cent of the overseas employment of Japanese banks with

Table 7.5: Geographical Distribution of Overseas Branches, Representative Offices, Local Banks and Japanese Staff

	Branches			Representative Offices			Local Banks			Total
	Branches	Japanese Employees	Employees of Local Nationality	Representative Offices	Japanese Employees	Employees of Local Nationality	Local Banks	Japanese Employees	Employees of Local Nationality	Total Japanese Employees
North America	36%	43%	25%	22%	19%	13%	17%	55%	39%	43%
Central and South America	3	2	7	14	15	16	11	9	51	5
Europe	33	38	27	13	14	10	32	20	3	31
Middle and Near East	0	0	0	12	11	9	4	1	0	2
Asia	25	16	40	22	24	37	29	14	6	17
Oceania	0	0	0	12	13	7	4	1	0	2
Africa	0	0	0	3	2	6	0	0	0	0
Others	0	0	0	0	0	0	4	0	0	0
Total	100	100	100	100	100	100	100	100	100	100

Figure 7.2 Geographical Composition of Overseas Bases

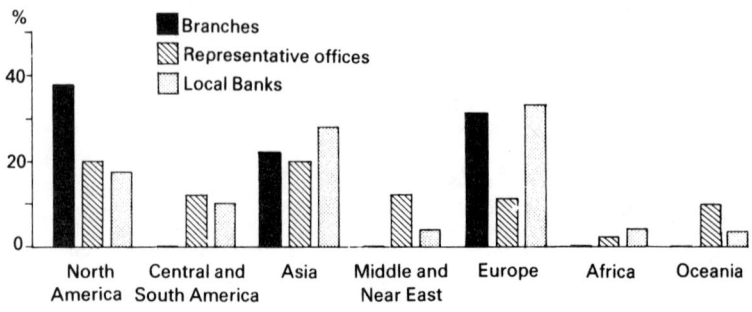

Figure 7.3 Geographical Distribution of Overseas Bases of Banks, Trade and Direct Investment

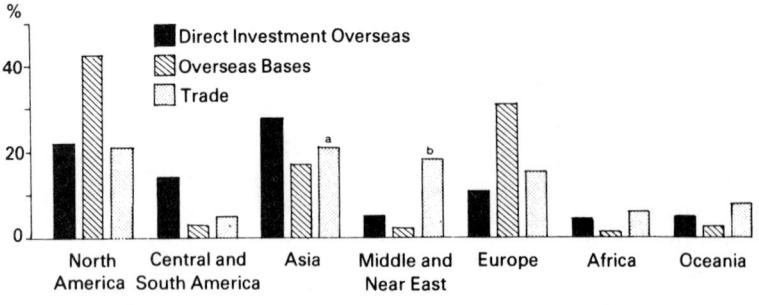

a. Southeast Asia
b. West Asia

only small percentages being in Central and South America (5 per cent), Oceania (2 per cent) and the Middle and Near East (2 per cent).

Figure 7.3 shows the relationship of the geographical distribution of overseas bases of banks, trade, and direct investment overseas. According to Figure 7.3, the spatial distinction of bank bases is quite different from the other two. In North America and Europe bank bases are over-represented in comparison with trade and direct investment, while in the Middle and Near East and other areas the reverse is the case. This may mean that even if the internationalisation of Japanese banks began in response to the internationalisation of their customers, banks' internationalisation has now taken a different direction. North America and Europe, in particular New York and London, are the two major international finance markets in which almost all fund-raising and a lot of loan accommodation is conducted. It is interesting to note that the geographical distribution of representative offices, whose main function is collecting information rather than conducting fund-raising and loans accommodation, is similar to figures for trade and direct investment overseas. It should be noted, however, that the present pattern of geographical distribution of bases reflects the decisions of banks within the framework of regulations and guidelines issued by authorities in Japan and overseas. It is quite likely that the present distribution may change with the progress of internationalisation. Our research shows that all Japanese banks want to establish new branches in the near future in North America, half of the banks want to establish branches in Europe and Asia, and a few want to establish branches in Central and South America, and the Middle and Near East. It seems, therefore, that North America will continue to be the most important area, with Asia, the Middle and Near East, and Central and South America gaining in importance, and Europe possibly becoming less important in this regard. This would mean that the distribution of branches would more closely parallel the distribution of trade and overseas direct investment.

These conclusions are based only on predictions of the future distribution of branches of Japanese banks which are already inter-nationalised, or in the process of internationalising. They do not take into account other banks, especially large regional banks and mutual loan and savings banks, which may establish overseas branches in the future. If they want to establish branches in the international finance markets, particularly in New York and London, the future distribution of branches of Japanese banks will not change as much as indicated earlier.[6] Our research suggests that the establishing of new representative offices will not differ greatly from the present pattern. This would reflect the fact that the function of these offices is not to conduct financial business themselves, but to collect local information on the region in which they are established.

When establishing local banks, Japanese banks must consider the advantages and disadvantages involved. For example, Japanese banks are not permitted to engage in securities business both domestically and overseas, so it is necessary to establish local banks abroad to carry out this business. Similarly, regulations prevent the establishing of new branches of foreign banks in

Australia, so foreign banks are compelled to establish non-bank financial companies (merchant banks, finance companies) instead. Whether they are established because of a purely economic decision or because it is the only alternative, the functions of local banks and overseas branches are complementary and valuable in helping banks meet the diverse needs of their customers under a variety of regulations and economic conditions. Therefore, provided there is no radical change in the present regulations governing the establishing of branches and local banks in various countries, or in general economic and financial conditions, there will be little change in the distribution of local banks.

The Operation of International Banking

There have been several phases in the process of the internationalisation of Japanese banking. Table 7.6 defines the content of each phase in terms of the internationalisation of customer companies, international banking operations, methods of internationalisation and the customers of the international operation.

In the first phase, the initial step is internationalisation of customers. Here, the customers are mainly engaged in import and export dealings with foreign companies, so the most important aspects of international banking are foreign exchange operations connected with foreign trade. Capital transactions with customers are limited to short-term finance (trade finance). In this phase, the main method of internationalisation is to enter into correspondence contracts with foreign banks. In the second phase, as direct investment overseas increases, banks raise the level of loans to Japanese-affiliated companies compared with foreign exchange business. Medium- and long-term capital transactions increase correspondingly. Banks aim to internationalise their business by building up a network of overseas branches and representative offices. In the third phase, the multinationalisation of big business develops, and foreign as well as Japanese companies become bank customers. International business extends to non-banking fringe activities, such as merchant banking and leasing, through the strengthening of branches and offices, capital participation, business affiliations and the establishing of non-bank fringe business firms. Banks seek the most profitable ways of fund-raising and lending. In the fourth phase, retail banking is conducted while at

Table 7.6: Phases of Internationalisation of Banking

Phases	1st Phase (National banking)	2nd Phase (International banking)	3rd Phase (in a broader sense)	
			3rd Phase (international full-service banking)	4th Phase (world full-service banking)
Internationalisation of customer companies	Export-import	Active direct overseas investment	Multinational corporation	
International operations in banking	Mainly foreign exchange operations connected with foreign trade. Capital transactions are mainly short-term ones.	Overseas loans and investments become important and medium- and longer-run capital transactions become important.	Non banking fringe activities such as merchant banking, leasing, consulting, and others are conducted.	
			No retail banking	Retail banking is done
Methods of internationalisation	Correspondence contracts with foreign bank	To strengthen own overseas branches offices	By strengthening of own branches and offices, capital participation, affiliation in business, establishing non-bank fringe business firms, the most profitable ways of fund-raising and lending are sought on a global basis	
Customers of international operations	Mainly domestic customers	Mainly domestic customers	Customers are of various nationalities	

Source: Mitsubishi Bank, *Chosa*, September 1974.

the same time the content of international operations and the methods of internationalisation advance and become more complex. The aspect of the fourth phase which distinguishes it from the third phase is the declining importance of the exploitation of new businesses and methods, and the concentration instead on deepening and strengthening the activities begun in the third phase. This change can be seen in the increasing ratio of international business to all banking business.

Our research shows that in 1977/78 four banks were in the fourth phase, seven in the third, and three in the second — in other words, it seems that, on average, banks have reached the third phase of internationalisation. This result is fairly consistent with the results of investigations into international banking business, as examined later in this section. Our research also confirms that the internationalisation of Japanese banking advanced slowly prior to the 1970s and rapidly in the first half of the 1970s, before slowing down again in the late 1970s.

What is the attraction, from the banks' viewpoint, of international business as compared with domestic business? The present study indicates that the major attractions are (1) diversification of banking business and customers; (2) high profitability; (3) high potential for growth; and (4) the existence of a large, flexible and free international finance market. Points (1) and (3) are consistent with the short-term objective of enlarging the number of customers, while points (2) and (4) are consistent with banks' proceeding to internationalise in order to attain high profitability in the free international market as opposed to the sluggish domestic financial market and the existence of various controls on domestic banking business. It should be noted, however, that risks which are absent in domestic business, such as exchange risk, country risk and availability risk, are present in international banking business. In addition, competition is much more severe in the free international market, and there are no control or safeguard institutions.

As mentioned previously, Japanese banks have branches in various countries to carry out their international business. We shall now examine the relative importance of banking business at the New York, London and 'others' branches (Table 7.7).

At the New York branch, trade finance is most important (9 of 12 banks), with loans to Japanese-affiliated companies taking second place. Fund-raising is a less important activity. At the

Table 7.7: The Order of Business in Each Branch

New York branch	(1) Trade finance, (2) Loans to Japanese-affiliated companies, (3) Fund-raising, (4) Loans to other companies, (5) Fringe business.
London branch	(1) Fund-raising, (2) Trade finance, loans to other companies, (3) Loans to Japanese-affiliated companies, (4) Fringe business.
Other branches	(1) Trade finance, (2) Loans to Japanese-affiliated companies, (3) Fund raising, (4) Loans to other companies, (5) Fringe business.

London branch, fund-raising is by far the most important activity (all banks), with trade finance and loans to non-Japanese companies being next in importance, and loans to Japanese-affiliated companies being last. It should be noted that four of the 12 banks listed loans to non-Japanese companies (i.e. not to Japanese-affiliated companies) as the second most important activity at the London branch. This suggests that some Japanese banks have already developed various kinds of international banking operations in the international finance market. At the other branches, the ranking of activities is similar to that of the New York branch, with trading finance being the most important, followed by loans to Japanese-affiliated companies, fund-raising and loans to non-Japanese companies. Typically, then, the relationship between the international operations at the various branches is that banks raise funds at London branches and make use of the funds for trading finance, loans to Japanese-affiliated companies and non-Japanese companies through New York and other branches.

Table 7.8 shows the geographical distribution of fund-raising for overseas operations. Almost all funds for overseas operations are raised by overseas branches, with very few being supplied by the head office. Japanese banks raise 51 per cent of funds in Europe, 35 per cent in America, 9 per cent in other regions and 6 per cent through head offices. This is consistent with the description of London branch activities given above.

Table 7.9 shows the maturity structure of the raised funds. About 80 per cent of all funds are short-term (within 12 months), with 20 per cent being long-term. In the case of upper-rank banks, the latter figure is less than 10 per cent. Table 7.10 shows the ratio of assets and liabilities in foreign currency to all foreign assets and liabilities. The ratio of short-term liability in foreign currencies in

Table 7.8: Sources of Funds for Overseas Operations

	Head Office	Overseas				Grand Total
		North America	Europe	Other	Total	
Total	5.85%	35.02%	50.55%	8.75%	94.15%	100%
Upper-rank group	8.20	29.60	53.93	8.26	91.80	100
Middle and lower group	5.00	37.52	46.31	11.16	95.00	100
Long-term group	3.00	41.08	50.75	4.83	96.67	100

Source: Bank of Japan; Tokoei Nenpo, MOF; Kokusai Kinyu Nenpo.

Table 7.9: Maturity Structure of Raised Funds and Loans

	Maturity Structure of Raised Funds		Maturity Structure of Loans	
	Short-term	Long-term	Short-term	Long-term
Whole	77.7%	22.3%	47.4%	52.7%
Upper-rank group	90.0	10.0	51.0	49.0
Middle and lower group	73.0	27.0	57.8	42.3
Long-term group	65.0	35.0	21.7	78.3

Source: Bank of Japan; Tokoei Nenpo, MOF; Kokusai Kinyu Nenpo.

Table 7.10: Percentage of Foreign Assets and Liabilities in Foreign Currency

	Short-term Assets	Long-term Loans[a]	Short-term Liabilities
1973	98.4%	100.0%	91.3%
1974	94.4	99.2	96.4
1975	93.2	98.1	95.8
1976	92.3	96.0	93.3
1977	91.3	92.6	94.1
1978	89.6	80.0	78.5

Note: a. Long-term loan figures are for the end of the fiscal year, while the other figures are for the end of the calendar year.
Source: Bank of Japan; Tokoei Nenpo, MOF; Kokusai Kinyu Nenpo.

1978 was 90 per cent. Fund-raising for overseas operations can be characterised as being predominantly foreign currency raised in Europe and North America, and the funds are mainly short-term.

Turning to the use of funds for international business, the main banking business relates to dealing in foreign exchange, trading finance, loans to non-residents and merchant banking. Foreign exchange dealing is growing steadily with the growth of the Japanese economy and foreign trade. As the stability and certainty of these dealings is very high, it constitutes the fundamental operation of international banking business. However, its relative importance has been decreasing due to the rapid increase in loans activity. The ratio of the trade bill in foreign assets of all banks was about 80 per cent in September 1970. This fell to about 35 per cent by September 1978 reflecting the growing importance of loans to non-residents.

Table 7.11 shows the distribution of loans among developed, developing and socialist countries. The developed countries' share is 51 per cent, that of developing countries is 42 per cent and socialist countries 7 per cent. It should be noted that the combined total of loans to developing and socialist countries is approximately half of all loans. The present study suggests that four out of ten banks want to increase the volume and share of loans to developing countries, and three want to increase the volume without changing the share. It can be said, therefore, that Japanese banks generally have a positive attitude towards exending loans to developing countries, despite the greater risk that may often be associated with such loans. These risks are both individual (the customer may have difficulty in repaying the loan) and country (due to political or economic instability) risks. It is interesting to

Table 7.11: Destination of Loans

	Advanced Countries	Developing Countries	Socialist Countries	Japanese-affiliated	Other Companies
Total	52.41%	39.58%	6.67%	44.59%	55.41%
Upper-rank group	60.25	36.00	3.75	44.25	55.75
Middle and lower rank group	48.60	42.40	9.00	47.70	52.30
Long-term group	48.33	45.00	6.67	37.50	62.50

note that banks which lend about 50 per cent of their loan funds to developing countries do not, according to our research, wish to increase the share of developing countries. This presumably reflects the associated risks.

Table 7.11 also shows that the shares of loans to Japanese affiliated companies and to non-Japanese companies are 45 per cent and 55 per cent, respectively. This confirms that the internationalisation of Japanese banks has already reached the third phase. While almost all Japanese banks place considerable importance on existing relations with Japanese customers when accommodating loans to Japanese-affiliated companies overseas, they do not always insist on an existing record of domestic transactions in Japan before granting loans to such affiliates. Therefore, Japanese banks aim to acquire new customers through internationalisation as well as maintain existing ones.

The percentages of short-term and long-term loans are 47 per cent and 53 per cent. Table 7.9 indicates that Japanese banks carry out 'maturity transformations', that is, short-term borrowing and long-term lending. The present survey suggests that Japanese banks accept this transaction as one of the functions of banks but remain rather wary of it. It should be noted that this maturity structure relates only to loans, and not to all assets. Complete data were not available, but the maturity structure of all assets and liabilities of the Japanese branches in London could be ascertained. According to the Bank of England, long-term assets and long-term liabilities as a percentage of all assets and liabilities in 1978 were about 15 per cent and 27 per cent, respectively. We may therefore conclude that Japanese banks carry out a moderate number of maturity transformations.

It was impossible to discover the proportion of loans to non-residents in foreign currency to total loans to non-residents. However, as Table 7.10 indicates, 80 per cent of all long-term loans to non-residents are in foreign currency, and about 90 per cent of all short-term assets are in foreign currency. It is therefore reasonable to assume that the proportion of both short- and long-term loans to non-residents in foreign currency to all loans to non-residents is over 80 per cent.

All banks are interested not only in trade finance and loans to non-residents but also in other related business, such as merchant banking, securities business, leasing, credit cards and so on. Among these, securities business and merchant banking are particularly important. Almost all banks express a strong interest in securities business, due not only to its inherent attractiveness, but also to a disadvantage (namely, Japanese financial law which prevents Japanese banks from carrying out securities business other than by owing affiliated local banks) which Japanese banks have in comparison with other banks in internationalising their business. In addition, as complicated business, such as syndicated loans and project finance, becomes more important, so too do the knowledge and know-how of merchant banking. Japanese banks want not only to provide funds for syndicated loans, but also to initiate, arrange and manage loans projects.

We now turn to some issues related to international banking business. As mentioned previously, the Eurodollar market is very important to international banking, especially for fund-raising. It is sometimes asserted that the market should be controlled by an authorised body, whose function would be to ensure stability. This reflects the fact that the Eurodollar market has no lender of last resort, and at times the market faces the risk of a collapse of confidence. Almost all banks, however, are against this idea, believing that the main advantage of the Eurodollar market is its freedom from control by monetary authorities, which promotes the rapid development of the market. Some banks, however, think that some international institution, or the monetary authorities of each country, should regulate and control banks so that an orderly market can be maintained if credit crises occur.

In relation to exchange rates, the adjustable peg system was changed to the managed float system in 1972 with the demise of the Bretton Woods agreement. Did the change affect the internationalisation of banking? Our research indicates that all Japanese banks either think the managed float system is preferable, or feel that the systems do not differ greatly. Many banks believe that the managed float system helps avoid drastic changes in exchange rates and helps establish stable exchange rates in accordance with market conditions. Two-thirds of banks believe that, under some circumstances, it is not necessary to maintain a 'square' exchange position, while one-third believe it is essential that it be maintained. It seems, therefore, that there is some flexibility in banks' attitude toward the exchange position.

To summarise the typical features of Japanese international banking which have been discussed so far.

(1) Almost all funds for overseas operations are in foreign currencies, and are raised in Europe (especially London) and North America. Funds are mostly short-term.

(2) Trading finance used to be overwhelmingly important in the accommodation of credit but, as Japanese companies and banks internationalise, loans to non-residents are becoming increasingly important.

(3) Japanese banks make about 50 per cent of their loans to developed countries, 40 per cent to developing countries and 10 per cent to socialist countries. Although some banks have reservations due to the associated risks, on the whole banks have a positive attitude towards developing countries.

(4) Loans to non-Japanese companies slightly outweigh those to Japanese-affiliated companies. Although, in principle, Japanese banks consider domestic transactions more important, they also want to acquire new customers through internationalisation.

(5) The ratio of long-term loans in the maturity structure is about 50 per cent. Japanese banks engage in maturity transformations, that is, short-term borrowing and long-term lending, and almost all the foreign assets of banks are in foreign currency. Japanese banks also conduct their international business by using foreign currencies.

(6) Japanese banks are interested in fringe business, such as securities business and merchant banking, as well as in banking itself.

(7) Japanese banks establish overseas bases in order to conduct various international business. Europe, especially the London branch, is the centre of fund-raising business, with New York and other branches conducting mainly trading finance and loans operations.

(8) From the features listed above, we can estimate that in the late 1970s, Japanese banking had reached the third phase of internationalisation.

(9) A description of the activities of a typical Japanese international operation would be that short-term funds in foreign currency are raised through the London branches, while credit in the form of short-term trading finance and long-term loans in foreign currency to non-Japanese as well as Japanese affiliate companies are accommodated through the other branches.

The Performance of Internationalisation

In this section, we examine the performance of internationalisation in Japanese banking. Figure 7.4 shows the actual proportion of total bank profits which comes from international business. Five banks give a figure of 11 to 15 per cent, three banks 0 to 10 per cent, one bank 16 to 20 per cent and one bank above 51 per cent. On average, the proportion seems to be 10 to 15 per cent. This figure is about equal to the proportion of staff in the international section to total bank staff. Comparing this actual figure with the feasible targets for profits shown in Figure 7.4, the feasible target exceeds the current figure by 5-10 per cent. The difference between the actual and feasible value of upper-rank banks is higher than that for middle and lower-rank banks (10 per cent as opposed to 5 per cent). This may suggest that the upper-rank banks are more willing to internationalise.

As discussed in the previous section, Japanese banks are

Figure 7.4 Comparison of Target and Actual Profits of International Sections

	0-10%	11-15%	16-20%	21-25%	26-30%	31-40%	41-50%	51%-
Upper Rank Group								
(1)		■		●				
(2)		■		●				
(3)								
(4)		■			●			
(5)				●				
Middle and Lower Rank Group								
(6)		■	●					
(7)	■	●						
(8)			■		●			
(9)								
(10)								■ ●
(11)	■	●						
Long-term Group								
(12)	■	●						
(13)		■	●					
(14)			●					
Total ●	0	3	3	3	2	0	0	1
Total ■	(3)	(5)	(1)	(0)	(0)	(0)	(0)	(1)

● Target for the proportion of profits from international business to all profits.
■ Actual proportion of profits from international business to all profits.

currently in the third phase of internationalisation. This can be compared with the position of other advanced countries' foreign banks. The proportion of profits from the international section to all profits of ten major American banks was 50.9 per cent in 1979 and 45.7 per cent in 1978. The figures for Citicorp were 82.2 per cent and 71.8 per cent, respectively. The figures for 1977 for three representative British banks (Barclays, National Westminster and Lloyds) were 38 per cent, 30 per cent and 22 per cent, respectively. Those for the Deutsche, Dresdner and Commerz banks in West Germany were 35 per cent, 30 per cent and 33 per cent, respectively in 1977. It will be noted that, with one exception, the figure for Japanese banks is considerably lower than that for these banks.

The present survey shows that almost all Japanese banks are aware of their relatively less-developed degree of internationalisation. The main ways in which Japanese banks regard themselves as less developed are in their networks of overseas bases, their ability to collect information and accumulate 'know-how', their ability to raise funds, to diversify international business (such as securities business), to localise banking business and to employ sufficient competent staff.

However, too much emphasis should not be given to the less-developed nature of internationalisation of Japanese banks because, if the degree of development is measured in terms of the number of branches or the volume of loans, rather than the ratio of international to total profits, Japanese banks are not much less advanced than other banks, with the exception of the major American banks. Table 7.12 shows the number of overseas bases that banks from various countries have in New York, London, West Germany and Japan. As a whole, Japanese banks are second only to American banks in number of overseas branches. Table 7.13 lists the 50 banks which fall into the category of 'lead managers', in terms of international syndicated loans and the issue of bonds in the international finance market. Column I of the table shows the syndicated loans, and Column II shows syndicated loans together with the issue of bonds. In Column I, it can be seen that Japanese banks as a whole rank higher than British and West German banks, and individual Japanese banks are not far inferior to European and Canadian banks, though they are considerably below the American ones. In Column II, on the other hand, West German banks rank higher, and Japan follows the USA, West

Table 7.12: Foreign Banks in Major Markets

1 Foreign Banks in Japan

	Banks	Branches	Representative Offices
USA	22	32	13
UK	7	9	10
France	6	7	8
West Germany	5	5	5
Singapore	4	4	0
Korea	3	4	7
Switzerland	3	3	4
Others	11	17	42
Total	61	81	89

2 Foreign Banks in West Germany

	Banks	Branches	Representative Offices	Local Banks
USA	13	27	14	5
Japan	10	12	8	2
France	4	16	5	0
UK	4	11	7	0
Others	21	27	90	2
Total	52	93	124	9

3 Foreign Banks in New York

	Banks	Branches	Agencies	Representative Offices	Local Banks
Japan	24	16	6	2	4
Italy	14	6	0	8	1
West Germany	11	9	0	2	0
France	11	6	0	4	4
Spain	11	0	8	3	0
UK	9	6	2	1	4
Canada	8	0	6	0	5
Others	73	16	30	9	8
Total	161	59	52	29	26

Continued on p. 218

Table 7.12 continued

---

4 Foreign Banks in London

	Banks	Branches	Representative Offices	Local Banks
USA	65	41	22	14
Japan	23	22	1	1
Italy	18	4	14	0
France	15	6	6	3
Spain	14	6	6	2
Switzerland	11	9	1	1
Australia	11	9	2	0
West Germany	10	8	2	0
Others	101	62	38	3
Total	268	167	92	24

Source: Kinyu Mondai Kenkyu Kai (1979).

Table 7.13: Achievements of Leading Managers in Terms of Country with Syndicated Loans and Issue of Securities, 1978

	Order 1-10		Order 11-25		Order 26-50		Order 1-50		Share of Achievements of Leading Managers	
	Iᵃ	IIᵇ	Iᵃ	IIᵇ	Iᵃ	IIᵇ	Iᵃ	IIᵇ	Iᵃ	IIᵇ
USA	6	5	1	3	4	4	11	12	42.7	38.6
Canada	1	1	4	3	2	3	7	7	14.9	12.4
Japan	1	0	3	4(3)ᶜ	3	4(3)ᶜ	7	8(6)ᶜ	10.9	11.2(9.1)ᶜ
West Germany	1	2	2	1	2	1	5	4	8.3	12.6
UK	1	1	1	1	3	3	5	5	8.7	7.9
France					4	4	4	4	3.5	3.7
Netherlands			1	1	1	1	2	2	2.1	2.5
Switzerland			1	1	1	1	1	2	2.1	3.4
Belgium					1	1	1	1	0.5	0.7
Consortium		1	2	1	5	3	7	5	6.2	6.9
Total	10	10	15	15	25	25	50	50	100	100

Notes:

a. Achievements of leading managers with syndicated loans.
b. Achievements of leading managers with syndicated loans and issue of securities.
c. The figure in brackets means figure of banks except securities companies.

Source: Kinyu Mondai Kenkyu Kai (1979).

Germany and Canada, with a figure of 10.9 per cent. This figure takes account of the activities of Japanese securities companies, however. If these are excluded, the figure for the six Japanese banks falls to 9.1 per cent; while West Germany's 12.4 per cent is achieved by only four banks. This relative rise of West German banks and fall of Japanese banks compared with that of foreign banks may be described as follows.

(1) In terms of the degree of internationalisation measured by the proportion of total profits obtained from international dealings, Japanese banks are considerably less developed than major American banks and other advanced countries' banks.

(2) Japanese banks are less developed than major American banks, in general and individually, in all the areas described above — number of branches, volume of loans, and proportion of total profits obtained from international profits.

(3) In comparison with West German and other advanced banks, Japanese banks, both individually and as a whole, are not as inferior in terms of loans activities and number of branches. However, because Japanese banks cannot conduct securities business, they are not competing with West German banks in this area. This may be a reflection of the less-developed degree of internationalisation in Japanese banking.

Difficulties and Limitations in the Internationalisation of Japanese Banking

This chapter has examined the internationalisation of Japanese banking, especially with regard to city banks, long-term credit banks and a specialised foreign exchange bank, in terms of aims and motives, the establishing of overseas bases, overseas banking business and the performance of internationalisation. It has been clear that the level of internationalisation of Japanese banking is lower than that of American and European banks. In this section, we shall examine the difficulties and limitations in the process of internationalisation, and discuss some of the problems in promoting it further.

There are two types of limitation in the process of internationalisation of banking — internal and external. Internal limitations are basically management problems while external limitations arise from general economic conditions and various regulations imposed on banks. The main internal limitations as perceived by the banks are, in order of priority, the shortage of staff competent to carry out internationalisation, the inability to collect adequate information and know-how, and the lack of an adequate system of operations for internationalised banking business.

The shortage of competent staff causes bankers greatest concern. As internationalisation progresses, the content of the international banking operation becomes more complicated, moving from mainly foreign exchange and trade finance business to loans to non-residents and to syndicated loans business. For example, in any project involving the development of resources, finance is extremely important, and banks must play an important role. This extends from the funding of the project through to playing a role in its formation, promotion and programming, as well as supervising its progress. It is thus necessary for banks to have staff competent in the fields of economics, finance, tax, law, information collection, research and investigation, and business administration. Many banks feel that acquiring staff with expertise in these areas is a matter of urgency.

As is generally known, a system of lifetime employment prevails in Japan. It is thus quite difficult for banks to acquire competent staff from outside, with the exception of some senior staff from monetary authorities. Consequently, it is unavoidable for most banks to train their own staff by sponsoring their study at overseas universities, training them in overseas banks or providing in-house training. It takes considerable time, therefore, for a bank to acquire staff with a high level of expertise in international banking. Although this may put Japanese banks at a disadvantage in terms of promoting rapid internationalisation, it is possibly to their long-term advantage because the trained staff are likely to remain with the bank and contribute to its international activities over many years.

Information and know-how on international business are extremely important in terms of the development of international banking operations and in assessing and avoiding associated risks. The perceived lack of such knowledge within their operations is causing banks concern. As mentioned earlier, Japanese banks make use of foreign currency in their international operations. This gives rise, *inter alia*, to exchange risk and availability risk. In addition, with the increase of non-Japanese firms (including foreign governments) as customers, the rising volume of loans to developing countries and the increase of long-term and large-scale loans to resource developers, it has become increasingly necessary for banks to collect information and analyse both the individual risk associated with the business and the risk of the country concerned. It is therefore necessary for banks to have a current, comprehensive collection of information on the politics and economy of different countries as well as on the individual customers. It may be necessary to organise small research groups to study country risk objectively, separately from the private banks. In any event, prediction of the future is a most difficult problem, and is seen as one of the main current limitations on the future development of internationalisation.

The third internal limitation perceived by banks was the lack of an adequate system of operation for internationalised banking business. Japanese banks intend to overcome this problem through localisation of the banking operation — that is, by ensuring that their international operations conform with the culture, national character, economic practices and laws of each country, and by providing clear-cut definitions and the assignment of broad powers to the local staff in charge.

There are also three external limitations on the internationalisation of banking, revealed in the present study. These are general world economic conditions (which are reflected in the economic growth rate, price level, exchange rate, interest rate and so on of individual countries and the international market), the Japanese economic situation (which is reflected in the position of the Japanese economy in the world economy), and the regulations and administrative guidelines from Japanese and overseas authorities on international banking operations.

In the 1970s when the internationalisation of Japanese banking was increasing rapidly, the world economic situation was not as good as it had been in the 1960s. It was characterised by turbulence in the international monetary system, the introduction of the floating exchange rate system, the oil crisis and sky-rocketing oil prices, unrest in the financial system due to the bankruptcy of the Herstatt Bank, high interest rates and the coexistence of high inflation rates and increased unemployment. The general economic situation had effects on both developed and developing countries, especially the latter, with countries like North Korea, Turkey and Peru having difficulties with debt repayment. The prospect for the 1980s is not particularly optimistic, which may be disadvantageous for the internationalisation of finance activities, with economic depression making it more difficult to measure country risk.

Japan was no exception in experiencing the difficulties of the world economy. The oil crisis at the end of 1973 and the failure of economic management caused the Japanese economy to get into difficulties, experiencing negative economic growth and sky-rocketing prices. However, the Japanese economy fared reasonably well in the 1970s, compared with other developed countries, with her ranking based on GNP, trade and capital exports rising. As mentioned earlier, the internationalisation of Japanese banking was promoted by the internationalisation of the Japanese economy. However, it is not certain whether this pattern can continue in the 1980s. The growth of the Japanese economy in the midst of the stagnation of the world economy, which formed the background for the internationalisation of Japanese banking, depended on overseas rather than domestic demand. For this reason, it is said that Japan's pattern of economic growth and the so-called 'closed market' have produced considerable friction between Japan and other developed countries. If the Japanese economy must in future depend much more on the domestic market and less on overseas markets, the incentive for internationalisation of Japanese banking from the economy will weaken. However, it may be that the problem of friction over trading issues will be settled through the increase of overseas investment, and that the incentive will continue to work. Even so, it will be necessary for Japanese banks to find ways of diversifying their business with non-Japanese firms in order to develop their internationalisation.

Besides the economic conditions surrounding Japanese banks, financial conditions, especially the internationalisation of the yen, are very important in considering the internationalisation of Japanese banking. One of the features of the internationalisation is that Japanese banks have promoted it through the use of foreign currency, without any significant internationalisation of the yen. This places Japan at a disadvantage compared with American banks, in that the latter can use its domestic currency as international currency, which is not possible for Japan. According to the results of a survey reported here, almost all bankers think the internationalisation of the yen, and thus the internationalisation of the money and capital market, is extremely important as it will enable them to enjoy the same advantages (easiness, stability and efficiency in the use and raising of funds) as the American banks. It should be noted, however, that some banks (for example the specialised foreign exchange banks) have attained a similar level of internationalisation as American banks without the internationalisation of the yen, demonstrating that it cannot be regarded as a prerequisite for the internationalisation of Japanese banking. In addition, it would be simplistic to discuss the internationalisation of the yen solely in terms of the internationalisation of Japanese banking, as the former would have widespread effects on the balance of payments, monetary conditions and the financial markets, and the management of monetary policy in Japan. Viewed in this light, it is possible to understand the argument of some banks that the internationalisation of the yen is a different problem from the internationalisation of banking. However, in general terms, it seems that, for the reasons mentioned above, the former does promote the latter.

The third external limitation on internationalisation is the various regulations and guidelines imposed on Japanese banks. Almost all banks think that regulations on foreign exchange operations, the establishing of overseas bases and other international banking operations constitute a significant limitation. In particular, many banks are greatly concerned at the regulation of the establishing of overseas bases, because this is the way they have pursued their internationalisation.

The present study shows that almost all banks (11 banks) agree that the present licensing policy of the Japanese monetary authorities regarding the establishing of new overseas branches (the so-called 'one new branch every three years' licence) should be liberalised. One bank regards the present policy as good, while another thinks it should be strengthened because of the undue competition between Japanese banks, which was reflected in the Japan rate in the Eurodollar market in 1974, and the low-interest lending rates in the American market in the late 1970s. It is natural that some banks are concerned about the market disorder brought about by such behaviour, and this illustrates one of the features of Japanese banks' behaviour — *yogonarabi ishiki*, worrying about comparison with other banks. However, even if such undue competition does exist, it is by no means certain that the cost of competition exceeds the benefit, or that strengthening controls on

establishing branches would solve the problem. One of the important factors for the development of the international finance market
is that it is a 'free' market, regulated not by controls, but by
rational and prudent management on the part of the banks themselves.

The second aspect of the regulation of the internationalisation
process is exchange control. Control of foreign exchange was
liberalised during the 1960s and 1970s. However, this liberalisation was not based on the amendment of the foreign exchange
law, whose spirit is 'the prohibition of dealing in foreign exchange
in principle', but on the liberalisation of the application of the law
by the monetary authorities. It was thus only a partial liberalisation. From the banks' viewpoint, internationalisation based on
their own long-term aims has been hindered by regulations on, for
example, the exchange position, long-term non-resident loans and
the taking in of private, untied loans. Many banks are particularly
concerned about the control of the exchange position (the difference between foreign assets and foreign debts). The aim of this
control is to check speculation in foreign exchange, and to regulate
the flow of funds in yen and foreign currencies. Initially, the
authorities demanded that the exchange position be in equilibrium.
Then, with the liberalisation of foreign exchange, a limited over-
selling was permitted. These regulations prevented Japanese banks
from becoming more international. In December 1979, however,
the foreign exchange law was revised, leading to 'free foreign
exchange dealing in principle'. Although regulation of the
exchange position remains in the amended law, it permits banks to
take in united loans and liberalises long-term loans to non-
residents. This makes it possible, therefore, further to promote
international banking operations through its effects on the internationalisation of the yen and of the money and capital markets
(Hiroo Fukui, 1980; Kaname Seki, 1981).

A further regulatory constraint on Japanese international
banking relates to securities. The present laws prohibit bankers
from issuing or accepting securities, and this principle is also
applied to overseas banking.[7] Japanese banks cannot do business
except through local finance companies, even if the monetary
authorities in the foreign country are willing to permit it. As a
result of this guideline, Japanese banks are at a disadvantage
compared with other foreign banks, which can issue both deben-
tures and syndicated loans, and usually offer customers a choice.

The reason for this guideline is the separation of securities dealing and banking. The application of the domestic finance system to the overseas market results in a conflict with standard international banking procedures. The fact that maintenance of the domestic financial order has taken precedence over the development of international banking is a source of concern to bankers.

Conclusions

The main points of this paper can be summarised as follows:

(1) The internationalisation of Japanese banking has developed primarily due to the development and internationalisation of the Japanese economy itself, although there are some aspects in which the banks have taken the initiative.

(2) A feature of the internationalisation of Japanese banking is that it has not been accompanied by internationalisation of the yen or the money and capital market.

(3) The internationalisation of Japanese banks has been based on the establishment of overseas branches, representative offices and local banks. Generally, they raise funds in foreign currencies though the international market (especially London branches) and lend funds to Japanese and non-Japanese firms overseas through other branches, especially in New York.

(4) The present phase of the internationalisation of Japanese banking is the third phase, in which banks enlarge the number of their customers to include both Japanese and non-Japanese firms, and to diversify their business to include merchant banking, and so on. By strengthening their branches and representative offices, they seek to globalise their profits by improving and extending capital participation, business affiliations, fund-raising, and so on. The ratio of international business to total banking business for Japanese banks is considerably lower than that for major American and European banks, although the size of the international business carried out by Japanese and major European banks is similar.

(5) There have been and will continue to be some limitations and problems facing the development of the internationalisation of Japanese banking. Some of these are listed below. First, it will

be necessary to train competent staff and establish an operational system to cope with increasingly diverse and complex international business. Secondly, the economic circumstances which fostered the development of the internationalisation of Japanese banking will change, providing a bleaker environment with the prospect of problems such as friction over trade issues and increasing protectionism. Thirdly, despite the liberalising of previous controls on international banking which should stimulate the internationalisation of the yen, the Japanese money and capital market and, consequently, Japanese banking, problems may arise as banks have to practise self-regulation. Fourthly, despite liberalisation, there are still some areas (such as securities business) in which the domestic finance system takes precedence over standard international banking practice.

In summary, Japanese banks will face intense competition in international banking business in an economic environment which is at the same time more harsh and more liberal. In order to survive in these conditions, Japanese banks will need to be self-reliant which, in turn, depends upon their ability to acquire competent staff and establish an effective system of international operations.

Notes

1. Main members of the teams besides ourselves included; Professor Y. Noritake (Kobe University), Professor R. Mikitani (Kobe University), Professor N. Miyata (Kagawa University), and Associate Professor N. Niwa (Toyama University).
2. The following banks cooperated in our research: City banks — Dai-ichi Kangyo, Daiwa, Fuji, Hokkaido Takushoku, Mitsubishi, Mitsui, Sanwa, Sumitomo, Taiyo Kobe, Tokai. Long-term credit banks — Nihon Choki Shinyo, Nihon Kogyo, Nihon Saiken Shinyo. Specialised foreign exchange bank — Bank of Tokyo. Regional bank — Hokuriku. We would like to express our appreciation for their cooperation.
3. Critically important for this research has been the report of the Financial Research Group (Kinyu Mondai Kenkyu kai) 'kokusaika ni tomonau wagakuni no kinyukikan no arikata' (Japan, Ministry of Finance, 1979). We have made use of the data attached to this report.
4. The grouping of banks is as follows — upper-rank group (Dai-ichi, Fuji, Mitsubishi, Sanwa, Sumitomo); middle and lower-rank group (Daiwa, Hokkaido Takushoku, Mitsui, Taiyo-Kobe, Tokyo); long-term group (Nihon Choki Shinyo, Nihon Kogyo, Nihon Saiken Shinyo). It should be noted that the Bank of Tokyo is grouped in the middle and lower-rank group.

5. Overseas financial affiliates with equity links with Japanese banks.

6. According to Japan, Ministry of Finance (1979), local banks seem to want to establish branches or representative offices in the international financial market.

7. However, long-term credit banks and specialised foreign exchange banks are permitted to issue bank bonds.

8 THE GLOBAL INVESTMENTS OF A BRITISH INTERNATIONAL DEVELOPMENT AGENCY

C.M. Rogerson

Introduction

Recent geographical research on multinational corporations (MNCs) has attracted considerable interest with work being pursued on both theoretical and empirical fronts (Hamilton and Linge, 1981; Taylor and Thrift, 1982). Many of the propositions and categories which guided initial forays into the geography of multinationals are now being challenged. In particular the assumption that MNCs display homogeneous and universal characteristics demands reappraisal. There is, for example, mounting empirical evidence which demonstrates that there are marked differences in the spatial expansion paths of MNCs based in core, semi-peripheral and peripheral economies (cf. Tucker, this volume). Such differentials have been revealed in the context of enquiry into those MNCs which are ostensibly or primarily in private ownership. But there exists another category of MNC not falling under the aegis of the private sector. This is the set of MNCs the operations of which are governed by various statutory obligations which affect them uniquely. Included within this category of MNCs are institutions like the World Bank, the International Monetary Fund and several public corporations established by national governments, particularly in Western Europe. Although this somewhat disparate collection of organisations is small relative to the proliferation of private sector MNCs, the individual members of this group may be enormously influential. In particular, the impact of this category of non-private sector MNCs is strongly experienced in peripheral capitalist societies as many of these organisations were founded as national or international development agencies.

This chapter addresses the global spread of one international development agency which abides by certain statutory provisions laid down in the United Kingdom where the organisation was founded and is still based. Established in 1948 as the Colonial Development Corporation, the restyled Commonwealth Development Corporation (CDC) has always had as its *raison d'être* the identification and promotion of development possibilities in peripheral economies. By 1980 the CDC had capital commitments totalling over £500 million spread throughout nearly 50 countries in Africa, Asia, the Caribbean, Latin America and Oceania. In focusing solely upon the spatial attributes of this international development agency no attempt is made in this chapter to assess the success or otherwise of the CDC as a development corporation. Nor is detailed discussion possible on the particular organisational features and financial structures of CDC operations in the different milieu in which it is engaged. The information upon which the present study is based derives primarily from the annual reports of the CDC (1948 to 1980), a business history (Rendell, 1976) and an official British government survey on colonial development (Morgan, 1980a; 1980b).

CDC — Origins, Organisation and Growth

Before proceeding to an examination of the finer geographical fabric of CDC activities, it is necessary to sketch the background to the launching of the organisation as a development agency of the British government. In addition, the broad picture of the financial growth of the enterprise and the changing composition of its project commitments are elaborated.

The Colonial Development Corporation was conceived in 1948 with the passing of the Overseas Resources Development Act (ORDA) (Rendell, 1976; Morgan, 1980a). The Act's terms of reference provide for the creation of a multinational conglomerate with the object of 'improving the standard of living of the Colonial peoples by increasing their productivity and wealth' (CDC Annual Report, 1948). Three decades later the rationale for the CDC's existence was restated in the Commonwealth Development Corporation Act 1978, which charged the agency with the task of assisting the overseas countries in which it was permitted to operate in the development of their economies. Although the CDC has always functioned as a *de facto* agency for aid, the corporation does not offer grants. Rather, under the statutory obligation to pay its own way taking one year with another, CDC seeks to invest in development schemes which will yield a reasonable rate of financial return and, additionally, will assist with the development of the host country. The financing of CDC operations is through borrowings from the United Kingdom Exchequer which are repayable and interest-bearing. By virtue of these statutory guidelines, CDC can effectively only invest in those projects potentially capable of servicing their capital. In its operations the corporation is empowered to undertake projects, either alone or in associatiorr with others (national governments, private enterprise or other aid agencies), in the spheres of basic development, primary production and processing, and industry and commerce. Specifically excluded from the corporation's mandate, however, are projects of a 'social nature' such as schools, hospitals, government buildings or other buildings or works for the public service (CDC, 1981).

Overall control of CDC operations is maintained from the London head office, which has close liaison with both the British government and representatives of Commonwealth and other governments in London. As well as being the command centre for CDC activities, the head office acts as a source of specialist and technical advice and provides centralised services to its overseas ventures (CDC, 1981). Supporting the head office is a network of regional offices responsible for close relations with host governments and the instigation and investigation of new projects within their operational spheres. At the outset of CDC's operations, five regions were established to cover West Africa, Central Africa, Far East, East Africa and the West Indies. The expansion of the corporation has been accompanied by a restructuring of these regional responsibilities, the creation of two new regions for Southern Africa and the Pacific, and the changing location of several of the regional office centres (Table 8.1).

The capital commitments of CDC have risen continually, albeit unevenly, over the 30-year period spanned by this investigation (see Table 8.2). In the first two years of its operations CDC committed over £30 million. During the decade 1950-1960 financial obligations increased threefold. This rapid pace of expansion slowed somewhat between 1960 to 1970 when an increase of only 60 per cent in capital commitments was recorded. Nevertheless in the most recent decade (1970-1980) the rate of increase in new financing rose sharply, with a further trebling of capital commitments to £516 million by 1980.

Funds devoted to all CDC projects expanded over the study

Table 8.1: The Regional Organisation of the Commonwealth
Development Corporation

Regional Office		Comments
Caribbean	Bridgetown, Barbados	The regional office has shifted three times between Bridgetown, Barbados and Kingston, Jamaica. 1948 to 1955 the regional office was in Kingston; 1955 to 1969 in Bridgetown; 1969 to 1972 in Kingston. During 1972 two regional offices for the West and East Caribbean were established at Kingston (West) and Bridgetown (East). In 1976 Bridgetown again becomes the regional locus for all Caribbean operations.
Asia	Singapore	Singapore was the site of the regional office from 1948 to 1957. Between 1957 and 1970 Kuala Lumpur, Malaysia was the regional office. In 1970 Singapore was re-established as the regional centre for Asian operations.
Pacific Islands	Suva, Fiji	This region was established only in 1980 when Pacific operations were separated from those of Asia.
East Africa	Nairobi, Kenya	The regional office was established in 1948 at Nairobi and has remained there.
Central Africa	Lusaka, Zambia	The original regional office was situated in Blantyre, Malawi for the period 1948-1951. Salisbury, Rhodesia became the locus for Central African operations between 1951 and 1965. As a consequence of Rhodesian UDI in 1965, the regional office moved to Lusaka, Zambia.
Southern Africa	Mbabne, Swaziland	This region was established as a separate operational area in 1955. The regional office was located until 1980 in Johannesburg, South Africa, from where it was shifted to Mbabane, Swaziland.
West Africa	Monrovia, Liberia	From its inception in 1948 through to 1979 the West African region was run from Lagos. In 1979 the regional office was removed to Monrovia, Liberia.

Table 8.2: CDC's Total Capital Commitments, 1949-80

Year	Amount ('000)*
1949	14,187
1950	30,224
1960	109,448
1970	171,592
1980	516,176

Note: * Current prices.
Sources: CDC Annual Reports and Accounts.

period but this increase was uneven in sectoral terms (Figure 8.1). The initial commitments were overwhelmingly dominated by monies channelled into projects broadly subsumed under the rubric of renewable natural resources. In 1950 such commitments represented 60 per cent of the total. The balance of capital was spread evenly between power and water, housing, industry and minerals. In the following decade, CDC financing patterns underwent significant alterations as power and water and housing projects together accounted for 60 per cent of new funds. As a consequence, power and water projects eclipsed renewable natural resources as the prime sector for CDC activity by 1960 (Figure 8.1). A further notable aspect of the 1950s was the modest involvement of CDC in new sectors of activity, notably transport, hotels and, most significantly for the future, the first financial contributions to national and/or regional development corporations. In the decade of slowed growth (1960-1970), almost a third of fresh capital was directed towards these newly constituted development corporations. Of the remaining new obligations three-quarters went into the sectors of housing or industry. A final point of note for the years 1960-1970 is the stagnation of CDC's involvement in renewable natural resources. Whereas in the first years of the organisation, natural resources had enjoyed the major share of CDC monies, two decades later the sector had been surpassed in total commitments by both power and water and housing. At the close of the 1970s a markedly different picture emerges once more. The period of the 1970s witnessed a revival of CDC activities in renewable natural resources which absorbed 55 per cent of new finance. A graphic illustration of the extent of new CDC funding of renewable natural resource projects between 1970 to 1980 is that during that decade commitments to this sector

Figure 8.1: The Regional Pattern of CDC Operations, 1949-80

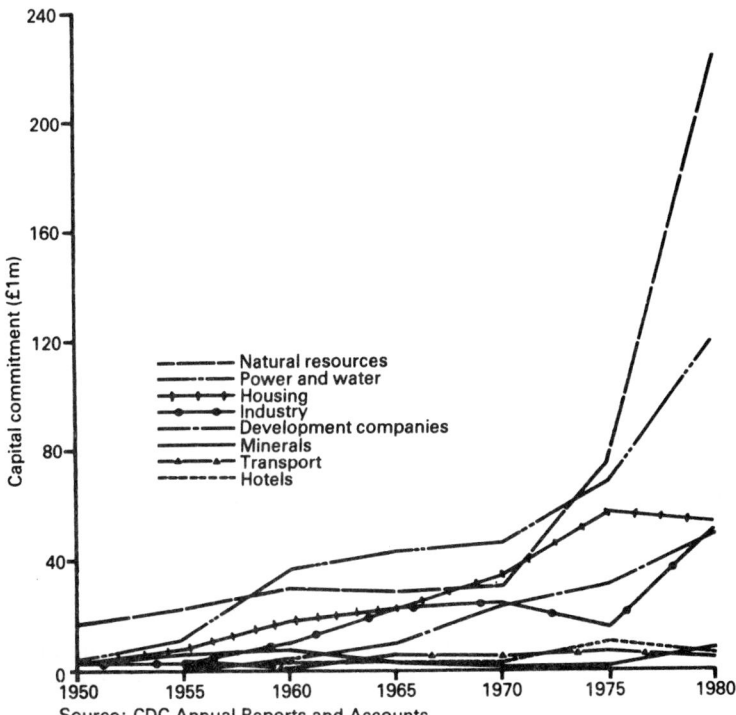

Source: CDC Annual Reports and Accounts

exceeded all CDC commitments in 1970. Also of significance in this latter phase of CDC growth was a near doubling of the organisation's involvement in power and water schemes. By 1980, little differentiation emerges in total CDC commitments to the sectors of housing, industry and development corporations. Together, the five sectors of renewable natural resources, power and water, housing, industry and development corporations account for 97 per cent of all CDC activities at the close of the study period. Sectors of minor significance to the CDC throughout the years surveyed were those of minerals, hotels and transport (Figure 8.1).

Analysis of the allocation of CDC funds on a regional basis (Figure 8.2) reveals a greater degree of consistency than the patterns of sectoral funding. Throughout the history of the CDC Africa has been the pre-eminent sphere of its operations. Aggre-

Figure 8.2: The Sectoral Pattern of CDC Operations, 1950-80

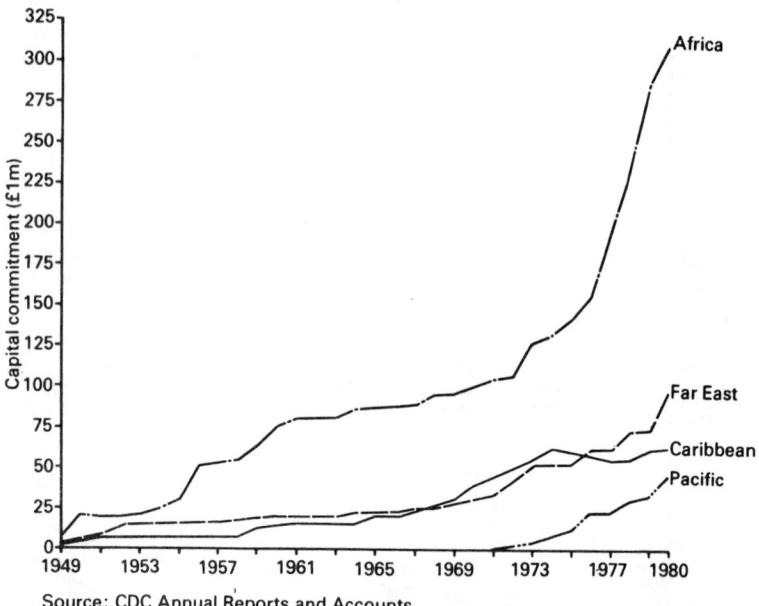

Source: CDC Annual Reports and Accounts

gating the data for West, Central, East and Southern Africa, the continent absorbs at its lowest point (1952) 44 per cent and at its peak level (1962) 69 per cent of all CDC finance. The pattern of commitments in the Far East and Caribbean regions is less volatile in absolute terms (Figure 8.2). Only since 1970 has the Pacific Islands emerged as a new arena and separate sphere for CDC activities. Some interesting findings are revealed if an analysis of the regional statistics is considered separately for *new* investments on a decade basis. Most striking is the fall of Africa's share of new commitments from 71 per cent for the period 1950 to 1960 to 40 per cent in the slow growth years of the 1960s. Renewed capital flows to Africa were, however, a feature of the 1970s when the continent drew over 60 per cent of new finance. During the 1960s when CDC reduced its relative commitment to Africa, the Caribbean region was the chief locus for new allocations. Beyond the boom years of the 1960s the share of the Caribbean in new investments dropped considerably as CDC revived its traditional interest in Africa, boosted its involvement in Asia (formerly the Far East) and committed itself heavily for the first time in the Pacific Islands. As measured on a regional basis by 1980 the respective shares of all CDC commitments were as follows: Africa 60 per cent, Asia 18 per cent, the Caribbean 12 per cent and the Pacific Islands 9 per cent. The small remaining share of CDC finance was accounted for by commitments to Cyprus and Gibraltar.

Set against this brief review of CDC's genesis, organisation and broad sectoral and regional commitments, attention is now focused upon a more detailed account and explanation of the changing geographical patterns of investment of this international development agency. In common with studies on the spatial expansion paths of private sector MNCs (cf. Taylor and Thrift, 1982) an historical approach is adopted to facilitate the task of reviewing CDC's international patterns of activity.

The Changing Spatial Fabric of CDC, 1948-80

During the years 1948 to 1980 the geographical pattern of CDC operations underwent several transformations. Interpretation of these shifts is best undertaken through chronicling the international spread and retreat of CDC activity in four broad periods: 1948 to 1955, in which the existence of CDC was threatened by the failure of many of its initial projects; 1956 to 1963, a period of further threat to the organisation in terms of the potential removal of part of its operational area; 1964 to 1970, watershed years in which CDC established the basis for expansion, securing formal recognition as part of Britain's international aid programme; and the decade 1970 to 1980, which witnessed a major expansion of CDC global operations, including an extension of its activities to countries outside of the Commonwealth.

False Start and Recovery, 1948-55

The birth of the CDC was heralded as 'the start of a new era in colonial progress' (*Crown Colonist*, 1947, p. 627). By means of the 'public corporation method of development' the British government intended 'to initiate productive activity in hitherto undeveloped areas of the world', (Wicker, 1955/56, p. 214). More precisely, the geographical sphere of CDC operations was delimited in the 1948 ORDA as encompassing those colonial territories to which the Colonial Development and Welfare Act 1940 then applied. The significance of this latter provision was in its exclusion from CDC's operational arena of the three newly independent territories of India, Pakistan and Ceylon as well as the white settler Dominions of Australia, Canada, New Zealand and the Union of South Africa, the Far East, the Caribbean and the Pacific. Although no statutory limits were set for CDC involvement in any colony, it was accepted that the organisation would strive for 'a measure of equitable geographical distribution of projects over Colonial territories as a whole' (Morgan, 1980a, p. 334).

The issue of equity in terms of the geographical spread of investments did not, however, notably influence the early spatial pattern of CDC activities. Nor evidently was commercial viability a sole criterion for capital approval. During the initial phase of the organisation the factors of 'need of the colony' and 'wishes of the colonial government' often emerged as paramount considerations (Wicker, 1955/56). But one further criterion was of critical significance in shaping the early geography of CDC operations. The post-World War II shortages of food and US dollars in the United Kingdom placed a premium on any projects which offered the possibility of earning or saving dollars. Sensitive to potential criticism that the CDC was functioning to 'exploit' the colonies for the benefit of the United Kingdom's balance of payments, the goal of promoting dollar-saving projects was married to that of 'colonial development'. The CDC's first annual report thus noted:

> In the short and in the long run, the objective of reducing the dollar deficit is closely linked with the objective of raising the standard living in the Colonies. This is most clearly seen in the West Indies. The colonies of this region import from dollar sources a considerable part of their requirements of food and manufactured goods. (CDC Annual Report, 1948)

That the course of CDC's early investments was vitally influenced by the search for dollar-savings is illustrated by the fact that of 28 CDC undertakings in 1950, eight were expected to earn or save dollars (Wicker, 1955/56).

The spatial pattern of CDC investments in 1950 (Figure 8.3) reflects these several pressures upon the choice of projects. With 50 schemes operating in 22 colonial territories, the geographical spread of the organisation was impressive. A perception of Africa as 'the most promising field for large-scale development' (CDC Annual Report, 1948) was evidenced in the initial concentrations

Figure 8.3: The Global Investments of CDC, 1950

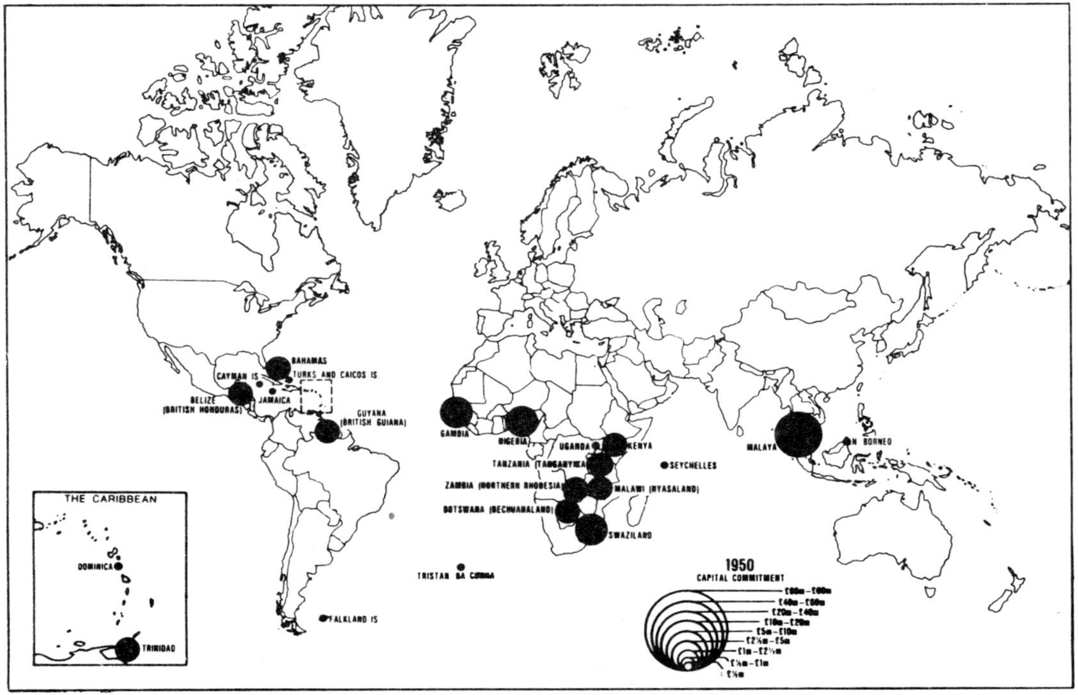

Source: CDC Annual Report and Accounts, 1950

of capital in territories such as Swaziland, Nigeria, Gambia, Kenya, Nyasaland, Bechuanaland, Tanganyika and Northern Rhodesia. Among the earliest projects in Africa were schemes for cattle ranching, fishing, poultry production, forestry, minerals and the production of tung oil; the functional spread of schemes demonstrated the emphasis upon projects which might produce either food or a saving of dollars.

Although Africa garnered the largest share of early CDC monies, the major single investment by colony in 1950 was in the Federation of Malaya where the CDC committed funds for rectifying the local housing shortage and for assistance with power development. The emphasis upon projects of this nature in Malaya contrasted with the focus on renewable natural resource developments in much of Africa. The CDC's investment patterns in the Far East illustrate a further facet of the organisation's operations. Those areas in the CDC realm with some endowments of capital and skill, such as Hong Kong and Singapore, were to be left largely to private enterprise for development. The CDC was, therefore, to seek out projects in territories, not so well endowed, which would not attract sufficient private development capital (Morgan, 1980a). Outside Africa and the Far East, other notable foci for early CDC operations were the Bahamas, British Guiana and British Honduras. Finally, that even the farthest outposts of the British Empire would not be overlooked is shown by CDC commitments to sealing and mutton production in the Falkland Islands and the crawfish industry of Tristan da Cunha (CDC Annual Report, 1950).

Increasingly after 1950 it became evident that the organisation had got off to a 'false start' (Rendell, 1976, p. 12) as many of the schemes to which it was committed began to show signs of failing. The CDC had over-extended its existing managerial capabilities and had engaged itself in a suite of projects with faint hope of profitability. This conclusion crystallised between 1951 to 1954. In three years some 15 projects were, for various reasons, abandoned (Table 8.3). Strikingly, the major losses were concentrated geographically in The Gambia and Nigeria and functionally weighted towards fisheries or fish-related schemes (Wicker, 1955/56). The most publicised failure was the scheme to produce eggs and poultry in The Gambia (Rendell, 1976; Morgan, 1980a). Once hailed as likely to become the world's largest chicken farm of its kind (Hennessy, 1950) the project was an abject disaster and by

Table 8.3: Schemes Abandoned by the CDC, 1951-53

Location	Project	Date Started	Date Abandoned	Reason for Abandonment
Bahamas	Andros Agricultural Development	1950	March 1953	Failure of crops and difficulties with Mexican produce in US market.
British Honduras	British Honduras Stock Farms	1950	March 1952	Commercially impracticable owing to heavy development expenditure.
British Somaliland	British Somaliland Camel and Sheep Abattoir	1951	March 1952	No demand for camel hides and local sheep not acceptable in UK meat market.
Dominica	Castle Bruse Estate, Dominica	1949	April 1952	Estate too remote.
	Fruit Packing Station, Dominica	1949	Oct. 1953	Too large to be operated economically with quantity of fruit offered.
Falkland Islands	South Atlantic Sealing	1948	Sept. 1952	Not enough seals and poor price for oils.
Gambia	Atlantic Fisheries	1949	Sept. 1951	Fishing and factory: vessel too expensive to run, and collapse of market price of shark-liver oil.
	Gambia Poultry and River Farms	1948	May 1951	Disease of poultry and failure of crops.
	Gambia Rice Farm	1949	April 1952	Uneconomic — capital cost of development too high.
Kenya	East African Ramie	1951	Sept. 1953	Poor crops.
Nigeria	Nigerian Fibre Industries	1950	Sept. 1953	Local products could not compete with imported jute sacks and cotton yarn.
	West African Fisheries	1951	May 1953	Numerous difficulties, including poor fishing and drop in demand for fish.
Nyasaland	Nyasaland Fisheries	1948	May 1951	Inefficient management and slump in price of Vitamin A oil.
Seychelles	Seychelles Fisheries	1950	July 1952	Catches of fish were not large enough to make the project commercially attractive.
Tanganyika	Kitario Gold Mine	1950	July 1951	Prospecting results poor.

Source: After Morgan (1980b), p. 93.

1954 the corporation had withdrawn entirely from the colony. This spate of failures emphasised not only the management problems of the CDC but perhaps, more importantly, the need to overhaul the statutory basis of the corporation, in particular the way in which it was vulnerable to enter into commitments as a result of being 'pressed' or 'urged' to do so by colonial governments (Morgan, 1980b).

As a consequence of this group of project failures some reorganisation and restructuring of CDC activities was set in motion. Most notably, the organisation was forced to shift the balance of its efforts from schemes which the CDC directly managed to those in which it was in partnership with either private enterprise or colonial governments. This changeover to financial investment without management responsibility was accompanied by an increase in loans to government corporations guaranteed by colonial government and functionally by a switch to investment in infrastructure projects (Wicker, 1955/56; Rendell, 1976). The ensuing recovery in the organisation's financial health led, however, to mounting criticism that the agency was leaning too heavily towards the funding of such 'safe' schemes (Rendell, 1976). A larger threat to the operations of the organisation emerged in 1956 with the danger that CDC would be forced to terminate activities in some of its more profitable operational spheres.

The Threat of a Reduced Operational Area, 1956-63

The question of the status of certain parts of the geographical sphere of CDC operations became an issue early on in the history of the organisation with respect to the case of Southern Rhodesia. In terms of the original statutory guidelines Southern Rhodesia was not a colonial territory defined by the 1948 ORDA not being a beneficiary of the Colonial Development and Welfare Acts. The eligibility of Southern Rhodesia changed with the formation in 1953 of the Federation of Rhodesia and Nyasaland. The CDC was now permitted to participate in projects within Southern Rhodesia but only on condition that such projects were shown to be of potential benefit to economic development in Northern Rhodesia or Nyasaland. It was on such grounds that the CDC was allowed to provide loans to Central African Airways, Southern Rhodesia African Housing and the Kariba Dam project. In 1956, however, the Colonial Office turned down a proposed CDC involvement in an iron and steel venture in Southern Rhodesia on the basis that its sanction would not offer benefits to the two other territories in the Federation. A 1956 amendment to ORDA regularised this decision, effectively excluding CDC from all further projects located in Southern Rhodesia (CDC Annual Report, 1956).

A more serious threat to the CDC also surfaced in 1956 when the very existence of the corporation was challenged (Rendell, 1976). The 1948 ORDA had defined the operational sphere of CDC activities in terms of those territories which were *dependent* at the time of Act's passing. No provision was made in the original Act as to what might happen in the event of territories attaining independence and/or opting to leave the Commonwealth. Such questions became very real with the impending independence of Ghana. In the absence of statutes to the contrary, it was an assumption of the CDC that it could continue to function in former colonies which had achieved political independence (Rendell, 1976). However, in 1956 the British government laid down the position that CDC should not embark on any new projects in colonies which had gained independence although it would be allowed to continue with existing projects and even invest more money in them if that was shown to be necessary (Rendell, 1976, p. 57). This policy held severe long-term implications for the organisation, especially in view of the scheduling of independence for Ghana and Malaya in 1957 and the prospect of many further grants of independence to follow. A government White Paper of 1957 duly confirmed the position that independent countries in the Commonwealth would have to rely primarily upon private enterprise and the support of institutions such as the World Bank for their economic development. The CDC then faced the possibility that within a short time-span the core of its operational area may be excised. The CDC would be forced to concentrate its efforts in the diminishing rump of colonial territories which offered only limited scope for profitable operations.

The restriction of the CDC's geographical sphere of operations could have been the start of a long-term death knell. But the organisation responded in such fashion that the British government was eventually compelled to restore its sphere of operations. The CDC realised that it must maintain pressure upon the British government to revise the exclusion policy and, with this in mind, corporate priority was given to those operations which might assist in achieving this goal (Rendell, 1976). Although the CDC regretted 'intensely having been forbidden to assist Ghana' (CDC Annual Report and Accounts, 1956), the former colony had never been a major area for its operations because of the unfavourable political climate under Nkrumah's African socialism. Exclusion from Malaya was a far more serious blow, for in 1955 the colony was the leading focus for CDC monies (CDC Annual Report and Accounts, 1955). To minimise the impact of exclusion from Malaya and a clutch of territories approaching independence, the CDC took the initiative in establishing substantial new investments before the 'cut-off' of independence. One important vehicle for the continuing channelling of post-independence funds was through the setting-up of development corporations in partnership with territorial governments (Rendell, 1976; Morgan, 1980b).

A further twist to the debate on the geographical sphere of the CDC's operations arose in the context of the Southern Cameroons, a territory ruled by Britain under mandate and administered as part of Nigeria until that country attained independence in 1960. The problem, posed was whether the CDC should invest funds in a territory likely to leave the Commonwealth. An approach was made to the CDC during 1957 to participate in the operations of the Cameroon Development Corporation. Despite impending Nigerian independence and the prospect of Southern Cameroons leaving the Commonwealth, the CDC was swayed on commercial criteria to commit funding. Indeed, in 1960 the organisation took on the role of managing agents for the Cameroon Development Corporation. The following year, however, the Southern Cameroons joined the Cameroon Republic, attaining independence outside the Commonwealth. Through this chain of events the CDC found itself with an investment in an independent non-Commonwealth state but one into which it could no longer channel additional funds (Morgan, 1980b).

The map of the CDC's operations in 1960 (Figure 8.4) shows the influence of these several events upon the pattern of its investments. The number of territories in which the organisation was committed had risen to 26 (CDC Annual Report, 1960). However, broad geographical advance of the CDC's activities was matched by a retreat from certain territories in which early projects had resulted in failure. Most striking was the withdrawal from The Gambia but other colonies abandoned by the CDC included Seychelles, Falkland Islands and Turks and Caicos

Figure 8.4: The Global Investments of CDC, 1960

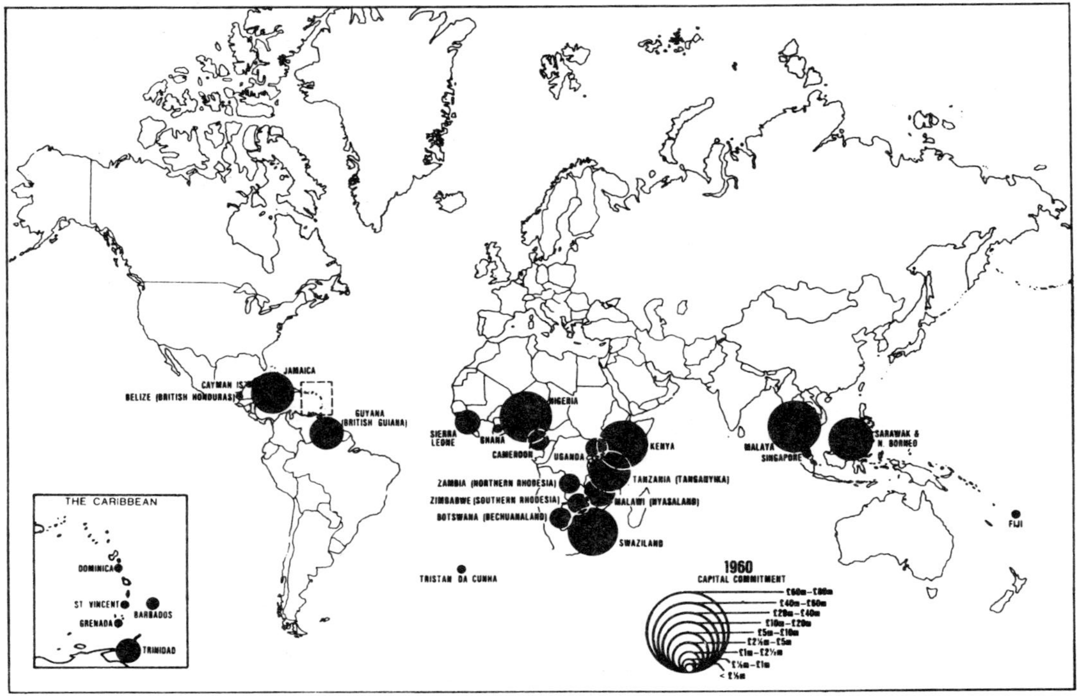

Source: CDC Annual Report and Accounts, 1960

Islands. In the decade 1950 to 1960 the greatest sum of investments (in descending order of magnitude) was made in Swaziland, Malaya, Kenya, Tanganyika, Nigeria and Jamaica. Operations in Swaziland were viewed as one of the CDC's great success stories with major investments in schemes for forestry development and a showpiece smallholder irrigation project for the production of sugar (Rendell, 1976). In Malaya the CDC was instrumental in launching three major projects in housing, land and industrial development which were recognised by the independent government as cornerstones of the country's economic progress. After being blocked from pursuing further projects in independent Malaya, the axis of CDC efforts shifted to the opening up of plantations in the still dependent territories of North Borneo and Sarawak. Excepting a major commitment to housing development in Jamaica, in the rest of the Caribbean growth was sluggish. This was explained largely by the absence of any major potential for the large-scale agricultural projects of the kind in which the CDC was gaining an international reputation (Phillips and Collinson, 1976).

The growing successes of the CDC in terms of its developmental objectives heightened pressures on the British government for a reinstatement of the corporation's former operational sphere. By 1962, the policy of debarring the CDC from newly independent territories had halted new growth (other than in existing projects) in Ghana, Malaya, Nigeria, Jamaica, Trinidad and Tobago, Singapore, Sierra Leone, Tanganyika and Uganda. Shortly to be added to this list were Kenya, Nyasaland, Northern Rhodesia and the territories of Borneo and Sarawak which were to be absorbed into the Federation of Malaysia. In 1963, the survival of the CDC was assured by the passing of the Commonwealth Development Act, removing the ban on CDC participation in new projects within territories which became independent in the Commonwealth and restoring to the CDC's operational sphere all those territories which had been previously removed. The reinstatement of former territories did not, however, apply to the Cameroons or ex-British Somaliland (now part of the Somali Republic), territories which had left the Commonwealth. Finally, the 1963 Act was noteworthy for one further action, the change in the corporation's name, from Colonial to Commonwealth Development Corporation (Morgan, 1980b).

Establishing the Basis for Future Growth, 1964 to 1970

The period of the late 1960s has been termed a 'watershed' in the evolution of the CDC (Rendell, 1976). By 1970, the organisation had secured formal recognition of its role as part of the United Kingdom aid programme and created the essential bases for the succeeding decade's major growth of CDC activities.

That a major expansion in CDC operations did not eventuate in the late 1960s, after the re-establishment of its former operational sphere, was partly the result of the financial downturn in the United Kingdom economy but, perhaps more significantly, was the consequence of unfavourable political circumstances in several territories in which the organisation might have expanded. Events following Rhodesian UDI in 1965 placed the CDC in an awkward position with respect to its activities in both Ghana and Tanzania, whose governments broke diplomatic ties with the United Kingdom. The break with Tanzania was particularly disturbing, for the former colony of Tanganyika had become the fifth largest focus for CDC operations by 1960 (CDC Annual Report, 1960). With diplomatic ties severed, the CDC could contemplate no new commitments to the territory (CDC Annual Report, 1966). The corporation's operations in parts of Asia were no less threatened by political uncertainties of the mid-1960s. In particular, the confrontation between Malaysia and Indonesia militated against expansion of the CDC's important schemes for natural resource developments in East Malaysia. Further violence occurred in West Africa in 1966 with military takeovers in Ghana and Nigeria. But with the removal of the Nkrumah regime, the military coup in Ghana was viewed in a favourable light raising 'hopes that CDC may expand its operations' (CDC Annual Report and Accounts, 1966). However the prospects for the CDC in Nigeria worsened by 1967 with the outbreak of civil war. Other turbulent political environments which affected CDC activities during this period appeared in Guyana, Trinidad and Sierra Leone.

The geography of the CDC's worldwide operations in 1970 (Figure 8.5) bears the mark of these political events. The cut-off of CDC funds from certain territories and the outbreak of political strife in others caused some shifting of investments during the decade 1960 to 1970. Although Africa as a whole suffered a relative downturn in commitments, the two leading territories for CDC operations in the 1960s were Kenya and Swaziland. In the

Figure 8.5: The Global Investments of CDC, 1970

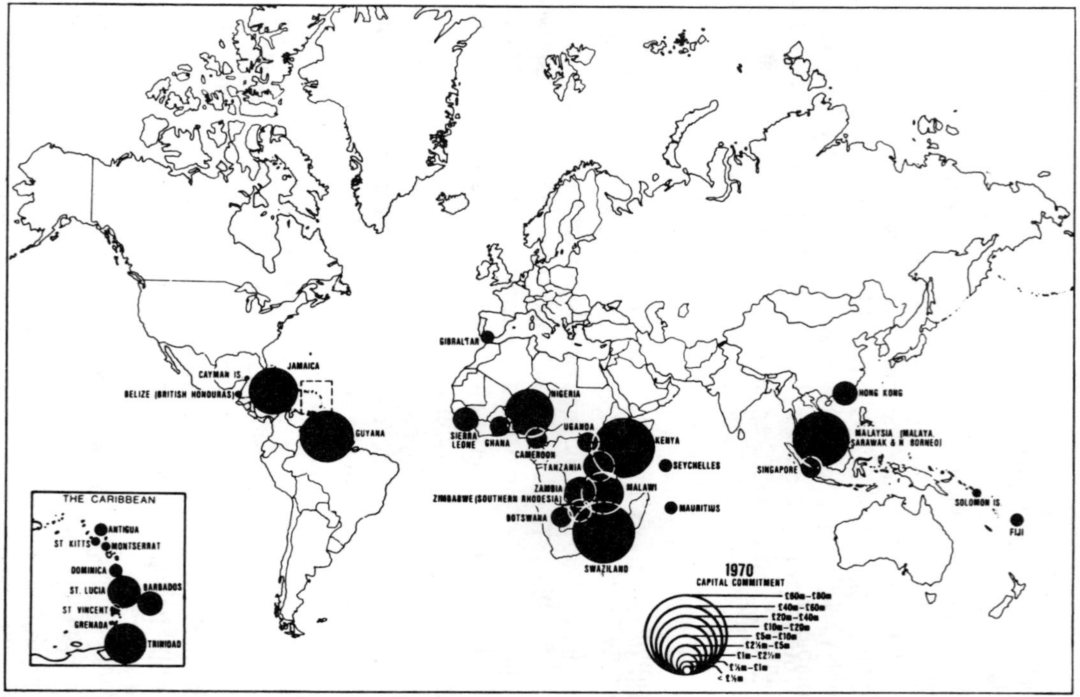

Source: CDC Annual Report and Accounts, 1970

former case, the CDC invested heavily in a smallholder tea scheme, power and housing. In the latter, the commitments were to extend further the highly successful sugar developments (CDC Annual Report, 1970). Together, these two territories accounted for approximately one-third of new CDC commitments during the decade. The balance was weighted towards investments in the relatively political stable environments of the Caribbean. In particular, Jamaica recorded an impressive growth, with finance directed primarily towards the areas of housing and property development. And, notwithstanding political tension, the CDC also invested substantially in Guyana, channelling funds to a smallholder sugar scheme, housing and power supply. In Asia the only notable growth of CDC investment was in the oil palm and cocoa plantations of Sabah and Sarawak, which were later threatened by the confrontation of Malaysia with Indonesia. Yet by 1970, Swaziland and Malaysia were still the major loci for CDC operations followed in order by Kenya, Jamaica and Guyana. The number of territories in which the organisation had financial commitments by 1970 rose to over 30 (CDC Annual Report, 1970).

If events in the external political environment of the CDC were not particularly favourable to the organisation's growth, this was not the case in terms of relations between CDC and the British government. After the 1963 reintroduction of its former geographical operational arena, the CDC began to press for a reduction in the interest charged on its financial borrowings from the British Treasury (Morgan, 1980b). The attempt to obtain subsidised funds was part of a strategy which sought recognition of the CDC's important developmental role (Rendell, 1976). Sympathetic consideration was sought for the fact that the CDC alone among major national or international development agencies, did not receive funds which enabled on-lending or investment at lower than market rates of interest. In order to compete with lending arrangements offered by organisations such as the World Bank, subsidised funds were sought. Fortuitously for the CDC, in 1964 an in-coming Labour government established a Ministry of Overseas Development with the specific object of stimulating British aid to developing countries. In 1967, after prolonged negotiations, the United Kingdom government accepted the principle that the rate of interest charged to the CDC should be subsidised so that the corporation might play a full and integral part in Britain's aid programme (Rendell, 1976). In light of this watershed decision, Morgan (1980b, p. 245) argues that the CDC began 'to see its future in the field of aid where it quoted with understandable pride the view of others that its work was "as effective a form of aid as any in the world"'. Due recognition of the vital role that the organisation might assume in the future was accorded in the doubling of CDC borrowing powers in 1969 (Rendell, 1976). In addition, the organisation was given a further extension in its geographical sphere of operations with the lifting of the restriction to activities within the Commonwealth. Henceforth, CDC could seek ministerial permission to expand in any developing country. The grant of this worldwide extension was greeted cautiously as indicated in the Annual Report of 1969:

> For its part, the Corporation contemplates that the area should be expanded for the time being only by a natural extension of its existing organisation through the regional offices and to countries where conditions are broadly similar to those of the countries in which the Corporation is already operating. (CDC Annual Report and Accounts, 1969)

It is against such a background that the CDC initially obtained approval for the potential extension of operations to Cameroon, Ethiopia, Indonesia and Thailand (CDC Annual Report, 1970).

The Decade of Major Expansion, 1970 to 1980

The consolidation and extension of the CDC's position as one of the major international agencies for aid and development was the dominant theme in the years 1970 to 1980. Frequently, the activities of CDC were likened to those of the World Bank, with whom there was considerable cooperation. None the less, important differences distinguished the CDC's operations from those of the World Bank and other leading development agencies. The World Bank only offered loans directly to governments or with government guarantees on loans whereas the CDC rarely made loans to governments and in only a minority of cases were loans government-backed (CDC Annual Report, 1970). In addition, the CDC was noted in international developmental circles for its ability 'to support the provision of risk capital and long-term finance with a comprehensive range of management and technical services' (CDC Annual Report, 1974).

That the CDC could carve out a distinctive niche in the league of international development operations was greatly facilitated by an agreement in 1972 whereby the British government would make funds available at concessionary rates of interest for the specific purpose of developing renewable natural resources. This was precisely the field in which CDC had accumulated the greatest amount of managerial expertise (Rendell, 1976). The decision to finance natural resources at concessionary rates opened up several new agricultural ventures for CDC participation (CDC Annual Report, 1972). Further stimulus to CDC investment in natural resources arose from the 1975 review of Britain's aid programme. A government White Paper emphasised the importance of directing British aid towards the poorest countries, especially in the wake of the oil price increases of the early 1970s. More particularly, the objective of channelling aid to the poorest groups within these countries highlighted the need for special attention to be devoted to projects for rural development. As a consequence of this aid review, the CDC was to aim between 1975 and 1979 to place its new capital commitments predominantly into the poorest countries and sectorally into an increased commitment to renewable natural resource projects (CDC Annual Report, 1975).

It was as a consequence of these developments that the CDC committed the bulk of its funding during the 1970s towards agricultural projects. Particular emphasis was placed upon using the concept of a nucleus estate as the catalyst of rural development (Phillips and Collinson, 1976). Around the nucleus or demonstration estate, smallholder farmers would be encouraged to settle. The central unit, besides undertaking processing functions, supplied peasant farmers with planting material, advice and services, credit for development as well as a guaranteed market for produce. In some smallholder schemes, central processing units were established without nucleus estates. In others, the processing unit served as the focal point for small farm development. Projects involving the use of nucleus estates and central facilities were instigated to promote the production of crops such as sugar, tea, coffee, cocoa, rubber and oil palms (Phillips and Collinson, 1976; Rendell, 1976).

Extensive new CDC investments in renewable natural resources were therefore a strong feature of the late 1970s. Between 1975 and 1980 some £148 million was steered towards the promotion of such schemes. By the end of the study period the CDC was

engaged in 66 agricultural projects in 23 different countries representing a total commitment of over £22 million (Figure 8.6). By
far the majority of these projects were in Africa, which accounted
for nearly two-thirds of the total. Favoured countries for agricultural operations included Kenya (five projects, investment of £28
million), Swaziland (seven projects, investment of £38 million),
Malaysia (seven projects, investment of £29 million), Papua New
Guinea (two projects, investment of £18 million), and Malawi
(seven projects, investment of £17 million) (see Figure 8.6). Taken
together the ten largest commitments in natural resources (Table
8.4) represented finance of over £100 million or one-fifth of all
CDC monies by 1980. In reviewing the progress of the CDC's
involvement in natural resources, one final point of note is the
striking commitment to new projects, for the first time in the
Pacific Islands, especially in Papua New Guinea, Fiji and the
Solomon Islands (Figure 8.6, Table 8.4).

Besides a revived interest in the development of natural
resources, one further factor was to re-cast the geography of CDC
operations by 1980. The provision under the Overseas Resources
Development Act 1969 which allowed the CDC to extend, with
ministerial permission, its sphere of operations, became a significant influence in the 1970s. Progressively, the CDC took advantage of this clause to increase from four to 17 countries the number
of additional states in which it might operate (Table 3.5). The
grant of ministerial approval did not automatically imply a commitment on the CDC's behalf to invest funds; by 1980 no funds
had been advanced to the permissible territories of Bangladesh,
Ecuador, Rwanda, Sri Lanka, Tunisia and Zaire. Nevertheless, by
1980, the CDC had committed over £90 million to ten non-
Commonwealth states constituting almost one-fifth of all fundings
(Figure 8.7). The most important investments were in natural
resource schemes in Cameroon, Ivory Coast, Indonesia and Liberia, and housing in Thailand. Within West Africa the volume of
investment outside the Commonwealth was so great that by 1980
it exceeded that in the Commonwealth states of the region (CDC
Annual Report, 1980). This shift in the balance of the CDC's
West African commitments was also generated by legislative measures introduced in Nigeria, the traditional focus for CDC
investment in the region, which required greater local control over
certain categories of enterprise. The CDC's failure to be excluded
from the provisions of the Nigerian Enterprises Promotion Decree

Figure 8.6: The Global Investments of CDC in Renewable Natural Resources, 1980

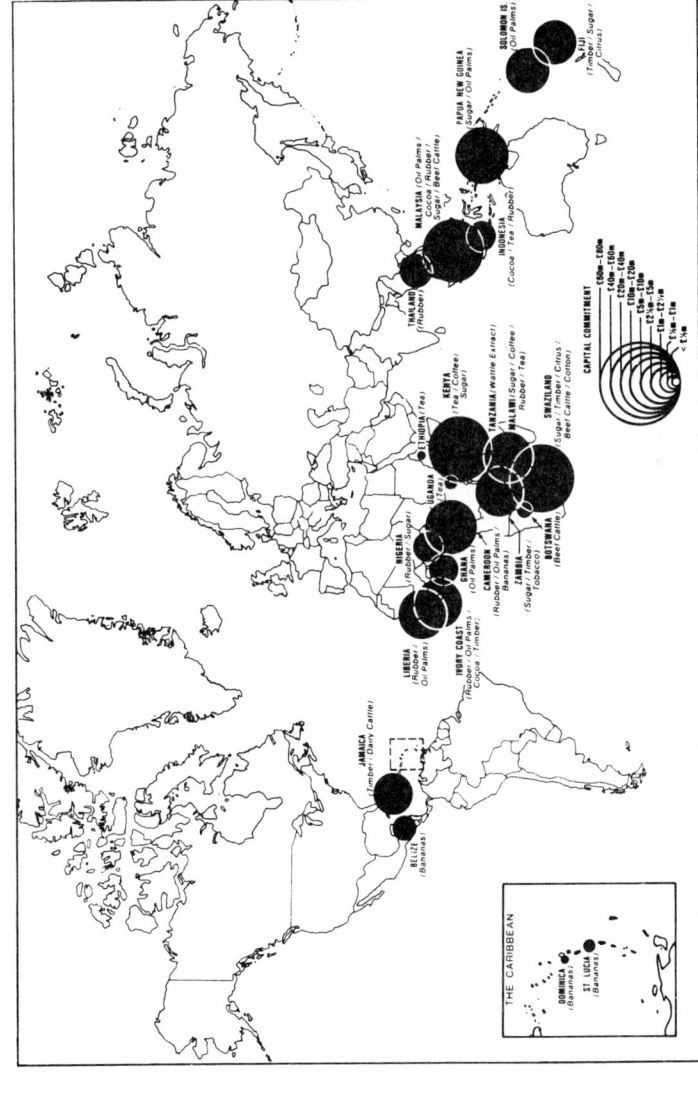

Source: CDC Annual Report and Accounts, 1980

Table 8.4: Major CDC Projects in Renewable Natural Resources

Location	Year Started	Estimated CDC Commitment (1980)	Project
Kenya	1960	15.2 million	Kenya Tea Development Authority
Swaziland	1957	13.0 million	Mhlume Sugar
Swaziland	1950	12.7 million	Swaziland Irrigation Scheme
Cameroon	1979	12.0 million	La Société Hévea Cameroun
Papua New Guinea	1980	9.4 million	Ramu Sugar
Malaysia	1948	9.3 million	B.A.L. Estates
Papua New Guinea	1976	9.0 million	Higaturu Oil Palms
Solomon Islands	1970	7.3 million	Solomon Islands Plantations
Kenya	1979	7.2 million	Smallholder Coffee Improvement
Liberia	1979	7.0 million	Decoris Oil Palm

Source: CDC Annual Reports.

Table 8.5: Developing Countries in which CDC may Operate Subject to Ministerial Approval

Year	Countries
1969	Cameroon, Ethiopia, Indonésia
1970	Thailand
1972	Tunisia, Zaire
1973	Costa Rica, Ivory Coast
1974	Rwanda
1976	Sudan
1977	Ecuador, Liberia, Philippines
1979	Bangladesh, Honduras
1980	Sri Lanka, Zimbabwe

Source: CDC Annual Reports.

was responsible not only for a net fall of capital commitments but also the transfer of regional operations to Liberia (CDC Annual Report, 1977).

Statutory changes in CDC's charter formed the backdrop to both the extensive rise in the organisation's global activities and their geographical spread in the 1970s. The map of CDC's operations in 1980 illustrates the importance of these new foci for the organisation, in the Pacific and in certain non-Commonwealth countries of West Africa and East Asia (Figure 8.8). Nevertheless, the most outstanding feature of the spatial pattern of the organisation by 1980 was in its commitments to territories in which CDC had enjoyed a long period of successful involvement. Kenya

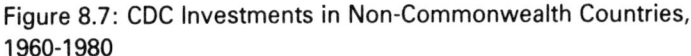

Figure 8.7: CDC Investments in Non-Commonwealth Countries, 1960-1980

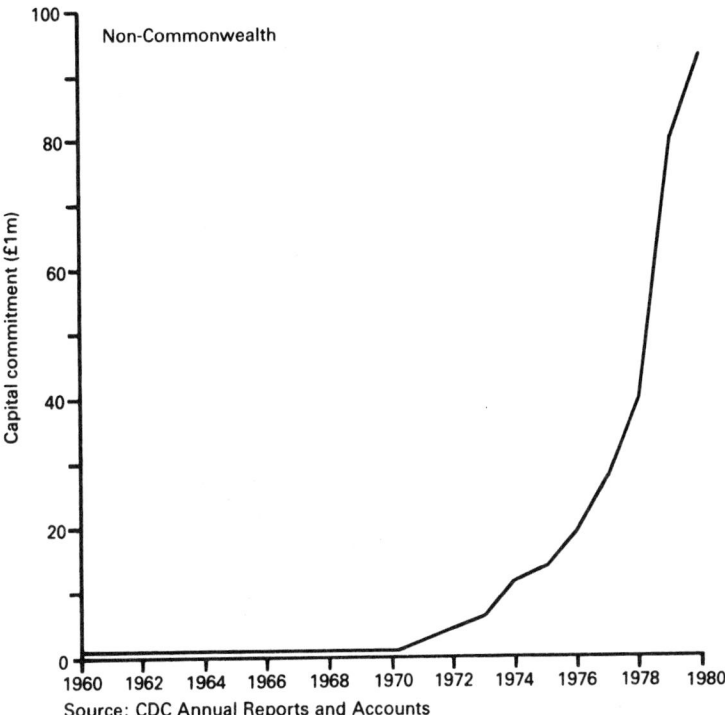

retained its status as the organisation's most favoured territory (Figure 8.8) gaining an additional £50 million of committed funds during the 1970s. Much of this new finance was channelled towards the end of the decade after the guidelines had been set down for British aid to be concentrated upon the poorest developing countries. After 1975, two-thirds of CDC funds were absorbed by only seven countries; Kenya, Malawi, Malaysia, Cameroon, Tanzania, Swaziland and Papua New Guinea. Of particular note was the strong recovery during the 1970s of CDC operations in Malaysia which at the close of the study period had grown to again become the second most popular territory. Finally, in contrast to the CDC's renewal of commitments to certain long-established spheres of operation, from others it retreated. Countries in which a net fall in capital commitments was recorded between 1970 to 1980 were Guyana, Nigeria, Trinidad and Uganda.

Figure 8.8: The Global Investments of CDC, 1980

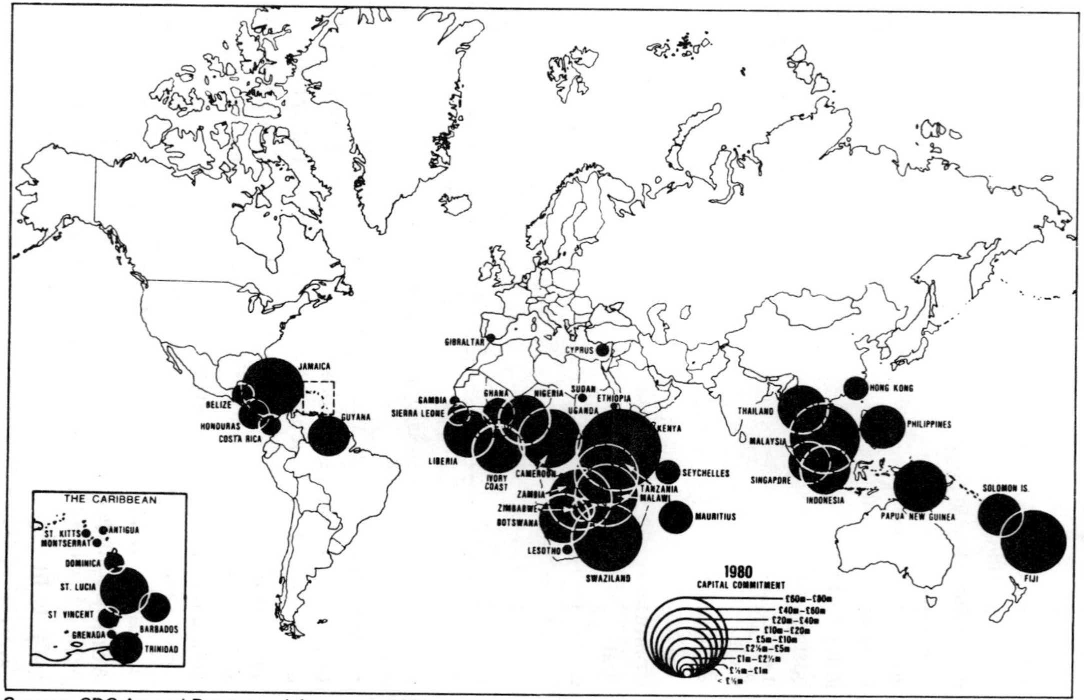

Source: CDC Annual Report and Accounts, 1980

Conclusions

This chapter has sought to open up a new dimension in the geographical literature on MNCs. Hitherto the central focus of research has concerned the category of private sector MNCs within which the majority of MNCs would be situated. It has been argued, however, that beyond this group of MNCs there are a number of influential organisations which qualify to be called MNCs but which are governed in their activities by official statutes laid down either by national governments or by international agreements. Peripheral capitalist societies are the most common hosts to this latter form of MNC as many such organisations are engaged in the business of international aid and development. The present study has attempted to unfold the spatial pattern of evolution of one such international development agency, the Commonwealth Development Corporation.

The broad lessons to be drawn from the case study of the Commonwealth Development Corporation are threefold. First, the spatial attributes of this type of MNC are inexplicable without explicitly recognising the statutory provisions under which the organisation is ruled. Second, the CDC's successful pressuring of the British government to recast its charter of operations illustrates the extent to which a nominally public enterprise may exhibit a degree of autonomy in relation to its parent state. Third, when a public enterprise is charged with the responsibility of breaking even financially, the principles underlying its changing international spatial organisation may parallel those of the private sector MNC. The significance of organisations such as Commonwealth Development Corporation merits a place on the research agenda of geographers for further empirical research and debate concerning similar multinational organisations operating under national or international statutes.

Acknowledgements

Mr P.J. Stickler is thanked for the preparation of the maps accompanying this chapter, and Gordon Pirie is thanked for his critical comments on an earlier version.

9 FRUITS OF INDEPENDENCE? PHILIPPINE CAPITALISTS AND THE BANANA EXPORT INDUSTRY

Peter Krinks

Although the concept of dependency has been severely attacked when claimed to be a theory of underdevelopment, it seems acceptable when used to describe situations under which poorer countries appear unable to progress autonomously because they are said to depend on advanced capitalist (or socialist) countries for investment capital, for technology and information to raise productivity, and for markets. In such usage, it may be more or less appropriate but there is no question of testing its validity. However, tests may be carried out on hypotheses that may be clustered under the descriptive umbrella of dependency, as was done by Newfarmer and Topik (1982). Because analysts of dependency stress the dominant role of the global capitalist system, there is a simple modulation to analysis of multinational corporations and the claim that they pre-empt development of indigenous economies by squeezing out local entrepreneurs in the most dynamic sectors of the host economy. In a search for testable hypotheses, Moran (1978) drew on earlier writers to suggest that MNCs are likely to concentrate on investing in industries with the greatest barriers to entry (based on scale, research and development capacity, and the significance of advertising and the technology and skills of marketing). Local investors may have specific skills, contacts or resources that encourage the establishment of joint ventures but these often appear transitory, with MNCs buying out local partners. On the other hand, Moran suggests that product-cycle analysis predicts increasing local competition to MNCs as new processes are standardised, markets probed, financial feasibility demonstrated, and uncertainty reduced: 'The pace and extent of the economic counter-challenge to foreign capitalist penetration in the Third World, however, has received surprisingly little rigorous study among either dependencia or non-dependencia analysts' (Moran, 1978, p. 87).

Analyses of economic transformations in Brazil by Evans

256

(1979) and by Newfarmer and Topik (1982) show that investment by a triple alliance of local capitalists, the state and foreign capitalists was responsible for growth that no individual group could have generated alone. Nevertheless, successful Brazilian firms were taken over or were squeezed out of dominant positions by foreigners so that the authors concerned considered the transformation to be dependent development. Similar conclusions were reached by Fernandez (1979) for Colombia, where, again, industrialisation was begun by local entrepreneurs, recently with participation by state enterprises, but also with increasing dominance in certain sectors by foreign corporations, some of which have taken over Colombian firms. Moreover, the state relied on foreign loans for 70 per cent of its development expenditure in the late 1970s. Fernandez suggests that the growth of early capitalism into imperialistic capitalism has constrained the growth of later forms into dependent capitalism, where, although the state is a powerful economic agent, its perceived financial needs render it partly subservient to the interests of foreign capital.

In contrast to such views that support the 'squeezing out' hypothesis, Cypher (1979) cites evidence from several countries that local capitalists and governments have competed much more successfully against MNCs than the dependency model allows, and he concludes that 'the degree of asymmetry of interdependence can be altered' (p. 39). Moran (1978), too, had noted the potential for host countries to deal successfully with MNCs, particularly since there are conflicts and competition among the MNCs themselves, but Newfarmer and Topik (1982, p. 58) point out that one should not overlook the possibility that state policy may be influenced by a fusion of class interests between local and foreign capitalists. This line of argument suggests the need to identify the people or groups involved in policy decisions relating to MNCs, at the level of both government and the corporate partners and/or competitors of MNCs. This should clarify, first, whether any groups have strong interests in asserting autonomy from the technological and financial dominance of foreign interests. Second, it should trace their performance in pursuit of such a goal, with an eye for possible shifts in relationships to other local and foreign interest groups. It is sometimes argued that in less developed countries, the historical relationships established under colonialism give to a *comprador* bourgeoisie interests that differ from those of emergent industrialists so that there will be conflict, in which external forces will side with the *compradores* to limit erosion of their privileges.

In contrast, Resnick (1973) has described a 'second path of capitalism' that may be traced by merchant capitalists developing under colonial conditions, yet capable of establishing an independent capitalism. Using the Philippines as an illustration, he shows how some of the landed class used the proceeds of commercial agriculture to become urban merchants. In the early twentieth century, some of these capitalists, side by side with citizens of the colonial powers and with Chinese residents, invested in agricultural processing and industries with a locational advantage, such as printing, glass, chemicals and construction goods; the required capital came not only from trading profits but also from continued family agricultural enterprises. After independence in 1946, the state introduced various measures to foster the growth of industries and of supporting financial institutions, but this did not provoke significant conflict over control of policy between industrialists and the merchant or landed class fractions because most of the few score dominant families were represented in all sectors: agricultural, financial and industrial enterprises. (This phenomenon, although with different origins, has been described in countries that include Chile (Zeitlin and Ratcliffe, 1975), Colombia (Fernandez, 1979), and Thailand (Hewison, 1981), not to mention, of course, the advanced centres of finance capitalism.) In the Philippines, family links spread through the organs of the state and into foreign enterprises (by way of joint ventures or of employment in such enterprises). This is not to deny that differences of interest exist within the dominant group, whose homogeneity is in any case also diluted by the prominence of resident but non-citizen Chinese business families.

The measures of the 1950s to stimulate industrialisation simultaneously encouraged a new wave of foreign investment in manufacturing. This raised the question of whether emerging Philippine capitalism could, by asserting economic and political power, enhance its autonomy, to accumulate capital and direct it into more complex industrial production, financial services, and the capitalist transformation of agriculture, all sectors of the economy in which foreign interests had not grown as rapidly as in manufacturing. In the world context, it would clearly need a strongly nationalist state to nurture opportunities for local accumulation of capital; most observers would agree that, despite the past decade of authoritarian government and increasing roles of state organisations, the Philippine state has failed to prevent the dilution of national control in important parts of the economy. The most critical observers say that the state has gone out of its way to facilitate penetration by alien corporations by providing access to land, credit, financial incentives and joint ventures with state bodies. Regardless of intentions, the state's scope for policy-making has been massively constrained by commitments to foreign lenders, especially the World Bank and IMF (Feder, 1982). Only a limited number of local capitalists have been able to thrive with individual or joint ventures, and from the late 1960s, many of the opportunities occurred in the hitherto lagging agricultural sector as it became eligible for the government's fiscal incentives to encourage export production.

In this chapter the Philippine banana industry is examined to see whether at any point it could serve as a new channel for autonomous accumulation of Filipino capital that could further nationalist development. The investigation is linked to the points cited earlier from Moran, although in the context of agriculture rather than manufacturing.

In principle, there should be few barriers to entering the banana industry because, in the tropics, the fruit is widely grown commercially at scales ranging from family smallholdings to plantations, with a range of sophistication in techniques and in sources of finance and with marketing by government agencies, cooperatives, or local or transnational corporations. Nevertheless, in practice, the great majority of the fruit for export has been produced on plantations and marketed, up to the late 1960s, by either the United Fruit Company or Standard Fruit and Steamship Company.[1] 'There are few tropical food crops that require the high capital investment involved in banana production, marketing and distribution' (UNCTAD, 1974, p. 21). In part, this high cost is necessary for high productivity in the fields and quality control in distribution, particularly since the late 1950s when United Fruit and Standard Fruit introduced new varieties of bananas, branding and packing in boxes, associated with advertising to expand market shares, so that their lagging profits revived.

The Philippine Banana Export Industry

The Philippine banana industry developed in the late 1960s in response to the removal of restrictions on entry to the Japanese market in 1963. Before then, Japan had been supplied almost exclusively from Taiwan. Although independent Ecuadorean producers and exporters took a temporary lead in 1963, the Taiwanese smallholders very rapidly raised their output to dominate again, but there was scope for Filipinos to compete because the island of Mindanao was free of the typhoons which sometimes damaged Taiwan's groves; moreover, with only a five-day voyage to Japan, the Philippines had a freight advantage over Latin American exporters.

In the Philippines, the import-substituting industrialisation of the 1950s had been checked and many infant industries had closed down or been bought out by foreign investors. In contrast, exporters and commercial enterprises had benefited and the Japanese banana market appeared as a new source of profits for those with access to suitable land. A number of people quickly developed small plantations (usually less than 20 hectares), selling to Japanese firms already importing from Taiwan, but quality was poor and for several years sales were only a few thousand dollars (Dangilan, n.d.). Neither the Filipinos nor their Japanese buyers possessed the changed production and packaging technology that had recently revived the profits of the American MNCs, and the Filipino firms failed to try to buy such technology independently (perhaps from growers in Ecuador or other Latin Americans), while the government's agricultural extension service offered only outdated advice to prospective growers.

Simultaneously with these efforts, the American multinationals knew that they had to capture a major share of the Japanese market to maintain their competitive performance and they recognised the locational advantages of a Philippine base. In 1962, United Fruit entered a joint venture with several Japanese firms to import United's 'Chiquita' brand bananas, initially from Central America (Read, 1982, p. 10) and then, in 1963, they engaged in highly confidential negotiations with the Philippine government for United's subsidiary Mindanao Fruit Corporation to lease and convert 8000 hectares of an agricultural penal colony into a banana plantation. An outcry by Filipino nationalists prevented consummation of the deal, and cost United Fruit its lead in the race to build a Philippine base, but they did not drop out. Neighbouring the penal colony were several 1024 hectare plantations, one of which, Tadeco, was owned by Antonio Floirendo, a close political associate of President Marcos (elected late in 1965).[2] In 1968, Floirendo signed a purchasing and technical advice agreement with Mindanao Fruit for the establishment of a banana plantation on his Tadeco land, aided by a loan guaranteed by United Fruit. The following year, he entered a so-called joint venture contract with the Bureau of Prisons (under the Department of Justice) to use approximately 3000 hectares of the penal colony as a banana plantation, with provision for unlimited later expansion on identical terms.[3] Once again, nationalists claimed that the agreement betrayed national interests. They forced an investigation, but its critical findings were over-ridden by the Department of Justice, except that an amendment to the contract required Tadeco to keep its accounts separate from those of the Bureau's shares.[4]

Among the advantages conferred on Tadeco by the contract were an extraordinarily low payment for use of the Bureau's land and low labour costs through use of prisoners as part of the workforce (David *et al.*, 1981, pp. 16-17).[5] In addition, it benefited from economies of scale through operating a single contiguous block of its own and Bureau land, reaching over 5000 hectares by 1981. Undoubtedly, some of the benefits of low costs accrued to United Fruit and added to the benefits of vertical integration after it had become sole owner in 1967 of the Japanese importing firm, Kyokuto Fruits (David *et al.*, 1981, p. 44). Not surprisingly, Tadeco became the most profitable of the banana plantations (Table 9.1). Its establishment costs had been covered by 1973 and in 1975 it earned its peak profit of 21.5 million pesos ($US3 million). Since the company had registered under the Board of Investment's export incentives scheme, it paid no income tax until 1977.

It is ironic that although United Fruit was first in attempting to establish a Philippine base, it was the last of three American MNCs actually to get a project on-stream. The first was Castle and Cooke, which operated through rather complex arrangements. Its first step was to set up Standard (Philippines) Fruit Corporation (Stanfilco) as a 66 per cent-owned joint venture with a Philippine holding company, House of Investments, in which Castle and Cooke had 17 per cent equity.[6] Its Filipino major partners in House of

Table 9.1: Financial Performance of Tadeco, 1973-82 (million pesos, current values)

Paid-up capital[a]	65.5
Total assets[a]	290.0
Outstanding loans[a]	146.0
Net income[b]	105.4
Income tax paid[b]	33.3
Retained earnings	15.3
Stock dividends[b]	55.0
Stockholder equity	90.3

Notes: a. 1982.
b. 1973-82.
Source: Financial statements on file at Securities and Exchange Commission.

Investments were already associated with Castle and Cooke through Dole Philippines, Inc. (Dolefil), set up in 1963 with 80 per cent equity held by the American corporation. The Filipinos were lawyers and businessmen associated with the Rizal Commercial and Banking Corporation (RCBC), and included J.P. Enrile, later the Secretary of Justice and then Minister of Defence under President Marcos. The President of Dolefil, G.P. Velasco, later became Marcos's Minister for Energy. In the same year, the government's National Development Corporation acquired 5500 hectares, mostly occupied by small-scale settlers and, almost certainly unconstitutionally, leased the land to Dolefil for 25 years (renewable). This time, nationalist protest was unsuccessful (Tanada, 1965, pp. 53-67).

Stanfilco made the first effective entry into the Philippine banana industry in 1966, by setting up an independent growers' scheme under which it contracted to buy the output of small growers to whom it would supply all necessary inputs, including advice and credit. The great majority of growers owned no more than 10 hectares (David *et al.*, 1981). Stanfilco also contracted to set up and operate as manager a plantation of 1024 hectares owned by a provincial family. At more or less the same time, the Manila and Hawaii-based stockholders set up three corporate subsidiaries of the House of Investments[7] to establish plantations up to 1024 hectares in size by leasing from large landowners. All of these producers sold their output to Stanfilco, who in turn sold to Castle and Cooke Worldwide in Hong Kong. In 1979, another provincial enterprise set up a small (112-hectare) plantation selling directly to Castle and Cooke. By then, Castle and Cooke marketed the output of 6770 hectares, and held 28 per cent of the Japanese market. By 1980, however, the costs of operating the dispersed small growers' scheme had become a main cause of frequent losses for Stanfilco and Castle and Cooke decided to merge it with the more profitable Dolefil.[8] The consolidation of accounts since then has prevented further analyses of the banana operations. Even before that, the figures for the individual subsidiaries (as shown in Table 9.2) were complicated by such facts as that much of the equipment used on the interspersed farms of nominally distinct companies came from a common pool.

Among the banana enterprises that preceded the entry of the giant multinationals was Hijo Plantation, owned by an American closely linked with a Japanese buyer, Fuji Fruits. Lacking financial resources, in 1966 he sold almost all his stock to a consortium comprising Fuji Fruits (28 per cent) and the owners of a Manila bank, his main creditor (65 per cent).[9] The same group simultaneously bought the neighbouring Twin Rivers Plantation, but they lacked the knowledge to develop large-scale banana operations until 1968, when another American multinational, Del Monte, entered the global banana trade and began contracting with local producers.[10]

Table 9.2: Financial Performance of Subsidiaries of Castle and Cooke (million pesos, current values)

	Period	Checkered Farms	Diamond Farms	Golden Farms	Stanfilco	Dolefil
Paid-up capital	1981	2.4	0.8	1.4	16.1[a]	64.7
Total assets	1981	21.8	25.9	17.2	172.7[a]	504.9
Stockholders' equity	1981	4.7	1.4	1.6	−1.6[a]	175.9
Outstanding loans	1981	15.2	23.6	14.8	150.9[a]	265.0
Income tax	1973-81	4.1[b]	1.5	2.0[c]	1.4[d]	33.2[e]
Net income after tax	1973-81	7.7	1.6	3.2[c]	−18.1[d]	49.8[e]
Retained earnings	1981	2.3	0.6	0.3	−17.7[d]	111.3
Dividends	1973-81	6.1	0.9	3.7	1.0[d]	NIL[e]

Notes: a. 1979, before merger with Dolefil.
b. 1973 plus 1975-81.
c. 1974-81.
d. 1973-79.
e. 1979-81. (Dolefil declared a cash dividend of 8.2 million pesos in 1982).
Source: Financial statements on file at Securities and Exchange Commission.

It was vital for Del Monte, as a new entrant in the trade, to build its market share by taking part in the Japanese market, and its strategy was to contract with large-scale producers to achieve a supply base of at least 5000 hectares. Rather than set up a new local subsidiary, like Castle and Cooke's Stanfilco, Del Monte used Philpack to provide technical services to its growers and as a conduit for production loans, either directly or as guarantor, while the purchasing contracts were with Del Monte International.

By 1972, eight Filipino corporations had contracts with Del Monte; they had planted 4243 hectares with a further 1750 hectares planned (Philippines, 1973). However, several corporations soon expressed discontent, partly on the issue of cost and quality of technical services and partly because they considered that Del Monte gained a disproportionate share of the selling price in Japan (David *et al.*, 1981, pp. 20-2). Therefore, three corporations used their newly acquired skills in banana production to set up independent plantations selling directly to Japanese importers (see Table 9.3). The first and most significant of these was the Hijo group.

The owners of Hijo plantation contracted to sell to Del Monte only the output of that plantation, and they developed Twin Rivers as an independent supplier to the minority owner, Fuji Fruits. Keen to play a bigger part in the industry, in 1969 they set up Davao Fruits Corporation as a 60:40 joint venture with the Japanese importer, Sumitomo Shoji Kaisha, which needed to augment its Taiwanese and Ecuadorean supplies to compete with the American MNCs. Whereas Fuji Fruits played a sleeping partner role in management of the earlier two companies, the Filipinos found that Sumitomo's members of the new board preferred to express opinions. Nevertheless, control was firmly in Filipino hands and the trading relationship was said to be effectively at arm's length.[11] The new company grew very quickly. By 1972 it had planted 2400 hectares on land leased from small owners, and already held 8.5 per cent of the Japanese market. The following year its share exceeded 11 per cent, and fluctuated within one percentage point of that through to 1980 (Japan Banana Importers Association, 1980, p. 101). In 1979, Davao Fruits Corporation ranked 147th by gross revenues in the list of the top 1000 corporations in the country, published annually by the leading business journal, *Business Day* (1980). Table 9.4 shows that its leading competitors in the banana industry were then Stanfilco and

Table 9.3: Ownership Groups in the Philippine Banana Industry

1973	Marketing[a] Company	1980	Marketing[a] Company	1983	Marketing[a] Company
Stanfilco	C	Dolefil	C	Dolefil	C
Checkered	C	Checkered	C	Checkered	C
Diamond	C	Diamond	C	Diamond	C
Golden	C	Golden	C	Golden	C
Hijo	D	Hijo	D	Hijo	I
Twin Rivers	I	Twin Rivers	I	Twin Rivers	I
Davao Fruits	I	Davao Fruits	I	Davao Fruits	I
		S.E.I.	I	S.E.I.	I
No Grouping					
Tadeco	U	Marsman	D	Marsman	D
Delta	D	Nova Vista	D	Nova Vista	D
Dizon	D				
Evergreen	D	Delta	D	Delta	D
Farmingtown	D	Evergreen	D	Evergreen	D
Lapanday	D	Farmingtown	D	Farmingtown	D
Marsman	D			Lapanday	D
A.M. Soriano	D	A.M. Soriano	D	Guihing	D
Cadeco	I	Soriano Fruits	I	Cadeco	D
S.E.I.	I				
Mount Apo Fruit	I	Lapanday	D	A.M. Soriano	D
Mabuhay	I	Guihing	I	Soriano Fruits	D
Desidal	I	Cadeco	I		
				No Grouping	
		No Grouping		Tadeco	U
		Tadeco	U	Dizon	D
		Dizon	D	Sarangani	C
		Sarangani	C		
		Ceased Operations			
		Desidal, Mabuhay,			
		Mount Apo Fruit,			
		Napungas			

Notes: a. C — Castle and Cooke; D — Del Monte; U — United Brands; I — Independent. Company names are abbreviated for convenience of presentation.
Source: Articles of Incorporation of the companies, including amendments, augmented by personal communications from company officers.

Tadeco, while its associate companies, Hijo and Twin Rivers, were midway in the list.[12]

Table 9.4 also indicates that the banana producers gradually lost prominence as their sales in a limited market failed to keep pace with revenues of corporations in more dynamic sectors. The period involved was also that of the 'second oil shock' when costs of industries heavily reliant (like banana plantations) on petroleum and chemicals escalated rapidly. One result was a shake-out in the

Table 9.4: Banana Producers Among Leading Corporations Ranked
by Gross Revenues

	1978	1979	1980	1981	1982
Dolefil	n.a.	n.a.	41	39	46
Stanfilco	73	104	n.a.	n.a.	n.a.
Tadeco	105	113	148	160	132
Davao Fruits	140	147	330	177	174
Twin Rivers	405	486	640	742	631
Hijo	385	508	755	(549)	u.
Guihing	n.a.	n.a.	n.a.	n.a.	679
Lapanday	u.	514	(791)	(712)	(764)
AMS Farming	u.	(726)	931	837	724
Farmingtown	862	878	1247	1143	922
Checkered Farms	987	933	1012	1120	1080
Evergreen	u.	1186	1209	u.	u.
Delta Farms	u.	—	—	1626	1400
Golden Farms	1049	1132	(1388)	1502	1359
F.S. Dizon	—	—	—	—	1502
Cadeco	—	—	—	1187	1666
Soriano Fruits	—	—	—	—	1886
Diamond Farms	—	—	—	1910	2000
Desidal	851	801	n.a.	n.a.	n.a.

Notes: Figures in brackets are not in published lists but interpolated using data from
corporate financial statements.
n.a. Not applicable (not yet in industry or ceased operations).
u. Data unavailable.
— Revenues not high enough to be listed.
Source: Annual issues of *Business Day, 1000 Top Corporations in the Philippines.*

Philippine banana industry, with the collapse or takeover of
smaller or less efficient producers, especially those that had leapt
on the banana bandwagon in its heyday of the early 1970s.

At that time, the prospects for the banana industry attracted
many individuals and corporations, apart from the groups already
discussed.[13] Three large Japanese trading companies and one
smaller company sought Filipino partners for joint ventures, and
two more offered loans to their existing Filipino suppliers of timber
to set up banana plantations. The resulting links are shown in
Table 9.5.

In all cases except Napungas (which operated for only two
years), the Filipino owners exercised managerial control. However,
this independence was ill-fated. By 1980, the last four companies
in the list had gone bankrupt or ceased banana production. Cadeco
had been taken over by the owners of Lapanday, S.E.I. by the
owners of the Hijo group and Soriano Fruits survived in a marginal

Table 9.5: Minor Japanese Participation in the Philippine Banana Industry

Japanese	Filipino	Financial Link	Percentage Share in Japanese Market 1977
Mitsui-Norin Kaisha	Cadeco	15 per cent equity	0.3
Toyo Menka Kaisha	S.E.I.	30 per cent equity	0.8
	Soriano Fruit	Loan	0.7
Mac Trading Co.	Mabuhay	40 per cent equity	1.3
Ataka and Co.	Desidal	Loan	3.2
Sanko Trading Co.	Mt. Apo Fruit	Loan	0.7
Nakano and Co.	Napungas	30 per cent equity	n.a.

Source: Articles of Incorporation, financial statements and interview responses. Market share from JBIA (1980, p. 94).

condition. Many factors, including poor management and grossly excessive debt–equity ratios, were involved in these failures (Krinks, 1981), but one contribution came from the intervention of the state.

Just after martial law was imposed late in 1972, the largest growers, led by Mr Floirendo, successfully urged the government to prevent over-supply and price-collapse by limiting the area of production to 21,000 hectares, distributed among 19 companies with existing exports. Despite the president's Letter of Instruction (LOI) No. 58, several late entrants nevertheless maintained or even enlarged their plantings, but were unable to cope with problems of poorer land and inadequate scale. The restrictions were undoubtedly a sensible measure, but they were imposed precisely as devised by the larger corporations who stood to benefit most, and at a time when the industry was recording very high profits.[14]

The small or late-established independent companies were not the only ones to experience difficulties. Two of Del Monte's producers — Delta and Farmingtown — were mismanaged and were bought by Filipino employees and associates of Del Monte in 1979 and 1981 respectively. The owners of a third producer, Evergreen, sold to the same buyers in 1980 in order to re-invest in another business.[15] By 1981, then, Del Monte controlled three of its eight corporation growers, but three others — Hijo, Lapanday and A.M. Soriano — still had their associate companies marketing separately, so it is necessary to follow through these assertions of independence.

After the rapid expansion of his A.M.S. Farming Corporation, the provincial entrepreneur A.M. Soriano set up several other companies as well as Soriano Fruits, including a Manila office. His main ambition appeared to be to tackle the MNCs in their own court, so he established a pineapple cannery and leased land for a plantation to supply it. Part of the capital for the three ventures came from his two banana companies. For a variety of reasons, the cannery had not become profitable by 1984. It thus had not repaid funds to the banana enterprises[16] and presumably diverted excessive executive time from them. These factors contributed to A.M.S. Farming's losses of over P 12 million between 1979 and 1981, and by 1982 a major banking creditor had taken a seat on the board of A.M.S. (AMSFC, 1982). Soriano was forced to switch Soriano Fruits' output from Toyo Menka to Del Monte, who took over technical management of both companies. They arranged a consolidation of all A.M.S. Farming's debts, some of which had been at interest rates up to 21 per cent, into short-term loans at 6.5 and 7 per cent, guaranteed by Philpack, which required all cheques over P 10,000 to be countersigned by its staff.[17] This appeared to be the end of one attempt to produce and market bananas independently of the MNCs.

Lapanday Agricultural Development Corporation was a joint venture between some of the owners of the 2nd and 14th biggest banks in the Philippines, all Filipino citizens.[18] It was the fourth company to contract with Del Monte and it quickly achieved both the highest productivity and the highest profit per hectare. From 1971 to 1976 its net income was over P 24 million from just over 600 hectares; in the same period it had built stockholders' equity to P 2 million and distributed P 4.4 million in cash and P 9.6 million in stock dividends. It then converted an associated company, Guihing Agricultural and Development Corporation, to a banana plantation selling directly to a Japanese importer, and the following year bought out Cadeco, one of the failing small producers that marketed through Mitsui-Norin. Guihing rapidly became very profitable, with a net income of P 13.8 million in 1981 and stockholders' equity of P 28.6 million. Cadeco too returned to profitability with a large injection of capital. However, both independents were funded in part out of Lapanday's retained earnings just at a time of low margins and declining productivity, partly caused by excessive use of chemical inputs. In addition, Lapanday began to experience difficulties with anti-government rebels operating in the area. Company financial statements reported that its security forces cost over P 1 million in 1981 and

1982. Late in 1981, Lapanday broke its contract with Del Monte in a dispute over responsibility for spoiled fruit. For a while it sold to Sumitomo but continued productivity problems and the added freight costs from selling the fruit cif rather than fob were discouraging. In 1982, Lapanday lost almost P 16 million, and the owners decided that they had better use for their funds so they sold two companies to the same combination of Del Monte associates and the third to a single senior executive of Del Monte.[19] Thus, another another assertion of independence ended.

This left the Hijo group outstanding. One of the problems Davao Fruits had faced all along was that of shipping. The company alone did not have enough mature hectarage at any one time to fill a refrigerated ship ('reefer') quickly enough to avoid expensive demurrage costs; worse, delay would contribute to fruit spoilage.[20] It therefore encouraged other independents to load on the ships it hired (usually those belonging to Compania Maritima; occasionally from Everett Lines). However, in mid-1981, Del Monte refused to allow this, so that Davao Fruits had to rely on hiring ships just when other independent producers were going out of business or being taken over. It was generally assumed locally that Del Monte, as a world-ranking trader, could get concealed discounts from ship-owners that would not be available to a smaller enterprise such as Davao Fruits which, therefore, had to operate on smaller margins.[21] The loss of support from independents, especially Lapanday and Guihing, was a crisis for the owners of the Hijo-Davao Fruits group. Through 1982, they negotiated with Del Monte for termination of Hijo's marketing contract so it could then sell to Sumitomo and, on 29 September, they concluded an agreement, conditional on Del Monte's success in contracting to buy the output of Lapanday and Guihing.[22] Such success was ensured by the sale of these companies to Del Monte's employees.

At the end of 1982, then, the Hijo group was one of only eight separate ownership groups and the only one not marketing through an American MNC (Table 9.3). It had a plantable area of almost 6300 hectares, enough to exercise an influential voice in the Japanese market and in the less significant Middle Eastern market. However, even though the management was Filipino, it was undoubtedly Sumitomo's funds and role as a global trading company that made possible the group's continuation as a force in the industry.

During 1982 and 1983, the four competitors discussed the problems of over-supply in the face of shrinking demand in Japan and eventually agreed that an informal division of market shares would be the most beneficial response, leaving competition for other markets and also in cost-cutting and productivity. The agreed quotas were 27 per cent for each of the American companies and 19 per cent for the Hijo group, which accepted this reluctantly. No public statement was made as to how the agreement would be operated, but it was not needed immediately because a drought of several months in 1983 cut production below the level of demand. The quota arrangements promised a period of stability in the industry provided that the Filipino owners of the Hijo group maintained their interest. One indication that this seemed likely was the establishment of another group company, Eden Fruits and Vegetables Co. Inc., which began exporting local *lakatan* bananas rather than the Cavendish variety that had been the mainstay since the 1960s. With its superior taste, *lakatan* commanded a price premium in Japan and by 1982 Eden Fruits achieved gross sales (including other products) of P19 million, making it 1566 in rank among the biggest corporations (*Business Day*, 1983, p. 186).

One other question of stability in the industry was whether Del Monte might be interested to take over its remaining producers not yet under its firm control, that is, F.S. Dizon & Sons, Inc., the Marsman Estate Plantation and its associate company Nova Vista Management and Development Corporation. The latter two companies were part of the agricultural activities of a large conglomerate covering mining and pharmaceuticals and whose parent company, Marsman & Co., was ranked 171 in 1982 (*Business Day*, 1983, p. 46). While the failure of some other banana ventures by Manila-based companies shows that size of parent need not ensure survival, the profitability of these two companies and Marsman's long-established agricultural concerns suggest it is likely to maintain its involvement. As for F.S. Dizon, he has operated agricultural enterprises in Luzon as well as Davao for several decades. From 1978 to 1981, his banana plantation suffered from nematodes and he blamed Philpack for inadequate technical advice. He had to relocate at considerable cost but by 1982 returned to profitability. He too seems unlikely to sell out, despite having debts of P36 million against assets of P45 million and stockholders' equity of only P3.4 million.

Reference has been made to corporate entrepreneurs in the banana industry being based in Manila or the second biggest city, Cebu City, because the industry attracted some of the most financially powerful groups in the country, although not all of these committed themselves heavily. The industry was seen as just another area for profit, because such groups had extremely diverse interests, centring on financial institutions but spreading widely across primary, secondary and tertiary activities (Simbulan, 1966, pp. 105-12). To take one example, the dominant owners of the group of corporations associated with Hijo Plantation are mostly major stockholders in the Far East Bank and Trust Company (FEBTC), in which about a quarter of the equity is held by a subsidiary of Chemical Bank of New York and by Mitsui Bank. In 1979, FEBTC had 161 director-interlocks with 112 major companies, including the country's biggest investment house, 38 of the largest agribusiness enterprises (from crop production to fertiliser and processed foods), cement and construction industries, rubber, electrical machinery and appliances, communications and transport equipment, paper, real estate, education and hotels (Doherty, 1979). Much the same could be said of the base groups of several other banana corporations — according to Doherty ten banking groups dominate the Philippine economy, and members of six of these have equity in banana corporations. Few of the corporations were established by small entrepreneurs without connections, and it was mostly these that failed.

Given the characteristics of many of the investors and of the prospects for the banana industry in its early years, it is not surprising that there were few problems of initial finance. As noted above, the MNCs provided loans to growers or guaranteed them, borrowing from both foreign and domestic sources. Unfortunately, most details are confidential, but it is known (from financial statements and *Business Day*, 26 May 1969) that United Fruit guaranteed an initial loan to Tadeco of at least $US 1 million from a Boston bank, when Tadeco's paid-up capital was less than P 50,000 and its net worth probably no more than double that. Del Monte (through Philpack) had a direct loan exposure to growers of over P 30 million (almost $US 5 million) in 1976, of which an unknown proportion was borrowed from local banks.[23] As Table 9.6 shows, Philpack had to make provision for the loans by banana growers that it had guaranteed at Philippine banks, and it also advanced money to growers on demand notes and promissory

Table 9.6: Advances from Philippine Packing Corporation to Banana Growers (million pesos, current values)

	Direct Advances	Loans from Local Banks Co-signed or Guaranteed	Notes Receivable[a]	Total Exposure
1973	7.4	u.	35.1	42.5
1974	17.2	u.	40.8	58.0
1975	21.7	7.2	52.7	81.6
1976	30.5	3.6	48.9	83.0
1977	20.7	n.a.	34.6	55.3
1978	10.2	45.9	5.4[b]	61.5
1979	12.9	51.2	4.6	68.7
1980	4.5	n.a.	0.5	5.0
1981	18.5	49 approx.	8.7	76.2
1982	17.2	214 approx.	0	231.2

Notes: a. These are demand notes secured by mortgages. They include an unspecified amount due from debtors other than banana producers.
b. The 1981 statement mentions allowance for losses of P 26.3 million on receivables from growers.
u. Not identified in statement; probably nil.
n.a. Not available.
Source: Annual financial statements for 1974, 1975, 1976, 1978, 1979, 1981 and 1982.

notes. A clear preference emerged for guaranteed loans rather than actual commitment of funds, and the rapid increase from 1978 mainly reflects support of its employees when they took over banana corporations. Castle and Cooke's loans to its subsidiary Stanfilco amounted to P 50 million by 1978, (repayable in US dollars), and Stanfilco also owed its associate Standard Fruit & Steamship Co. P 35 million, while its debts to Philippine banks were P 63 million. In turn, Stanfilco had advanced P 50 million to its small growers.

Most of the Filipino corporations had no difficulty in borrowing also from local banks (sometimes, from those linked to the borrower by director interlocks),[24] but in later years those with poor records had to turn increasingly to dollar loans from foreign and local banks, and in a period of a deteriorating exchange rate repayments compounded their crucial problems of cash flow. This contributed to the takeover of two of Del Monte's growers. The ease of credit and laxness of government supervision meant that some Filipino corporations were set up with what had, over years, become the acceptable financial practice of massive debt–equity ratios — one, for instance, borrowed P 12 million to augment a paid-up capital of only P 50,000 (and later collapsed with P 23 million debts). On the other hand, the more responsible corporations, including Hijo and Marsman, quickly repaid debts to the MNCs using internally-generated funds or borrowed from local banks to give themselves greater independence. It was these companies that were able to survive, or even make profits, in the very tight market after 1978.

By 1981, seven corporations had failed or sold out without ever issuing dividends — in fact, two of these had stockholders' deficits exceeding P 18 million, considerably more than the value of their assets. In some cases, there were unproven allegations of use of funds from the corporations for the benefit of the major stockholders who, therefore, accumulated privately despite the public losses of their companies. It is necessary to note that all the banana producers were closely held or family corporations, as is usual in the Philippines where only 6 per cent of all corporations have their shares traded on the stock exchanges. Probably, because of the interlocking nature of the socio-financial networks of the wealthy — what Zeitlin (1975) calls 'kinecon groups' in Chile — owners of failing corporations were not penalised but merely sold off their assets, some having their debts condoned.

In contrast with the hopes of the early 1970s, only a minority of the corporations flourished. Chief among these was Tadeco: its privileged access to government land at low rent enabled it to declare stock dividends of P55 million in 1973-82 (in this period it did not distribute cash dividends). By 1982, its assets reached P290 million, and undoubtedly it was this major source of accumulation that financed Floirendo's emergence as a multinational entrepreneur, though his close association with President Marcos ensured that all his other enterprises flourished. Until his association with United Fruit, Floirendo had owned three or four modest provincial businesses (including a Ford motor agency and a piggery). The banana profits allowed expansion of all of these, as well as the establishment of at least two new agricultural enterprises and ancillaries in trucking, insurance, agricultural equipment and chemical supply, and agricultural aviation. Floirendo set up a new Ford agency in Manila and also began investing in other companies, beginning with Purefoods Corporation, a major meat processor that was a customer of his stockfarm and ranked 90th among corporations in 1981; other significant companies are Rizal Commercial and Banking Corporation, Delgado Bros (operators of the Manila Hilton), and Citibank's local subsidiary, FNCB-Finance. About 1980, Floirendo bought a sugar refinery in the USA for $11 million (Hawes, 1981, p. 12) and was rumoured to own real estate in Britain. As his interests expanded, he set up Anflo Management and Investment Corporation in Manila as a general manager and consultant for all his enterprises, following well-established Filipino practices of having an 'apex firm' above a group of affiliates (Makil, Reyes and Koike, 1983). Thus, the banana industry made possible Floirendo's progress from provincial to national élite, from *comprador* to transnational entrepreneur.

The second group of corporations that successfully made the banana industry a viable source of accumulation was, as noted earlier, the Lapanday group but the owners had no motivation beyond profit and willingly sold out in 1982, believing that Sumitomo's limited commitment to the banana trade constrained its ability to compete against the specialist American MNCs.[25] That is, they recognised that they could assert their independence in production, but they would remain dependent in international marketing.

The Hijo group also made the banana industry a source of accumulation, with a combined distribution of dividends of nearly P5 million in cash and over P5 million in stock between 1973 and 1981 (Table 9.7). The group's uses of the funds generated are not clear because the owners, all based in Manila, were, as noted above, well-established in a very wide range of enterprises. In

Table 9.7: Financial Performance of Companies in Hijo Group (million pesos, current values)

	Period	Hijo Plantation	Twin Rivers	Davao Fruits	S.E.I.
Paid-up capital	1981	28.7	11.7	10.3	5.0[a]
Total assets	1981	64.4	30.6	69.5	6.1[a]
Stockholders' equity	1981	37.2	9.3	20.2	4.2[a]
Outstanding loans	1981	17.0	18.0	35.6	0[a]
Income tax	1973-81	8.1	3.6	2.6	negligible[b]
Net income after tax	1973-81	38.2	10.4	10.4	−0.7[b]
Retained earnings	1981	5.3	−2.6	9.2	−0.8[a]
Dividends, cash	1973-81	9.4	3.2	2.0	0[b]
Dividends, stock	1973-81	7.8	4.7	2.7	0[b]

Notes: a. 1980. No data available for 1981. Company taken over by group in November 1978.
b. 1979-80.
Source: Corporate financial statements.

terms of the national economy, the benefit was diluted by the foreign ownership of 24 per cent of Hijo, 27 per cent of Twin Rivers, and 40 per cent of Davao Fruits. In this context, it is paradoxical that the officers of the Hijo group were among the most explicitly nationalist in their interview statements on asserting an independent challenge to the dominant role of the American MNCs, while their own companies had significant foreign ownership and they and their associates in Manila were involved in various other ventures with Japanese and American partners (Tsuda, 1978).

A final point to make on the financial aspects of the corporations is that, as would be expected in a capitalist system, there was a trend to centralisation and concentration of ownership. Sixteen separate groups entered the industry (forming, with subsidiaries, 25 corporations), but, by 1983, the processes of failure and takeover reduced the total to eight groups, of which only two had a majority of provincial rather than metropolitan or foreign ownership.

Discussion and Conclusions

Leaving aside the issue of the desirability of agribusiness in the Philippines, the story of the industry as sketched above seems to indicate failure by Filipino capitalists independently to take advantage of a new opportunity. Rather than asserting control by hiring the needed skills in production and marketing, the entrepreneurs compromised their autonomy by the nature of the contracts and other arrangements they made with the dominant MNCs. These then left far less scope for later attempts at independent production and marketing when the MNCs were firmly established in the Japanese market. How far a more autonomous approach would have succeeded is, of course, hypothetical; more than one MNC executive suggested the Filipinos would have been 'eaten alive' by the importers, though that was certainly not true for the suppliers to Sumitomo. The control of shipping was also a problem as here the Americans had an advantage, but this problem might also have been surmountable at an early stage as Compania Maritima built up its reefer fleet for the industry. Financially, too, several Filipino corporations found themselves stifled through debt to the foreigners, although there is no doubt that the industry could have been initially financed from Filipino sources and maintained in part from retaining rather than distributing earnings.

Organisationally, Filipinos in banana industry joint ventures with Japanese seem to have retained control in two cases (to the extent of leading the ventures to collapse). This contrasts with findings in the manufacturing sector. For instance, David and Tsuda (1978) concluded, 'In practice, the Filipino capitalist often has no qualms about surrendering organisational control as long as he is assured his share of the profits'; a view supported by several other observers and related partly to a cultural attribute and partly to perception of restricted opportunities for independence after the partial denationalisation of the manufacturing and finance sectors in the 1960s and 1970s. If this is valid for the majority of Filipino potential entrepreneurs, it seems to coincide with the findings by Evans on Brazilian development and with the stereotype of *compradores*.

In a situation where the opportunities for national capitalists are seen as constrained, one might expect that state action could make a difference. Given the size and importance of the Japanese market in the 1960s, there would have been a large opportunity cost to traders in *not* investing in such a convenient production centre as the Philippines, so that the government had a significant potential bargaining weapon. It was not used. As shown above, the main direct state intervention in the banana industry was to impose restrictions on planting and, although this had been requested by Filipinos, they were all suppliers of or joint ventures with aliens acting against late developers, mostly independent Filipinos. The independents might have retained a greater share of final value by selling directly to Japanese buyers, cutting out MNC traders (though the complexities of the trade make this benefit hypothetical).

As for less direct intervention, the state's export incentives were available to all banana corporations, with or without foreign participation, as part of the government's drive for exports and for foreign investment. It continues to favour MNC investment in food and agriculture so that recent years have seen rapid expansion in rubber, palm oil, pineapples, fisheries, and others. At the same time, there has been increasing state participation and control in some major commodity areas, notably sugar and coconuts/copra. This is paralleled by a trend for the state to enter joint ventures with aliens and to take over ailing manufacturing and financial companies (particularly those earlier excessively favoured because they belonged to associates of the president). To a degree, this means the state is pre-empting part of the domain of local capitalists and broadening its scope for direct accumulation rather than through its fiscal processes. It has been suggested that the government is using its powers in these ways to counter the strength of the longer-established oligarchs but, as Wurfel (1979) argues, 'the occasional policy conflicts between industry and export agriculture ... are ... muted by the bridge of family ties between both sides', and between them and government.

The increasing role of the state ought to enhance its position *vis-à-vis* foreign corporations, but in practice this appears not to be so. Whatever civil servants believe individually, they are subject to the highly centralised authority of the president and the senior bureaucrats, and it is clear they do not give priority to autonomous development.[26] Given the long-established connections between local and foreign capitalists, it seems unnecessary to blame this on policy constraints imposed by the World Bank and IMF, as argued by Feder (1982). Essentially, the situation fits the generalisations of Clairmonte and Kavanagh (1983), where governments have facilitated the expanding control of MNCs in processing, marketing and distribution, working with local oligarchies and resulting in the elimination of small and medium-sized enterprises.

At the same time, in the Philippines the process of penetration is not entirely one way. While the economy is open to foreign capital it has also been possible for Filipinos to invest overseas (until the crisis of 1983). The example of Floirendo has been mentioned. Others include at least two private banks, the country's major construction company, the government's Land Bank, which bought a Californian bank in 1980, and the United Coconut Mills monopoly, which bought the largest copra mill in France (Hawes, 1981, p. 13). These dealings are, of course, insignificant in global terms but they do qualify the image of total dependence. Such use of funds is clearly different from the secret bank deposits customary among the Filipino élite. On the other hand, it might be more productive if the accumulated funds were invested within the Philippines (David and Tsuda, 1978, p. 16).

In summary, then, of the participants in the Philippines banana industry in 1983, in the Castle and Cooke group both production and marketing were under control of the MNC. In the Del Monte group, the Americans controlled the marketing and, via associates, the production phase of six of their nine growers. United Brands controlled marketing for its partner but the production unit, Tadeco, was under clear Filipino ownership and control. As for the Sumitomo group, it was the Japanese MNC that controlled marketing, but Filipinos controlled the production phase.

In relation to the initial propositions, it was the production skills, research capacity and marketing techniques of the American MNCs that opened up a field of profits where local capitalists had made inadequate pioneering efforts. As the production skills diffused, local capitalists drew on their resources (and linkages with Japanese buyers) to set up their own failure: a threat of over-supply, which led the early producers to use their links with an authoritarian government to restrict entry to the industry. With limited scale of operations, the later entrants had limited scope in the marketing stage. Over-supply destabilised the distribution system in Japan and small participants could not adequately compete with global traders. In a temporarily dynamic industry, it was the MNCs who in effect determined the growth path, scale and techniques; most Filipino operators were either unwilling or inadequately prepared to meet the challenges of confronting MNCs in their specialist area.

Appendix

Abbreviated Corporate Name	*Full Name*
A.M.S.	A.M.S. Farming Corporation
Cadeco	Cadeco Agro-Development Philippines, Inc.
Checkered	Checkered Farms, Inc.
Davao Fruits	Davao Fruits Corporation
Delta	Delta Farms, Inc.
Desidal	Desidal Fruits, Inc.
Diamond	Diamond Farms, Inc.
Dizon	F.S. Dizon and Sons, Inc.
Dolefil	Dole Philippines, Inc.
Evergreen	Evergreen Farms, Inc.
Farmingtown	Farmingtown Agro-Developers, Inc.
Golden	Golden Farms, Inc.
Guihing	Guihing Agricultural and Development Corporation
Hijo	Hijo Plantation, Inc.
Lapanday	Lapanday Agricultural and Development Corporation
Mabuhay	Mabuhay Agricultural Corporation
Marsman	Marsman Estate Plantation, Inc.
Mount Apo	Mount Apo Fruit Enterprises, Inc.
Napungas	Napungas Agro-Development Corporation

Nova Vista	Nova Vista Management and Development Corporation
Sarangani	Sarangani Cattle Company, Inc.
S.E.I.	S.E.I. Agricultural Development Corporation
Soriano Fruits	Soriano Fruits Corporation
Stanfilco	Standard (Philippines) Fruit Corporation
Tadeco	Tagum Agricultural Development Company, Inc.
Twin Rivers	Twin Rivers Plantation, Inc.

Notes

1. Contemporary titles for the various companies have been retained. United Fruit Company merged in 1968 with A.M.K. Corporation to become United Brands. Standard Fruit & Steamship Co. was bought in 1964 by Castle and Cooke of Hawaii. As appropriate, Castle and Cooke and its joint-venture subsidiaries are referred to as Dole Philippines, Inc. (or Dolefil), a pineapple producer, and Standard (Philippines) Fruit Company, Inc. (or Stanfilco), the banana producer. In 1980, Stanfilco was merged with Dolefil. Del Monte, Inc. of California had a long-established pineapple-producing subsidiary, Philippine Packing Corporation, or Philpack. For its banana trade it used its subsidiaries Del Monte International in Brussels and Del Monte Products Inc. of Liberia. In 1979, Del Monte was bought by R.J. Reynolds of Atlanta. It remained a distinct division, but by 1983 Reynolds officers had moved into all significant financial and administrative positions.

2. According to several local business people (including a family member), Floirendo had long-established links with national politicians, obtaining the Tadeco land in 1951 after special release from public reservation by the president. By the mid-1960s, it is said that Floirendo's provincial businesses were close to bankruptcy and this lay behind his oath of support to President Marcos in 1965 (confidential sources). During the period of martial law (1972-81), Floirendo's brother-in-law was made a member of the Interim National Assembly, and in 1984 he became Minister of National Resources.

3. The first expansion of 1000 hectares took place in 1973. Terms are from a copy of the contract deposited in Office of the Provincial Assessor, Tagum, Davao del Norte.

4. It is noteworthy that the Secretary of Justice who signed the contract was J.P. Enrile, probably President Marcos's closest political associate and mentioned earlier as contributing to Dolefil's establishment and access to Philippine land. Enrile is of the Ilokana ethnic group, like the president. It is notable, too, that during the investigation, Tadeco's case was handled by the law firm of E. Angara, another close associate of the president. The investigator's report was summarised in the press (e.g. *Manila Times*, 27 December 1971), but after martial law was declared in 1972, it was available only in 'underground' copies.

5. One executive of the company stated confidentially in 1984 that Tadeco was still paying to the Bureau only P250 per hectare plus 10 centavos per box exported, while some other corporations were paying rents of over 1000 pesos per hectare to local landowners (field notes).

6. Minor participants in the House of Investments have been a Japanese bank, Fidelity Bank of Philadelphia and Continental International Finance Corporation Ltd, a wholly-owned subsidiary of Continental Illinois National Bank (House of Investments Annual Report, 1977). The same subsidiary held 30 per cent of Rizal Commercial and Banking Corporation. A further 10 per cent was held by Sanwa Bank (Doherty, 1979, p. 5).

7. In 1982, House of Investments' subsidiary, Checkered Farms, bought the 280 hectares it had been leasing from the Philippine Women's Educational Association. In 1983, the subsidiary, Diamond Farms, bought the 1024 hectares it had leased from a prosperous Davao family, which needed cash to pay estate duties on the death of the head of the family.

8. Filipino observers have expressed doubts as to the validity of the size of Stanfilco's losses, pointing out the opportunities for transfer-pricing in its ownership and trading makeup. Unfortunately, no data are available to clarify the issue.

9. Information from corporate officers and from Amended Articles of Incorporation, on file at Securities and Exchange Commission (SEC).

10. A brief sketch of Del Monte's entry into the banana trade is given by Litvak and Maule (1977).

11. Personal communication from company officers, 1980 and 1983.

12. The lists are not entirely accurate because companies sometimes fail to submit their financial statements to SEC. Thus, the absence of a company from one year's list does not necessarily mean that it ranked below 1000. The list's coverage has gradually expanded from 200 to 2000 corporations.

13. An account of the establishment, ownership and performance of each company is given in Krinks (1981), and additional information appears in David *et al.* (1981).

14. Despite the demonstrably high profits of the early 1970s, government continued to allow corporations to register for tax benefits under the Export Incentives Act: 13 corporations (out of a total of 26) registered, one as late as 1979. From 1975 to 1977 alone, the total value of benefits (or tax lost to the government) was P107 million (BOI, 1981).

15. Some former owners and officials of these companies have commented confidentially that Del Monte 'choked its growers with loans'. Some also argued that Philpack's technical management should have helped them raise productivity to avoid takeover. However, it was obviously other factors that produced a capital deficiency of P 18.5 million in Delta Farms Inc. in 1979, and P 7.1 million in Farmingtown Agro-Developers in 1981, while Evergreen Farms moved from a stockholders' equity of P 14.1 million in 1979 to P 0.6 million in the year of sale. It is notable that Philpack repaid P 8.4 million to Delta *after* the takeover, correcting charges made previously for interest and service fees (financial statement for 1980). Under the new owners, Delta achieved a small profit in 1981, while Farmingtown earned P 12.2 million in 1982.

16. In 1982, stockholders voted to convert A.M.S. Farming's loan of P 1.9 million into equity in the pineapple company (Minutes of the annual stockholders' meeting, 1982).

17. Personal communication from a confidential source. Other details are from 1982 financial statements.

18. However, the Bank of the Philippine Islands was itself 20 per cent-owned by J.P. Morgan Overseas Capital Corporation. For a time in the 1970s, Insular Bank of Asia and America had 30 per cent of its equity held by Bank of America and 10 per cent held by Dai-Ichi Kangyo Bank (Doherty, 1975, p. 5; *Business Day*, 1981, pp. 217-18).

19. Personal communication from the former chairman of Lapanday. It is notable that most of the companies sold to Del Monte experienced massive apparent plummeting of stockholders' funds in the year of, or prior to, sale.

20. The average reefer would take about 150,000 cartons (of 12 kg each). Shipping issues are discussed in UNCTAD (1974, pp. 41-62).

21. An interesting potential conflict of personal and family interest lay in the background. The dominant stockholder in Compania Maritima was J.P. Fernandez,

who also held stock in Hijo Plantation and its associate Apo Fruits Corporation, while one of his sisters was married to a senior executive in Del Monte's Philippine operations. Another was married to one of the owners of Farmingtown Agro-Developers, the banana producer bought out by Del Monte in 1981. It may be assumed that potential conflict was best resolved by operating on strict commercial principles. (Source: Corporate records at Securities and Exchange Commission and a confidential informant.)

22. A copy of the agreement is on file in the office of the Provincial Assessor, Davao Del Norte.

23. One former executive stated confidentially that in the late 1960s Philpack borrowed P 120 million from local banks for the banana project. In 1977, Philpack borrowed P 355 million locally for all its projects (David, 1981, p. 102).

24. For instance, in 1979, Davao Fruits Corporation borrowed P 18 million from the Far East Bank and Trust Co. Dolefil borrowed from Rizal Commercial and Banking Corporation, to the extent of P 110 million by 1980.

25. Personal communication, October 1983, in an interview with one of the former owners, who believes that economic progress is served by the sale of land or businesses whenever the price is right, without fear of concentration of ownership.

26. This is the basis of the extended nationalistic complaint by a local capitalist in Lichauco (1973).

10 THE ROLE OF FOREIGN MANUFACTURING IN BRITAIN'S GREAT RECESSION

Alan R. Townsend and Francis W. Peck

Introduction

Contemporary discussion of the 'globalisation' of activities in large multinational companies has mainly emphasised their expansion of production in the Third World. Less attention has been given until recently to the contraction of such corporations within industrialised countries which has characterised the period 1977-81. It is widely believed that after 1979 there was a tendency for foreign-owned corporations to close plants in the UK to the benefit of plants in other countries, paralleling an increase in investment abroad by UK-owned corporations (*Barclays Review*, August 1982). This chapter examines the evidence that foreign-owned plants played a disproportionate role in the loss of employment in Britain's recession, both in the country at large and in particular geographical areas including those supported by past government policy.

In addressing this question it quickly becomes apparent that past experience provides little context for the study of contraction in foreign-owned plants. The established literature on 'multinationals' mentions only briefly the possibility of plant closure, although Brooke and Remmers (1978) see the abandonment of operations early in the career of a plant as a possible outcome of too rapid growth.

The international literature on multinational investment tends to accept that its expansion serves to benefit the developed core regions of a country. Soon after Holland (1975) put that proposition, it was factually contradicted for the UK. For instance, Keeble (1976, p. 140) showed the distribution of 'moves' to the UK by sub-region of destination to be occurring well away from the earlier dominant core of the South East. It is particularly clear that 'first-time greenfield investments' concentrated in Scotland; in the period 1966-75 it attracted 10,900 out of 34,000 jobs from abroad (Pounce, 1981). However, very few of these jobs arose from moves occurring after 1972, except in developments related to preparations for the production of oil from the North Sea.

The Census of Production (Department of Trade and Industry) provides our main statistical framework. Despite occasional deficiencies in this source, the main geographical pattern which emerged from data for 1963, 1971, 1973 and 1975 was of the growth of employment (influenced by government regional policy) in 'peripheral regions' and of relative but not absolute decline in the 'core', the South East (Dicken and Lloyd, 1976; McDermott, 1977; Watts, 1979; Dicken and Lloyd, 1980). Significant differences between different nationalities of ownership were reflected by Watts (1979) and in papers on US investment (Dicken and Lloyd, 1976), European countries (Watts, 1980) and West Germany (Watts, 1982).

Foreign corporations experienced an overall expansion in jobs of 72 per cent from 1963 to 1975. However, Smith (1982) and Watts (1982) noted a change in the geographical pattern of the growth in the last few years of that period; Scotland and Northern Ireland were attracting less expansion and *closures* were increasing in number. The higher incidence of foreign-owned manufacturing plant closures in the 'assisted areas' between 1972 and 1975 was related to two factors: first, their increased peripherality with regard to the market of the EEC after 1973, and, second, the increased importance of acquisition as opposed to greenfield investment after 1971. Both sets of circumstances may have encouraged foreign companies to focus their rationalisation strategies on these peripheral regions during the recent recession (Smith, 1982). The reversal of core–periphery relationships is taken a stage further by recent research on Scottish foreign-owned manufacturing. Unlike earlier decades, when it was fairly well-established that such multinational firms exhibited greater employment robustness than indigenous firms in times of recession and, at best, went solidly against the trend displayed by older, declining industries, in recent years in Scotland the witnessing of large numbers of closures among long-established multinational enterprise plants is a 'totally new experience and one not readily understood' (Hood and Young, 1982). This chapter utilises data of net change from the Censuses of Production for 1977, 1979 and 1981 as a framework within which to assess more detailed evidence for the main trend of that period, that of rationalisation and closure in a period of mounting international recession. The detailed evidence comprises all reports of gross job losses, by names of companies involved, from the *Financial Times*; all cases occurring under foreign ownership were extracted by reference to annual editions of *Who Owns Whom*. (For further details of the data set as a whole, see Townsend and Peck, 1985.) The order of the analysis is one which works 'from the whole to the parts', beginning in the next section with the aggregate performance of the foreign-owned sector as a whole. Subsequent sections deal with data by nationality, region, sub-region and type of local area.

The Reversal of Expansion Trends, 1977-81

Clearly, any downturn in foreign-owned manufacturing activity in the UK is a serious departure from a past history of investment in the country's 'growth industries'. Following the changing trend of the period from 1972 to 1975, it is now clear that later editions of the Census of Production record a dramatic about-turn: manufacturing employment in foreign-owned establishments in the UK was 925,700 in 1975, 1,013,800 (peak) in 1977, 974,200 in 1979 and 858,100 in 1981.

As in domestically-owned industry, job losses had become the dominant component of employment change by 1980, and it would be surprising if the foreign-owned sector showed no further continuing reduction beyond 1981 (data for all years represent average numbers employed during the year, including part-time workers). The decline of 155,700 between 1977 and 1981 may be disaggregated *separately* by country of ownership, sector and region. This chapter uses this framework of aggregate change to assess the contribution of the principal named companies reported in the *Financial Times* over this period. (The work is complementary to case studies of UK corporations, as in Peck and Townsend, 1984.) There is as yet comparatively little work on this period of change. The area where analysis of government data is most advanced is that of Scotland, where Hood and Young (1982, p. 9) estimate a net employment reduction of 28,300 in overseas-owned units from 1975 (108,200) to 1982 (80,500), involving at least two job losses for every one increase (p. 35). Units which closed in this period at their peak provided nearly 45,000 jobs in Scotland. Our own *Financial Times* record, of all kinds of job loss reported by company, covers gross job losses in Scotland of 25,200, in 1977-81.

The net UK decline of 155,700 jobs is the resultant of several components of change — not only openings, closures, expansions and contractions, but also the acquisition and sale of companies and plants in a period of markedly increased 'interpenetration' of holdings between industrialised countries. Over the period as a whole the Census of Production actually records an increase in both the number of foreign enterprises (corporations) engaged in manufacturing in the UK, and an increase in the number of factory establishments which they owned (see Table 10.1).

A comparison with the UK private manufacturing record shows that foreign manufacturing enjoyed better productivity (on both the measures used in Table 10.1) than UK-owned plants in all major industries in 1977. By 1981 this position was less clear and the average ratio of foreign to domestic productivity had fallen from being a third better to a quarter better. The main feature of foreign corporations' performance was one of reduced manning in the general population of plants, rather than closures; the average foreign factory reduced its employment from 382 in 1977 to 304 in 1981, whereas the average UK factory on the same Census of Production measures, declined from 64 to 53. Many UK corporations were attempting to 'catch up' on international standards of increased productivity (for examples, see Peck and Townsend,

Table 10.1: Basic Dimensions of Change, 1977-1981, Private Sector Manufacturing

	1977		1981	
	Foreign-owned	Total UK	Foreign-owned	Total UK
Enterprises	1,370	89,822	1,522	90,068
Establishments	2,654	107,691	2,825	108,276
Employment (000s)	1,013.8	6,883.4	858.1	5,777.9
Net output per capita	£9,519	£7,057	£15,265	£12,222
Ratio of foreign-owned to UK		1.35		1.25
Gross value added	£8,185	£6,102	£12,355	£10,027
Ratio of foreign-owned to UK		1.34		1.23

Note: The revised definition of manufacturing in the Standard Industrial Classification of 1980, compared with that of 1968, caused a 0.23 per cent reduction in the coverage of UK manufacturing, as evident in a 'data-bridge' for 1979; this adjustment is ignored in tables and text of this chapter.

Source: Department of Trade and Industry, *Census of Production.*

1984), but the foreign plants in the UK still shared many of the same trends of rationalisation, intensification and technical change.

National Change in Ownership

For the purpose of locational analysis, Watts (1979) divided enterprises into three groups of countries: the USA, with notable representation in the South East and Scotland, the EEC, with a marked emphasis on the South East and East Anglia, and a residual group of 'others'. Table 10.2 shows that these groups performed differently in the three time-periods. Because of its proportionate importance (Dicken and Lloyd, 1976), and because it showed continuous and above average decline, the USA accounts for a large part of the total pattern of change; this disproportionate reduction contributes to some diversification in the overall national composition of ownership, with the 'other' group actually showing net increases during 1977-81, largely attributable to early stages of penetration from the 'Pacific Basin', i.e. Japan and Australia. There is, however, a different grouping, of traditional UK trading partners, Canada, the Netherlands and Switzerland, which sustained rates of job loss comparable with those of the USA. The table also reveals the continuing impetus from the UK's entry into the EEC in 1973, suggested by the evidence that factory employment of other member states in the UK peaked in 1979 and not in 1977.

Direct analysis by industry is prevented by the revision in 1980 of the industrial classification. However, the concentration of foreign-controlled employment in a relatively small number of enterprises and establishments enables us to assess the dominant elements of change in terms of job losses at named plants reported in the *Financial Times*. The names of leading corporations for job loss are introduced in the final column of Table 10.2.

The source of this type of information in the rest of this chapter is a comprehensive survey of all reports of job loss in the *Financial Times*, undertaken from October 1976 to September 1981. In UK manufacturing at large it provides a 43.1 per cent coverage of recorded redundancies. (For definitions and principal results, see Townsend and Peck, 1985.) However, its coverage of 100,400 job losses attributed to foreign companies is crudely equivalent to 64.5 per cent of the net loss of 155,700 jobs with which we are dealing

Table 10.2: Net Employment Change by Nationality of Foreign-owned Manufacturing in UK, 1977-81

	1977	1979	1981	Change 1977-81 No.	Change 1977-81 Per cent	Leading Corporations for Job Loss, 1977-81
USA	711,800	661,500	568,100	−143,700	−20.2	General Motors (9100); Singer (5700)
Canada	66,500	63,400	51,800	−14,700	−22.1	Massey Ferguson (5800)
EEC, including	136,800	152,600	127,400	−9,400	− 6.9	
Netherlands	63,200	58,700	46,100	−17,100	−27.1	Philips (2400); Akzo (600)
France	32,100	49,200	40,900	+8,800	+27.4	Peugeot-Citroen (10,900)
West Germany	19,400	22,300	22,100	+2,700	+13.9	Hoechst (1000); Grundig (1000)
Italy	2,000	1,300	1,200	−800	−40.0	Fiat (800)
Eire	9,800	10,000	8,900	−900	− 8.2	Jefferson-Smurfitt (300)
Other, including	98,700	96,700	110,800	+12,100	+12.3	
Switzerland	52,100	48,500	42,800	−9,300	−17.9	Ciba-Geigy (3000)
Sweden	19,500	20,100	21,000	+1,500	+ 7.7	SKF (1400)
Australia	12,900	13,000	21,600	+8,700	+67.4	Wormald (1300)
Japan	1,100	1,700	3,000	+1,900	+27.3	Toshiba (1200)
Other	12,900	13,400	22,400	+9,500	+73.6	
Total	1,013,800	974,200	858,100	−155,700	−15.4	

Sources: Census of Production; *Financial Times* data-file.

Table 10.3: Foreign Corporations Responsible for 1000 or more Job Losses in the UK, as Reported in the *Financial Times*, 1976-81

UK Name	Nationality	Rank by UK Turnover[a]	Jobs Lost	Location(s) of Job Losses (leading 3 in order of importance)	Main Product Affected
Peugeot-Citröen	France	336	10,900	Strathclyde,* Coventry, Luton	Motor cars
General Motors	USA	75	9,100	Luton, Cheshire,* Southampton	Motor cars
Massey-Ferguson (UK)	Canada	114	5,800	Coventry, Peterborough, Strathclyde*	Tractors, diesel engines
Singer (UK)	USA	553	5,700	Strathclyde*	Sewing-machines
Hoover	USA	250	5,100	Mid-Glamorgan,* Strathclyde,* London	Domestic appliances
International Harvester of GB	USA	289	4,200	Doncaster, Bradford, Lancashire	Tractors, commercial vehicles
Goodyear Tyre & Rubber (GB)	USA	251	3,700	Wolverhampton, N. Ireland,* Strathclyde*	Tyres, etc.
Ford Motor Co.	USA	10	3,200	London, Merseyside,* Swansea*	Motor cars
Ciba-Geigy (UK)	Switzerland	143	3,000	Essex, Manchester	Photographic materials
ITT Industries	USA	557	2,800	N. Ireland,* Brighton, Hastings	Television sets & electronics
Philips Electronic & Associated Industries	Netherlands	76	2,400	Suffolk, Lancashire, Co. Durham*	Television sets & electronics
Monsanto	USA	210	2,300	Strathclyde,* Co. Durham,* N. Ireland*	Artificial fibres
Firestone	USA	579	2,100	London, Clwyd*	Tyres, etc.
Marathon Manufacturing	USA	—	1,900	Strathclyde*	Oil rigs
Heinz	USA	193	1,700	Wigan,* N. Ireland,* London	Tinned food
Paccar	USA	—	1,600	Cheshire	Commercial vehicles
Champion	USA	—	1,500	Bradford	Woollen cloth
Borg-Warner	USA	368	1,400	West Glamorgan,* Hertfordshire	Vehicle components
SKF (UK)	Sweden	—	1,400	Strathclyde,* Luton	Bearings

Table 10.3 continued

Wormald International Holdings (UK)	Australia	374	Manchester	Mechanical engineering
Toshiba	Japan	—	Plymouth, Cornwall*	Television sets
Alcoa	USA	479	Swansea,* Gwynedd, Buckinghamshire	Aluminium products
Ronson	USA	—	Surrey, Tyne & Wear*	Cigarette lighters
Hoechst UK	W. Germany	147	N. Ireland,* W. Yorkshire, Newcastle*	Chemicals, paint
Grundig	W. Germany	—	Belfast*	Electrical goods
Total		75,400		

Notes: *Locations in development areas assisted under British government regional policy, 1976 (including special development areas).
a. As listed in *Times 1000, 1981-82* (Times Books, London).
b. 2400 job losses in the joint enterprise Rank-Toshiba.

from the Census of Production. Computer-sorting enables us to rank the leading corporations for job loss, of whatever nationality of control (Table 10.3).

Table 10.2 shows that there is a contrast between the USA, in which the two leading corporations account for only 10 per cent of aggregate job loss, and several of the other countries in which the scale of change is sufficiently small to be heavily influenced by the decisions of individual corporations. There are a number of reasons why recorded losses may not always be compared directly to the 1977 total figure for the same country. Chief among these is that certain job losses were in holdings acquired only after 1977. The most notable case is that all the reported French job losses were in Peugeot-Citröen, in respect of their acquisition of the European operations of the US company, Chrysler, in 1979. Many of their job losses occurred in the Linwood, Strathclyde, plant where 4700 workers were made redundant on 22 May 1981 (Sims and Wood, 1984). These are some of the principal reasons why the recorded apparent net gain for France was accompanied by heavy job losses. This French car-making group is the leading corporation responsible for job losses in the UK, as is shown in the ordered list in Table 10.3. Below it in the list are *nine* further vehicle-manufacturing and component groups, immediately General Motors of the USA and Massey-Ferguson of Canada. The rest of the list is dominated by USA corporations, as one would expect from Table 10.2, although the foot of the list includes rationalisation of relatively recent investments made by Australia, Japan and the Federal Republic of Germany. Eighteen of the 25 corporations in the list are shown, in the third column, to be among the leading 1000 corporations in UK domestic industry in their own right. There are comparatively few leading foreign corporations with less than 1000 job losses. As an indication of the concentration of job losses in a relatively small number of foreign corporations, it is notable that the 25 corporations of Table 10.3 provide 75,400 job losses, equivalent to nearly half the net change for the period.

Over half the locations reported in Table 10.3 involve the government's 'assisted areas' under regional industrial policy. If we ignore intermediate areas, this leaves 26 (those shown by asterisk) of the 56 cases noted as occurring in special development areas and development areas (as defined near the start of our study in 1976), together with Northern Ireland; the core–periphery dimension appears to provide an important axis of decision-making in these mobile industries of the post-war period, reflecting in part the passing of maturity in past investment.

The Regional Pattern of Job Losses

The general thrust of comment in previous literature, and first indications of what we have said above, might be that job losses in foreign-owned establishments were disproportionately weighted towards 'peripheral regions', and perhaps more concentrated there than job losses at large. The Census of Production confirms that variations in job losses across the UK regions do provide some core–periphery contrasts. Table 10.4 shows that the foreign-owned sector contributed a greater proportion of its losses in the 'periphery' than did UK private industry; a feature of Scotland and Northern Ireland which received a full 15 per cent of UK job losses from this source, which was, none the less, heavily under-represented in Wales and the North. The foreign source was consistently under-represented in all regions of the 'manufacturing heartland', but was a most important origin of job losses in the South East, experiencing over one-third of total losses of this kind. In absolute terms, however, the greatest impact of foreign job losses was concentrated in the South East. *Relative* to the scale of private sector job losses in different regions, the foreign sector was most important in East Anglia, the South East, Scotland and Northern Ireland, in each of these accounting for more than one in six of all job losses.

The question arises whether these variations in the distribution of foreign losses are due to variations in the *initial distribution* of activity, as at the start of our period, and whether they represent a worse performance than UK private industry in respective regions. The initial regional distribution of employment in foreign-owned establishments is available for manufacturing establishments for the year 1977, and provides the basis of Figure 10.1, and the first column of Table 10.5. From inspection of this table (column 3), it is clear that when we standardise for the size of 'initial' foreign employment in 1977 the average apparent loss of 15.4 per cent is *exceeded* in the 'periphery' and *under-represented* in the 'core', but the difference in performance is not large. The high level of *absolute* losses which we recorded in the South East is entirely due

Table 10.4: Regional Distribution of Net Job Losses in Foreign and all Other Private Manufacturing Corporations

| | Net Loss of Employment in Manufacturing, 1977-81 | | | | Foreign as proportion of total |
| | Foreign | | UK Total | | |
	No.	Per cent	No.	Per cent	
'Periphery', including	40,000	25.7	352,500	23.5	11.3
N. Ireland	4,000	2.6	28,300	1.9	14.1
Scotland	19,800	12.7	140,300	9.3	14.1
Wales	5,700	3.7	77,800	5.2	7.3
North	10,500	6.8	106,100	7.1	9.9
'Manufacturing heartland', including	51,600	33.2	746,500	49.7	6.9
North West	20,200	13.0	248,800	16.6	8.1
Yorkshire and Humberside	15,100	9.7	161,900	10.8	9.3
East Midlands	3,000	1.9	89,100	5.9	3.4
West Midlands	13,300	8.6	246,700	16.4	5.4
'Core', including	63,800a	41.1	403,600	26.9	15.8
South West	(600)a	(0.4)	44,600	3.0	—
East Anglia	7,900	5.1	25,400	1.7	31.1
South East	56,500	36.4	333,600	22.2	16.8
Total UK	155,700a	100.0	1,502,600	100.0	10.4

Note: a. Column total and sub-total incorporate a recorded net gain of 600 jobs in the South West, and rounding error.
Source: Census of Production.

Figure 10.1: Foreign-owned Manufacturing Plants in the UK: Reported Job Losses, 1977-81 in Relation to Total Employment in 1977

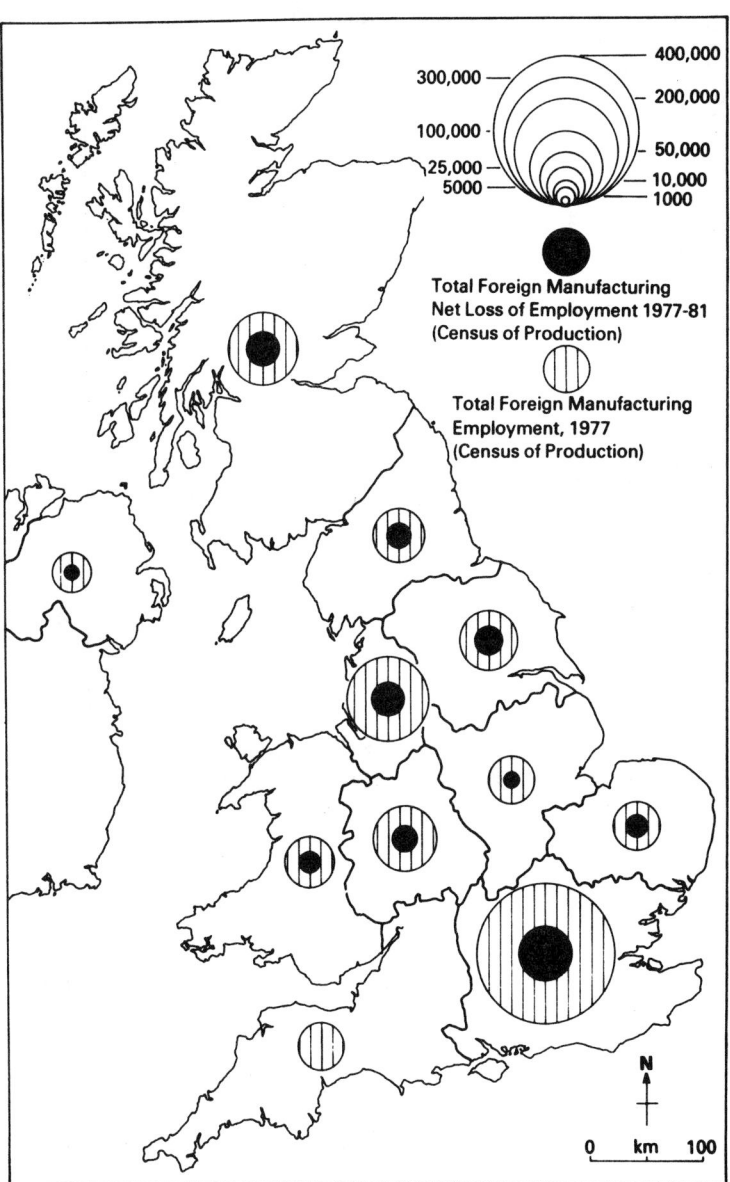

Table 10.5: Net Job Losses Reported in Manufacturing in the UK, 1977-81, Related to 1977 Total Employment

| | Total in Manufacturing, 1977 | Foreign-owned Establishments | | All Private Sector Establishments |
| | | Net Loss of Employment, 1977-81 | Apparent Rate of Loss | Apparent Rate of Loss |
			Per cent	Per cent
'Periphery', including	234,100	40,000	17.1	23.2
N. Ireland	28,800	4,000	13.9	19.7
Scotland	101,300	19,800	19.5	22.7
Wales	51,100	5,700	11.2	24.8
North	52,900	10,500	19.8	24.0
'Manufacturing heartland', including	325,800	51,600	15.8	22.5
North West	135,200	20,200	14.9	24.2
Yorkshire & Humberside	65,000	15,100	23.2	22.5
East Midlands	44,300	3,000	6.8	15.3
West Midlands	81,300	13,300	16.4	25.0
'Core' including	453,900	63,800[a]	14.1	16.5
South West	42,200	(600)	—	10.6
East Anglia	44,500	7,900	17.8	12.6
South East	367,200	56,500	15.4	18.2
Total	1,013,800	155,700	15.4	20.6

Note: a. Column total and sub-total incorporate a recorded net gain of 600 jobs in the South West.
Source: Census of Production.

to the well-established concentration of plants in the South East, where there was a reduction of 15.4 per cent, and the apparently low level of losses which we recorded in the West Midlands reflects the small scale of foreign investment in that region. On the other hand, the 'periphery' showed a poor performance in relative as well as absolute terms, though it is also clear that the North and Scotland showed a worse record than Northern Ireland and Wales.

Using information on named corporations from the *Financial Times*, it is now possible to examine the corporate context within which these job losses occurred. The worst rate of loss among UK regions, one of 23.2 per cent, occurred in Yorkshire and Humberside (Table 10.5). Almost half of the jobs involved (but no more) may be accounted for by the decisions of two American firms, which were shown on Table 10.3; the International Harvester Co. of Great Britain announced seven successive rounds of redundancies at its factories at Bradford and Doncaster, while Champion Industries closed down one of Bradford's largest woollen mills after acquiring the indigenous company, Associated Weavers. Scotland's loss of nearly 20 per cent of its foreign-owned jobs is better understood and documented from Hood and Young (1982), and from the *Financial Times*, whose main Scottish reports are for Peugeot-Citröen, Massey-Ferguson, Singer (UK), Hoover, Goodyear Tyre and Rubber, Monsanto, Marathon Manufacturing, and SKF (UK); Singer (UK) closed a factory which had existed near Glasgow for 99 years, one of the very oldest American investments in Britain.

By comparison, evidence is hard to find for a net loss of 10,500 jobs in the North. The lack of any cross-tabulation of foreign manufacturing employment by region *and* industry prevents any 'shift-share' interpretation of Table 10.5. (Outline cross-tabulations for 1977 were published for Wales by the Welsh Office, 1981, and for Scotland by Horn and Hetherington, 1982.) None the less, the main conclusions of Table 10.5 appear to be robust ones; that above average foreign losses in Scotland and the North give the regions of the 'periphery' as a whole a worse rate of loss than the 'manufacturing heartland', which in turn has performed worse than the 'core' regions. Before the 1981 Census of Production was published, the same ranking of three broad sections of the country was evident from *Financial Times* data. It was tested for robustness in the face of variable coverage among plants in all types of ownership; applying the 'worst' assumptions for poor coverage in the 'core' and 'manufacturing heartland', and the 'best' in the 'periphery', the results were similar to Table 10.5 (Townsend and Peck, 1984).

We have yet to compare the 'performance' of foreign-owned manufacturing jobs with that of UK private sector manufacturing (last column of Table 10.5) in the different regions of the UK, and indeed in the UK at large. In fact, all the evidence suggests, again somewhat contrary to public impression, that net job losses in foreign-owned manufacturing corporations stood at a lower level than in UK-owned plants. Table 10.5 enables us to assess whether this was true in all regions, bearing in mind the considerable inter-regional variation of manufacturing decline in general. At the height of recession conditions between 1979 and 1981, that decline was identified from redundancy data (1980) for establishments in all types of ownership as being at its worst in the West Midlands, Wales and the North West (Townsend, 1982; 1983; Martin, 1982). Many of the sharpest contractions of employment were in nationalised industries such as the British Steel Corporation (Townsend and Peck, 1985) and in British Shipbuilders (Peck and Townsend, 1984).

The Census of Production data are valuable for our present purposes in excluding nationalised industries, and in providing a direct comparison between rates of loss in all private sector establishments and the sub-set of foreign-owned establishments (Table 10.5), in both cases including Northern Ireland (unlike other sources). On this basis, it is clear that the lower rate of net job loss, compared with UK-owned firms, is *common to most regions*, in fact, to 9 of the 11 standard regions. The exceptions are Yorkshire and Humberside (as discussed above), and East Anglia (dominated by a few cases in vehicles); the 'best performances' relative to UK industry at large occurred in the South West, Wales and the North West. There were, of course, gross job losses in South West England, including those of Toshiba (Table 10.3), but these were completely and uniquely offset by acquisitions and expansions. In Wales, there were redundancies at branch plants, but also new developments by Japanese firms and by the Ford Motor Company, which sustained only moderate redundancies at its Halewood (North West) plant.

The differences in performance between UK and foreign-based firms is at its smallest in the South East. One general interpretation might be that the early importance of the South East for investment from the USA meant that it had a number of structural features in common with the general industrialisation of the South East since the 1930s. Much post-war growth by multinationals was dispersed outside the South East to the 'periphery' but also included new acquisitions in, for instance, the Midlands. Thus the general contrast in age of investment, structural conditions and working practices was at its greatest in the provinces and its smallest in the South East. On this hypothesis it would not be surprising if employment decline in foreign plants showed further variation between older and newer 'sub-regions' of investment.

The Sub-regional Pattern of Job Losses

It is a commonplace of contemporary analysis that disaggregation by region is inadequate, both for making inferences about process (if that is possible at all; Sayer, 1980), and for tracing effects in local labour market areas. Very few analyses have traced changes in foreign corporations' activity beyond the regional tables of the Census of Production. Notable exceptions include the work of Lloyd and Mason (1979) on the conurbations of North West England. In this chapter, however, we have already referred to sub-regional locations in Table 10.3. The table showed the strong impact of some closures where the international corporation had only one plant in the UK (as with Singer, Strathclyde), but more commonly a distribution of job losses between a number of UK plants. Using the same source of data collated systematically from the *Financial Times*, we may sum job losses by area, and map and tabulate them by individual sub-regions. This gives a 64 per cent coverage overall, but varies from region to region from 100 per cent in Scotland to below 40 per cent in the South East and East Anglia.

Figure 10.2 shows the distribution of job losses, from this source and by administrative areas of Great Britain (metropolitan districts and counties in England and Wales, together with regions of Scotland). This map demonstrates quite clearly that employment trends in foreign-owned plants within individual regions are the product of highly diverse trends at a sub-regional or local scale, partly reflecting the localisation of foreign investment in some sub-regions. In Scotland, for example, foreign job losses are highly localised in Strathclyde, while in Wales, they are concentrated in Mid- and West Glamorgan. The same is true of the North West,

Figure 10.2: Reported Job Losses in Foreign-owned Manufacturing Plants, 1977-81: Total and USA

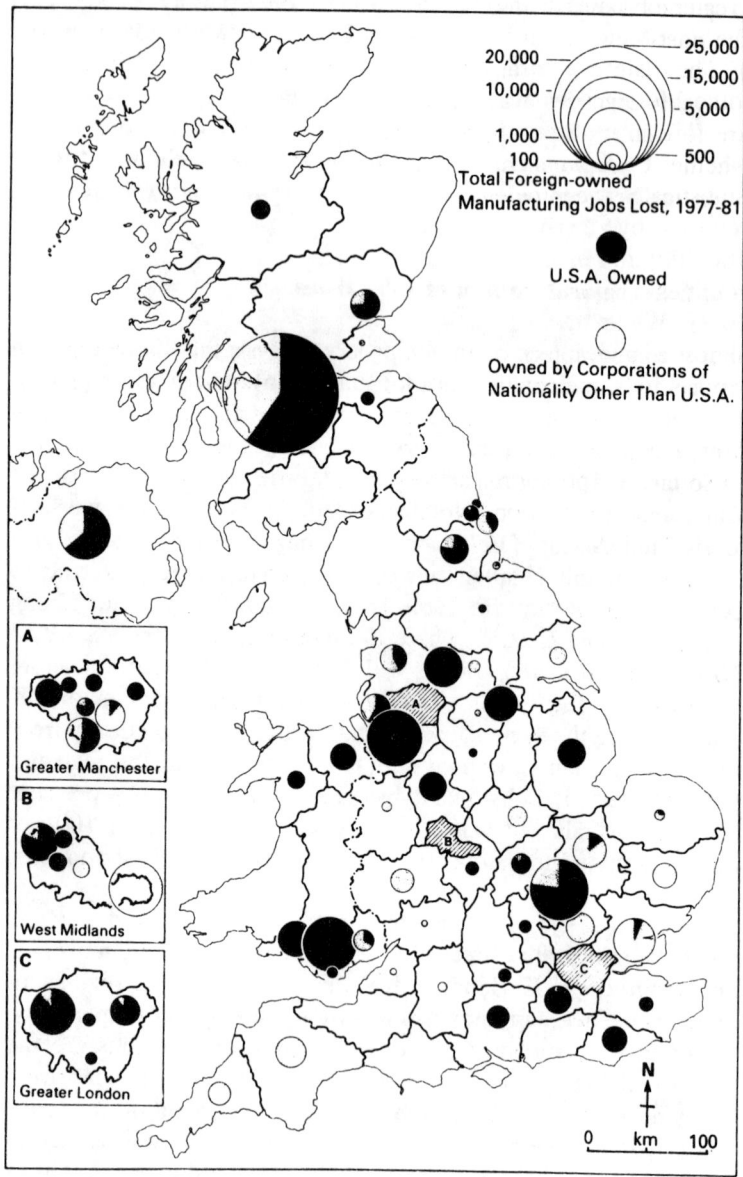

where foreign job losses are concentrated in Cheshire (see Table 10.6). It is also significant that some individual counties have experienced greater job losses than some regions; e.g. Bedfordshire had more than the East Midlands or Northern Ireland.

The data are also divided between 'American' (USA) and 'other' foreign ownership. They enable us to ask how widespread are foreign multinationals' job losses in the UK sub-regions, and whether USA firms are always the dominant source of these losses. Statistically, the American job losses represent 70 per cent of those reported by all nationalities of firm in this source (70,800 out of 100,400) and their level of geographical concentration as between counties is naturally close to the overall average (as shown in Table 10.7). While the overall distribution of American job losses is almost as widespread as in 'all ownerships', there is an absence of reports from the South West, and few from the Northern region. There are comparatively high figures from the South East, and from government 'assisted areas' (see Table 10.8).

So far, the analysis has moved from a regional to a sub-regional scale, and there is clearly considerable variation in the scale of foreign job losses within individual regions. This analysis can be

Table 10.6: Reported Job Losses in Foreign-owned Manufacturing by Leading Counties (including regions of Scotland)

1. Strathclyde	23,100	6. Cheshire	5,000
2. W. Midlands county	8,400	7. Mid-Glamorgan	4,700
3. Greater Manchester	6,300	8. Northern Ireland	4,500
4. Bedfordshire	5,700	9. Essex	3,000
5. Greater London Council	5,200	10. W. Yorkshire	2,600

Source: *Financial Times* data, October 1976-September 1981.

Table 10.7: Concentration of Reported Manufacturing Job Losses by County (including regions of Scotland)

Proportion of job losses in	USA Ownership	Other Foreign	All Foreign	All Ownerships
5 counties	46.3%	73.2%	48.5%	39.8%
10 counties	65.2%	95.1%	68.3%	54.8%
Total job losses	70,800	29,600	100,400	511,400

Source: *Financial Times* data, October 1976-September 1981.

Table 10.8: Leading Counties for Reported Job Losses in USA-owned Manufacturing (including regions of Scotland)

County	Jobs Lost (sum)	Jobs Lost	Leading Corporations Name	Product
1. Strathclyde	13,900	5700	Singer (UK)	Sewing machines
		1900	Marathon Manufacturing	Oil rigs
		1500	Hoover	Domestic appliances
		1000	Goodyear Tyre & Rubber (GB)	Tyres, etc.
2. Cheshire	5000	3400	General Motors	Motor cars
		1600	Paccar (formerly Fodens)	Commercial vehicles
3. Greater London	4700	1500	Ford Motor Co.	Motor cars
		1500	Firestone	Tyres
		1000	Hoover	Domestic appliances
4. Mid-Glamorgan	4700	2400	Hoover	Domestic appliances
5. Bedfordshire	4500	4400	General Motors	Motor cars

Source: *Financial Times* data, October 1976-September 1981.

taken one step further to the level of individual companies and plants. Table 10.8 demonstrates that within high-loss sub-regions themselves, job losses are often associated with one or a few major foreign corporations. In general terms, therefore, the map of aggregate job loss in foreign-owned establishments has been created by relatively few key decisions within a few large companies. In Strathclyde, for example, 5700 job losses out of 13,900 total were accounted for by Singer (UK). In Cheshire 3400 job losses were attributed to General Motors out of a total of only 5000. The mention of corporations' names does not of itself take us far in understanding why job losses have occurred but it does indicate strongly that this understanding needs to involve case studies of corporate decision-making (Peck and Townsend, 1984). Studies of this kind need to focus on how decision-makers discriminate between plants under their control in different countries, and, we now see, in the same country. In effect, those which had sites in many parts of the UK discriminated in different ways between prosperous and less prosperous areas. A common pattern was to inflict a greater absolute number of job losses in the South East, but to impose proportionately greater ones at 'assisted area' plants. For instance, job losses were relatively greater at General Motors' Vauxhall plant at Ellesmere Port, Cheshire than at Luton, Bedfordshire, and at Ford's Merseyside plant than at Dagenham, Greater London.

The non-American job losses show a somewhat different geographical pattern statistically and on Figure 10.2. The figure shows a concentration between the Thames and the Wash, in two regions identified by Watts (1979) for a concentration of EEC-controlled factory employment. However, the leading counties are those of Strathclyde (where both Peugeot-Citröen and Massey-Ferguson closed plants) and the West Midlands (where the same corporations had redundancies); see Table 10.9.

Clearly, individual areas of the UK may have 'very diverse experience of selective closure' (Hood and Young, 1982), and there is very little suggestion of a decisive role for local industrial linkages in the rationalisation patterns of leading foreign corporations. The essential first step for detailed research is to assess the pre-existing pattern of all factories and other land uses in a corporation (including plants without job losses and those under other operating names) before superimposing the pattern of job losses upon them, whether they be ones of rationalisation, intensification

Table 10.9: Leading Counties for Reported Job Loss in Foreign but non-USA-owned Manufacturing (including regions of Scotland)

County	Jobs Lost (sum)	Jobs Lost	Leading Corporations Name	Product
1. Strathclyde	9200	7400	Peugeot-Citröen	Motor cars
		1000	Massey-Ferguson (UK)	Tractor parts
2. West Midlands	5300	2600	Peugeot-Citröen	Motor cars
		1900	Massey-Ferguson (UK)	Tractors
3. Essex	2800	2500	Ciba-Geigy	Photographic materials
4. Greater Manchester	2700	1300	Wormald International	Mechanical engineering
5. Northern Ireland	1600	1000	Grundig	Electrical goods

Source: *Financial Times* data, October 1976-September 1981.

or technical change (Massey and Meegan, 1982), or a mixture.

Sub-regional variation is also, however, a function of history, chiefly of past acquisition activity but also of 'greenfield investments'. It is safe to say that the overall distribution of foreign manufacturing jobs was more dispersed from conurbation cores than UK-owned plants, and that they were thus an important channel through which recession conditions affected the manufacturing sector of counties such as Essex or Surrey. The logic of these statements is to imply that foreign manufacturing job losses were working against any continual urban–rural shift in employment losses in recession conditions. We can safely say that in the majority of conurbations, foreign sources played a below average role in manufacturing job losses. At a maximum the foreign source accounted for only 12 per cent of *reported* job losses in metropolitan counties, compared with an apparent ratio which was twice as large in Greater London and four times larger in Strathclyde. However, closer dissection is possible still in time and place. Our data set has been classified more closely by year, by types of settlement, and by types of 'assisted area', to assess more precisely the relevance of this source of job losses to policy analysis.

The Relationship to Government 'Assisted Areas'

The debate about the influence of multinational corporations' investment on UK employment has largely been conducted in terms of government 'assisted areas' under regional policy. Naturally, many parts of the UK which rely on foreign investment have expressed fears that this dependence may induce a greater rate of job loss in periods of recession. Similar fears have surrounded the influx of foreign establishments to some New Towns, and into smaller towns where the incoming firm may monopolise the local labour market. Our data-set, which contain 251 incidences of job loss, allows us to assess the extent to which different types of settlement, and different assisted areas have been affected by foreign job losses in each year from 1977 to 1981; analysis at this degree of disaggregation in time and space is obviously not possible in any published sources in the Census of Production.

A study was conducted of the incidence of job losses in foreign-owned plants as between different types of settlements, such as New Towns, 'traditional industrial towns', etc. The weight of job losses clearly fell in the latter before 1980, when redundancies became very widespread. In the first three years studied, however, all cases of foreign job loss over the size of 600 redundancies fell in 'assisted areas', all except one (at Bradford) in long-established development areas. A study of 'assisted areas' is therefore allowed to take precedence here over one based on settlement types.

Recent studies of patterns of redundancy during the 1976 to 1979 period appear to show strong negative differentials most noticeable in peripheral regions as a whole (Townsend, 1982, p. 1402). As industry entered more general recession, however, in 1979, all the indications point to a change in these patterns, with continuing elements of a 'North–South' division in employment performance more dominated by the general effects of manufacturing decline (Regional Studies Association, 1983, p. 44). A more precise set of areas for studying plants under the influence of regional policy, including many owing their origins to it, is afforded by directly taking the government's assisted areas, defined here as in 1976. At that date the main special development areas and most development areas were in Scotland, Wales and Northern Ireland, together with the Northern region, although they also included Merseyside in the North West region. The intermediate areas, mainly in the North West and in Yorkshire and Humberside, had enjoyed such regional policy status only since 1972 and had little opportunity of attracting greenfield investment by foreign corporations. We might, therefore, expect some differences in their experience of these first few years of significant disinvestment by foreign corporations. Table 10.10 dissects 251 cases of reports involving job loss at foreign-owned plants.

As one would expect from the historical background to foreign investment in the UK, and from analyses immediately above, there is some overall bias toward assisted areas in the cases reported in Table 10.10. This is accompanied by a significant bias in terms of employment. Non-assisted areas are under-represented in this set of results at least until 1979, and the incidence of reports in the foreign-owned plants of intermediate areas is unremarkable. Conversely, if we take development areas, special development areas and Northern Ireland together we find their share of UK cases declining steadily from 49 per cent (1979) to 42 per cent (1980), and 33 per cent (1981). There is, included within the figures, some similarity in the pattern of closures. This, of course, partly reflects the national manufacturing incidence of recession (Martin, 1982;

Table 10.10: Cases of Reported Job Loss in Foreign-controlled Manufacturing Establishments; by Government Development Status and Year

		Non-assisted	Intermediate Area	Development Area	Special Development Area	Northern Ireland	Total Cases Analysed
1977	No.	1	0	2	2	0	5
	Per cent	20.0	0	40.0	40.0	0	100.0
1978	No.	5	5	1	8	0	19
	Per cent	26.3	26.3	5.3	42.1	0	100.0
1979	No.	11	8	4	12	2	37
	Per cent	29.7	21.6	10.8	32.4	5.4	100.0
1980	No.	39	10	11	18	7	85
	Per cent	45.9	11.8	12.9	21.2	8.2	100.0
1981	No.	46	24	5	24	6	105
	Per cent	43.8	22.9	4.8	22.9	5.7	100.0
Total	No.	102	47	23	64	15	251
	Per cent	40.6	18.7	9.2	25.5	6.0	100.0
All Ownerships	Per cent	44.6	22.6	8.9	20.5	3.3	100.0

Source: *Financial Times* data, October 1976-September 1981.

Townsend, 1982), but is also fully compatible with a model of gradual withdrawal from branch plants under accelerating difficulties.

Our study period is thus divided into two by the arrival of 'mass redundancy' in 1980. Trends between 1977 and 1981 show a noticeable break after 1979, consistent with the UK-owned firms in our data-sets. In the early period the 'assisted areas' in general, and the special development areas in particular, were worst hit by job losses, whereas in 1980-81 there was a marked relative decline in corporate job losses in assisted areas and relative increases in losses in non-assisted areas. Whereas we found that the urban–rural contrasts in patterns of job loss over time (i.e. the reduced share met in conurbations) were largely, if not totally, a consequence of *different* corporations shedding labour at different times and in different places, these North–South contrasts also reflect some regularity in the behaviour of major corporations, including several significant foreign-owned examples. These are, in fact, the now familiar cases of Peugeot-Citröen, Massey-Ferguson and Hoover, who announced their job losses in the Midlands and London well after their redundancies in 'assisted areas'. Equally, however, the pre-1980 period involved only 25 of the 96 corporations in our data-set; the remaining 71 included (in order of their UK turnover) Ford, Ciba-Geigy, Hoechst, Alcan, Nestlé, Fiat, Burroughs, Cummins, Honeywell and Borg-Warner. Five of these are controlled from countries other than the USA, which we saw earlier had a tendency, as a group, to defer job losses until 1979-81 and to have lower location quotients in the peripheral regions.

Where individual corporations did allocate job losses to 'assisted areas' before others, this points in many cases to discrimination between plants in the same industrial product heading. This opens the door to many possible avenues of inquiry, one of which is explored here because of its immediate relevance to foreign-owned corporations. It is possible that the recession has disproportionately affected branch plants in the peripheral regions, after having accounted for differences in industrial composition. In this way it is hypothesised that companies faced with the need to cut capacity more often closed or reduced employment in more distant branch plants rather than equivalent plants within the head office regions. The idea that such branch establishments are discriminated against in closure decisions is of course not new, and indeed the evidence of such behaviour from former time-periods is extremely inconsistent (Watts, 1981).

All but 15 of the 96 foreign corporations in our data set had identifiable UK headquarters in the UK. To a remarkable extent these headquarters were concentrated in South East England (53 cases), including central London (18). There was no other focus of relevant head offices anywhere in the remaining regions of the UK (17 cases in all). A study of our data showed that reports of job loss at foreign-owned plants, between 1977 and 1981, related more often to 'long-distance' control than at UK-owned plants (distances $> 500\,km$ including all plants in Northern Ireland), and less often to 'short-distance' control ($< 100\,km$) (to be read in the light of regional distributions seen in Table 10.5). This feature varied in significance over time with long-distance cases becoming steadily and relatively less important from 1977 to 1981, and short-distance cases becoming more important from 1979 to 1981. The latter feature was not, however, accompanied by proportionate increase in actual closures at shorter distances. These results are compatible with the view, noted also for UK corporations, that, on average, foreign corporations met difficulties in a fairly normal trading period, 1976-79, by running down, and in some cases closing, more distant plants, and in severe recession also produced job losses (though without a full complement of closures) nearer to headquarters, commonly in the South East.

Given that most UK headquarters are in or near London, and that most 'assisted areas' are at a distance from London, these results are not surprising, and lead us to the view that the two variables are partial surrogates for each other within the general pattern of the 'branch-plant' economy. The hypothesis that 'multinational corporations close their branch plants first' does have some descriptive statistical validity in this, their first general period of rationalisation in the UK.

Fortunately, the most prominent case in this paper (which is in our most prominent industry, vehicles) is already documented in other research. Sims and Wood (1984) assessed that there was no alternative to the foreign rescue of the Rootes Group, including the Linwood, Strathclyde plant by Chrysler UK.

In reality Linwood was increasingly used as a dumping ground for making outdated models. As these functions naturally declined so did Linwood's chances of being developed as an integral part of Chrysler's operations in Europe. Indeed Chrysler UK's management continued to concentrate its new capital investment in the Midlands and so marginalise production in Scotland. (Sims and Wood, 1984, p. 56)

The same authors conclude that there was very little that could be done to preserve the plant from closure after acquisition by Peugeot-Citröen in January 1979.

In the light of the results of this section, one is inclined to agree with Hood and Young (1982) that the short-term pursuit of jobs in the favourable conditions of the 1960s led to longer-term problems for Scotland at large, and for Strathclyde in particular. A number of the new foreign plants suffered from technological change in terms of process and product innovations. Others fell prey to European-wide production and marketing strategies, increasingly introduced after Britain's entry to the EEC in 1973. The writers stress, however, that there was a very diverse experience of selective closure in Scotland as between different corporations; where a Scottish plant did suffer disproportionately this was due to an aspect of labour relations. The Peugeot-Citröen closure was 'obviously' likely in terms of performance over the years, and Singer's closure of the Clydebank factory was related primarily to relative performance in Europe. However, Hoover's eventual decision to close their London (Perivale) factory rather than their distant plants in the 'assisted areas' of mid-Glamorgan and Strathclyde stands as testimony to the amount of behavioural variation in this field.

Conclusions

Foreign corporations have clearly played a significant part in a manufacturing recession for the first time in UK history. Yet some of our results work contrary to general impressions and are counter intuitive:

(1) The rate of job loss per thousand manufacturing workers in foreign-owned plants is a quarter lower than that in UK-owned plants. Only in two regions is the rate higher.
(2) In absolute terms, the worst affected regions are the South

East, the North West, Scotland and Yorkshire and Humberside (in that order).

(3) Relative to 1977 levels of employment in foreign-owned factories, the worst affected regions were Yorkshire and Humberside, the North, Scotland and East Anglia.

(4) The least affected regions were the South West, Wales and East Midlands, three of the smaller regions identified by Keeble (1980) with better than average manufacturing performances in the period 1971-76. The list is similar if considered relative to UK private manufacturing performance. A principal reason for the lower rate of job loss in foreign-owned plants than in British ones would appear to be the higher productivity standards of the former at the beginning of the study period. The main feature, however, which distinguishes the foreign-owned plants is their greater average size, which creates 'lumpy' effects for individual labour market areas when selective rationalisation is undertaken in multi-plant corporations.

When we disaggregate the cases we have studied by corporation, nationality, sub-regional location, type of location, and the date of occurrence of job losses we find considerable variation. Indeed, it is clear that there are difficulties in writing about a single population of foreign-owned multinational corporations in the UK. They are dominated statistically by USA-owned plants, which, because of their greater age and more widespread regional distribution, had a different pattern of job losses compared with other nationalities. A number of large corporations with multi-plant holdings run fairly autonomously in the UK are difficult to distinguish from UK corporations of similar size and merger history.

On the whole it is clear that foreign corporations' patterns of disinvestment broadly reflected those of UK-based private corporations when adjusted for initial concentrations in certain regions. This is notably the case in respect of a concentration of losses in the years 1976 to 1979 in 'assisted areas' more distant from London, and in a gradual spread to non-assisted areas including further locations of post-war greenfield investment in the years 1979 to 1981. This is, however, only an average picture; there are, as we saw, corporations which placed the balance of their job losses in assisted areas, and others which actually 'favoured' assisted areas from the start of this period.

As a whole, however, foreign cases accentuate the contrasting experience of 'peripheral' and 'core' areas. Where foreign-owned corporations have created serious unemployment it has arisen from their concentration of investment in large sites. Of course, these events must be seen in the general European pattern of planning and investment. However, the monitoring of our overall data on 1633 occasions of job loss reveals relatively few in which withdrawals from the UK, whether by British or foreign corporations, are *directly* attributable to openings in the Third World.

ECONOMIC CRISIS AND CORPORATE
RESTRUCTURING: MULTINATIONAL
CORPORATIONS AND THE PAPER, PRINTING
AND PACKAGING SECTOR IN BRISTOL

Keith Bassett

Introduction

An increasing number of studies have begun to be published
exploring the impacts of the post-1978 recession on industrial
decline at the regional and urban level. An analysis of the role of
multinational corporations has figured prominently in many such
research studies. There are two obvious reasons for this focus.
First, large corporations (usually multinational in scale) control a
large proportion of total manufacturing employment at local as
well as national scales. Decisions made by these corporations can
clearly have major impacts on employment levels either directly or
through multiplier effects on smaller suppliers and subcontractors.
Secondly, the study of decision-making in large multinationals
provides a direct way of linking local events such as closures and
redundancies to broader macro-economic forces at the national
and even global scale. Multi-level corporate structures and their
interlinkages thus provide an important transmission mechanism
between forces at different spatial scales.

There are, however, pitfalls that need to be avoided in studying
multinational corporations in this context. At one extreme it could
be argued that attempts to construct a highly generalised 'Theory
of the Multinational Corporation' have not proved very successful
or revealing. There is a danger, however, that in reaction to excessive abstraction, research rebounds to the other extreme of
multiplying detailed case studies of individual companies with no
common theoretical framework. Recent attempts at comparative
analyses in terms of corporate strategies of rationalisation, intensification and technical change (Massey and Meegan, 1982; Peck
and Townsend, 1984) go some way towards a theoretical framework but a lot more work is clearly needed in this direction.

This chapter hopefully avoids some of the worst pitfalls by

311

attempting to link a detailed comparative study of corporate decision-making to broader processes of capital accumulation within a specific industrial sector. The first section explores the nature of industrial decline in Bristol and the contribution of multinational corporations to that decline. The chapter then focuses more narrowly on a particular industrial sector (Paper, Printing and Packaging), identifies the broader economic pressures on this sector, and traces contrasting corporate responses to these pressures. Particular emphasis is given to those responses which have had significant impacts on the local economy. A concluding section evaluates the findings and tries to place them in a wider theoretical context.

Industrial Decline and Multinationals in the Bristol Economy

The analysis begins by exploring the nature of manufacturing decline in Bristol. This analysis forms the essential preliminary step to asking how important multinational companies have been in accounting for this decline.

The Bristol built-up area, with a population of around 500,000, constitutes the major city of the South West region and has had a long history of relative commercial and industrial prosperity. Aided by the growth of its aircraft industry, rearmament, and the monopolistic market position of its tobacco and confectionary multinationals, the city escaped the worst effects of the 1930s' slump with unemployment levels well below the national average. In the 1950s the city prospered in the upswing of the long post-war boom. Industrial employment began to decline in the 1960s by about 0.1 per cent per annum, but this was a rate close to the national average and was more than offset by faster growth in service employment. The completion of the M4 and M5 motorways and the Severn Bridge in the 1960s improved access to other parts of the country. Then, in the 1970s, things began to change dramatically.

There is general agreement that the late 1960s and early 1970s saw the emergence of major changes in the growth patterns of the industrialised countries, although there is considerable disagreement as to the causes of these changes (contrast, for example, Mandel (1975) and Beenstock (1983)). Following Aglietta (1976) and others it can be suggested that the onset of economic crisis in the 1970s signalled the end of the post-war 'golden age' of intensive capital accumulation and monopoly regulation, and from de Vroey (1984), it can be argued that the subsequent crisis phase is a complex interaction of both structural and cyclical effects on an international scale. One of the most important manifestations has been the decline of industrial employment in the developed economies, and in the UK in particular, and the relocation of certain forms of manufacturing production overseas (Fröbel, Heinrichs and Kreye, 1980). How have these broader processes been manifested in the Bristol economy?

Change in Employment Structure, 1971-81

Table 11.1 provides basic information on the employment structure in Bristol in 1971 and the changes experienced over the following decade. In 1971 around 36 per cent of employment was in manufacturing (slightly below the national average) compared to over 57 per cent in services. However, within the manufacturing sector as a whole over 64 per cent of total manufacturing employment was concentrated in three industrial sectors: Vehicles (mainly Aerospace); Food, Drink and Tobacco; and Paper, Printing and Publishing. These are three traditional industries which have dominated the Bristol manufacturing economy since the 1920s.

Table 11.1: Employment in the Bristol Travel-to-Work Area, 1971 and 1981

	Empl. 1971	% 1971 total empl.	Empl. change 1971-81	% Empl. decline 1971-81	Empl. change p.a. 1971-78	Empl. change p.a. 1978-81
Manufacturing Industry	107,423	35.7	−23,663	−22.0	−2189	−2779
Major sectors						
Vehicles	27,539	9.2	−2,099	−7.6	−527	+530
Food, Drink, Tobacco	24,671	8.2	−9,000	−36.5	−737	−1279
Paper, Printing, Publishing	16,338	5.4	−7,342	−44.9	−450	−1396
Mechanical Engineering	9,859	3.3	−2,078	−14.4	−241	+88
Metal goods, n.e.s.	5,147	1.7	−1,479	−28.7	−207	+9
Electrical Engineering	4,667	1.5	−273	−5.8	−97	+136
Chemicals, etc.	3,749	1.2	+1,352	+36.0	+318	−292
Metal manufacture	3,426	1.1	−2,078	−60.6	−245	−120
Service industry	172,207	57.3	+21,799	+12.6	+3516	−937
Total	300,600	100.0	−1,249	+0.4		

Source: Department of Trade and Industry, *Census of Production.*

Between 1971 and 1981 total employment remained roughly stable but this overall figure concealed major structural changes. Total manufacturing employment fell by 23,663 (−22 per cent) whilst total service employment grew by 21,799 (+12.6 per cent). Two comments immediately follow.

First, in terms of aggregate employment levels, the Bristol economy came through the decade fairly well, and certainly much better than many of the cities in the West Midlands and the North. This was almost entirely due to rapid service sector growth. Unemployment levels remained generally below the national average although the differential was not as high as the above service employment figures might suggest; the vast bulk of the service sector jobs (over 95 per cent) were for women and did not generally absorb the predominantly male workforce displaced from the manufacturing sector. Secondly, it is clear that the popular image of Bristol's prosperity relative to the country as a whole conceals the fact that the manufacturing sector rapidly declined at a rate (−22.0 per cent) close to the national average (−24.9 per cent). Manufacturing in prosperous Bristol was plainly affected by the broader processes of deindustrialisation experienced in other major cities where service sector growth did not act as a buffer.

Matters become more complex, however, when these figures are disaggregated by time-period and sector. Comparing the period 1971-78 with the phase of deepening recession after 1978 brings out the ominous fact that service sector growth only offset manufacturing decline in the former period. After 1978 manufacturing job loss p.a. accelerated *and* service sector growth was stopped and reversed.

Once the manufacturing sector is disaggregated important variations in employment growth and decline immediately emerge. Over 69 per cent of the total manufacturing employment decline was accounted for by two major sectors; Food, Drink and Tobacco, which lost 9000 jobs, and Paper, Printing and Publishing, which lost 7342 jobs. The key Vehicles (Aerospace) sector only declined by 7.6 per cent and without its stability the manufacturing sector would have fared as badly in employment terms as the national average. Moreover, the rate of job loss in the first two sectors accelerated after 1978 whilst the Vehicle sector actually grew slightly fuelled by defence contracts.

In conclusion, it is evident that the Bristol economy underwent major transformations in the 1971-81 period affecting both industrial and service sector employment. There was a pattern of industrial decline (excluding Aerospace) and a reversal of service growth.

Corporate Structure and Change, 1978-83: Aggregate Effects on Manufacturing Employment

The contribution of major corporations to the decline of industrial employment is an important topic. The Bristol case has been explored in some detail elsewhere (Bassett, 1984) and only some of the main conclusions are summarised here by way of background.

In 1978-79, there were 20 major companies with plants in the city employing at least 5000 workers. Estimates in the present study indicate that these 20 companies controlled at least 58 per cent of total manufacturing employment. All these companies operated on a multinational scale and only two had their headquarters in the city. Figure 11.1 identifies the companies and shows the location of their corporate headquarters. The dominance of London-based multinationals is evident.

The deepening recession from 1978-79 onwards produced a range of corporate responses that had a major impact on employment in the city and on patterns of ownership and control. Closures, the introduction of new technology, and intensification of labour processes in these major corporations combined to produce around 6000 job losses between 1978 and 1981 or approximately 70 per cent of the total manufacturing job loss in the city. At the same time there was a spate of acquisitions and disinvestments that had significant impacts on the pattern of ownership in the city. (See Bassett (1984) for details.)

This brief summary substantiates the importance of multinational corporations in accounting for local economic change. To proceed further to an analysis of the processes at work behind these changes requires some kind of framework to avoid a proliferation of case studies of individual corporations.

Economic Pressures and Corporate Strategies: A Simple Framework

It is important to pursue an analysis at several different levels. At a general level it is important to disaggregate the broad processes of capital accumulation in an international economy to explore the

Figure 11.1: Headquarters of Corporations Owning Plants Employing More Than 500 Workers in Bristol: 1978/79

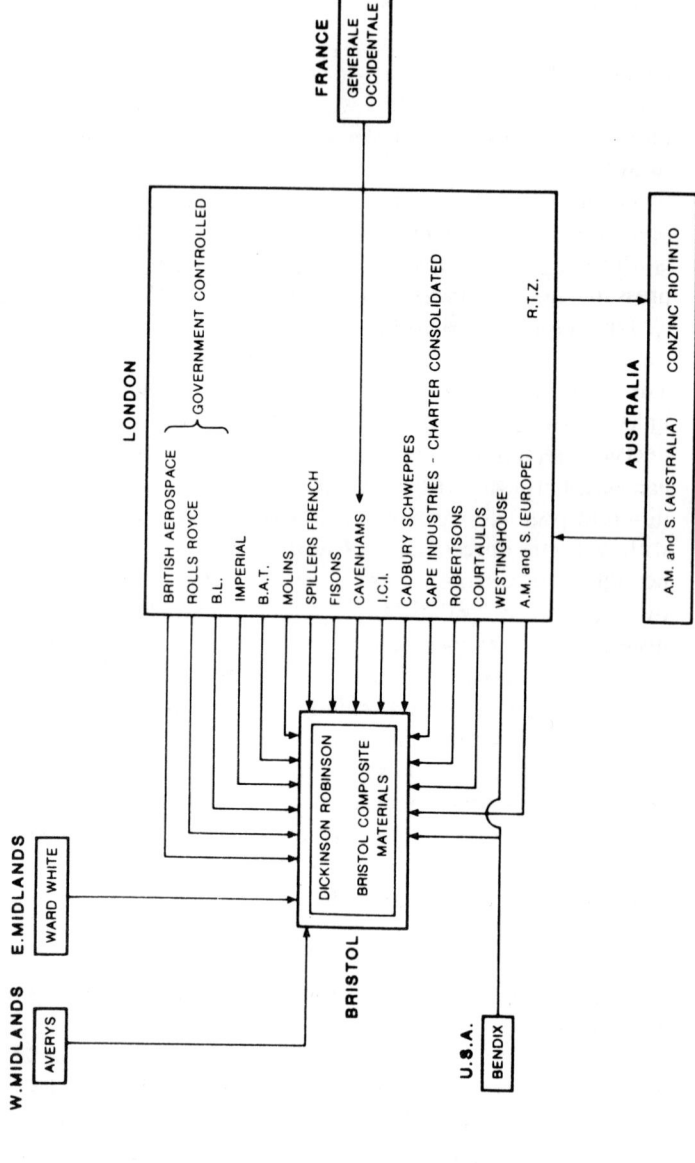

specific problems of capital accumulation in different industrial sectors (Figure 11.2). The present economic crisis, for example, has clearly hit different industrial sectors in different ways and to differing degrees, reflecting a whole range of market, technological and labour relations factors. It is then important, at a more disaggregated level, to explore the way these sectoral pressures are mediated through the varying responses of companies, particularly major corporations which have a presence in those sectors. The more general level of analysis thus establishes the broader structural framework within which individual firm decisions are made. Since most major multinationals are simultaneously involved in several sectors of production the company's response in one sector is affected by its decisions in other sectors where the economic pressures and constraints may be quite different.

To explore the role of multinational corporations in detail it is necessary to look at corporate linkages and corporate strategies. The study of *corporate linkages* involves the identification of the links between individual plants in the local economy and the decision-making centres of the corporation. Increasingly, the links are likely to be through separate divisional structures covering different product areas with their own headquarters and staff and with varying degrees of autonomy from the overall corporate headquarters. Several different plants in the local economy owned by the same corporation may be linked back to the corporate headquarters through different divisional structures. Of course, such structures are not fixed but are themselves subject to change as corporate strategies unfold.

Corporate strategies may take a variety of interrelated forms. Figure 11.2 presents a simple classification that embraces both changes in corporate structures and changes in the nature and organisation of production. These strategies unfold through a hierarchy of decisions in response to forces at different levels. At the headquarters level the corporation makes its response to broader international and national forces which affect the overall profitability of the corporation and the relative profitability of its product divisions. At this level choices are made between longer-term patterns of investment and disinvestment both between geographical areas and major product divisions. Decisions at this level become constraints on the management in different product divisions who may be given specific profitability targets and ceilings on investment. Different divisions may adopt different

Figure 11.2: Corporate Strategies in Response to Recession

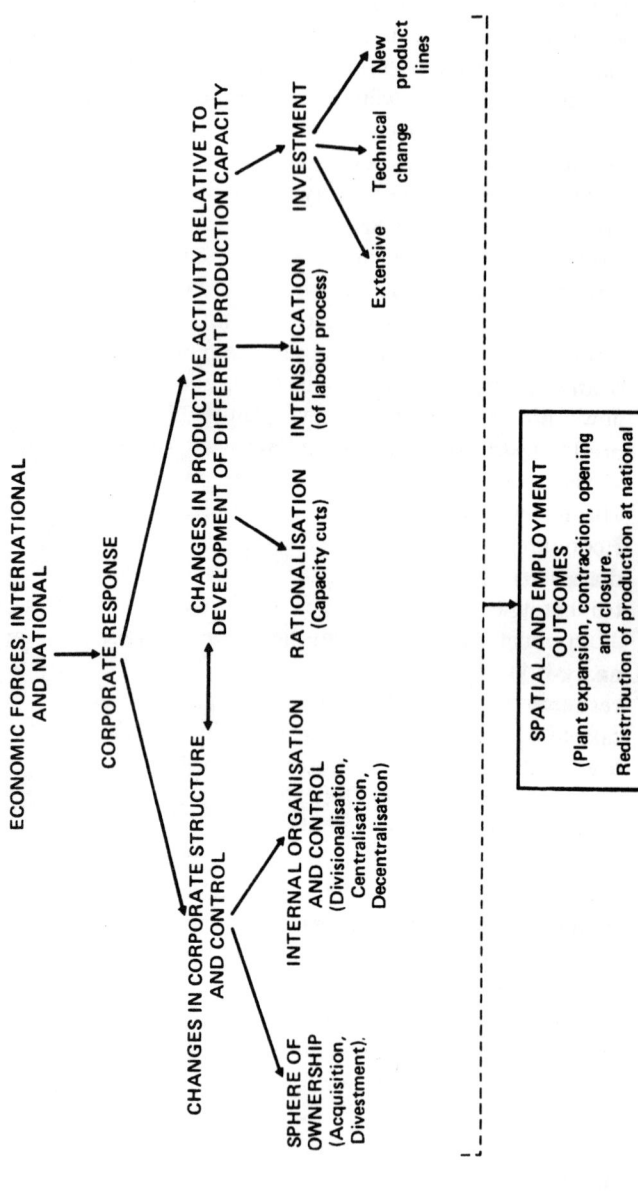

strategies of diversification, investment, contraction and closure which then impose constraints on the management of individual plants in different local economies. Which plants are most affected, and how, will depend upon factors such as their age, product line, labour relations and location (relative accessibility and linkages to other plants).

The intersection of these different restructuring processes produces a complex pattern of locational changes. Spatial variations in plant openings, closures, contractions and expansions reflect the uneven development of the firm in space. Different plants may also be linked to different stages of product cycles. Using the terminology of Taylor and Thrift (1983) we can identify *leader* subsidiaries benefiting from innovation and investment in new product development; *intermediate* subsidiaries mass-producing standardised products in expanding markets; and *laggard* subsidiaries producing long-established products approaching obsolescence in diminishing and increasingly competitive markets. Economic crises and corporate restructuring will affect these subsidiaries in different ways, accelerating some product cycles and truncating or terminating others.

In conclusion, it is necessary to explore a number of levels of analysis in order to account for patterns of local economic change resulting from multinational corporate strategies. The next section takes up some of these themes in the Bristol context.

Sectoral Change: The Paper, Printing and Packaging Industry

The Paper, Printing and Packaging sector has been chosen for detailed study. The discussion in section 1 highlighted this sector as a major component of Bristol's industrial structure and a major contributor to employment decline. Understanding the reasons for decline in this sector is therefore important for understanding the process of industrial decline in Bristol as a whole.

The Components of Sectoral Change: Narrowing Down the Problem

The Paper, Printing and Packaging sector in Bristol employed 16,338 people in 1971. In the 10 years between 1971 and 1981 employment declined by 44.9 per cent. Over 57 per cent of the total job loss was concentrated in the period 1978 to 1981.

The first point to note is that the overall 44.9 per cent decline in employment in Bristol was far higher than the 13.7 per cent decline nationally in this sector. A shift-share analysis (Bishop and Simpson, 1973) reveals the following components behind this decline.

$$\text{Actual change} = \frac{\text{national}}{\text{component}} + \frac{\text{structural}}{\text{component}} + \frac{\text{differential}}{\text{component}}$$

$$-7342 \quad = \quad 1310.9 \qquad -931.1 \qquad -5099.9$$

The differential component, which represents the difference between the expected employment change (based on national trends and local economic structure) and the actual change, is by far the largest component. This suggests that the sector contracted faster than expected in terms of employment because of factors specific to the industry in the area.

We can take the analysis a step further by disaggregating sectoral change to component Minimum List Headings. Table 11.2 details the relative changes at the local and national levels. The national figures reveal that there are really two sub-groups of industries here. Group A includes the more basic paper and

Table 11.2: Employment Change in the Paper, Printing and Packaging Sector, 1971-81, Bristol and Great Britain

Minimum List Heading						Great Britain
				% 1981		
	Total employment			Total	% change	% change
	1971	1978	1981	Empl.	1971-81	1971-81
481 Paper and board	3,331	2,026	363	4.0	−89.1	−36.0
482 Packaging products	7,674	6,657	4,314	47.9	−44.0	−18.3
483 Manuf. stationery	206	101	285	3.2	+38.3	−29.3
484 Paper and board, n.e.s.	239	575	107	1.2	−55.2	−24.0
485 Printing and publishing: newspapers	6	878	884	9.8 ⎫	−24.2	−3.5
486 Printing and publishing: periodicals	1,432	354	206	2.3 ⎭		
487 Other printing, publishing, etc.	3,686	2,595	2,837	31.5	−23.0	−7.4
Total SIC 18	16,338	13,186	8,996	100.0	−44.9	−13.7

Source: Department of Trade and Industry, *Census of Production.*

packaging industries, whilst Group B includes printing, publishing, bookbinding, etc. The rates of employment decline of Group A industries were all much higher than the rates for Group B industries.

The same differentiation between Group A and Group B industries was roughly apparent in Bristol but with important variations. First, apart from Manufactured Stationery (a small sector), all Minimum List Headings declined faster than the comparable national totals. Secondly, the Paper and Board and Packaging industries in Bristol accounted for a much larger proportion of the overall sector employment than nationally (67.3 per cent compared to 26.6 per cent) and accounted for a larger share of total sector decline. In fact, the Paper, Board and Packaging industries in Bristol accounted for 88 per cent of the total employment loss in the sector as a whole between 1971 and 1981. In all sub-sectors the rate of decline increased noticeably after 1978 as the recession deepened. The Paper and Board industry almost disappeared during this period.

We have now narrowed down the problem area. We need to focus particular attention on the factors behind the dramatic decline in the Paper, Board and Packaging industries in Bristol after 1978. The logical starting-point is to examine the economic pressures upon these industries at a national and international level to establish the framework for corporate decision-making in these industries.

Economic Pressures on the Paper and Board and Packaging Industries

The Paper and Board and Packaging industries were subject to a range of pressures, both national and international, and long- and short-term, in the period under consideration. The balance of pressures was not the same in each industry so it is necessary to disaggregate further and treat them separately.

Paper and Board.   The Paper and Board industry (MLH 481 and 484) lost almost 33,000 jobs nationally in the decade as the consequence of widespread mill closures and redundancies. Sixty-eight paper and board mills were reported to have closed between 1971 and 1982 in the UK, 32 of them between 1978 and 1982 when decline accelerated (*Paper, Review of the Year*, 1983). A number of key factors lay behind this contraction.

(a) Longer-term structural factors. Changing comparative advantages have led to major geographical shifts in production over the past 15 years or so. Nordic producers have had the advantage of low-cost energy and local raw material supplies. The ending of tariffs with EFTA in the late 1960s opened up formerly protected European markets to these producers (*Financial Times,* 1982a). Twenty years ago they exported mainly pulp but subsequent investment in integrated pulp, paper and board mills led to the increasing export of paper and board. Smaller, non-integrated European mills have not been able to compete in the production of commodity grade papers (for newsprint, and so on) and mill closure was a European phenomenon in the 1970s. EEC producers' advantage in being closer to their customers than Nordic producers has also been eroded in recent years by the acquisition of European merchants and producers by Nordic companies (*Financial Times,* 1981).

(b) Shorter-term and cyclical factors. The longer-term locational disadvantages of UK producers have been reinforced by shorter-term factors particularly in the post-1978 period.

(c) Recession and exchange rate disadvantages. The post-1978 recession in the UK has had a significant impact on demand for consumer goods which has worked its way through to affect the demand for paper and packaging materials such as board. The government's monetarist financial strategy also had the effect of pushing up the exchange rate and thus increasing the import prices of basic fibre for UK producers.

(d) High energy costs. UK producers have complained bitterly about having to pay much higher energy costs than their competitors in the 1980s. The energy element in their production rose from 7 per cent to 15 per cent of total average manufacturing costs between 1974 and 1980 (NEDO, 1981). UK energy costs were higher than their EEC competitors and substantially higher than Nordic and North American producers.

(e) Foreign subsidies. UK producers have also alleged that a number of EEC governments have been providing indirect subsidies to their own producers either to keep down fuel costs or to keep open ailing plants.

In order to survive these structural and cyclical pressures the major UK companies have had to specialise in products that (a) are of higher quality than mass-produced products from overseas mills; (b) require a mix of pulps (thus outweighing the advantages of integrated mills); (c) are produced from local materials (waste paper and home-grown timber); and (d) are difficult or costly to transport (e.g. tissues) (*Financial Times*, 1982b). These responses have produced substantial changes in the output and structure of the industry. The move towards quality products in particular has often necessitated investment in new, technologically-advanced, computer processes.

Packaging. The packaging industry discussed here covers packaging derived from paper and board and allied products. Packaging products derived from glass, steel, tin, etc. are included in different industrial sectors. The packaging industry as a whole underwent major changes in the last decade, changes which particularly affected those products made from paper and board (*Financial Times*, 1982b).

(a) Longer-term structural factors. The growth of supermarkets led to an increasing demand for new forms of packaging attractive to self-service customers. Changes in social habit, reflected in the rapid growth of the take-away food industry, generated demands for new packaging materials such as film and aluminium foil. These shifts in demand and changes in raw material costs encouraged growth in the production of flexible containers embodying plastics and laminates at the expense of more traditional containers made of metal and glass, paper and board.

(b) Shorter-term and cyclical factors. The recession effectively checked the growth of what had previously been one of the major UK growth industries. The contraction of consumer demand rapidly worked its way through to consumer packaging materials. Again, exchange rate differentials made it cheaper to import many mass-produced materials from overseas, increasing the competitive pressures on home producers. Further pressure on home producers resulted from rapid changes in supermarket packaging styles and the proliferation of 'special offers' as competition increased in the food industry.

Again, the large multinational corporations which dominate the industry (Labour Research, 1983) responded by cutting out less profitable and competitive packaging lines, and switching to more specialised forms of packaging often requiring substantial investment in new technology.

Corporate Structure and Corporate Response in the Bristol Paper, Board and Packaging Industries

We are now in a position, having identified the broader patterns of sectoral change, to examine the details of corporate structure and corporate response which had a particular impact in Bristol.

The Paper and Board and Packaging industries in Bristol are dominated by a handful of major multinational corporations. As a rough estimate, almost 90 per cent of employment in the late 1970s was in subsidiaries of four multinational companies. The Imperial Group controlled the St Anne's Board Mills which, with 1700 employees, dominated the Paper and Board industry. In the Packaging industry, DRG (the Dickinson Robinson Group) had its headquarters in the city and had five major factory sites in different locations. The Imperial Group and British and American Tobacco plc (BAT) between them controlled four important factories through their joint ownership of Mardon Packaging International. Courtaulds had ultimate control of the local Colodense factory. Apart from DRG, these corporations all had their headquarters in London. In each case Paper and Board or Packaging activities were only one division of the corporation's total activities, although in each case an important one.

In most cases the plants had been long established in the city, although ownership had sometimes changed. Companies such as Imperial and DRG had roots in the industry going well back into the nineteenth century. At various times there had also been strong linkages between these companies. Mardon Son and Hall (part of Mardon Packaging International) had manufactured cigarette cartons and cards for Wills in the nineteenth century before becoming part of the Imperial Tobacco Company (the precursor of the Imperial Group) in 1901. Imperial and BAT jointly established the St. Anne's Board Mills in 1913. DRG was involved in the establishment of the Colodense plant just before the Second World War, and also provided many packaging products for Wills, Imperial and the tobacco industry.

In summary we are dealing here with a long-established industrial structure with a history of local corporate and market linkages. Most of these Paper, Board and Packaging plants had been first established before 1945. As such they represented a particular phase of capital accumulation in the growth of their respective corporations. Subsequent phases of capital accumulation, as we shall see, had often taken these companies away from this sector of production and away from the Bristol area.

To explore the dynamics of corporate change and their local impacts, two of these multinational companies are chosen for detailed comparative study — DRG and the Imperial Group. The following sections explore the structure of each company, its linkages to the Bristol area, and the factors behind its pattern of corporate response in the post-1978 recession.

DRG and Bristol

Historical background. DRG is the only major multinational company in any sector with its headquarters in the city. The company assumed its present form in 1966 as the result of a merger between the old-established Bristol firm of E.S. and A. Robinson and the equally long-established firm of John Dickinson, based in South East England.

Elisha Robinson established his firm in Bristol in 1844 to supply paper bags and wrapping paper to the retail trade (Darwin, 1945). The firm grew rapidly and consolidated its position by acquiring rights to a new American paper bag-making machine in 1873. The company had two substantial factories in Bristol by 1887. The first subsidiary was acquired in 1917, and rapid expansion took place in the 1920s and early 1930s. New packaging and paper factories were built in Bristol, which formed the core of the company's activities, and the Bristol engineering firm of Strachan and Henshaw (making printing and paper-making machines) joined the group in 1920. Paper and Board mills were built or acquired in Scotland and the London area and the first overseas company established in Cape Town in 1921. Further developments and acquisitions, both at home and overseas, followed after the Second World War and in 1966 the firm merged with John Dickinson which had developed a wide range of related paper, printing and stationery interests. The location of the headquarters in Bristol reflected the dominant role of Robinsons in the establishment and running of the new company. The new company employed 26,000 at home and overseas, its activities covering paper and board, envelopes and stationery, adhesive tapes, packaging products, printing, engineering and marketing.

Corporate structure and spatial location. Figure 11.3 shows the structure of the company in 1981. The UK operations were

Figure 11.3: DRG: Company Structure 1981 (Main Operating Units and Divisions)

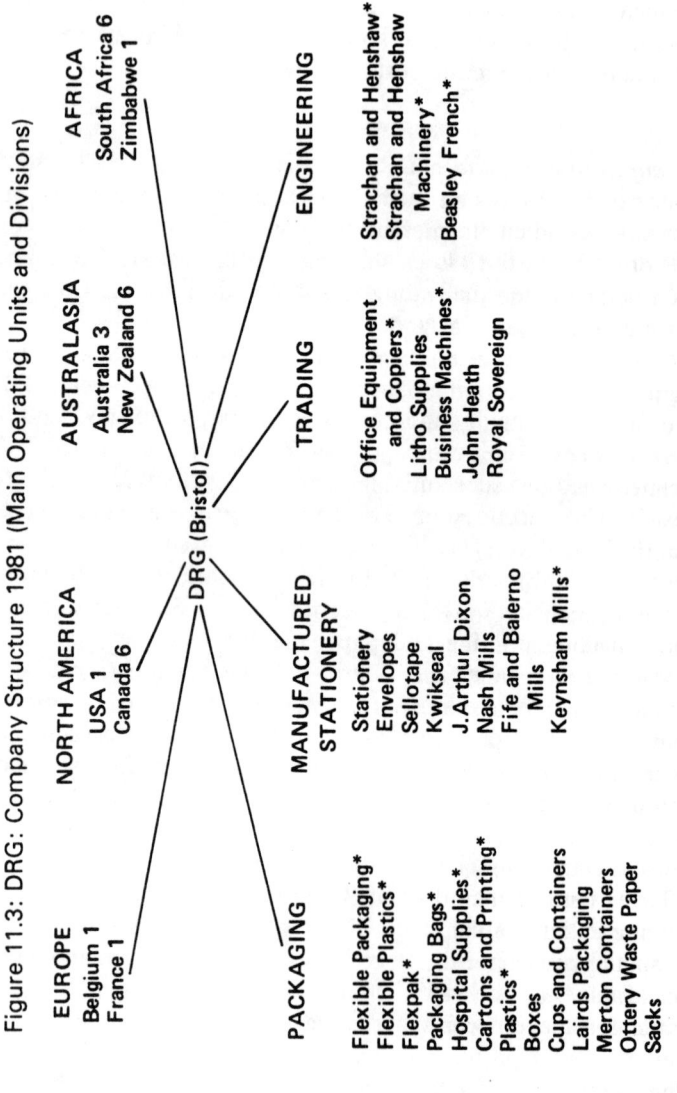

EUROPE	NORTH AMERICA	AUSTRALASIA	AFRICA
Belgium 1	USA 1	Australia 3	South Africa 6
France 1	Canada 6	New Zealand 6	Zimbabwe 1

DRG (Bristol)

PACKAGING	MANUFACTURED STATIONERY	TRADING	ENGINEERING
Flexible Packaging*	Stationery	Office Equipment and Copiers*	Strachan and Henshaw*
Flexible Plastics*	Envelopes	Litho Supplies	Strachan and Henshaw Machinery*
Flexpak*	Sellotape	Business Machines*	Beasley French*
Packaging Bags*	Kwikseal	John Heath	
Hospital Supplies*	J.Arthur Dixon	Royal Sovereign	
Cartons and Printing*	Nash Mills		
Plastics*	Fife and Balerno Mills		
Boxes	Keynsham Mills*		
Cups and Containers			
Lairds Packaging			
Merton Containers			
Ottery Waste Paper			
Sacks			

*Operating unit located in Bristol

grouped into four 'business groups' with their own group directors and management structures. Figure 11.4 shows the distribution of the main operating units illustrating the clustering of activities in certain areas of the country with a particular concentration in Bristol. The Packaging and Engineering groups were strongly represented in Bristol but the Manufactured Stationery group was more oriented to the South East. The corporate structure then had a distinctive spatial form reflecting different phases of investment and acquisition.

Corporate response to recession.   The impact of the recession and other external factors on the company are well brought out by the profitability and employment figures in Figure 11.5.

Profits rose until 1979 and then turned sharply downwards. For UK operations the decline in profits reached bottom in the first half of 1981, when the company achieved an operating profit of just £1.1 million over the six-month period, with a slow recovery beginning in the second half of the year. The continuing worldwide recession, however, prevented any recovery in overseas profits. In 1982, the slow recovery in UK profits continued, but total profits declined because of a further slump in overseas earnings. By 1983, however, UK profits were showing a 'splendid recovery' (DRG Company Accounts, 1983) and overseas profits were also improving. Overall, profits rose for the first time since 1979.

The company responded to the recession and declining profitability with an extensive programme of rationalisation and reorganisation both at home and overseas. This shows up clearly in the employment figures. Total employment declined 39 per cent from 25,886 in 1977 to 15,878 in 1983, whilst UK employment declined less, by 30 per cent or 7806 jobs. The major job losses, both at home and overseas, came after 1980. The sale of South African subsidiaries made the major contribution to the decline of overseas employment in 1982-83.

To explore further the impact of recession it is necessary to examine its differential effects on different company divisions and the spatial impacts of the resulting rationalisation and reorganisation. Table 11.3 below sets out the differences in UK trading profits for the different company sectors in the critical period 1980-82. Total profits slumped £3.7 million between 1980 and 1981 before staging a recovery. The table shows that the biggest drops were in Manufactured Stationery (a drop of £2.6 million

Figure 11.4: DRG: Main Operating Units, 1978

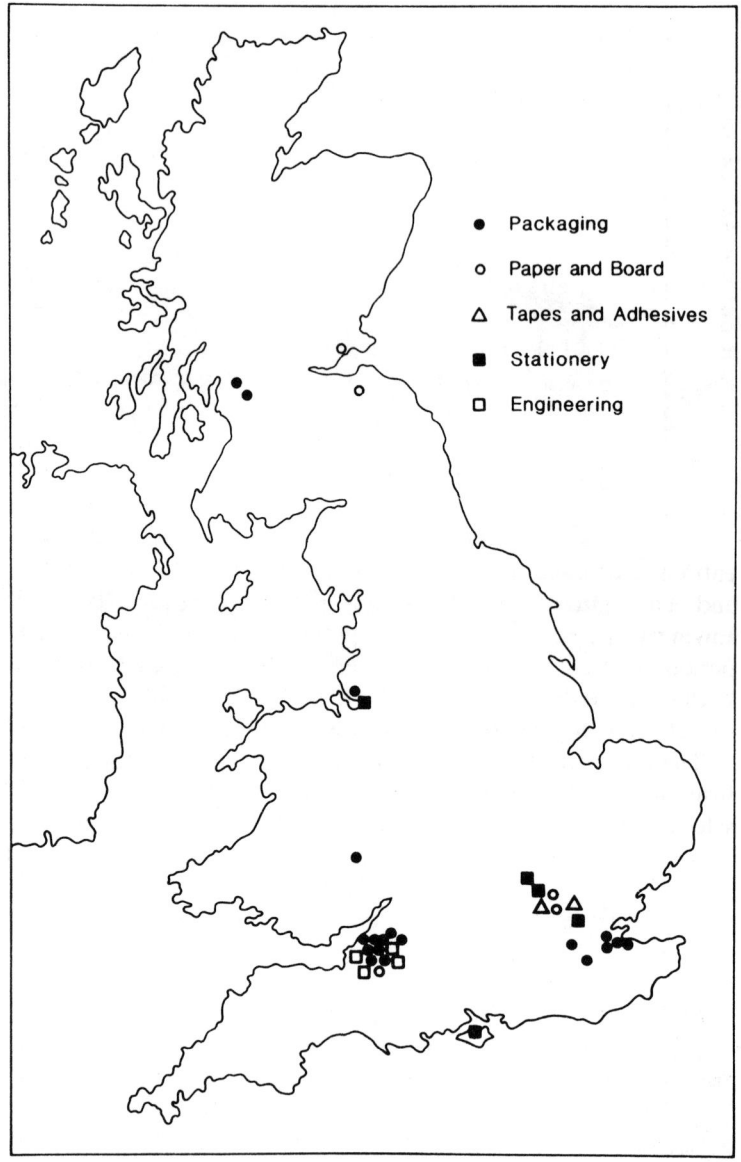

Figure 11.5: DRG: Trading Profits and Employment

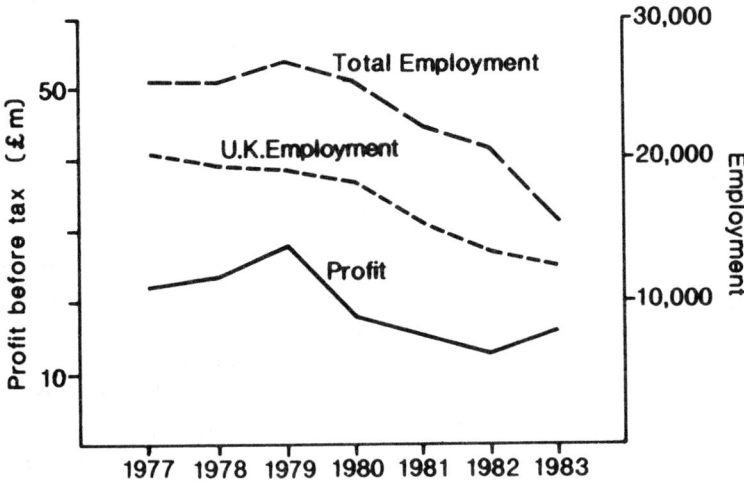

entirely accounted for by the collapse of Paper and Board profits) and Packaging (a drop of £2.4 million). The Trading and Engineering sectors actually increased their profits during this period of slump. The recovery in 1982 was due to the recovery in Packaging and Manufactured Stationery and the continuing success of Trading and Engineering.

The success of the Trading sector was partly due to the diversification into office equipment supplies (including microcomputer sales and servicing) through acquisition of the A.C. Barratt group

Table 11.3: DRG: UK Trading Profits (£ million)

	1980	1981	1982
Packaging			
Consumer	4.1 } 6.2	2.8 } 3.8	} 4.2
Industrial	2.1 }	1.0 }	}
Manufactured Stationery	3.5 } 5.6	3.5 } 3.0	} 4.0
Paper and Board	2.1 }	−0.5 }	}
Trading	1.3	1.9	2.5
Engineering	1.8	2.5	2.6
Total	14.9	11.2	13.3

Source: Annual Reports (various years).

of companies (although profits remained below expectations in this sector even in 1983). The success of the Engineering sector was largely due to the success of Strachan and Henshaw, the Bristol-based subsidiary, in securing defence contracts for underwater weapons-handling equipment and contracts from the nuclear industry for waste-handling equipment. The recession therefore had its biggest impacts on the Packaging and Paper and Board sectors and the consequent restructuring of these sectors had important impacts on the firm's Bristol employment.

Corporate strategies and the packaging sector. Successive company reports identified a number of key factors in the decline of profits in this sector. The basic factor was perceived to be the decline of consumer demand, particularly after 1980, and widespread destocking by retailers and wholesalers. Other contributory factors cited included the strength of sterling and import penetration, high energy costs relative to foreign competitors, and the obsolescence of some packaging products due to shifts in the pattern of demand. The company responded with a number of interrelated policies.

First, older and less profitable products were phased out and plants closed. Corrugated board was phased out in Glasgow, plastic cups in Liverpool, and rigid boxes in Bristol.

Secondly, investment was made in new technology to increase productivity in surviving operations where competition was intense. For example, there was substantial investment in new litho machines and computer-controlled equipment in carton production and printing in Bristol.

Thirdly, new investment was ploughed into the expansion of certain specialist activities where growth prospects were considered to be good. The two product areas that received particular emphasis were medical packaging and plastic containers. Bristol became the UK centre for the development of medical packaging and a new company was acquired to strengthen the US operations in this field. New investment went into plastics production at Yate, near Bristol, and a new specialist plastics company acquired in Corby in 1982.

Corporate strategies and the paper and board sector. As the profitability figures show, this basic sector of production was particularly hard hit during this period, mainly by lower demand, overseas competition and high energy costs. Excess capacity was emerging as early as 1977 and the following year the Croxley (Herts) paper mill was closed. The closure of the Kent Kraft Mills and the Merton Board Mills, both in the London area, followed in 1981 and 1982. These capacity cuts fell mainly on the former John Dickinson plants in the South East. The only Bristol plant, at Keynsham, specialising in the production of high-quality coated papers, was one of the more profitable survivors in this contracting sector.

Overall impacts on the Bristol economy.   In summary, a complex pattern of responses can be seen at work — reorganisation, capacity cuts and closures, new investment and acquisition — which affected different sectors to different degrees and had different spatial impacts. The various strategies in combination produced a particular pattern of employment effects in the Bristol area. Although some new jobs were created they were outweighed by losses, resulting in a net decline of around 18 per cent between 1978 and 1983. This was significantly less than the 37 per cent drop in the company's UK employment. The Bristol core of the company's employment was thus to some extent protected from the wider rundown although the net loss of over 1000 local jobs was not insignificant. The vast majority of the net loss of jobs was in the company's packaging plants in the city.

The analysis so far, therefore, enables us to establish some of the connecting links between wider changes in the national and international economy and local changes in the Packaging and Paper and Board sectors. To establish more of the links it is necessary to turn to the analysis of another multinational with strong ties to the Bristol economy.

Imperial and Bristol

The responses of the Imperial Group to recession provides an interesting set of contrasts to DRG with different impacts on the local economy. We can here link local changes in the paper and board and packaging industries to wider economic forces through a different pattern of corporate mediations.

Historical background.   The Imperial Group has also had long associations with the city through the historic ties of many of its present subsidiary companies. The tobacco firm of Wills was founded in 1786 in the city and grew to dominate the British tobacco industry from its Bristol headquarters in the late nineteenth century (Alford, 1973; 1976). The Wills company played a leading role in the formation of the Imperial Tobacco Company in 1901. Thirteen tobacco companies came together as a defensive response to the threatened entry of the giant American Tobacco Company into the British market. In the following year five other companies joined including the Bristol printing and packaging firm of Mardon Son and Hall which had close ties to Wills and the tobacco industry. In 1902, Imperial and the American Tobacco Company effectively signed a truce and set up BAT as a jointly-owned company to take charge of the export and overseas marketing of their branded products.

Bristol was clearly a core area in the foundation phase of Imperial. It was also the site of new investment during the subsequent phase of consolidation and growth in tobacco, paper, board and packaging down to the 1960s (Imperial Group, 1979). In 1913 Imperial and BAT collaborated to set up the St Anne's Board Mills in the city to supply carton board for packaging (Imperial acquired BAT's share in 1921) and Imperial also established Ashton Containers in 1918 to supply other forms of packaging material. Bristol was thus the site for important 'upstream' investment out of tobacco.

In the 1960s Imperial, whose headquarters had been shifted to London, began a major diversification phase out of tobacco, board and packaging that led to the acquisition of a wide range of brewery and food interests. This phase largely passed Bristol by, although a local brewery was incorporated into the group with the takeover of Courages in 1972. By the late 1970s, therefore, Bristol remained an important area for Imperial's activities but largely as a location for its older-established board, packaging and tobacco interests rather than its new growth sectors.

Imperial also retained a large share ownership in BAT which had grown to become a major multinational in its own right. In 1962 Imperial and BAT set up a new jointly-owned multinational, Marton Packaging International, and transferred to it Bristol firms such as Mardon Son and Hall and Ashton Containers.

Corporate structure and spatial location. The structure of Imperial in 1978 is illustrated in Figure 11.6. At this time the company employed 87,000 people worldwide, its component subsidiaries organised through four main divisions, Bristol being

Figure 11.6: The Corporate Structure of the Imperial Group: 1978

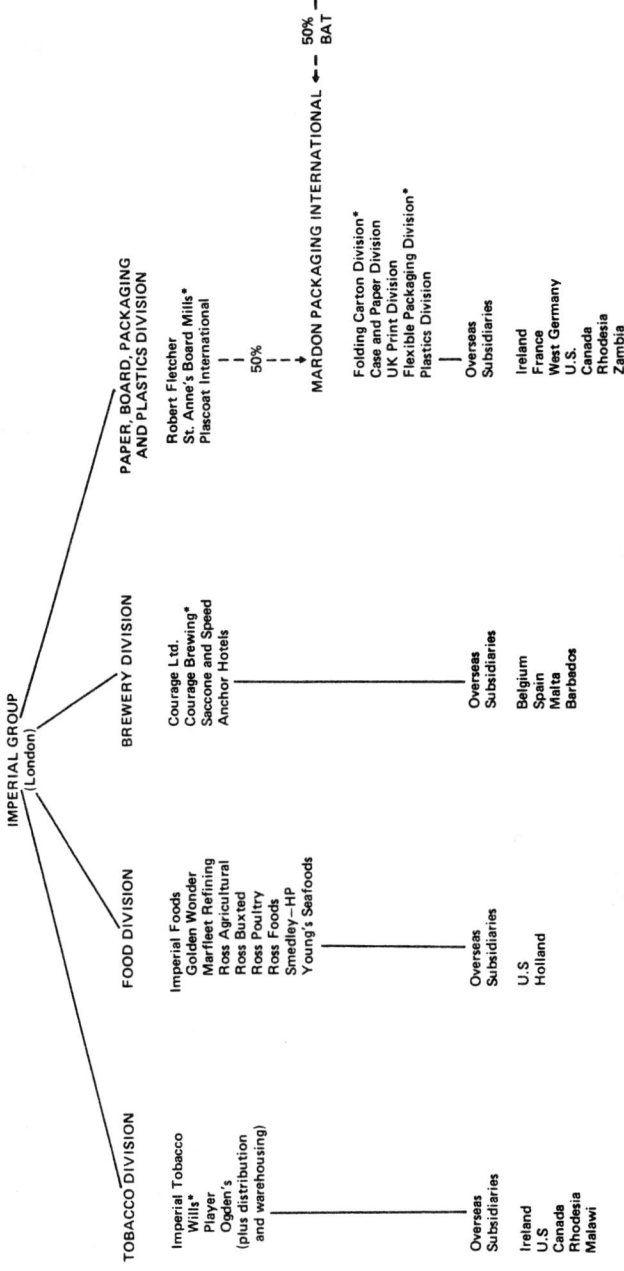

IMPERIAL GROUP
(London)

TOBACCO DIVISION

Imperial Tobacco
Wills*
Player
Ogden's
(plus distribution
and warehousing)

Overseas
Subsidiaries

Ireland
U.S
Canada
Rhodesia
Malawi

FOOD DIVISION

Imperial Foods
Golden Wonder
Marfleet Refining
Ross Agricultural
Ross Buxted
Ross Poultry
Ross Foods
Smedley—HP
Young's Seafoods

Overseas
Subsidiaries

U.S
Holland

BREWERY DIVISION

Courage Ltd.
Courage Brewing*
Saccone and Speed
Anchor Hotels

Overseas
Subsidiaries

Belgium
Spain
Malta
Barbados

**PAPER, BOARD, PACKAGING
AND PLASTICS DIVISION**

Robert Fletcher
St. Anne's Board Mills*
Plascoat International

50%

MARDON PACKAGING INTERNATIONAL ◄— 50% - - -
BAT

Folding Carton Division*
Case and Paper Division
UK Print Division
Flexible Packaging Division*
Plastics Division

Overseas
Subsidiaries

Ireland
France
West Germany
U.S.
Canada
Rhodesia
Zambia

(*Plant located in Bristol)

strongly represented in three of them and in the jointly-owned
Mardon Packaging International.

Figure 11.7 shows the distribution of the main UK plants.
Bristol stands out as the centre of an important cluster of major
plants. In the city the Wills tobacco plants employed around 4000.
The St Anne's Board Mills employed over 1700 in the production
of high-quality folding board (one of the largest sites in Europe).
The various factories of Mardon Son and Hall and Ashton
Containers employed around 4500 more, all jointly owned with
BAT.

Corporate response to recession.   The problems faced by Imperial
are graphically illustrated in Figure 11.8. Imperial's profits rose
until 1979 and then plummeted to a trough in 1981. In response to
this crisis a new managing director was appointed and a major
programme of rationalisation and reorganisation launched. A
rapid recovery in profits ensued.

The scale of rationalisation shows up in the employment figures.
Total employment dropped by over 20 per cent (26,000 jobs)
between 1980 and 1982, and UK employment dropped by 17.4
per cent (15,000 jobs).

As with DRG a clearer picture of the restructuring process can
be obtained by looking at performance figures by major divisions
and product areas (Table 11.4). The first point to note concerns
the divisional structure itself. A new division, Howard Johnsons,
appears in 1980 for the first time and the Paper and Packaging
sector has shrunk to 'other activities' relatively insignificant in
financial terms. The process of change, which had important
implications for the Paper and Board industry, started in 1979.
The Tobacco division, the traditional bedrock of Imperial's activities, had been hard hit by a combination of factors in the 1970s.
Tobacco taxes were increased in successive budgets, domestic
demand declined, and Imperial faced increasing competition in
UK and European markets from BAT following the ending of
their longstanding territorial trading agreements under EEC law.
in 1979, Imperial further distanced itself by selling its shares in
Mardon Packaging International to BAT. The Bristol firms of
Mardon Son and Hall and Ashton Containers thus passed to a new
multinational. The proceeds of the sale (over £280 million) partly
covered the purchase of Howard Johnson, the US restaurant and
hotel chain, as Imperial sought to diversify further out of its

Figure 11.7: Imperial Group: Main Operating Units, 1979

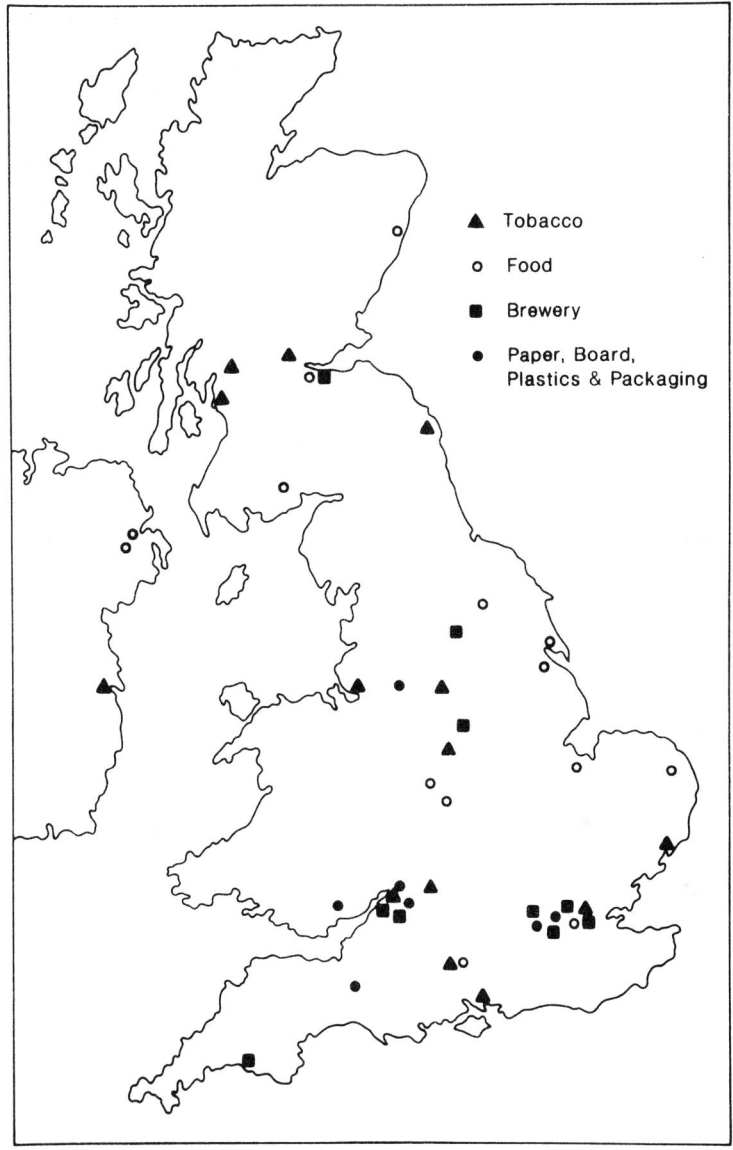

Figure 11.8: Imperial Group: Trading Profits and Employment

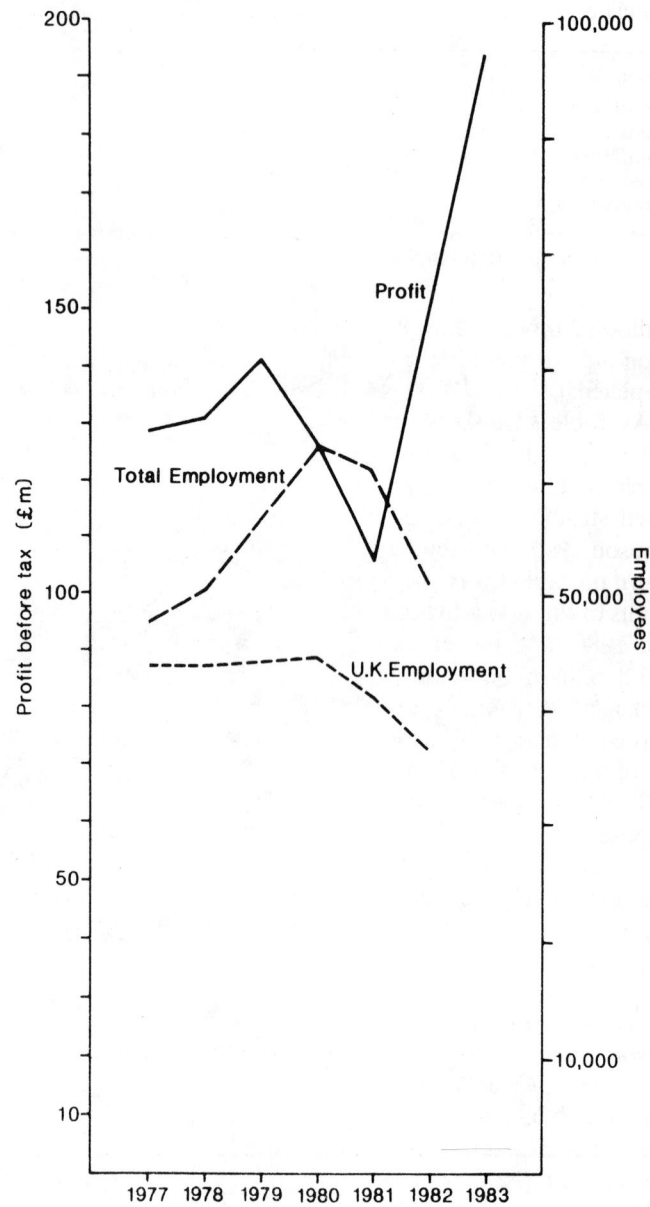

Table 11.4: The Imperial Group: Operating Profits by Division (£ million)

Division	1979	1980	1981	1982	1983
Imperial Tobacco Ltd	82.4	85.5	68.7	84.0	96.6
Imperial Brewing and Leisure	37.7	40.8	50.4	58.5	71.6
Imperial Foods	19.7	16.1	20.8	23.3	27.7
Howard Johnson	—	11.5	20.5	15.6	19.4
Other activities	−1.1	−5.4	−0.3	0.5	0.5

Source: Annual Reports (various years).

traditional tobacco and paper and packaging activities. The acquisition did not provide the expected return and Imperial's problems deepened.

As Table 11.4 shows, the drop in overall profits between 1979 and 1981 was related to the relative performance of the different divisions. The Brewing and Leisure division did well and contributed steadily increasing profits throughout the period. Howard Johnson also contributed to overall profitability although the return on capital was lower than expected. However, the operating profits of the Food division slumped by £3.6 million between 1979 and 1980, and the operating profits of the Tobacco division by £16.8 million between 1980 and 1981, and the losses of the Packaging division ('other activities') increased by £4.3 million. This combination of factors precipitated the differential restructuring of these divisions.

The loss-making poultry business, employing over 9000, was disposed of and this contributed to a modest turnaround of the Food division's profits the following year. The Tobacco division was extensively restructured with the closure of factories in Glasgow, Stirling and Bristol and the concentration of administrative functions in Bristol.

Corporate strategies and the paper, board and packaging sector. Over a three-year period Imperial all but moved out of paper and packaging production. Following a trading loss of £6 million the St Anne's Board Mills were closed in 1980. The plant, one of the largest in Europe, used imported woodpulp from Scandinavia and waste paper from the UK, and supplied companies such as Wills and DRG with folding board for packaging. Losses increased in the late 1970s and closure was finally approved in

1980. Imperial put the losses down to a number of related factors, chief of which were the advantages of Scandinavian producers in having access to local timber and abundant energy, heavy competition in the market for mass production grades, high UK energy costs, the effects of the rise in the exchange rate on import costs for raw materials, and the effects of the recession on the overall demand for consumer products. Efforts to find a buyer for the plant failed and its closure wiped out 84 per cent of Bristol's employment in the paper and board sector.

Following the closure of the Board Mills, Imperial sold Plascoat International in 1982, reducing its Paper and Board division to one subsidiary making cigarette papers and part-ownership of a film conversion company.

Overall impacts on the Bristol economy.   The interlinked changes outlined above had a major impact on the Bristol economy and the paper and board sector in particular. Bristol experienced some loss of jobs as the result of the rationalisation in the Brewery division but the major job losses resulted from rationalisation and reorganisation of the Tobacco and Paper and Packaging divisions. In tobacco, Bristol lost a cigar factory but gained additional jobs from management and administration functions for the division as a whole. The net loss of jobs was approximately 1000 between 1980 and 1984. The closure of the St Anne's Board Mills added another 1700 job losses to this figure.

Discussion

Through the analysis of the corporate strategies of these two major corporations alone we have accounted for almost all of the employment decline in the Paper and Board industry in Bristol and approximately half of the employment decline in the Packaging industry. To account for the balance of the job loss would require similar studies of major multinational corporations such as BAT and Courtaulds and of two or three much smaller, locally-based, single-plant firms.

The explanation of local job loss has involved the integration of different levels of analysis. The discussion of the impacts of broader national and international economic forces on different sectors and sub-sectors provided a framework for the analysis of particular corporate strategies. The analysis of individual corporations established links between their strategies in the sector under study and their interrelated strategies across other sectors of the economy. Finally, the particular impacts of these interlinked policies on the Bristol area were identified. Local economic changes in a key sector were thereby linked to broader economic forces through a complex chain of corporate mediations. Comparing and contrasting the two chains of mediation presented here leads to a number of general observations.

Profitability Crises

Both corporations had been involved in restructuring exercises throughout the 1970s but the profitability crises they faced after 1979 triggered more rapid and widespread changes. In terms of percentage decline DRG faced the more severe crisis. Its profits dropped 55 per cent between 1979 and 1982 before recovering, whilst Imperial's profits dropped 25 per cent between 1979 and 1981 before staging a more rapid recovery.

Restructuring Strategies

Corporate-wide. DRG had embarked upon a steady programme of restructuring from the late 1970s onwards involving reorganisation of its divisional structure, investment in new growth areas and increasing productivity in basic mass-production sectors. After 1979 this strategy was accelerated and coupled with the closure or rundown of plants in sectors such as paper where overseas competition was acute. The company also attempted to diversify to a limited extent through the acquisition and expansion of subsidiaries providing office and computing services. This represented a move away from production itself to a closer involvement with consumer services.

Imperial's response to profits decline involved a more concentrated phase of restructuring involving major management reorganisation and a more complex and wide-ranging package of closures, disposals and acquisitions. Given Imperial's greater size and resources major acquisitions (such as Howard Johnson) were possible on a scale beyond DRG. Nevertheless, Imperial's diversification strategy also represented a move closer to consumer markets and services, although on a larger scale and less related to existing activities.

The two restructuring strategies were not accompanied by the same organisational changes in terms of centralisation or decentralisation. DRG appears to have operated through a more decentralised management structure throughout the period. In a published interview in 1980 (*Investors Chronicle*, 1980) the then managing director referred to a decentralised structure made up of separate profit centres. He considered the central board to be managing a portfolio, not expecting the same return from each business at each point in time. This management structure seems to have been maintained over the subsequent period. The Imperial Group, on the other hand, went through a phase of increasing centralisation after 1980 following the dismissal of its chairman, who had favoured more autonomy for divisions and subsidiaries, and the appointment of a successor who favoured much greater central control as a means of restoring profitability (*Observer*, 1984).

There are also interesting contrasts to be made in terms of the international dimensions of overall corporate strategy. Many studies have pointed towards the outflow of capital from Britain through the investment policies of multinational corporations resulting in a shift production overseas and job loss in Britain (e.g. Fröbel, Heinrichs and Kreye, 1980; Gaffikin and Nickson, 1984). In the case of DRG and Imperial the employment outcomes do not quite fit this pattern.

In 1977, Imperial employed around 47,000 people, only 8.3 per cent outside the UK. Largely as a result of overseas acquisitions, total employment rose to 63,000 in 1980 with 28 per cent of the total overseas. However, between 1980 and 1982 overseas employment actually fell more sharply than UK employment (−26 per cent compared to −18 per cent), although in 1982 overseas employment remained substantially above its 1977 level both in absolute and percentage terms. In the case of DRG, however, overseas employment actually contracted at a faster rate than UK employment over the whole 1979-83 period. Overseas employment accounted for less than 25 per cent of total employment in 1983 compared to around 30 per cent in 1979. This decline was accounted for by the sale or closure of overseas plants in Australia, Canada and New Zealand and the disposal of the bulk of the company's South African subsidiaries following profit decline and management errors. The different corporate strategies adopted by DRG and Imperial clearly had different effects in terms of the international distribution of jobs during this period.

Restructuring and the paper, printing and packaging sector. The impacts of corporate-wide restructuring on the paper, printing and packaging sector also varied. These industries were far more central to DRG's corporate structure than they were to Imperial's both in terms of assets, employment and intra-firm linkages. Paper, printing and packaging formed the core of DRG's activities but had been reduced to a more peripheral status in Imperial's organisation. Imperial had the option of closing or disposing of almost all its activities in this sector without disrupting its entire organisation. Basic paper and board activities could be axed without damaging other divisions and joint ownership with BAT provided an opportunity for disposing of a number of packaging subsidiaries at one go. DRG, more firmly tied to the paper, printing and packaging sector, preferred a strategy of selective investment and disinvestment within the sector.

Restructuring Strategies and Bristol

The strategies of both corporations had major impacts on Bristol. The precise effects reflected a number of factors, in particular the specific product areas represented in Bristol and the age and profitability of plants. As a key site for Imperial's basic paper and board production, Bristol was strongly affected by the decision to end production in the face of intense international competition. As a site for a number of packaging plants jointly owned with BAT, Bristol was also affected indirectly by Imperial's sale, to realise capital for overseas diversification, of Mardon Packaging International to BAT.

Bristol was affected in different ways by DRG's decisions in this sector. Bristol was not a major site for basic paper and board production for DRG and was less affected by major closures and rationalisations. The city was affected by rationalisation and technical change in basic packaging production but also benefited from selective investment in other sectors such as medical packaging and plastics. Whereas Bristol was a site for less profitable and older Imperial plants, it was a site for a wider range of DRG's plants covering different product areas with different growth prospects.

Finally, the fact that Bristol was also the headquarters for DRG may have made a difference. This may have operated through closer management ties with local plants as well as through the initial establishment of new activities (e.g. business systems) near the headquarters location.

In summary, changes in investment and employment in the Bristol paper, printing and packaging industry resulted from the intersection of a whole series of interrelated factors at different spatial scales involving both the paper, printing and packaging sector and other industrial sectors related to paper, printing and packaging only in terms of common corporate ownership. Thus, the availability of funds for investment in the sector under study, and the pressures for closure and rationalisation, depended not only on market conditions and profitability in that sector but also market conditions and profitability in other industrially unrelated sectors. It was the different patterns of corporate ownership that brought these factors together in varying and complex ways.

What we have uncovered are some of the processes behind the reworking of an older layer of corporate investment in the city. The point was made in an earlier section that many of these plants dated originally from before the war and represented a particular phase of corporate growth in the corporations under study. Subsequent rounds of investment in different product areas have reworked this original layer to different degrees. In the case of Imperial subsequent investments had their greatest impacts elsewhere whilst DRG's investments have more continuously reworked the original layer of investment in Bristol. The post-1978 recession phase has seen an accelerated reworking of these earlier layers of investment.

Finally, it is important to note the limitations on the explanations offered here. Some of the complex processes behind job losses in a particular industrial sector in a particular locality, Bristol, and in a particular economic context have been uncovered. The large negative differential component in the shift-share analysis reflected the spatial outcomes of a range of essentially non-spatial corporate strategies. However, it is not entirely clear that these strategies were the result of consciously worked-out and rational decisions by identifiable key decision-makers. It is apparent that the corporations, although identifiable units in terms of boundaries of ownership, sprawl over quite different sectors of the economy and as such are best conceptualised as *sites* for the intersection of a complex range of often contradictory and competing economic forces. Strategic response is heavily constrained by overall profitability, resource availability and adopted or imposed 'success' criteria. Corporate strategy unfolds in a context of limited information and uncertainty and can only be implemented through negotiation and compromise with various levels of management, unions and the workforce. Much more work is needed on the real nature of the 'corporate strategies' described here and their underlying determinants.

Further work is also needed on the way that corporate strategies impact upon the labour market and the nature of labour processes. This work can best be carried out at the level of the individual plant and is the subject of current research which uses the findings of this paper as a general framework for plant-level interviews and surveys.

12 ONE PERSPECTIVE ON THE ENTERPRISE PERSPECTIVE

Bob McNee

What would you do if you were called a 'pioneer of the enterprise perspective' in geography and asked to reflect on the emergence of a 'geography of multinationals'? I accepted with haste: how often does one get to play the sage?

A Country Boy and Future Shock

I would like to be able to describe my initial attempts to study multinational corporations (MNCs) as some sort of 'triumph of the intellect'. However, the truth is quite otherwise.

In 1952, I began teaching economic geography in an economics department in an élitist (though public) university on the western edge of a large and expanding black residential area or 'ghetto' (Harlem) in the major city (New York) of the most economically powerful network in the history of the world. That great economic system was expanding rapidly in those years and the almost unchallenged hegemony of the American global empire. The key instrument for that expansion was a modern social invention, the MNC. For those with eyes to see, there was abundant visual evidence of the rise of the MNC in New York itself: an office-building boom dwarfing the one which had made New York's skyline world-famous (McNee, 1966). In the 1950s was I responsive to such evidence before my eyes? Of course not — no one had given me 'permission' to make that kind of connection.

I had few qualifications for examining MNCs other than a kind of child-like curiosity, nor was I well-equipped to try to understand the 'ghetto' engulfing the campus. No one had given me 'permission' to look critically at that process either. I saw little connection between mass impoverishment in the city (or the world) and the increasing concentration of economic and social power.

I had been born on a ranch in Montana, reared on tenant farms in Minnesota, exposed on at least a superficial level to the socio-economic diversity of the world (navy service in many

344

countries/dissertation research in the *mezzogiorno*), briefly introduced to twentieth-century industrial struggles and non-bourgeois interpretations of them (as a post-war undergraduate in an allegedly 'radical' municipal university in Detroit), and well-trained (at Syracuse University) in a kind of geography that was of very limited value in interpreting such experiences. It was a kind of geography daily becoming less and less useful for interpreting twentieth-century economic landscapes. Indeed, I was better equipped, in 1952, for studying the geography of the Edwardian era than that of the mid-twentieth century. Events in the turbulent twentieth century are still outrunning my ability to comprehend them. But I am not as far in the rear as I once was (or such is my conceit).

Future shock is a central problem for all twentieth-century social 'science'. Unfortunately, social 'scientists', myself included, are reluctant to write off their investments in outmoded forms of analysis. Fortunately, I had a high tolerance for conceptual ambiguity, perhaps the primary need in studying MNCs.

Another great need is luck. I stumbled into a golden research opportunity. Required by my economist colleagues to use Zimmerman's pioneering book as a text, I came to understand, for the first time, the compelling role of energy costs in economic geography (Zimmerman, 1933). Inspired, in 1956, I obtained a six-weeks fellowship with Socony Mobil at its New York headquarters (through the Foundation for Economic Education, a capitalist-libertarian organisation). I was able to ask naive questions in each of the functional (production, transportation, refining, marketing, and so on) divisions of the firm and thereby to be puzzled by the spatial complexity of such a large organisation.

The firms in the programme hoped professors might be less anti-business if they had the chance to meet managers as people and to ask professional questions. Perhaps they intuitively considered professors as class allies. Another programme intended to improve the image of 'Big Business' was that of the National Planning Association. With support from the Carnegie Foundation, it published a series of partially candid reports on American business abroad, including studies of General Electric in Brazil and Casa Grace in Peru. Those case studies are still valuable today not only because of their data but also for their evidence of how American multinationals saw themselves at the time and hoped others would see them.

Such programmes were justified within MNCs as 'public relations'. But, they can also be seen as a quest by the professional managerial class of the MNCs for 'understanding'. Their social role was a relatively new one — that of 'world managers' — and they perceived themselves very differently from the way outsiders perceived them (Barnet and Muller, 1974, pp. 45-71). Economists and economic geographers, whether Marxist or bourgeois, tend to underrate the importance of managers and management. According to traditional theory, it is the market which is the organiser of the economy. So why bother to study the internal patterns of a firm, including its managerial structures? When you have imagined one firm, you have seen them all, so to speak.

However, the executives of Socony Mobil knew that they were playing a critical role in shaping the emerging world economy, no matter what traditionalists might think. Perhaps they wanted affirmation, an appreciative audience, and thus were willing to answer naive questions from a young professor from City College. This, despite the popular image of City College at the time as 'the big Red Schoolhouse' (courtesy of Senator Joseph McCarthy). Subsequently, the author obtained other corporate fellowships. During the turbulent 1960s, the cleavage between one set of career bureaucrats (the managers) and another (the tenured professoriat) widened. Fellowship programmes of that type were casualties. I have found few professors or managers who seem aware of the ideological and class bases for their negative stereotypes of each other.

Initially, I stubbornly tried to fit my observations of Socony Mobil into the established boxes of geographic thought. Giving up at last, I turned to the 'regional concept', assuming it was 'the wave of the future' in geography rather than what it was; an excellent summary of the accumulated wisdom of an ageing generation (Whittlesey, 1954). Thus was born the 'company region', a 'special type of planned economic region, somewhat resembling other planned regions, both economic and political, but having distinctive characteristics of its own' (McNee, 1958, p. 322). Though the analogy to 'accepted' ideas in geography was vague and imprecise, it helped others *to visualise* 'company geography'. It 'gave permission' to dream new dreams, to conceive of worlds not imagined before. That was its principal value.

The 'company region' gave some 'legitimacy' to the study of MNCs, though not much. For a decade, 1958 to 1968, such research was only marginally 'legitimate'. Interesting, to be sure, but where did it 'fit in', where could it lead? The emphasis on case studies made it seem hopelessly outdated in the springtime of the 'new geography'. A famous paper by Berry and Garrison was published in the same issue of *Economic Geography* (Berry and Garrison, 1958). Those of a thoroughly theoretical turn of mind saw 'company geography' as consistent with the 'new geography'. But others were less attuned to the theory-building thrust of the 'new geography', interpreting that term primarily as simplistic bourgeois 'positivism' and 'quantification'.

The problem of intellectual 'legitimacy' is central in a time of rapid socio-economic change. I sought to deepen my understanding of the economic, managerial and organisational literature relevant to further case studies. But the resulting manuscript was considered 'too economic' and 'not geographic' enough. So I added an introductory section implying, with justice, that Vidal de la Blache and other heroes of the geographic past supported my endeavours. The article, using the term 'geography of enterprise', was published in Europe, where there was less avoidance of theory (McNee, 1960). The term 'geography of enterprise' was substituted for 'company regions' to foster 'legitimacy'. It is so much more 'scholarly' and 'scientific' sounding, don't you think?

In the 1960s, 'legitimacy' was advanced immeasurably by a theory-minded cluster of professors and graduate students at the University of Washington, including Gunter Krumme, Guy Steed, Morgan Thomas, Edward Ullman and others. They and their students and the students of their students account for much of the advance in the study of enterprise and the MNC. In the 1970s advancement came at many places around the world, especially Britain, Canada, Australia and New Zealand; soon 'legitimacy' was no longer a concern. However, the most important factor in the change may have been the wide media attention given to MNCs that came in the 1970s. Despite much 'liberal' and so-called 'radical' rhetoric, the professoriat as a social class is conservative, even reactionary. Its response to 'future shock' tends to be withdrawal into comforting old formulae. I fit my class except that I have a high tolerance for conceptual ambiguity and am lucky.

Pragmatic Advances Toward Theory

Initially, MNC research was necessarily pragmatic. That is, much of the effort was on 'discovering the facts', using any concept, model, theory or whatever that appeared to lead toward that end. Pragmatism has its advantages, especially at first. However, theoretical incoherence and methodological disunity, recurrent complaints, follow as the night the day from a continued pragmatic approach. Perhaps enough 'facts' have been discovered. Perhaps it is time to step back, stressing theoretical coherence and consistency to a higher degree. A recent book on 'industrial organisation and location' (actually, an analysis of the spatial dimensions of formal organisations) is suggestive of what the author means (McDermott and Taylor, 1982). That study uses a case study (the electronics industry of the United Kingdom); the approach to the case study is detailed, coherent and rigorous. The issue is not whether case studies have been outgrown (a very unlikely event in my opinion). The issue is whether specific case studies go beyond the simplistic approaches used initially by myself and others.

In 1958, I called for studies of firms involved in 'mass-production industries such as steel, aluminium, automobiles, and chemicals' (McNee, 1958, p. 337). A fairly obvious list, if you assume vertical integration to be of great importance, as I did. Gradually, case studies have appeared on steel (Fleming and Krumme, 1968; Heal, 1974), aluminium (Savey, 1981), automobiles (Bloomfield, 1981; Kortus and Kaczorowski, 1981; Krumme, 1981) and chemicals (Chapman, 1974; Clarke, 1982; Watts, 1982). Perhaps over-impressed by vertical integration, I did not list such industries as electrical products or clothing (Steed, 1981; Newfarmer and Topik, 1982).

Though I was impressed with the spatial dimensions of vertical integration, I left room for 'company regions organized primarily for purposes of financial manipulation', which might be 'somewhat amorphous, random, and incoherent in regional terms' (McNee, 1958, p. 323). I also referred to conglomerates:

> some companies have sought economic stability by diversification into quite dissimilar lines of production, such as corn flakes and laundry equipment. The parent company region might then include several loosely associated company regions, with great

regional unity at the local or provincial levels, but great regional disunity in terms of the whole company. (McNee, 1958, p. 323)

I did not develop that point. However, I think it should be explored in depth. As Taylor and Thrift have noted, 'there may be no single development sequence for all organisations, but rather a series of development sequences' (Taylor and Thrift, 1982, p. 19). However, that series may involve much more than distinctions among small firms, national oligopolistic firms, and the like; they may depend very much on the kind of spatial integration that is attempted, i.e. the kind of business organisation involved.

My list of industries (steel, aluminium, automobiles, chemicals) distinctly did *not* include a very important group: those firms directly involved with renewable resources such as forestry or farm crops. Hayter has illuminated much about the organisational aspects of forestry (Hayter, 1976; 1978;1981). Although there are many agricultural MNCs, they have not attracted much research attention. Perhaps this will be remedied by James Wilson, who has had years of experience on the inside of a major firm, Cargill. If I had been writing my 1958 paper with today's hindsights, I would have stressed the need for research on how such firms enhance or destroy environmental quality. But concern for the environment was at a low ebb in the confident, expansionist 1950s. Unfortunately, there has not been much effort by others to correct my blindness.

All my case studies were of American firms. Fortunately, this initial bias or overemphasis has been balanced by studies of British, German, French and other MNCs (Krumme, 1981; Savey, 1981; Bloomfield, 1981; Clarke, 1982). Likewise, there have been tantilising glimpses into the organisational structures of the Eastern European countries (Hamilton, 1974; Bora, 1981; Kortus and Kaczorowski, 1981). Also, there have been studies of state corporations, as in Quebec (Bradbury, 1982). There are state corporations, such as E.N.I. (Ente Nazionale Idracarburi), the Italian state corporation for petroleum, that operate in ways quite at variance from the 'received wisdom' about state corporations. Bradbury has opened a significant research door. The various efforts to expand the vision beyond the American and the 'private' will no doubt continue, including, one hopes, more interpretation of MNCs originating beyond the North Atlantic Basin.

I was impressed by the ways in which the early geography of

Socony Mobil had conditioned all subsequent geographies (McNee, 1958, pp. 328-30). Therefore, spatial evolution was the focus of my study of Sunoco (McNee, 1963). I found there was an underlying tension between those Sunoco bureaucrats preoccupied with the maintenance, smooth functioning, and perfection of an existing spatial system and other Sunoco bureaucrats who were more spatially innovative, more willing to risk the security of the system through radical spatial changes. In some periods, the latter group would win, thus creating new geographies. But both kinds of bureaucrat were a necessary part of the 'company team', the excesses of one balanced those of the other. Consequently, I was intrigued by the kind of radical spatial change described recently for ICI (Clark, 1982). The kind of intense documentary interest that would be necessary for detailed case studies of spatial evolution is not common among industrial geographers today. It would be useful if historical geographers could be weaned away from their current preoccupations to study the evolution of many firms in depth, using the documentary sources from within and without the firm.

Of course, spatial evolution as a more generalised process has been studied increasingly and to great benefit, as in studies of acquisitions, market capture, locational matching and internal adjustments following mergers. Likewise, the processes of spatial evolution have been clarified by the development of general models (Hayter and Watts, 1983; Taylor and Thrift, 1982, p. 19). Spatial evolution research developed much more rapidly than I thought possible in 1958. Such research has the dual value of contributing to knowing what governments might do to regulate corporate growth and providing ways to analyse corporate economic history more effectively.

Unfortunately, many of the early studies of corporate control function locations were rather superficial, mere manipulations of the kinds of 'facts' available in the annual *Fortune* survey. To know the location of 'corporate headquarters' is not to know very much unless one knows what the corporation centralises and what it disperses and the manner in which dispersals are spatially organised. Thus, I wrote in 1958:

> corporation regions have an internal nodal structure, with one or more foci, including a major focus, the home office. Lines of transportation and communication link the foci to the outer-

most limits of the region. There is an ever-changing flow of authority between the center and the parts, for in large corporations the decision-making process is very complex. The intricacy of this process is only partially indicated by the directly observable system of direct operations, affiliates, subsidiaries, and branches. (McNee, 1958, p. 323)

It is only recently that research on corporate control functions has gone very far beyond that simple and obvious statement. But now progress should be rapid.

Wealth Unchaperoned by Virtue

'Experience shows us', wrote the poetess Sappho over 2500 years ago, 'wealth unchaperoned by virtue is never an innocuous neighbour' (Barnard, 1958, fragment 86). The wealth and power of MNCs are necessarily of public concern wherever they operate and whatever their protestations of 'virtue'. In my initial paper, I commented briefly on 'the problem of social control of corporate growth' (McNee, 1958, p. 337). However, by the 1980s I had come to see this as a major research priority, calling for policy-oriented research that would enable governments to be more effective in regulating MNCs (McNee, 1981). I attributed this advance in wisdom to the many fine studies of the economic impacts of MNCs in both developing and developed nations. One of the most interesting recent policy-oriented studies has been Steed's study of Canadian threshold firms (Steed, 1982).

Recently, Peet has warned against the dangers of *assuming* (nation) states must necessarily be opposed to MNCs, a point which is well taken (Peet, 1982, p. 275). However, it is equally a mistake to assume states to be simple systems or that national capitalists will necessarily cooperate at all times and in all places with international capitalists. Reality tends to be messy. Peet also warns of the 'great diversionary potential' of a focus on MNCs rather than the more generalised processes of international capital (Peet, 1982, p. 275). This is a safe enough posture if one is a member of the tenured professoriat, but what if one is a governmental bureaucrat? I contend that states which exhibit any degree of independence, for whatever historical reason, need to have a variety of sophisticated interpretations of MNCs available for their use. To argue otherwise is to cooperate in mystification and to encourage apathy. As Krumme says, 'whether the operations of MNCs contribute more to the economic development of the host environment than to undesired imbalances and exploitation, remains to be seen' (Krumme, 1983, p. 520). MNCs are not the only form of exploitation and hierarchical domination in the world. Governments are usually in the position of choosing among 'evils' (as they define them).

Marxism and the Corporate Environment

In my 1958 paper, I stressed 'the importance of institutions as space organisers, and especially the firm as a man-created framework or system within which decisions on spatial interaction are made' (McNee, 1958, p. 337). I wanted to look at the *managerial structure*. Some call this a 'micro approach'. More accurately, it is an 'open the box' approach, in contrast to the traditional 'black box' approach to the firm of both Marxist and bourgeois geographers. Some people still prefer black boxes, resulting in recurrent assertions that no more case studies of individual MNCs are needed (though the number of detailed case studies completed is really quite small).

Traditionalists prefer studying the *environment* of the firm. Marxist geographers have been even more reluctant than bourgeois geographers to look inside that black box. The author considers ideology to be at work here. Bourgeois 'science' has provided 'organisational theory' derived from apologists for capitalistic hierarchy, domination, alienation and 'rationality', such as Max Weber. So the use of such theory in studying the firm is not threatening to someone with a bourgeois mind-set. However, Marx and his successors did not develop a comparable Marxist theory. This does not mean it could not be done, just that it has not been done yet.

Therefore, the most significant contributions of Marxist geographers to the understanding of the MNC have been in relation to the functioning of the global economy, the *environment* of individual MNCs. For example, Harvey's explanation and development of Marxist analysis, impressive even to know-nothings such as me, has little new to say about the MNC. Harvey does note a transition from national firms to MNCs and says 'the sheer scale and complexity of organisation — in both government and business — have changed out of all recognition in the last two hundred years' (Harvey, 1982, p. 137). He also notes that the MNC can produce in a specific geographic location 'what it would take many years of concentration through accumulation to bring about' and this in only 'the twinkling of an eye' (Harvey, 1982, p. 139). This is a fact of rather great geographic importance.

One of the great advantages of Marxist thought is that it does not deny history as bourgeois mythology so often does (Barthes, 1972, p. 151). Harvey has examined the structural evolution of large firms to some extent. He quotes Chandler on the history of changes in managerial structures within large corporations effectively but does not go on to other interpretations of such managerial change. However, consistent with his goal of clarifying and developing traditional Marxist analysis, he does not stray far from an emphasis on the economic environment rather than the firm itself. Someone of Harvey's analytic powers could illuminate within the MNC should he decide to open that black box for himself. For example, I liked his comment that 'the local integration of multinational firms makes the decision to stay put or close down a branch plant in a particular place a difficult one. And within the hierarchy of the multinational firm, what makes sense at one level does not necessarily make sense at another' (Harvey, 1982, p. 423). In short, Harvey has at least momentarily lifted the lid of the black box and peeked inside.

Traditionally, Marxists have stressed the *economic* environment to the virtual exclusion of the cultural environment. However, in recent years there has been a revival of interest in Gramsci's concept of cultural 'hegemony'. Peet has given us a fascinating interpretation of consumer culture (Peet, 1982, pp. 289-302). This is of great value for the study of the MNC because the structure and behaviour of organisations are clearly affected by their *symbolic environments* as well as the more obvious aspects of economic and cultural environments (Meyer and Scott, 1983). I agree with Enzensberger, quoted by Peet, to the effect that the main function of advertising and allied industries is to 'sell' the existing socio-economic order (Peet, 1982, p. 292). The most vivid expression of this point of view is by James Baldwin:

The music of the commercial simply reiterates the incredible glories of this great land, and one learns, through advertising, that it is, therefore, absolutely forbidden to the American people to be gloomy, private, tense, possessed; to stink, even a little, at any time; to grow gray, to wrinkle, to be sexless; to have unsmiling children; to be lustless of eye, hair, or teeth; to be flabby of breast, belly or bottom; to be gloomy, to know despair, or to embark on any adventure whatever without the corroboration of the friendly mob. (Baldwin, 1978, p. 433)

As Berger, Bloomberg, Fox, Dibb and Hollis say, 'publicity is the culture of the consumer society. It propagates through images that society's belief in itself' (Berger, 1972, p. 139). Peet has described the spread of this consumer culture around the world through the MNC (Peet, 1982, pp. 299-302).

Kropotkin, Reclus, and All That

If the geography of enterprise is to develop beyond its current embryonic stage then the most significant characteristics of organisations — hierarchy, centralisation, decentralisation, control and management (élites) — need to be addressed not only in terms of a narrow economic functionalism but also in terms of alternative approaches to society and 'the good life'. In 1984, we cannot pretend that George Orwell's vision should not be a part of the discussion about MNCs and their meaning. We cannot pretend (with a straight face, that is) that bourgeois 'organisational theory' was 'immaculately conceived', unaffected by the nature of the bourgeois society that gave it birth and nourished it. The dominance of hierarchical bureaucratic systems in modern life, *whether in bourgeois states or Marxist states*, may be the most significant social, political and economic difference between our time and that of the past. But, as Barthes points out, bourgeois mythology 'deprives the object of which it speaks of all history' (Barthes, 1972, p. 151). Thus, the rule of the new bureaucratic élites does not appear strange to most people; rather, it appears to be 'natural' based on 'eternal verities'. If geographers are to develop theories about MNCs that have real value and staying power, then they must penetrate bourgeois mythology and examine hierarchy, centralisation, decentralisation, control and management (élites) with more 'objectivity' than they have evidenced to date.

One way to achieve some distance from contemporary society

and its myths is to examine the ideas of social anarchists such as Peter Kropotkin and Elisee Reclus. Although both Kropotkin and Reclus were highly respected in both geographic and social anarchistic circles in their day, few geographers today seem aware of their contributions in either context. But recently, geographers have begun a reconsideration of their work (Breitbart, 1981; Dunbar, 1981).

Social anarchistic behaviour involves *spontaneous* cooperative effort to achieve goals *consensually* arrived at, rather than the non-spontaneous hierarchical ritual and hierarchical assignment of tasks which is so characteristic of the MNC. In the past, much economic behaviour was of that spontaneous kind. Today, it is found more commonly among the poor, the socially disadvantaged, and the alienated than among the white middle classes. That is, it survives in the interstices not yet fully 'organised' by the bureaucratic élites. Conceptually, such behaviour is of great interest. However, since it is partially outside of the market economy it is largely ignored by bourgeois social 'scientists'.

Social anarchists centred in London were among the most significant radical thinkers of the nineteenth and early twentieth centuries. However, Marxism gradually gained the ascendancy. Then, after the October Revolution of 1917, the ideas of social anarchists such as Goldman, Kropotkin, Reclus, Bakunin and Proudhon went into eclipse. Kropotkin, an anarchist as well as a geographer of renown, died in disappointment in 1921 (Goldman, 1970, p. 865). In the 1930s, there was an anarchist revival in Spain. Anarcho-syndicalists were remarkably successful in practice as well as in theory. But they were crushed in the civil war (Guerin, 1970, pp. 114-43). It is easier to exterminate a people than it is their ideas, as Goldman noted in 1938 (Guerin, 1970, p. 142).

Recently, interest in social anarchism has revived again. Feminists often come to social anarchism intuitively, through efforts to overcome the hierarchical conditioning of patriarchal society (Lewis, 1979, pp. 163-97). Gradually the buried anarchistic tradition has been rediscovered (Kornegger, 1979; Leighton, 1979). Feminists have become sensitive to the links between the training of boys for a lifetime of violence, competition and male bonding and social organisations such as religious orders, universities, governmental bureaux and the MNCs. Feminists have also become sensitive to the denigration of 'feminine' behaviour, such as cooperation, caring and nurturing and the related denigration of cooperatives as an economic alternative to the bureaucracies of bourgeois or Marxist states (David and Brannon, 1976; Tolson, 1977; Vetterling-Braggin, 1982; Coward, 1983).

Social anarchism shares with Marxism a highly critical view of all forms of capitalism (including the MNC) and a desire for equality and freedom. But beyond these general aspects the two traditions differ markedly. Social anarchism does not consider itself a 'science'. It is more a cluster of ideas; many of its adherents have been active in the artistic avant-garde. History is not viewed linearly, as in the Marxist tradition. There is no assumption of 'progress' or historical inevitability. History is viewed as a continuing struggle between rulers and ruled (in the MNC context, 'managers' and 'managed') in which future outcomes are always in doubt. Though social anarchists consider economic production and ownership of the means of production very important, they do not overlook other basic aspects of culture, including the most routine aspects of ritual and patterning in daily life. For them, psychocultural conditioning is of central importance: the role of internalised patterns of hierarchical thought. Hence they believe 'the revolution' begins here and now, and that it requires the linking of personal change and social change. Not surprisingly, anarchists such as Goodman have contributed much to educational theory and practice (Goodman, 1962). Most of the historic differences between Marxist and anarchist thought persist, but there are some ways in which the conceptual gap between them is being narrowed (Benello, 1979, pp. 168-9).

Peet and other Marxist and bourgeois ideologues often use the word 'anarchy' to mean chaos and disorder (Peet, 1983, p. 107). Similarly, those who assume contemporary bourgeois 'masculine' and 'feminine' gender roles are rooted in biology rather than socioeconomic history also assume social anarchistic thought is 'impractical'. Likewise some have dismissed social anarchistic thought as 'utopian'. But even 'negative utopias' such as George Orwell's have their value in clarifying our thinking. As Bookchin, a leading contemporary anarchist, says 'utopia redeems the future' (Bookchin, 1980, p. 284).

Anarchists oppose the state and organisations such as corporations because they conceive them as instruments for maintaining social inequalities. This does not mean they are against all social organisations. Quite the contrary. Social anarchists support voluntary, consensual organisations. They oppose the *insti-*

tutionalisation of organisation, the establishment of a special group of people whose job it is to organise other people (Walter, 1979, p. 148). They agree with Marxists that most property should be public rather than private but they consider *control* more important than ownership *per se*. *Bureaucratisation*, whether in the context of 'public property' or 'private property' is of central concern. This concern has intensified as the world has become increasingly ruled by 'careerists', whether bourgeois or Marxist. But the concern is not new. Indeed, part of Bakunin's opposition to Marx's programme was the fear of 'a new class, a new hierarchy of real and pretended scientists and scholars', who would be 'a minority ruling in the name of knowledge' (de Leon, 1979, p. 76). According to Bakunin 'the ridiculous cult of the superiority of the intellectual could arise only with the bourgeoisie' (Dolgoff, 1980, p. 424).

Since anarchists are individualistic their ideas differ in detail. The views of Reclus and Kropotkin are of special interest to geographers. Reclus thought questions of production and consumption should be made by 'communities of association of free labourers who have transcended avarice and the lust for power' (Dunbar, 1981, p. 161). That does sound just a wee bit utopian, doesn't it? Kropotkin stressed cooperation and 'mutual aid'. The purpose of his 'decentralist vision' was to achieve personal freedom and growth for everyone in the context of social responsibility (Breitbart, 1981, p. 151). What would he say today of the problems of centralisation and decentralisation, of the global spread of vast corporate systems coupled with the efforts of disaffected people to create communes and other forms of cooperative behaviour in their very shadow?

The overriding problem for MNC research is how to create theory with some staying power, some validity over a period of time, not just 'theory' which may be overturned by the next news from New York, London, Paris, Moscow, Tokyo or other major 'transactional cities'. Gottman's term 'transactional cities' aptly fits a world in which bureaucratic agreements so often take the place of the market (Gottman, 1983). Valid theory can be created only by acquiring some conceptual distance from bourgeois mythologies (Barthes, 1972). Such theory cannot be built simply by listening for the latest pronouncement from the Harvard School of Business. Nor can it be built by laying the ideas in journal articles end to end in a chain. So much in those articles is thoroughly 'depoliticised' (i.e. the political agenda is hidden). As Barthes says, mythology is depoliticised speech (Barthes, 1972, pp. 142-5). Bourgeois 'organisational theory' is of value, but only so long as its limitations are recognised. For example, an otherwise fascinating study of 'industrial organisation and location' is marred by the apparent assumption that something supposedly 'neutral' such as 'technology' is at the centre of the corporate system (McDermott and Taylor, 1982).

As Ehrlich says, bourgeois organisational theorists tend to 'see organisational authority as legitimate, non-coercive, and fundamentally rational' (Ehrlich, 1979, p. 97). However, the feminist movement has shown the patriarchal prejudice in most of what we used to consider 'organisational rationality'. Bourgeois 'organisational theory' seldom even mentions the state, though in fact the state (with all of its coercive power) is the ever-present validating agent for the MNCs and other formal organisations. Similarly, bourgeois 'organisational theory' gives short shrift to voluntary and ephemeral associations, so central to social anarchist thought (Ehrlich, 1979, pp. 108-10). In short, bourgeois theorists reflect bourgeois ideological assumptions.

I am not asserting that social anarchistic thinking must necessarily be embraced by all geographers studying the MNC. Rather, I am asserting that social anarchism *or any other point of view not sanctioned* by *bourgeois mythology* provides perspective, a different window on the world. Theory-building of lasting value requires such perspective.

Final Comments: The Effect of Ideology on Writing Styles

Reclus probably wrote more geographic prose than anyone else before or since. As a social anarchist, he studiously avoided anything supportive of authoritarian hierarchies. Therefore, he avoided authoritarian or Cartesian prose, the kind of writing widely (though dubiously) known as 'scientific' nowadays. Though he was, in fact, more of an 'authority' than most of his contemporaries and many of those posing pompously as 'geographic authorities' today, he cared nothing for such posing. He wrote in 'the tone of a pleasant conversation' (Dunbar, 1981, p. 162). He was sensitive to the support for an authoritarian and hierarchical social order that would be provided by geographic descriptions that were themselves authoritarian in nature. He tried, instead, to assume an egalitarian posture.

I consider myself to be a social anarchist of sorts, and Reclus a most worthy model for all geographers today. Therefore, please overlook any lapses in this essay into authoritarian (i.e. 'scientific') prose. Only the inexperienced think Reclus's 'tone of a pleasant conversation' is easy to emulate in our authoritarian, hierarchical world. It is so much easier to be a pompous bore (editors are less threatened by bores than by rebels).

REFERENCES

Abumere, S.I. (1982) 'Multinationals and Industrialisation in a Developing Economy: The Case of Nigeria', in M.J. Taylor and N.J. Thrift (eds), *The Geography of Multinationals* (Croom Helm, London), pp. 158-77.

Adrian, C. and Evans, C. (1984) 'Borg-Warner (Albury Wodonga): A Lead Firm in a Regional Economy?', in M.J. Taylor (ed.), *The Geography of Australian Corporate Power* (Croom Helm, Canberra), pp. 159-71.

Aglietta, M. (1976) *A Theory of Capitalist Regulation* (New Left Books, London).

Agmon, T. and Lessard, D.R. (1977) 'Financial Factors and the International Expansion of Small-country Firms' in T. Agmon and C.K.P. Kindleberger (eds), *Multinationals from Small Countries* (MIT Press, Cambridge, Mass.), pp. 197-219.

Aldrich, H.E. (1979) *Organisations and Environment* (Prentice-Hall, Englewood Cliffs, N.J.).

Alexander, I. (1982) 'Office Suburbanisation: a New Era', in R.V. Cardew, J.V. Langdale and D.C. Rich (eds), *Why Cities Change* (George Allen & Unwin, Sydney), pp. 55-75.

Alford, B.W. (1973) *W.D. & H.O. Wills and the Development of the United Kingdom Tobacco Industry, 1786-1965* (Methuen, Andover, Hants).

Alford, B.W. (1976) 'Strategy and Structure in the U.K. Tobacco Industry', in L. Hannah (ed.), *Management Strategy and Business Development* (Macmillan, London), pp. 123-45.

Ambrose, P. and Colenutt, R. (1975) *The Property Machine* (Penguin Books, Harmondsworth, Middlesex).

Amin, A. (1985) 'Restructuring and Spatial Decentralisation in Fiat', in R. Hudson and J. Lewis (eds), *Dependent Development in Southern Europe* (Methuen, London).

Andreff, W. (1984) 'The International Centralisation of Capital and the Re-ordering of World Capitalism', *Capital and Class*, 22, pp. 59-80.

Angly, P. (1983) 'Keating Springs to Defence of FIRB', *National Times*, 2 September, pp. 41-2.

Anwar, A. (1980) 'Trade Strategies and Industrial Development in Indonesia', in R. Garnaut (ed.), *ASEAN in the Changing Pacific and World Economy* (Australian National University Press, Canberra), pp. 207-31.

ASEAN Forecast (AF), December 1982.

Asia Corporate Profile (1983) *Asia 1983 Measures and Magnitudes* (Asian Finance Publications Ltd, Hong Kong).

Asia Research Bulletin (ARB), 13 August 1983.

—— (1983) 'Residence Permits Offered to Major Investors', 13(4), p. 1090.

Asian Business (1983) 'Irresponsible Asian Investment', April, pp. 49-50.

Asiaweek (1982) 'The Crack of Dawn', 7 May, p. 21.

—— (1983a) '1997: How Businessmen Feel', 29 July, pp. 48-9.

—— (1983b) 'An Office Glut in Kuala Lumpur', 23 September, pp. 45-8.

Australian Property News (1983) 'Lewis in Canberra — Joint Venture Office Project', September, p. 72.

Awanohara, S. (1982) 'Off the Beaten Track', *Far Eastern Economic Review*, 177(38), 17 September, pp. 84-7.

—— (1983) 'Shaking the Industrial Cocktail', *Far Eastern Economic Review*,

121(33), 18 August, pp. 39-58.

BKPM (Badan Koordinasi Penamanan Modal) *Laporan Perkembangan Penanaman Modal,* Jakarta (various editions).

—— (1981) *Priority List for Foreign Investment of the Year 1981* (Jakarta).

BPS (Biro Pusat Statistik) *Sensus Industri 1974/75* (various publications).

Baldwin, J. (1978) *Just Above My Head* (Dell, New York).

Bank of Indonesia (1982) *Report for the Financial Year 1980/1981* (Jakarta).

Barak, R. (1981) *Foreign Investment in US Real Estate* (Law and Business Inc., New York).

Barnard, M. (1958) *Sappho, A New Translation* (University of California Press, Berkeley).

Barnet, R.J. and Muller, R.E. (1974) *Global Reach, the Power of the Multinational Corporations* (Simon & Shuster, New York).

Barthes, R. (1972) *Mythologies* (Jonathan Cape, London; first published in French, 1957).

Bartholomew, J. and Rowley, A. (1980) 'The Hongs Close Ranks', *Far Eastern Economic Review,* 7 November, pp. 115-18.

Bassett, K. (1984) 'Corporate Structure and Corporate Change in a Local Economy: The Case of Bristol', *Environment and Planning A,* 16, pp. 879-900.

Beenstock, M. (1983) *The World Economy in Transition* (George Allen & Unwin, London).

Bellam, M. (1980) *A Question of Balance: New Zealand Trade in the South Pacific* (New Zealand Coalition for Trade and Development, Wellington).

Benello, C.G. (1979) 'Anarchism and Marxism: a Confrontation of Traditions', in H.J. Ehrlich, C. Ehrlich, D. DeLeon and G. Morris (eds), *Reinventing Anarchy* (Routledge & Kegan Paul, London), pp. 156-71.

Bennett, R.B., Merchan, J.E. and Metcalfe, J.S. (1981) *Motives for Australian Direct Foreign Investment* (Bureau of Industry Economics, Working Paper 23, Canberra).

Benson, J.K. (1975) 'The Interorganisational Network as a Political Economy', *Administrative Science Quarterly,* 20, pp. 229-49.

Berger, J. (1972) *Ways of Seeing* (Penguin Books and BBC, New York).

Berry, B.J.L. and Garrison, W.L. (1958) 'A Note on Central Place Theory and the Range of a Good', *Economic Geography,* 34, pp. 304-11.

Beynon, H. (1975) *Working for Ford* (EP Publishing, Wakefield).

Blackbourn, A. (1982) 'The Impact of Multinational Corporations on the Spatial Organisation of Developed Nations', in M.J. Taylor and N.J. Thrift (eds), *The Geography of Multinationals* (Croom Helm, London), pp. 147-57.

Bloomfield, G.T. (1981) 'The Changing Spatial Organization of Multinational Corporations in the World Automotive Industry', in F.E.I. Hamilton and G.J.R. Linge (eds), *Spatial Analysis, Industry and the Industrial Environment, Vol. 2. Industrial Systems* (John Wiley, New York), pp. 357-94.

Bluestone, B. (1984) 'Coping with Labour and Community: Capitalist Strategies in the 1980s', *UNIDO CRP 34* (UNIDO, Vienna).

—— and Harrison, B. (1984) 'The Economic State of the Union in 1984. Uneven Recovery, Uncertain Future', paper delivered at a meeting of Progressive Economists, January.

Bookchin, M. (1980) *Toward an Ecological Society* (Black Rose Books, Montreal).

Bora, G. (1981) 'International Division of Labor and the National Industrial System: The Case of Hungary', in Hamilton and Linge (eds), *op. cit.,* pp. 155-83.

Borner, S., Burgever, B., Stuckey, B. and Wehrle, F. (1984) 'The Changing

International Division of Labour and the Internationalisation of Swiss Industry', *UNIDO CRP 3* (UNIDO, Vienna).

Bradbury, J.H. (1982) 'State Corporations and Resource-Based Development in Quebec, Canada: 1960-1980', *Economic Geography*, 58, pp. 45-61.

Breitbart, M.M. (1981) 'Peter Kropotkin, the Anarchist Geographer', in D.R. Stoddart (ed.), *Geography, Ideology and Social Concern* (Barnes & Noble, Totowa, N.J.), pp. 134-53.

Brewer, A. (1980) *Marxist Theories of Imperialism. A Critical Survey* (Routledge & Kegan Paul, London).

Brooke, M.Z. and Remmers, H.L. (1978) *The Strategy of Multinational Enterprise* (Pitman, London).

Browning, H.C. and Singelmann, J. (1978) 'The Transformation of the US Labour Force: the Interaction of Industry and Occupation', *Politics and Society*, 8, pp. 481-509.

Buckley, P. (1983) 'New Theories of International Business: Some Unresolved Issues', in M. Casson (ed.), *The Growth of International Business* (George Allen & Unwin, London), pp. 34-50.

Budiono Sri Handoko (1984) 'Rural–Urban Relations in a Non-growing Growth Centre: the Cilacap Case Study', Workshop on Urbanization and the Household Economy (Universiti Sains Malaysia, Penang).

Bureau of Industry Economics (1983) 'Characteristics of Major Industries Supplying Tourist Services in Australia', *Bureau of Industry Economics Information Bulletin 5* (Australian Government Publishing Service, Canberra).

—— (1983a) *Australian Direct Investment in New Zealand,* Information Bulletin 3 (Australian Government Publishing Service, Canberra).

—— (1983b) *Australian Direct Investment in the ASEAN Countries,* Information Bulletin 4 (Australian Government Publishing Service, Canberra).

—— (1984) *Australian Direct Investment Abroad: Effects on the Australian Economy*, Research Report 14 (Australian Government Publishing Service, Canberra).

Business Day (1980, 1981, 1983) *Business Day 1000 Top Corporations in the Philippines* (Business Day Corporation, Quezon City).

Cameron, N. (1979) *The Hongkong Land Company Ltd. A Brief History* (Hongkong Land Company, Hong Kong).

Canberra Times, 10 November 1982, p. 1.

Carnoy, M. and Castells, M. (1984) 'After the Crisis?', *World Policy Journal*, May.

Casson, M. (ed.) (1983) *The Growth of International Business* (George Allen & Unwin, London).

Castells, M. (1984) 'Technological Change, Economic Restructuring and the Spatial Division of Labor', *UNIDO CRP 35* (UNIDO, Vienna).

Caves, R.E. (1982) *Multinational Enterprise and Economic Analysis* (Cambridge University Press, Cambridge).

Chapman C. (1983) 'Realty Blues', *Asian Business*, 11 June.

Chapman, K. (1974). 'Corporate Systems in the United Kingdom Petro-Chemical Industry', *Annals of the Association of American Geographers*, 64, pp. 126-37.

Chase-Dunn, C. (1984) 'Urbanisation in the World-System: New Directions for Research', in M.P. Smith (ed.), *Cities in Transformation. Class, Capital and the State* (Sage, Beverly Hills), pp. 111-20.

Chen, E.K.Y. (1981) 'Hong Kong Multinationals in Asia: Trends, Patterns and Objections', in K. Kumar and M. McLeod (eds), *Multinationals from Developing Countries* (Lexington Books, D.C. Heath), pp. 79-99.

Citizen (1983) 'Breweries Moves into Ciskei', 14 August.

Clairmonte, F. and Kavanagh, J. (1983) 'Transnational Corporations and the Struggle for the Global Market', *Journal of Contemporary Asia*, 13, pp.

446-80.

Clarke, I.M. (1982) 'The Changing International Division of Labour within ICI', in M.J. Taylor and N.J. Thrift (eds), *The Geography of Multinationals* (Croom Helm, London), pp. 90-116.

—— (1984b) 'Global Chemical Corporations: their Form and Impact in Australia', in M.J. Taylor (ed.), *The Geography of Australian Corporate Power* (Croom Helm, Canberra), pp. 125-55.

—— (1984) 'The Spatial Organisation of Corporations: a case study of the multinational chemicals industry with specific reference to ICI', unpublished PhD thesis, The Australian National University.

Clark, G.L. and Massey, D. (1984) 'A Research Agenda on Multinational Enterprises and the Spatial Division of Labour', in B.T. Robson and J. Rees (eds), *Geographical Agenda for a Changing World* (Social Science Research Council, London), pp. 78-85.

Coakley, J. (1984) 'The Internationalisation of Bank Capital', *Capital and Class*, 23, pp. 107-20.

Coase, R.H. (1937) 'The Nature of the Firm', *Economica*, n.s. 4, pp. 386-405.

Cohen, R.B. (1981) 'The New International Division of Labour, Multinational Corporations and the Urban Hierarchy', in M.J. Dear and A.J. Scott (eds), *Urbanisation and Urban Planning in Capitalist Society* (Methuen, London), pp. 287-315.

Colonial Development Corporation (CDC) Annual Reports and Accounts, 1948-1962.

Commonwealth Development Corporation (CDC) (1963-80) Annual Reports and Accounts, 1963-1980.

—— (CDC) (1981) *Investment Facilities* (CDC, London).

Connell, R.W. (1983) 'Class Formation on a World Scale', in *Which Way Is Up? Essays on Class, Sex and Culture* (George Allen & Unwin, Sydney) pp. 162-86.

Coriot, B. (1980) 'The Restructuring of the Assembly Line: a New Economy of Time and Control', *Capital and Class*, 11, pp. 234-43.

Coward, R. (1983) *Patriarchal Precedents* (Routledge & Kegan Paul, London).

Cowling, K. (1982) *Monopoly Capitalism* (Macmillan, London).

Cutler, M. (1975) 'How Foreign Owners Shape our Cities', *Canadian Geographical Journal*, 90, June, pp. 39-48.

Cypher, J.M. (1979) 'The Internationalization of Capital and the Transformation of Social Formations: A Critique of the Monthly Review School', *Review of Radical Political Economics*, 11(4), pp. 33-49.

Daly, M.T. (1982a) *Sydney Boom. Sydney Bust* (Allen & Unwin, Sydney).

—— (1982b) 'Finance, the Capital Market and Sydney's Development', in R. Cardew, J.V. Langdale and D.C. Rich (eds), *Why Cities Change* (George Allen & Unwin, Sydney), pp. 43-53.

—— (1984) 'The Revolution in International Capital Markets: Urban Growth and Australian Cities', *Environment and Planning A*, 16, pp. 1003-20.

Dangilan, V. (n.d.) 'Prospects of the Banana Industry in the Philippines', unpublished typescript prepared for Development Bank of the Philippines.

Darwin, B. (1945) *Robinsons of Bristol, 1844-1944* (E.S. & A. Robinson Ltd, Bristol).

David, D.S. (1981) *Transnational Corporations and the Philippine Banana Export Industry*, Report to UN CTC/ESCAP Unit on TNCs (Bangkok).

—— and Brannon, R. (1976) *The Forty-Nine Percent Majority: The Male Sex Role* (Addison-Wesley Publishing Company, Reading).

—— and Tsuda, M. (1978) 'The Politics of Major Japanese-Filipino Joint Ventures: A Sociological View', *The Philippines in the Third World Papers*, No. 8.

Davidson, W.H. and Haspeslagh, P. (1982) 'Shaping a Global Product

Organisation', *Harvard Business Review*, 60, pp. 125-32.

Davies, D. (1981) 'The Keswicks are Coming ...' *Far Eastern Economic Review*, 18 August, pp. 84-7.

—— Lee, M. and Rowley, A. (1983) 'Exit a Man of Property', *Far Eastern Economic Review*, 18 August, pp. 84-7.

DeLeon, D. (1979) 'Anarchism on the Origins and Functions of the State: Some Basic Notes', in H.J. Ehrlich, C. Ehrlich, D. DeLeon and G. Morris (eds), *Reinventing Anarchy* (Routledge & Kegan Paul, London), pp. 70-83.

de Vroey, M. (1984) 'A Regulation Approach Interpretation of the Contemporary Crisis', *Capital and Class*, 23, pp. 45-66.

Delta Corporation Annual Report (*Delta A.R.*) (1978, 1983).

Department of Trade and Industry, *Census of Production* (relevant tables in alternate years) (HMSO, London).

Dicken, P. and Lloyd, P.E. (1976) 'Geographical Perspectives on United States Investment in the United Kingdom', *Environment and Planning*, 8, pp. 685-705.

—— (1979) 'The Corporate Dimension of Employment Change in the Inner City', in C. Jones (ed.), *Urban Deprivation and the Inner City* (Croom Helm, London), pp. 32-62.

—— (1980) 'Patterns and Processes of Change in the Spatial Distribution of Foreign-controlled Manufacturing Employment in the United Kingdom, 1963-75', *Environment and Planning A*, 12, pp. 1405-26.

Doherty, J.F. (1979) *A Preliminary Study of Interlocking Directorates Among Financial, Commercial, Manufacturing and Service Enterprises in the Philippines* (Manila).

Dolgoff, S. (1980) *Bakunin on Anarchism* (Black Rose Books, Montreal).

Donges, J.B., Stecher, B. and Wolter, F. (1974) *Industrial Development Policies for Indonesia* (J.C.B. Mohr, Tubingen), pp. 357-405.

—— (1980) 'Industrialization in Indonesia', in G. Papanek (ed.), *The Indonesian Economy* (Praeger, New York), pp. 357-405.

Draper, N. and Smith, H. (1960) *Applied Regression Analysis* (John Wiley, New York).

Dun and Bradstreet (1977-81) *Who Owns Whom: United Kingdom and Republic of Ireland*, Vols 1 & 2 (Dun and Bradstreet, London).

Dunbar, G.S. (1981) 'Elisee Reclus, an Anarchist in Geography', in D.R. Stoddart (ed.), *Geography, Ideology and Social Concern* (Barnes & Noble, Totowa, New Jersey), pp. 154-64.

Dunning, J.H. (1979) 'Explaining Changing Patterns of International Production: In Defence of the Eclectic Theory', *Oxford Bulletin of Economics and Statistics*, 41, 269-65.

—— (1981) *International Production and the Multinational Enterprise* (George Allen & Unwin, London).

—— (1983) 'Changes in the Level and Structure of International Production: The Last One Hundred Years', in M. Casson (ed.), *The Growth of International Business* (George Allen & Unwin, London), pp. 84-139.

—— and McQueen, M. (1982a) *Transnational Corporations in International Tourism* (Center on Transnational Corporations United Nations, New York).

—— and McQueen, M. (1982b) 'The Eclectic Theory of the Multinational Enterprise and the International Hotel Industry', in A.M. Rugman (ed.) *New Theories of the Multinational Enterprise* (Croom Helm, London), pp. 79-106.

—— and Norman, G. (1983) 'The Theory of the Multinational Enterprise: An Application to Office Location', *Environment and Planning A*, 15, pp. 675-92.

Economic Development Board (1982) *A Guide to Investment in Fiji* (Economic Development Board, Suva).

Economist Intelligence Unit (1983) *Hong Kong: Economic Prospects to 1987*, Special Report No. 156 (Economist Intelligence Unit, London).

Ehrlich, H.J. (1979) 'Anarchism and Formal Organizations — Some Notes on the Sociological Study of Organizations from an Anarchist Perspective', in Ehrlich, Ehrlich, DeLeon and Morris (eds), *op. cit.*, pp. 96-112.

Evans, P. (1979) *Dependent Development. The Alliance of Multinational, State and Local Capital in Brazil* (Princeton University Press, Princeton, N.J.).

Evans, P.B. (1981) 'Recent Research on Multinational Corporations', in R.H. Turner and S.F. Short (eds), *Annual Review of Sociology*, Vol. 7 (Sage, Beverly Hills), pp. 199-223.

Feagin, J.R. (1982) 'Urban Real Estate Speculation in the United States: Implications for Social Science and Urban Planning', *International Journal of Urban and Regional Research*, 6, pp. 35-60.

Feder, E. (1982) 'The World Bank and Underdeveloped Agriculture', *Journal of Contemporary Asia*, 12, pp. 34-60.

Fennema, M. (1982) *International Networks of Banks and Industry* (Martinus Nijhoff, The Hague).

Ferguson, R. (1977) 'Linear Regression in Geography', *Concepts and Techniques in Modern Geography (CATMOG), No. 15* (Geo. Abstracts, Norwich).

Fernandez, R.A. (1979) 'Imperialist Capitalism in the Third World: Theory and Evidence from Colombia', *Latin American Perspectives*, 6(1), pp. 38-64.

Fiji, Central Planning Office (1975) *Fiji's Seventh Development Plan 1976-1980* (Central Planning Office, Suva).

—— (1980) *Fiji's Eighth Development Plan 1981-1985* (Central Planning Office, Suva).

Financial Times', 'Nordic Producers Scent Blood', 26 May 1981.

—— 'Pulp Paper and Board', 16 March 1982a.

—— 'The Long Battle to Survive', 29 October 1982b.

Fleming, D. and Krumme, G. (1968) 'The Royal Hoesch Union: Case Analysis of Adjustment Patterns in the European Steel Industry', *Tijdschrift voor Economische en Sociale Geografie*, 59, pp. 177-99.

Forbes, D.K. (1982) 'Energy Imperialism and a New International Division of Resources: the Case of Indonesia', *Tijdschrift voor Economische en Sociale Geografie*, 73(2), pp. 94-108.

—— (1984a) *The Geography of Underdevelopment: A Critical Study* (Croom Helm, London).

—— (1984b) 'Corporate Relocation: Australian Companies in Indonesia', in M.J. Taylor (ed.), *The Geography of Australian Corporate Power* (Croom Helm Australia, Sydney), pp. 47-65.

—— (1984c) 'Industrialisation and Urbanisation in Indonesia', Workshop on Urbanisation and the Household Economy, University Sains Malaysia, Penang.

—— and Rimmer, P.J. (1983) 'Vers une Réinterprétation de L'Integration de l'Asia du Sud-est dans L'Économie Mondiale', *L'Espace Geographique*, 12(3), pp. 161-72.

—— Kissling, C.C., Taylor, M.J. and Thrift N.J. (1985) *Economic and Social Atlas of the Pacific Basin* (Allen & Unwin, Sydney).

Foreign Investment Review Board (1977-82) *Foreign Investment Review Board Report* (Australian Government Publishing Service, Canberra).

Fothergill, S. and Gudgin, G. (1982) *Unequal Growth: Urban and Regional Employment Change in the UK* (Heinemann, London).

Franko, L.G. (1976) *The European Multinationals* (Harper & Row, London).

—— (1983) *The Threat of Japanese Multinationals: How the West Can Respond* (Wiley, Chichester).

Fraser, I. (1981) 'Room on the West Coast', *Far Eastern Economic Review*, 20

March, pp. 62-3.

Friedman, H. and Meredeen, S. (1980) *The Dynamics of Industrial Conflict: Lessons from Ford* (Croom Helm, London).

Friedman, J. and Wolff, G. (1982) 'World City Formation: an Agenda for Research and Action', *International Journal of Urban and Regional Research,* 6, pp. 309-44.

Fröbel, F. (1982) 'The Current Development of the World Economy: Reproduction of Labour and Accumulation of Capital on a World Scale', *Review,* 5, pp. 507-55.

—— Heinrichs, J. and Kreye, O. (1980) *The New International Division of Labour* (Cambridge University Press, Cambridge).

Gaffikin, F. and Nickson, P. (1983) *Jobs, Crisis and the Multinationals. Deindustrialisation in the West Midlands* (Russell Press, Birmingham).

Gallie, D. (1978) *In Search of the New Working Class: Automation and Social Integration within the Capitalist Enterprise,* Studies in Sociology, 9 (Cambridge University Press, Cambridge).

Gershuny, J. and Miles, I. (1983) *The New Service Economy* (Frances Pinter, London).

Gibson, K.D. and Horvath, R.J. (1983a) 'Aspects of a Theory of Transition within the Capitalist Mode of Production', *Environment and Planning D. Society and Space,* 1, pp. 121-38.

—— (1983b) 'Global Capital and the Restructuring Crisis in Australian Manufacturing', *Economic Geography,* 59, pp. 178-94.

Giddy, I.H. and Young, S. (1982) 'Conventional Theory and Unconventional Multinationals: Do New Forms of Multinational Enterprise Require New Theories?', in A.M. Rugman (ed.), *New Theories of the Multinational Enterprise* (Croom Helm, London), pp. 55-78.

Goldman, E. (1970) *Living My Life,* Vol. II (Dover, New York; originally published by Alfred Knopf, New York, 1931).

Goodman, P. (1962) *The Community of Scholars* (Vintage Books, New York).

Gottman, J. (1983) *The Coming of the Transactional City* (University of Maryland Institute for Urban Studies, College Park, MD).

Government of Canada (n.d.) *Foreign Investment Review Act, Businessman's Guide* (Government of Canada, Ottawa).

Greenberg, M.A. (1983) *Bibliography on Mobility of Capital Among Pacific Basin Countries,* Working Paper 5, Institute of Asian Research, University of British Columbia.

Greenfield, H.C. (1966) *Manpower and the Growth of Producer Services* (Columbia University Press, New York).

Grosse, R.E. (1982) 'Regional Offices in Multinational Firms', in A.M. Rugman (ed.), *New Theories of the Multinational Enterprise* (Croom Helm, London), pp. 107-32.

Grou, P. (1983) *La Structure Financière du Capitalisme Multinational* (Presses de la Fondation Nationale des Sciences Politiques, Paris).

Guerin, D. (1970) *Anarchism* (Monthly Review Press, New York).

Habir, M. and Rowley, R. (1983) 'The Extended (Corporate) Family of Liem Sioe Liong', *Far Eastern Economic Review,* 120(14), 7 April, pp. 51-6.

Håkanson, L. (1979) 'Towards a Theory of Location and Corporate Growth', in F.E.I. Hamilton and G.J.R. Linge (eds), *Spatial Analysis, Industry and the Industrial Environment. Vol 1. Industrial Systems* (John Wiley, Chichester).

Hamilton, F.E.I. (1974) 'Self-Management: The Yugoslav Case', in F.E.I. Hamilton (ed.), *Spatial Perspectives on Industrial Organization and Decision-making* (John Wiley, London), pp. 449-59.

—— (1976) 'Multinational Enterprise and the European Economic Community',

Tijdschrift voor Economische en Sociale Geografie, 67, pp. 258-78.
—— and Linge, G.J.R. (eds) (1981) *Spatial Analysis, Industry and the Industrial Environment: Vol. 2. International Industrial Systems* (John Wiley, Chichester).
Harvey, C. (1981) 'Foreign Investment in Manufacturing: The Case of Botswana's Brewery', in C. Harvey (ed.), *Papers on the Economy of Botswana* (Heinemann, London), pp. 209-19.
Harvey, D. (1982) *The Limits to Capital* (Basil Blackwell, Oxford).
Haselhurst, D. (1982) 'Multinationals Move in our Top Hotels', *The Bulletin*, 30 March, pp. 98-100.
Hawes, G. (1981) 'The State, TNCs and Agricultural Development in the Philippines', *The Philippines in the Third World Papers*, No. 24.
Hayden, E.W. (1980) *Internationalising Japan's Financial System* (Stanford University Press, Stanford).
Hayter, R. (1976) 'Corporate Strategies and Industrial Change in the Canadian Forest Product Industries', *Geographical Review*, 66, pp. 209-28.
—— (1978) 'Locational Decision-making in a Resource-based Manufacturing Sector: Case Studies from the Pulp and Paper Industry of British Columbia', *Professional Geographer*, 33, pp. 240-9.
—— (1981) 'Patterns of Entry and the Role of Foriegn-controlled Investments in the Forest Produce Sector of British Columbia', *Tijdschrift voor Economische en Sociale Geografie*, 72, pp. 99-113.
—— and Watts, H.D. (1983) 'The Geography of Enterprise: a Re-appraisal', *Progress in Human Geography*, 7, pp. 154-81.
Heal, D. (1974) 'Ownership, Control and Location Decisions: The Case of the British Steel Industry Since 1945', in Hamilton (ed.), *Spatial Perspectives on Industrial Organization and Decision-making* (John Wiley, London), pp. 265-84.
Heenan, D.A. (1977) 'Global Cities of Tomorrow', *Harvard Business Review*, 55, May-June, pp. 79-92.
—— and Keegan, W.J. (1979) 'The Rise of Third World Multinationals', *Harvard Business Review*, 57(1), pp. 101-9.
Hennessy, M.N. (1950) 'Fifty Thousand Chickens in the Gambia', *Crown Colonist*, 20, pp. 291-3.
Hewison, K.J. (1981) 'The Financial Bourgeoisie in Thailand', *Journal of Contemporary Asia*, pp. 395-412.
Hickson, D.J., Hinings, C.R., Lee, C.A., Schneck, R.E. and Pennings, J.M. (1971) 'A Strategic Contingencies Theory of Intra-organisational Power', *Administrative Science Quarterly*, 16, pp. 216-29.
Hiemenz, U. (1982) 'Industrial Growth and Employment in Developing Asian Countries: Issues and Perspectives for the Coming Decade', *Economic Staff Paper No. 7* (Asia Development Bank, Manila).
Hinings, C.R., Hickson, D.J., Pennings, J.M. and Schneck, R.E. (1974) 'Structural Conditions of Intra-organizational Power', *Administrative Science Quarterly*, 19, pp. 22-44.
Hiroo Fukui (1980) 'Gaikoku Kawase Oyobi Gaikoku Boeki Kanriho No Kaisei in Tsuite', *Finance*, 15 November.
Ho Kwun Ping (1979) 'Birth of the Second Generation', *Far Eastern Economic Review*, 104(20), 18 May, pp. 76-80.
Hobson, R. (1981) 'A Luxury Staging Post', *Far Eastern Economic Review*, 20 March, p. 61.
Holland, S. (1975) *The Socialist Challenge* (Quartet Books, London).
Hood, N. and Young, S. (1982) *Multinationals in Retreat, The Scottish Experience* (Edinburgh University Press, Edinburgh).

—— (1984) *Multinational Investment Strategies in the British Isles* (HMSO, London).

Horn, B. and Hetherington, D. (1982) 'Overseas Manufacturing Establishments in Scotland: Output, Investment and Employment', *Scottish Economic Bulletin*, No. 24.

Horne, J.L. (1980) *The Internationalization of Japanese Finance: A Preliminary Assessment*, Research Paper No. 69, Australia–Japan Research Centre, Australian National University.

Hout, T., Porter, M.G. and Rudden, E. (1982) 'How Global Companies Win Out', *Harvard Business Review*, 60(5), pp. 98-108.

Howie, I. (1977) *The Effects of Foreign Investment in Fiji*, Centre for South Pacific Studies, University of California, Santa Cruz, 6pp.

Imperial Goup (1979) *The Story of the Imperial Group*, Imperial Group Information Brochure, Group Public Affairs Department (Imperial Group Ltd, London).

Indonesia Development News (IDN) (1981) December.

—— *(IDN)* (1982) August.

—— *(IDN)* (1983a) March.

—— *(IDN)* (1983b) June.

—— *(IIF)* (1979a) October.

—— *(IIF)* (1979b) December.

—— *(IIF)* (1980) March.

Innes, D. (1983) *Anglo American and the Rise of Modern South Africa* (Heinemann, London).

Islands Business (1984) 'Why Motibhai is Winning', April, p. 40.

International Labour Organisation (1984) *World Labour Report 1. Employment, Incomes, Social Protection, New Information Technology* (International Labour Office, Geneva).

Japan Banana Importers Association (1980) *Monthly Bulletin of Banana Statistics*, No. 160, December.

Japan, Ministry of Finance (1979) 'Kinyu Mondai Kenkyukai' (Financial Research Group), *Kokusaika No Shinten Ni Tomonau Wagakuni Kinyukikan No Arikata*.

Jenkins, D. and Awanohara, S. (1979) 'Batam Tries to Go Places', *Far Eastern Economic Review*, 104(16), 20 April, pp. 45-50.

Jolliffe, J. (1983) 'Macao Profits from Doubts in Hong Kong', *Canberra Times*, 30 October, 1983, p. 14.

Jones Lang Wootton (1982) *A Comprehensive Real Estate Service* (Jones Lang Wootton, London).

—— (1980-83a) *South East Asian Property Review* (Jones Lang Wootton, Singapore).

—— (1980-83b) *International Property Review* (Jones Lang Wootton, London).

Kaname Seki (1981) 'Atarashii Kawase Kanri no Arikata', *Finance*, 16 November.

Kaplan, D.E. (1983) 'The Internationalisation of South African Capital: South African Direct Foreign Investment in the Contemporary Period', *African Affairs*, 82, pp. 465-94.

Kawahara, I. (1982) 'Present Status and Prospects of Export Processing Zones in Asia', *Exim Review*, 2(2), pp. 5-20.

Keeble, D. (1976) *Industrial Location and Planning in the United Kingdom* (Methuen, London).

Keeble, D.E. (1980) 'Industrial Decline, Regional Policy and the Urban–Rural Manufacturing Shift in the United Kingdom', *Environment and Planning A*, 12(8), pp. 945-62.

King, A.D. (1985) 'Capital City: Physical and Social Aspects of London's Role in the World Economy', *Development and Change*.

Kirby S. (1983) *Towards the Pacific Century. Economic Development in the Pacific Basin*, Economist Intelligence Unit Special Report 137 (The Economist Intelligence Unit, London).

—— and Cox, A. (1983) *The Politics of Modern Capitalism* (Harvester, Brighton).

Knight, K. (1976) 'Matrix Organisation — A Review' *Journal of Management Studies*, 13, pp. 111-30.

Kornegger, P. (1979) 'Anarchism: The Feminist Connection', in H.J. Ehrlich, C. Ehrlich, D. DeLeon and G. Morris (eds), *Reinventing Anarchy* (Routledge & Kegan Paul, London), pp. 237-49.

Kortus, B. and Kaczorowski, W. (1981) 'Polish Industry Forges External Links', in F.E.I. Hamilton and G.J.R. Linge (eds), *Spatial Analysis, Industry and the Industrial Environment, Vol. 2. International Industrial Systems* (John Wiley, New York), pp. 119-53.

Krinks, P. (1981) 'Corporations in the Philippine Banana Export Industry: A Preliminary Account', *The Philippines in the Third World Papers*, No. 28.

Krumme, G. (1981) 'Making it Abroad: The Evolution of Volkswagen's North American Production Plans', in Hamilton and Linge (eds), *op. cit.* pp. 329-56.

—— (1983) 'Review of *The Geography of Multinationals*', *The Professional Geographer*, 35, pp. 519-20.

Kumar, K. and McLeod, M.G. (1981) *Multinationals from Developing Countries* (Lexington Books, Lexington, Mass.).

Labour Research (1982) 'Company File: Packaging Companies', *Labour Research*, May, p. 227.

Lall, S. (1983) 'The Rise of Multinationals from the Third World', *Third World Quarterly*, 5, pp. 618-26.

Lamarche, F. (1976) 'Property Development and the Economic Foundations of the Urban Question', in C.G. Pickvance (ed.), *Urban Sociology* (Tavistock, London), pp. 85-118.

Langdale, J.V. (1983) 'Telecommunications in Sydney: Towards an Information Economy', in R. Cardew, J.V. Langdale and D.C. Rich (eds), *Why Cities Change* (George Allen & Unwin, Sydney), pp. 77-94.

Lecraw, D. (1977) 'Direct Investment by Firms from Less Developed Countries', *Oxford Economic Papers*, (n.s.), 29, pp. 442-57.

Lee, S.Y. and Jao, Y.C. (1982) *Financial Structures and Monetary Policies in Southeast Asia* (Macmillan, London).

Lefeber, L. and Datt Chaudhuri, M. (1971) *Regional Development Experiences and Prospects in South and Southeast Asia* (Mouton, The Hague).

Leighton, M. (1979) 'Anarcho-feminism', in Ehrlich, Ehrlich, DeLeon and Morris (eds), *op. cit.*, pp. 253-8.

Lethbridge, D. (ed.) (1980) *The Business Environment in Hong Kong* (Oxford University Press, Hong Kong).

Levine, J. (1972) 'The Sphere of Influence', *American Sociological Review*, 37, pp. 14-27.

Lewis, S.G. (1979) *Sunday's Women* (Beacon Press, Boston).

Lichauco, A. (1973) 'The Lichauco Paper. Imperialism in the Philippines', *Monthly Review*, 25(3), whole issue.

Linge, G.J.R. (1984) 'Developing-country Multinationals: A Review of the Literature', *Pacific Viewpoint*, 25(2), pp. 173-95.

—— and Hamilton, F.E.I. (1981) 'International Industrial Systems', in Hamilton and Linge (eds), *op. cit.*, pp. 1-118.

Litvak, I.A. and Maule, C.J. (1977) 'Transnational Corporations and Vertical Integration: The Banana Case', *Journal of World Trade Law*, 11, pp. 537-49.

Livesey, C. (1973-74) *New Zealand Investment in Fiji*, Vols. 1 and 2 (CORSO,

Wellington).

Lloyd, P.E. and Mason, C.M. (1979) 'Industrial Movement in North West England, 1966-75', *Environment and Planning A*, 11, pp. 1367-85.

—— and Reeve, D.E. (1982) 'North-West England 1971-1977: a Study in Industrial Decline and Economic Restructuring', *Regional Studies*, 16, pp. 345-59.

Makil, P.Q., Reyes, L.A. and Koike, K. (1983) 'Philippine Business Leaders', *Joint Research Program Series No. 37* (Institute of Developing Economies, Tokyo).

Mandel, E. (1975) *Late Capitalism* (New Left Books, London).

Manning, C. (1978) 'Pockets of Privilege Amidst Mass Poverty: Wages and Working Conditions in Indonesian Industry', in *The Life of the Poor in Indonesian Cities*, public lectures on Indonesia, Centre of Southeast Asian Studies, Monash University, Melbourne.

—— (1980) 'Segmentasi Pasar Tenaga Kerja di Sektor Industri di Java: Beberapa Implikasi Dari Studi Kasus Industry Tenun dan Rokok', *Prisma*, 9(11), pp. 85-93.

Marshall, J.N. (1982) 'Organisational Theory and Industrial Location', *Environment and Planning A*, 14, pp. 1667-83.

Martin, R. (1982) 'Job Loss and the Regional Incidence of Redundancies in the Current Recession', *Cambridge Journal of Economics*, 6, pp. 375-96.

Massey, D. and Catalano, A. (1978) *Capital and Land* (Edward Arnold, London).

—— and Meegan, R. (1979) 'The Geography of Industrial Reorganisation: The Spatial Effects of the Restructuring of the Electrical Engineering Sector under the Industrial Reorganisation Corporation', *Progress in Planning*, 10(3), pp. 155-237.

—— (1982) *The Anatomy of Job Loss* (Methuen, London).

McCawley, P. (1979) 'Industrialization in Indonesia: Developments and Prospects', *Occasional Paper No. 13*, Development Studies Centre (Australian National University, Canberra).

—— (1981) 'The Growth of the Industrial Sector', in A. Booth and P. McCawley (eds), *The Indonesian Economy During the Soeharto Era* (Oxford University Press, Kuala Lumpur), pp. 62-101.

McDermott, P.J. (1976) 'Ownership, Organisation and Regional Dependence in the Scottish Electronics Industry', *Regional Studies*, 10, pp. 319-35.

—— (1978) 'Overseas Investment and the Industrial Geography of the United Kingdom', *Area*, 9, pp. 200-7.

—— and Keeble, D. (1978) 'Manufacturing Organisation and Regional Employment Change', *Regional Studies*, 12, pp. 247-66.

—— and Taylor, M.J. (1982) *Industrial Organisation and Location* (Cambridge University Press, Cambridge).

McFarlane, B. (1982) *Radical Economics* (Croom Helm, London).

McNee, R.B. (1958) 'Functional Geography of the Firm, with an Illustrative Case Study from the Petroleum Industry', *Economic Geography*, 34, pp. 322-37.

—— (1960) 'Towards a More Humanistic Economic Geography: the Geography of Enterprise', *Tijdschrift voor Economische en Sociale Geografie*, 51, pp. 201-6.

—— (1963) 'The Spatial Evolution of the Sun Oil C *Association of American Geographers*, 53, p. 609.

—— (1966) 'New York', in J.H. Thompson (ed.), *Geography of New York State* (Syracuse University Press, Syracuse, New York), pp. 423-57.

—— (1981) 'Perspective — Use It or Lose It', *Professional Geographer*, 33, pp. 12-15.

McPhee, L. (1983) 'Becoming Dinki-di Now a Big Test for 20 Hopefuls', *Business Review Weekly*, 22-28 October, pp. 32-7.

Meyer, J.W. and Scott, W.R. (1983) *Organizational Environments, Ritual and*

Rationality (Sage, Beverly Hills).

Michalet, C.A. (ed.) (1981) *Internationalisation des Banques et des Groupes Financières* (CNRS, Paris).

Mollenkopf, J., Noyelle, T.J. and Cohen, R. (1984) *The Growth of Investment Banking, Corporate Legal Services and Management Consulting in New York City*, Report to the New York City Office of Economic Development, New York.

Moran, T.H. (1978) 'Multinational Corporations and Dependency', *International Organization*, 32(1), pp. 79-100.

Morgan, D.J. (1980a) *The Official History of Colonial Development: Vol. 2. Developing British Colonial Resources 1945-1951* (Macmillan, London).

—— (1980b) *The Official History of Colonial Development: Vol. 4. Changes in British Aid Policy 1951-1970* (Macmillan, London).

Morgan, K. and Sayer, A. (1983) 'The International Electronics Industry and Regional Development in Britain', University of Sussex, Urban and Regional Studies Working Paper 14.

Moulaert, F. and Salinas, P.W. (eds) (1983) *Regional Analysis and the New International Division of Labour* (Kluwer-Nijhoff, The Hague).

Murray, R. (ed.) (1980) *Multinationals Beyond the Market* (Harvester Press, Brighton).

NEDO (1981) 'Energy and the Paper and Board Industry', Report to the Paper and Board Sector Working Party, by the Energy Sub-committee, National Economic Development Office, London.

National Urban Development Strategy Project (1983) *Outline Urban Strategy*, Directorate of City and Regional Planning (Department of Public Works, Jakarta).

Nelson, D. (1983) 'A Sense of Déjà-vu', *Far Eastern Economic Review*, 18 August, p. 84.

Newbould, G.D., Buckley, P.J. and Thurwell, J. (1978) *Going International. The Success of Smaller Companies Overseas* (Associated Business Press, London).

Newfarmer, R.S. and Topik, S. (1982) 'Testing Dependency Theory: a Case Study of Brazil's Electrical Industry', in M.J. Taylor and N.J. Thrift (eds), *The Geography of Multinationals* (Croom Helm, London), pp. 33-60.

Nichols, T. and Beynon, H. (1977) *Living with Capitalism: Class Relations and the Modern Factory*, (Routledge & Kegan Paul, London).

Noyelle, T.J. (1983) 'The Implications of Industry Restructuring for Spatial Organisation in the United States', in F. Moulaert and P. Salinas (eds), *Regional Analysis and the New International Division of Labour* (Kluwer Nijhoff, Boston), pp.113-33.

O'Brien, P. (1980) 'The New Multinationals: Developing-country Firms in International Markets', *Futures*, August, pp. 303-15.

On Tap (1978) 'R4 Million Brewery for Transkei', December, p. 4.

Pacific Islands Monthly (1982) 'A New Look, and on the Go for Profitable 80s' July, pp. 59-61.

Palloix, C. (1975) 'The Internationalisation of Capital and the Circuit of Social Capital', in H. Radice (ed.), *International Firms and Modern Imperialism* (Penguin Books, Harmondsworth), pp. 63-88.

—— (1977) 'The Self-expansion of Capital on a World Scale', *Review of Radical Political Economics*, 9, pp. 3-27.

Panglaykim, J. (1979) *Emerging Enterprises in the Asia-Pacific Region* (Centre for Strategic and International Studies, Jakarta).

Pearce, R.D. (1983) 'Industrial Diversification Amongst the World's Leading Multinational Enterprises', in Casson, M. (ed.), *The Growth of International Business* (George Allen & Unwin, London), pp. 140-79.

Peck, F.W. and Townsend, A.R. (1984) 'Contrasting experience of recession and spatial restructuring in different British corporations: British Shipbuilders, Plessey and Metal Box', *Regional Studies*, 18, pp. 319-38.

Peet, J.R. (1982) 'International Capital, International Culture', in M.J. Taylor and N.J. Thrift (eds), *The Geography of Multinationals* (Croom Helm, London), pp. 275-302.

—— (1983) 'Introduction: The Global Geography of Contemporary Capitalism', *Economic Geography*, 59, pp. 105-11.

Perrons, D.C. (1981) 'The Role of Ireland in the New International Division of Labour: A Proposed Framework for Regional Analysis', *Regional Studies*, 15(2), pp. 81-200.

Pfeffer, J. (1972) 'Size and Composition of Corporate Boards of Directors: The Organisation and its Environment', *Administrative Science Quarterly*, 17, pp. 218-28.

—— (1981) *Power in Organisations* (Pitman, Boston).

—— and Salancik, G. (1978) *The External Control of Organisations: A Resource Dependence Perspective* (Harper & Row, London).

Philippines (1973) 'Presidential Letter of Instruction No. 58', Office of the President, Republic of the Philippines.

Phillips, T.A. and Collinson, M.P. (1976) 'The Organisation and Development of Small-Holder Schemes in the Programmes of the Commonwealth Development Corporation', in G. Hunter, A.H. Bunting and A. Bottrall (eds), *Policy and Practices in Rural Development* (Croom Helm, London), pp. 340-54.

Plasschaert, S.R.F. (1979) *Transfer Pricing and Multinational Corporations: An Overview of Concepts, Mechanisms and Regulations* (Saxon House, Farnborough).

Pounce, R. (1981) *Industrial Movement in the United Kingdom, 1966-75* (HMSO, London).

Pred, A.R. (1977) *City-Systems in Advanced Economies* (Hutchinson, London).

Pugh, D.S., Hickson, D.J., Hinings, C.R. and Turner, C. (1968) 'Dimensions of Organization Structure', *Administrative Science Quarterly*, 13, pp. 63-105.

Radice, H. (1984) 'The National Economy: A Keynesian Myth?', *Capital and Class*, 22, pp. 111-40.

Rand Daily Mail (1973a) 'Southern Sun on a Listing Course', January, p. 31.

Rand Daily Mail (1973b) 'Hotel Group to Get Cash Ahead of Schedule', 19 January.

Rand Daily Mail (1981a) 'Beer Boom Boosts SA Breweries by 60%, 5 November.

Rand Daily Mail (1981b) 'Boom in New Holiday Resorts', 28 October.

Rand Daily Mail (1982) 'SAB to Build Yet Another Brewery', 24 June.

Read, R. (1982) 'Corporate Foreign Direct Investment Strategies and Trade Liberalisation in Japanese Market for Bananas 1960-76', *Discussion Report in International Investment and Business Studies*, No. 60, University of Reading.

Rees, J. (1972) 'The Industrial Corporation and Location Decision Analysis', *Area*, 4, pp. 199-205.

—— (1978) 'On the Spatial Spread and Oligopolistic Behaviour of Large Rubber Companies', *Geoforum*, 9, pp. 319-30.

Regional Studies Association (1983), *Report of an Inquiry into Regional Problems in the United Kingdom* (Geo Books, Norwich).

Rendell, W. (1976) *The History of the Commonwealth Development Corporation* (Heinemann, London).

Resnick, S. (1973) 'The Second Path of Capitalism: A Model of International Development', *Journal of Contemporary Asia*, 3(2), pp. 133-48.

Rhodesia Herald (1932) 'Breweries Buy Hotels', 18 May.

Rhodesia Herald (1950) 'New Brewery for Bulawayo', 19 January.

Rhodesia Herald (1978) 'Delta — Top Company', 19 October.
Rhodesian Breweries Annual Reports (R.B. A.R.) (1960, 1962, 1967).
Rhodesian Breweries First Annual General Meeting (*R.B. A.G.M.*) (1948).
Rhodesian Breweries Minutes (*R.B. Minutes*) (1902, 1910, 1934).
Rhodesian Breweries Press Release (*R.B. Press Release*) (1969).
Rice, R. (1983) 'Industrial Location Study', Draft Report for World Bank, Jakarta.
Richard Ellis (1982) *Two Centuries of Service* (Richard Ellis, London).
—— (1980-83a) *International Property* (Richard Ellis, London).
—— (1980-83b) *South East Asia: The Property Market* (Richard Ellis, Singapore).
Richardson, R. (1979) 'Opening an Off-Shore Drive', *Far Eastern Economic Review*, 106(49), 7 December, pp. 93-4.
Robbins, S. and Stobaugh, R. (1973) *Money in the Multinational Enterprise* (Basic Books, New York).
Rogerson, C.M. (1981a) 'Industrialization in the Shadows of Apartheid: A World Systems Analysis', in F.E.I. Hamilton and G.J.R. Linge (eds), *Spatial Analysis, Industry and the Industrial Environment Vol. 1. International Industrial Systems* (John Wiley, Chichester), pp. 395-421.
—— (1981b) 'Spatial Perspectives on United Kingdom Investment in South Africa', *South African Geographical Journal*, 63, pp. 85-106.
—— (1982a) 'Multinational Corporations in Southern Africa: A Spatial Perspective', in M.J. Taylor and N.J. Thrift (eds), *The Geography of Multinationals* (Croom Helm, London), pp. 179-200.
—— (1982b) 'Patterns of Indigenous and Foreign Control of South African Manufacturing', *South African Geographer*, 10, pp. 123-34.
Ross, R. and Trachte, K. (1983) 'Global Cities and Global Classes: the Peripheralisation of Labour in New York City', *Review*, 6, pp. 393-431.
Rowley, A. (1981) 'Ready for a Second Take-off', *Far Eastern Economic Review*, 20 March, pp. 57-61.
—— (1982) 'Hongkong Land Sinks', *Far Eastern Economic Review*, 13 October, p. 101.
Rugman, A.M. (ed.) (1982a) *New Theories of Multinational Enterprise* (Croom Helm, London).
Rugman, A. (1982b) 'Internationalisation and Non-equity Forms of International Involvement', in A.M. Rugman (ed.) *New Theories of Multinational Enterprise* (Croom Helm, London), pp. 9-23.
Sabre (1975) 'SAB Abroad' p. 9.
Sassen-Koob, S. (1984) 'The New Labor Demand in Global Cities', in M.P. Smith (ed.), *Cities in Transformation. Class, Capital and the State* (Sage, Beverly Hills), pp. 139-71.
Savey, S. (1981) 'Pechiney Ugine Kuhlmann: A French Multinational Corporation', in Hamilton and Linge (eds), *Vol. 2. op. cit.*, pp. 305-27.
Sayer, R.A. (1980) 'Some Methodological Problems in Industrial Location Studies', paper presented to the Conference of the Industrial Activity and Area Development Study Group of the Institute of British Geographers, London School of Economics, May.
—— (1984) *Method in Social Science. A Realist Approach* (Hutchinson, London).
Shearlock, P. (1984) 'Bermuda's Not Short for Disaster', *Sunday Times*, 1 April, p. 32.
'Shrof' (1980) 'A Question of Management', *Far Eastern Economic Review*, 12 September, p. 73.
—— (1983) 'Now for the Real Simon Pure', *Far Eastern Economic Review*, 13 October, p. 93.
Simbulan, D.S. (1966) 'A Study of the Philippine Socio-Economic Elite, 1946-1963', unpublished PhD thesis, Australian National University.

Sims, D. and Wood, M. (1984) 'Car Manufacturing at Linwood: The Regional Policy Issues', *Clyde Valley Industrial Policy Archive* (Department of Politics and Sociology, Paisley College, Paisley).

Singelmann, J. (1979) *From Agriculture to Services* (Sage, Beverly Hills).

Smith, I.J. (1982) 'The Role of Acquisition in the Spatial Distribution of the Foreign Manufacturing Sector in the United Kingdom', in Taylor and Thrift (eds), *op. cit.*, pp. 221-51.

—— and Taylor, M.J. (1983) 'Takeover, Closure and the Restructuring of the United Kingdom Ironfoundry Industry', *Environment and Planning A*, 15, pp. 639-61.

Soehoed, A.R. (1982) 'Industrial Development During Repelita III', *Indonesian Quarterly*, 10(4).

Soja, E., Morales, R. and Wolff, G. (1983) 'Urban Restructuring: An Analysis of Social and Spatial Change in Los Angeles', *Economic Geography*, 59, pp. 195-230.

South African Breweries Minutes (*S.A.B. Minutes*) (1902, 1910, 1934).

South African Breweries Annual Report (*S.A.B. A.R.*) (1969, 1973, 1983).

South African Wine and Beer (1982) 'Pure Fruit Juices are Privileged', October.

Southern Sun Hotel Corporation, Annual Report (*S.S. A.R.*) (1976).

Spiers, N. (1983) 'Chinatown: Making its Mark on the Map', *The Bulletin*, 16 August, pp. 58-60.

Sricharatchanya, P. (1983) 'Tariff Take-off at Last', *Far Eastern Economic Review*, 122(44), 3 November, pp. 76-7.

Staab, M.J. (1980) 'The Production Location Problem and the Development of Industries on a Regional Basis in the ASEAN Countries', *The Developing Economies*, 18(1), pp. 65-96.

Stanback, T.M. and Noyelle, T.J. (1982) *Cities in Transition* (Allanheld and Osmun, Totowa, N.J.).

Star (1972) 'Beer: SA Brews Now Aims at Angola', 17 August.

Star (1982a) 'Sun Goes Down Under in New Casino Venture', 13 October.

Star (1982b) 'Apartheid Costs Sol Casino Win', 19 November.

Star (1982c) 'Southern Sun Plans R50 million Investment Abroad', 16 November.

Star (1983a) 'Southern Sun Scraps US Deal, but Still Talking', 16 May.

Star (1983b) 'SAB to Put Millions into Juice Venture', 12 May.

Steed, G.P.F. (1981) 'International Location and Comparative Advantage: The Clothing Industries and Developing Countries', in Hamilton and Linge (eds), *Vol. 2. op. cit.*, pp. 265-303.

Stewart, J. (1981) 'Land of Opportunity', *Far Eastern Economic Review*, 20 March, pp. 64-7.

Stopford, J.M. and Wells, L.T. (1972) *Managing the Multinational Enterprise* (Basic Books, New York).

Storey, D.J. (ed.) (1983) *The Small Firm: An International Survey* (Croom Helm, London).

Streeten, P. (1979) 'Multinationals Revisited', *Finance and Development*, 16(2), pp. 39-42.

Sunday Times (1971) 'Southern Sun Ties up Big Mozambique Deal', 11 July.

Sunday Times (1982a) 'Lesotho's New R10 Million Brewery', 3 October.

Sunday Times (1982b) 'SA Tourism Investments are Safe — Islands New Premier', 12 September.

Tamba, J.L. (1976) 'Kebijaksanaan Industrialisasi Dalam Rangka Pembangunan Daerah di Indonesia', *Ekonomi dan Keuangan Indonesia*, 24(1), pp. 63-70.

Tanada, L.M. (1965) *Nationalism: A Summons to Greatness* (Phoenix Publishing House, Quezon City).

Taylor, M.J. (1975) 'Organisational Growth, Spatial Interaction, and Location

Decision-Making', *Regional Studies*, 9, pp. 313-23.
—— (1983) *Business Organisation Segmentation and the Functioning of the Fiji Economy*, Report to the Fiji Employment and Development Mission, Suva.
—— (ed.) (1984a) *The Geography of Australian Corporate Power* (Croom Helm, Sydney).
—— (1984b) 'The Changing Pattern of Australian Corporate Investment in the Pacific Islands', in M.J. Taylor (ed.), *The Geography of Australian Corporate Power* (Croom Helm, Sydney), pp. 25-45.
—— (1984c) 'Business Organisations and Transfer of Value: Examples from Fiji', in D.K. Forbes and P.J. Rimmer (eds), *Uneven Development and the Geographical Transfer of Value*, Human Geography Monograph 16 (Research School of Pacific Studies, The Australian National University, Canberra), pp. 175-97.
—— and Thrift, N.J. (1979) 'Guest Editorial', *Environment and Planning A*, 11, pp. 973-5.
—— (1980) 'Large Corporations and Concentrations of Capital in Australia: a Geographical Analysis', *Economic Geography*, 56, pp. 261-80.
—— (1981a) 'Some Geographical Implications of Foreign Investment in the Semi-periphery: The Case of Australia', *Tijdschrift voor Economische en Sociale Geografie*, 72, pp. 194-213.
—— (1981b) 'British Capital Overseas: Direct Investment and Firm Development in Australia', *Regional Studies*, 15, pp. 183-212.
—— (1981c) 'Spatial Variations in Australian Enterprise: The Case of Large Firms Headquartered in Melbourne and Sydney', *Environment and Planning A*, 13, pp. 137-46.
—— (eds) (1982a) *The Geography of Multinationals* (Croom Helm, London).
—— (1982b) 'Models of Corporate Development and the Multinational Corporation', in Taylor and Thrift (eds), *op. cit.*, pp. 14-32.
—— (1982c) 'Industrial Linkage in the Segmented Economy: 1. Some Theoretical Proposals', *Environment and Planning A*, 16, pp. 1601-13.
—— (1982d) 'Industrial Linkage and the Segmented Economy: 2. An Empirical Reinterpretation', *Environment and Planning A*, 14, pp. 1615-32.
—— (1983a) 'Industrial Geography in the 1980s: Towards a Decade of Differences', *Environment and Planning A*, 15, pp. 1289-91.
—— (1983b) 'Business Organisation, Segmentation and Location', *Regional Studies*, 17(6), pp. 445-65.
—— (1983c) 'Organisational Structure and the Segmented Economy: The Case of the UK Electronics Industry', unpublished.
Teulings, A.W.M. (1984) 'The Internationalisation Squeeze: Double Capital Movement and Job Transfer within Philips-Worldwide', *Environment and Planning A*, 16, 597-614.
The Crown Colonist (1947) 'New Partnership for Empire Production', December, pp. 627-28.
The Economist (1983a) 'Out of the Wok, into the Fire', 286 (7280), 12 March, p. 72.
The Economist (1983b) 'Asia's Insecurity Market', 287 (7291), 28 May, p. 93.
The Economist (1983c) 'London Offices. Cheap at Twice the Space', 289 (7309), 1 October, pp. 83-4.
The Economist (1983d) 'Misery Inc.', 289 (7310), 8 October, p. 90.
The Economist (1983e) 'Here Come the Multinationals of the Third World', 23 July, pp. 61-2.
The Economist (1984) 'Jardine's puts 8000 Miles Between Itself and Hong Kong', 290 (7335), 31 March, pp. 65-6.
The Times (1983) *The Times 1000, 1982/83* (Times Books, London).

Thee Kian Wie (1981) 'Indonesia as a Host Country to Indian Joint Ventures', in K. Kumar and M. McLeod (eds), *Multinationals from Developing Countries* (D.C. Heath, Lexington, Mass.), pp. 133-44.

Thompson, G. (1982) 'The Firm as a Dispersed Social Agency', *Economy and Society*, pp. 233-56.

Thompson, J.D. (1967) *Organisations in Action* (McGraw-Hill, New York).

Thrift, N.J. (1983) 'World Cities, World Property Market', unpublished seminar paper, Department of Human Geography, Australian National University.

—— (1985a) 'All Change. The Geography of International Economic Disorder', in R.J. Johnston and P.J. Taylor (eds), *World in Crisis* (Blackwell, Oxford).

—— (1985b) 'Taking the Rest of the World Seriously? The State of British Urban and Regional Research in a Time of Economic Crisis', *Environment and Planning A*, 17, pp. 7-24.

Times Books (1983) *Times 1000, 1981-82* (Times Books, London).

Tolson, A. (1977) *The Limits of Masculinity, Male Identity and Women's Liberation* (Harper & Row, New York).

Townsend, A.R. (1981) 'Geographical Perspectives on Major Job Losses in the UK 1977-80', *Area*, 13, pp. 31-8.

—— (1982a) 'Recession and the Regions in Great Britain, 1976-1980: Analyses of Redundancy Data', *Environment and Planning A*, 14, pp. 1389-404.

—— (1982b) *The Impact of Recession: On Industry, Employment and the Regions, 1976-1981* (Croom Helm, London).

—— and Peck, F.W. (1984) 'Spatial Deployment through Plant Closures and Redundancy by Foreign Companies in the United Kingdom, 1976-81', paper presented to the symposium on Regional Development Processes/Policies and the Changing International Division of Labour, UNIDO Building, Vienna, August.

—— (1985) 'The Geography of Redundancy in Named Corporations', in M. Pacione (ed.), *Progress in Industrial Geography* (Croom Helm, London), pp. 174-218.

Tsuda, M. (1978) *A Preliminary Study of Japanese-Filipino Joint Ventures* (Foundation for Nationalist Studies, Quezon City).

Tucker, B.A. (1985) 'Locational Behaviour and Structural Change in an Oligopolistic Environment: The South African Brewing Industry', *South African Geographical Journal.*

Uckey, B. (1983) 'A Tube of Goo Sealed Local Boy's Success', *Business Review Weekly*, 22-28 October, pp. 101-2.

UNCTAD (1974) *The Marketing and Distribution System for Bananas*, TD/B/C.1/162, Geneva.

UNIDO (United Nations Industrial Development Organisation) (1980) *Export Processing Zones in Developing Countries*, UNIDO Working Papers on Structural Change, No. 19.

United Nations (1983) *Transnational Corporations in World Development. Third Survey* (United Nations Center on Transnational Corporations, New York).

Urry, J. (1984) 'Disorganised Capitalism', unpublished manuscript.

Utrecht, E. (1984) 'Fiji: A Client State', in E. Utrecht (ed.), *Fiji: Client State of Australasia* (Transnational Corporations Research Project, University of Sydney), pp. 1-66.

Van Der Bulcke. P., Boddewyn, J.J., Martens, B. and Klenmer, P. (1979) *Investment and Divestment Policies of Multinational Corporations in Europe* (Saxon House, Farnborough).

Vernon, R. (1979) 'The Product-Cycle Hypothesis in a New International Environment', *Oxford Bulletin of Economics and Statistics*, 41, 255-68.

Vetterling-Braggin, M. (ed.) (1982) '*Femininity', 'Masculinity', and 'Androgyny',*

A Modern Philosophical Discussion (Littlefield, Adams, Totowa, New Jersey).

Wallerstein, I. (1978) *The Capitalist World Economy* (Cambridge University Press, London).

Walter, N. (1979) 'About Anarchism', in Ehrlich, Ehrlich, DeLeon and Morris (eds), *op. cit.*, pp. 42-63.

Warr, P.G. (1983) 'The Jakarta Export Processing Zone', *Bulletin of Indonesian Economic Studies*, 19(3), pp. 41-62.

Watts, H.D. (1979) 'Large Firms, Multinationals and Regional Development: Some New Evidence from the United Kingdom', *Environment and Planning A*, 11, pp. 71-81.

—— (1980a) 'The Location of European Investment in the United Kingdom', *Tidjschrift voor Economische en Sociale Geografie*, 71, pp. 3-14.

—— (1980b) *The Large Industrial Enterprise: Some Spatial Perspectives* (Croom Helm, London).

—— (1981) *The Branch Plant Economy: A Study of External Control* (Longman, Harlow, Essex).

—— (1982) 'The Inter-regional Distribution of West German Multinationals in the United Kingdom', in Taylor and Thrift (eds), *op. cit.*, pp. 61-89.

Way, N. (1983) 'Keswick Whips Jardine and Land into Shape', *Australian Financial Review*, 1 September, pp. 10-11.

Wellings, P.A. and Crush, J.S. (1983) 'Tourism and Dependency in Southern Africa: the Prospect and Planning of Tourism in Lesotho', *Applied Geography*, 3, pp. 205-23.

Wells, L.T. (1977) 'The Internationalisation of Firms from Developing Countries', in T. Agmon and C.P. Kindleberger (eds), *Multinationals from Small Countries* (MIT Press, Cambridge, Mass.), pp. 133-57.

—— (1981) 'Foreign Investors from the Third World', in K. Kumar and M.G. McLeod (eds), *Multinationals from Developing Countries* (D.C. Heath, Lexington, Mass.), pp. 23-36.

—— (1982) 'Technology and Third World Multinationals', Multinational Enterprises Programme, Working Paper No. 19 (International Labour Office, Geneva).

—— (1983) *Third World Multinationals* (MIT Press, Cambridge, Mass.).

—— and Warren, V. (1979) 'Developing Country Investors in Indonesia' *Bulletin of Indonesian Economic Studies* 15(1), pp. 69-84.

Welsh Office (1981) *Welsh Economic Trends No. 7* (HMSO, Cardiff).

Wen Lee Ting and Chi Schive (1981) 'Direct Investment and Technology Transfer from Taiwan', in Kumar and McLeod (eds), *op. cit.*, pp. 101-14.

Whittlesey, D. (1954) 'The Regional Concept and the Regional Method', in P.E. Jones and C.F. Jones (eds), *American Geography. Inventory and Prospect* (Syracuse University Press, Syracuse, New York), pp. 19-68.

Who Owns Whom (1982) *Who Owns Whom — Australasia and the Far East 1981* (London).

Wicker, E.R. (1955-56) 'The Colonial Development Corporation (1948-54)', *Review of Economic Studies*, 23, pp. 213-28.

Williamson, O.E. (1975) *Markets and Hierarchies: Analysis and Antitrust Implications* (Free Press, New York).

—— (1981) 'The Modern Corporation: Origins, Evolution, Attributes', *Journal of Economic Literature*, 19, pp. 1537-68.

Wong, S.T. and Saigol, K.M. (1984) 'Comparison of the Economic Impacts of Six Growth Centres on Their Surrounding Rural Areas in Asia', *Environment and Planning A*, 16(1), 81-94.

Wood, C. (1983) 'Days of Dynasty Again', *Far Eastern Economic Review*, 19 April, p. 76.

World Bank (1981) 'Indonesia. Selected Issues of Industrial Development and Trade Strategy', East Asia and Pacific Regional Office, unpublished.

—— (1983) *World Development Report 1983* (Oxford University Press, New York).

Wurfel, D. (1979) 'Elites of Wealth and Elites of Power, The Changing Dynamic. A Philippine Case Study', *Southeast Asian Affairs 1979* (Institute of Southeast Asian Studies, Singapore).

Yannopoulos, G.N. (1983) 'The Growth of Transnational Banking', in Casson, M. (ed.), *The Growth of International Business* (George Allen & Unwin, London), pp. 236-57.

Youngson, A.J. (1982) *Hong Kong: Economic Growth and Policy* (Oxford University Press, Oxford).

Zagaris B. (1980) *Foreign Investment in the US* (Praeger, New York).

Zeitlin, M. and Ratcliff, R.E. (1975) 'Research Methods for the Analysis of the Internal Structure of Dominant Classes: The Case of Landlords and Capitalists in Chile', *Latin American Research Review*, 10(3), 5-61.

Zimmerman, E. (1933) *World Resources and Industries* (Harper, New York).

AUTHOR INDEX

Abumere S.I. 50
Adrian C. 24
Aglietta M. 312
Agmon T. 108
Aldrich H.E. 12
Alexander I. 173
Alford B.W. 332
Ambrose P. 179, 191
Amin A. 24
Andreff W. 3, 5, 15
Anwar A. 113, 131
Awanohara S. 133, 136, 139

Baldwin J. 354
Barnard M. 351
Barnet R.J. 346
Barthes R. 353, 354, 357, 358
Bartholomew J. 185
Bassett K. 24, 315
Beenstock M. 312
Bellam M. 57, 76
Benello C.G. 356
Bennett R.B. 63
Benson J.K. 13, 60
Berger J. 354
Berry B.J.L. 347
Beynon H. 24
Blackbourn A. 50
Bloomfield G.T. 348, 349
Bluestone B. 20
Bookchin M. 356
Bora G. 349
Borner S. 3
Bradbury J.H. 349
Breitbart M.M. 355, 357
Britton S.G. 70
Brooke M.Z. 282
Browning H.C. 144
Buckley P. 8
Budiono Sri Handoko 136

Cameron N. 180, 182, 183
Carney M. 20
Castells M. 20
Caves R.E. 7, 51, 106
Chapman C. 172
Chapman K. 348
Chen E.K.Y. 131

Clairmonte F. 277
Clark G.L. 16
Clarke I.M. 22, 23, 27, 46, 56, 348,
  349, 350
Coakley J. 19
Coase R.H. 13
Cohen R.B. 42
Connell R.W. 15
Coriot B. 24
Cutler M. 160
Cypher J.M. 257

Daly M. 110, 173, 174, 187, 190,
  191
David D.S. 356
David R.S. 277
Davidson W.H. 1
Davies D. 357
De Leon D. 283, 286
Dicken P. 23, 283, 286
Dolgoff S. 357
Donges J.B. 126, 127, 134
Draper N. 31
Dunbar G.S. 355, 357, 358
Dunning J.H. 5, 8, 10, 11, 144, 184

Ehrlich H.J. 358
Evans P.B. 106, 257

Feagin J.R. 145, 191
Feder E. 159, 277
Fennema M. 5, 15
Ferguson R. 31
Fernandez R.A. 257, 258
Fleming D. 348
Forbes D.K. 105, 107, 111, 115, 116,
  127
Fothergill S. 23
Franko L.G. 18, 60
Fraser I. 160
Friedman H. 142
Friedman J. 24
Fröbel 21, 47, 105, 312, 340

Gaffikin F. 19, 340
Gallie D. 24
Gershuny J. 144
Gibson K.D. 52

379

Giddy I.H. 107
Goldman E. 355
Goodman P. 356
Gottman J. 357
Greenfield H.C. 144
Grosse R.E. 51
Grou P. 5, 15
Guerin D. 355

Habir M. 106
Håkanson L. 50, 56
Hamilton F.E.I. 50, 110, 228, 349
Harvey C. 98
Harvey D. 15, 353
Haselhurst D. 177
Hawes G. 274
Hayden E.W. 194
Hayter R. 349, 350
Heal D. 348
Heenan D.A. 108, 142
Hennessey M.N. 238
Hickson D.J. 13, 25
Hiemenz U. 133
Hinings C.R. 25
Hiroo Fukui 224
Hobson R. 160, 162, 163
Holland S. 282
Hood M. 19, 201, 283, 308
Horn B. 295
Horne J.L. 194
Howie I. 76, 77
Hymer S. 6

Innes D. 86

Jenkins D. 138, 139
Jolliffe J. 162

Kaname Seki 224
Kaplan D.E. 87, 101, 102
Keeble D.E. 23, 282, 309
Kirby S. 3
Knight K. 61
Kornegger P. 355
Kortus B. 348, 349
Krinks P. 267
Krumme G. 86, 349, 352

Lall S. 86, 90, 107, 109, 110
Lamarche F. 191
Langdale J.V. 173
Lecraw D. 108
Leferbre L. 136
Leighton M. 355

Lethbridge D. 151
Levine J. 13
Lewis S.G. 355
Linge G.J.R. 107, 108, 109, 110
Livesey C. 69, 76
Lloyd P.E. 23, 297

McCawley P. 113, 114, 126, 127, 128, 131
McDermott P.J. 14, 22, 23, 26, 49, 51, 283, 348, 358
McNee R.B. 344, 346, 347, 348, 349, 350, 351, 352
McPhee L. 179
Makil P.Q. 274
Mandel E. 312
Manning C. 131
Marshall J.N. 26
Martin R. 304
Massey D. 21, 23, 26, 191, 202, 311
Meyer J.W. 353
Michalet C.A. 19
Moran T.H. 256, 257
Morgan D.J. 229, 236, 239, 240, 242, 244, 247, 248
Morgan K. 15
Moulaert F. 110
Murray R. 52, 61

Nelson D. 187
Newbould G.D. 1
Newfarmer R.S. 46, 256, 257, 348
Nichols T. 24
Noyelle T.J. 142, 146

O'Brien P. 108, 110

Palloix C. 105, 140
Peck F.W. 285, 296, 301, 311
Peet J.R. 15, 351, 353, 354, 356
Perrons D.C. 105
Pfeffer J. 12, 14, 60
Phillips T.A. 244, 249
Plasschaert S.R.F. 52, 61, 74
Pounce R. 282
Pugh D.S. 25

Radice H. 20
Read R. 260
Rees J. 50
Rendell 229, 238, 240, 241, 242, 244, 245, 247, 248
Resnick S. 258
Rice R. 127

Richardson R. 131
Robbins S. 74
Rogerson C.M. 57, 86
Rowley A. 171, 172
Rugman A.M. 7, 51

Savey S. 86, 348, 349
Sayer R.A. 11, 297
Shearlock P. 158
'Shroff' 185, 186, 190
Sims D. 288, 307, 308
Singelmann J. 144
Smith I.J. 70, 283
Spiers N. 165, 172, 178
Sricharatchnya P. 126
Staab M.J. 124
Steed G.F.P. 348, 351
Stewart J. 160
Stopford J.M. 60
Storey D.J. 76
Streeten P. 108

Tamba J.L. 127
Tanada L.M. 262
Taylor M.J. 1, 5, 18, 21, 26, 49, 50,
    51, 56, 57, 61, 63, 66, 67, 71, 72,
    74, 83, 86, 106, 110, 142, 228,
    235, 319, 349, 350
Teulings A.W.M. 23
Thee Kian Wie 110, 116, 119, 120
Thompson G. 50, 52
Thompson J.D. 12
Thrift N.J. 1, 20, 110, 142
Tolson A. 356

Townsend A.R. 21, 24, 284, 286,
    296, 304, 306
Tsuda M. 275, 276
Tucker B.A. 89
Tuckey B. 157

Utrecht, E. 56

Van den Bulke P. 19
Vernon R. 6

Wallerstein I. 105
Walter N. 357
Warr P.G. 140
Watts H.D. 21, 50, 283, 301, 307,
    348
Way N. 173, 190
Wellings P.A. 100
Wells L.T. 86, 90, 107, 108, 110,
    116, 119, 120, 131
Wen Lee Ting 131
Whittlesey D. 346
Wicker E.R. 235, 236. 238, 240
Williamson O.E. 7, 12, 13
Wood C. 186
Wurfel D. 277

Yannopoulos G.N. 19
Youngson A.J. 151

Zagaris B. 162, 163
Zeitlin M. 258, 273
Zimmerman E. 345

SUBJECT INDEX

Aceh 134, 136, 138
administrative ratio 31, 34, 36
agents and importers 79
agribusiness 275
Ambon 133
anarchism 355-8, 359
Angola 89, 95, 98
anti-government rebels 267
apartheid economy 103
Argentina 90, 109
ASEAN, industrial cooperation 124-6
Asian multinationals
  concentration in Jakarta 127-8
  investment in Indonesia 111-40
  regional distribution in Indonesia 126-33
  size 119, 120
  spatial strategies 120
assisted areas 288, 303, 306, 309
Auckland 162
Australia 27, 36, 46, 47, 54, 66, 68, 69, 72, 73, 85, 101, 102, 111, 116, 147, 151, 159, 163, 177, 183, 184, 206, 236, 286
Australian financial System 173
autonomy 13

Bahamas 238
balance of payments 74
Bali 133, 134
banana industry, role of the state 277
Bangkok 184
Bangladesh 250
banking 5, 19, 193-227
Batam Island 128, 133, 137, 138, 141
Bayview Harbour 173
Bechuanaland 90, 238
Bedfordshire 299, 301
Belgian Congo 90
Bermuda 93
Biak 133
Bisho 101
boards of directors 63
bonded warehouses 134, 136
Bophuthatswana 99
Botswana 97, 98, 100, 101
boundary spanning structures 12, 62

Bradford 304
branch plant economy 307
branch plants 40, 60, 72, 85, 306
Brazil 90, 108, 109, 110, 256, 257, 345
Bretton Woods Agreement 213
Brisbane 170, 172
Bristol 19, 312-43
  corporate structure and change 1978-83 315
  employment structure 1971-81 313-15
  impact of restructuring strategies 341-3
  paper and board and packaging industry 321-38
British Guiana 238
British Honduras 238
Broken Hill 90
Brunei 184
Bulawayo 90
bureaucratic elites 354
bureaucratic impediments 140
bureaucratisation 357
business-cycle 76
business organisation 22, 23, 49, 50, 53

Cabarita 36, 47
Calgary 160
Cameroon 244, 248, 250, 253
Canada 27, 160, 163, 216, 219, 236, 286
capital accumulation 15
capital intensity 31, 43
capital markets 193
capital retreat 87
capital transactions 206
Caribbean 234, 235, 236, 244
causes of industrial growth 312-13
Cebu City 271
Central Africa 230, 234
Central America 204
centralisation 86, 275
centrality 13, 18, 25-6, 61
Ceylon 236
charter 25
chemical export dynamics 38, 43

chemical sector growth 36, 38
Cheshire 299, 301
Chicago 150
Chile 258
China 97, 137, 155, 157, 184
Cilegon industrial zone 136
Ciski 99, 101
Clayton 36, 47
closely held corporations 273
Clydebank 308
Colombia 257, 258
colonialism 257
colonial trading companies 54, 63
Commonwealth Development
    Corporation
    British aid 249
    British aid programmes 235
    capital 230
    changing spatial distribution
        235-55
    control 230
    exclusion on independence 241-2
    growth 232-5
    independence movements 241
    interest rates 247
    organisation 230-1
    origins 229, 230
    regions of investment 233-5
    rural development 249
    sectors of investment 232-3
    sugar developments 247
    1948-1955 235-40
    1956-1963 240-8
    1970-1980 248-55
company closures 69-70
company failure 270, 273
company geography 346, 347
company region 346
comparative advantage 21, 322
comprador bourgeoisie 257
concentration of ownership 275
concentration through accumulation
    353
conservation/dissolution 54
consolidated group profits 66, 67, 68
contraction of foreign-owned
    manufacturing 284-6
contracts 79
Corby 330
core-periphery relationships 283
core regions 283
corporate
    autonomy 309
    competition, banana shipping 269

contraction 282
control 307, 350
co-operation 270
development 325-38
growth 86, 267
headquarters 315
performance 335-7
regions 350-1
response to recession 327-31,
    334-8
strategies 315-19, 330-1, 337-8,
    339-41
structure 311
Costa Rica 10
crisis in accumulation 313
Croxley 331
Cultural Revolution 155, 182
currency markets 193
currency stability 32
Cyprus 235

Dagenham 301
debt-equity ratios 272-3
decision-making 25, 52
Denver 162
dependency theory 256
development studies 52, 53
differentiation 12
disinvestment 68
diversification 87, 329
dual economy model 53

East Africa 230, 234
eclectic theory 8
economic cycles 322
economic development board 75
economic geography 345
Ecuador 250
EEC 137, 144, 286
effectiveness 12
efficiency 46
Ellesmere Port 301
employment change 30, 34
employment decline 286, 321, 327,
    334
energy costs 322
enterprise development 50
enterprise perspective 344
entrepreneurship 75
environmental domain 26, 27, 29, 31,
    36, 45
Essex 303
Ethiopia 248
Eurodollar market 213

Europe 147, 202, 205, 211
exchange rates 213, 322
export incentives 276
export-led growth 63, 73
export processing zones 128, 134,
    136, 137, 138

Falkland Islands 238, 242
family corporations 273
family firms 77
Far East 147, 230, 234, 236, 238
fast food operations 60
Federation of Malaysia 244
Federation of Rhodesia and
    Nyasaland 240
Fiji 49-85, 177
Filipino
    capitalists 276
    overseas investment 277
Fordism 104
foreign control 84
foreign exchange controls 224
foreign investment 38, 43, 49
    from the Third World 126
Foreign Investment Review Board 64,
    165, 166, 170, 177-9, 190
    conditions of approval 177
    examples of intervention 178-9
foreign ownership 55-74
franchising 60
fund-raising 209

Gambia, The 238, 242
garment relabelling 137
geographical transfer of value 74
Ghana 241, 244, 245, 424
Gibraltar 235
Glasgow 330
global corporations 56
globalisation 282
Gold Coast 172
government incentives 79
Greater London 303
Greece 10
greenfield investments 282
growth of South African breweries
    89-91
Guam 184
Guyana 245, 247, 253

Hawaii 183
Hereford 102
hierarchies 8, 10, 29, 317
Hilden 36

historical inertia 47
home market 78
Hong Kong 108, 109, 110, 111, 115,
    116, 117, 120, 124, 131, 136,
    137, 140, 143, 151, 238, 262
    banking, finance and insurance
        152-5
    capital outflow 157, 158, 159
    competition from other centres
        159
    eclipse of real estate market 158-9
    financial centre 151, 152, 157
    office space 155
    real estate market 155-7
    rise of producer services 151-8
    stock market 162
    withdrawal of producer services
        158
    1997 157-8
Hongkong Land Company 179-91
    change of chairman 186, 187
    diversification and
        internationalisation 180, 181
    growth 180-83
    in financial difficulties 186
    investment in hotels 183-4
    investment in offices and
        apartment blocks 183
    investment in retail business 184
    joint ventures 185
    London property market
        losses 185
    overseas investment in real estate
        183-4
    pre-war activities 180
    problems in Australia 187
    profitability 182
    recent history 185-91
    workforce expansion 182
Hong Kong property market fall 185
Honolulu 160, 162, 171, 190
hotel investment 134
hotel purchases in Sydney 174, 177

import-substitution 260
index of wealth and political
    democracy 38
India 29, 109, 116, 131, 136, 137,
    236
Indian entrepreneurs 77
Indonesia 18, 104-41, 245, 247, 248,
    250
    Asian direct investment 115-20
    Asian firm location 131-3

bureaucratic maze 133
foreign manufacturing 119
industry and government
    regulation 133-40
Investment Priorities List 134
manufacturing 113-14
'New Order' 112
openness to foreign investment
    113
industrial decentralisation 86
industrial decline 313
industrial economics 5-11
industrial restructuring 111
industrial zones and estates 134
integration 12
intellectual 'legitimacy' 347
intensification 286
interdependence 257
internalisation 2, 66, 76
internalisation theory 7, 8, 51
internationalisation of
    banking 193-5
    finance 142
    producer services 142, 143,
        144-51
    production 111-12, 140, 141, 142
international market structure 32, 43
international recession 283
inter-organisational relationships 27
inter-penetration of corporate
    investment 285
inter-regional trade 126
intra-organisational
    forces 46
    power 61
    relations 32
    relationships 27
Ivory Coast 250

Jakarta 110, 124, 127, 128, 134, 138,
    139, 141, 162, 163, 184, 244, 247
Japan 18, 111, 115, 116, 151, 260, 286
Japanese banks
    attractions of internationalisation
        208-15
    bank-led internationalisation 200,
        201
    comparison with West German
        banks 219
    competition 225-6
    correspondent bank contracts 201,
        202
    customer-led internationalisation
        200, 201

inadequate international systems
    221
information collection 205
international performance 215-19
international profits 215, 216
issues in internationalisation 194,
    199-201
less internationalised nature
    216-19
limitations of Japan's 'closed
    market' 222
local offices 202, 203, 204
long-term loans 212, 213
motives for internationalisation
    199-201
number of customers 199
overseas bank branches 202
phases of internationalisation
    206-8
pressures for internationalisation
    198, 199
regulations and guidelines 223-5
representative offices 202-4
shortage of information 220, 221
shortage of staff 220
short-term loans 212, 213
summary of internationalisation
    214
use of raised funds 211, 212, 213
world economic conditions 221,
    222
Japanese city banks 194
Japanese exchange rate, liberalisation
    195
Japanese funds 269
Japanese investment in the
    Philippines 266-70
Japanese local banks 205, 206
Japanese market 275, 276
Japanese trade liberalisation 195
Japanese trading companies 266, 269
Java 127, 128, 131
job generation 72
job loss 284, 285, 288, 309, 342,
    343
job mix 24
job stability 24
Johannesburg 97
joint ventures 124, 126, 260, 261,
    262, 264, 276

Kalimantan 127, 131, 134
Kenya 238, 244, 245, 247, 250, 252,
    253

Keswick family 180
Kuala Lumpur 162, 183

labour costs 31, 43, 45
labour dynamics 21-5, 26, 30-45
labour market 72
labour process 104
labour supply 131
landed class 258
length of group membership 34, 36, 38
Lhokseumawe industrial zone 136, 141
Liberia 250
Linwood 307
livelihood enterprises 80
Liverpool 330
loans from multinationals 271, 272
local accumulation 258
local business organisations, dynamics 80-4
local enterprise 74-84
locally owned firms 75, 76
location quotients 306
Lomanis industrial estate 136
London 150, 171, 205, 209, 212, 216, 230, 307, 308, 357
Lorenco Marques 95, 97
Los Angeles 160
Luton 301

Macau 162, 184
Madagascar 95, 97, 100
Main Beach 173
Malawi 250, 253
Malaya 238, 241, 242, 244
Malaysia 111, 116, 120, 160, 245, 247, 250, 253
managerial control 266
managerial structure 352
Manila 184
manufacturing decline 312
Marcos, President 261, 273
martial law 267
Martin Report 173
marxism and corporate environment 352-4
marxist theory 14, 15
mass redundancies 306
maturity structure of funds 209, 210, 211
Mauritius 95, 97, 101
maximising assumptions 50, 51
Melbourne 162, 170, 171, 173, 177

Menado 133
merchant capitalism 258
merchants 258
merger 70, 71
Mexico 108, 109
Middle East 202, 204, 205
Mindanao 260
mismanagement 267
Mmabatho 101
money markets 193
Montana 344
Moscow 357
Mozambique 89, 90, 95, 98, 100
multinational banking 15
multinational control of shipping 275
multinational corporations
    change in number 1
    change in size 1
    competitive context 16
    corporate context 16
    diversification 3
    dynamics 64-72
    fiscal character 5
    foreign production 1, 2
    local context 16
    nationality 3
    structural context 16
    structure 15
    trading patterns 72-4
multiple regression 31
multiplier effects 70, 311

Namibia 95
Ndola 90, 93
Near East 202, 204, 205
Netherlands 115, 116, 286
New Caledonia 176
new international division of labour 21, 47, 104
New Jersey 102
New South Wales 190
New Towns 303
New York 204, 205, 208, 209, 216, 344, 357
New Zealand 54, 57, 67, 69, 72, 73, 85, 111, 151, 176, 236
NICs 107, 140
Nigeria 238, 242, 244, 245, 250, 253
non-bank fringe business 206
North America 202, 204, 205, 211
North Borneo 244
Northern Rhodesia 90, 91, 238, 244
Northern Territory 170
North Korea 221

North Sumatra 127, 134
Nossi Be 97
Nyasaland 238, 240, 244

Oceania 202, 204
office boom 344
office location 142
office property 158-9
office sector employment 173
offshore banking 174
oil companies 113
oil crisis 222, 265
OLI theory 8, 9, 10, 11
open economies 27
organisational rationality 358
organisational structure 77, 78
organisation-environment
    relationships 45
organisation theory 11-14, 354
over-capacity 84
over-capitalisation 84
over-supply 278
over-supply of bananas 270
ownership change 286-91

Pacific Basin 141, 159, 191, 286
'Pacific Cross' 111
Pacific Islands 230, 234, 235
Padang 133
Pakistan 29, 236
Papua New Guinea 68, 176, 250, 253
Paris 357
patronage 81
pension funds 164
peripheralisation 64, 84
peripherality 26
peripheral regions 283, 306
periphery 291, 295
Perth 162, 170, 171
Peru 221, 345
Philippine banana industry 259-81
Philippines 19, 108, 111, 160, 163,
    260-81
    ease of credit 272
    industrialisation policies 258
plantations 68
plant closure 282, 283, 297, 304,
    321, 341, 342
plant-level analysis 23
plant status 32, 34, 36, 40
political hostility 103
political patronage 81, 84, 261, 262,
    273
Port Adelaide 36

positivism 347
power 13, 25, 30
power networks 13, 14
producer services
    definition 143, 144
    employment growth 144
    growth of output 144
    in world trade 144, 145
product-cycle model 6, 256
product cycles 319
production efficiency 24
production technology 36, 38, 43
productivity 31, 38, 40, 46, 285
profitability 342
profit maximisation 51, 74
profits 327, 339
property companies 179
Pulogadung industrial estate 136

Queensland 101, 170, 184

rationalisation 286, 301, 327, 341,
    342
real estate boom 155
real estate producer services,
    internationalisation 145-51
recession 282-310, 311
redundancies 295, 321
regional analysis 22-3
regional branch offices 173
regional concept 346
regional policy and job loss 303-8
relocation 47
restructuring 334
restructuring strategies 339-43
Reunion 97
Rhodesia 87
Riau 138
Rwanda 250

Sabah 247
Sal da Bandeira 95
Salisbury 89
San Francisco 160
Sarawak 244, 247
satellite local firms 78
scale of chemicals production 32, 34,
    43, 45
scale of production 32, 34, 40, 43, 45
Scotland 282, 284
'second tier' cities 146
sectoral change 319-24
'selective closure' 301
semi-periphery 5, 18, 86, 102, 103

services 3, 19
Seychelles 95, 97, 242
shift-share analysis 111, 320
ship repairing 70
Sierra Leone 244, 245
Silicon Valley, California 110
Singapore 27, 29, 108, 109, 111, 113,
    116, 120, 131, 133, 136, 137,
    138, 140, 152, 160, 162, 173,
    183, 184, 190, 238, 244
Singapore Chinese investors 174
Singapore developers 171
Slough 36, 46
small firm closures 266
sorghum beer 92, 93, 99
South Africa 86-104, 236
South African Breweries
    consolidation in Rhodesia 91-5
    expansion into advanced countries
        101-2
    outside the Rhodesias 95-7
    southward retreat 97-101
South America 147, 150, 202
South Australia 170
Southeast Asian investment
    Australia 162
    Australian real estate, growth
        163-70, pattern 170-3
    comparison with Japanese
        investment 165-6
    hotels 177
    North America 160, 161
    real estate 159-63
    second tier cities 162, 163
    Singapore 162
    Sydney 173-7
Southern Rhodesia 89, 90, 91, 240,
    241
South Korea 109, 110, 111, 116
South Sulawesi 128
South Sumatra 128
South Yara 172
spatial concentration of investment
    128
spatial organisation 17
specialisation 38
Sri Lanka 111, 124, 250
Stowmarket 36, 46
Strathclyde 297, 301, 303, 307, 308
structural contingency model 12, 50,
    51
subcontracting 80, 82, 83
sub-modes of production 52
subsidiaries 57-9, 64

subsidies 322
Sulawesi 131
Sumatra 131
supermarkets 184
Surabaya 110, 127, 131, 136
Surfers' Paradise 172
Surrey 303
Swakopmund 95
Swaziland 89, 90, 95, 97, 98, 238,
    245, 247, 250, 253
Switzerland 286
Sydney 143, 152, 165, 170, 171, 173,
    183, 184, 190
symbolic environments 353, 354

Tahiti 176
Taiwan 109, 111, 136, 260
takeover 64-5, 70, 266, 267, 270,
    274
Tanganyika 238, 244, 245, 253
tariffs 322
Tasmania 170
tax incentives 134
technical change 286
technology 40
Thailand 29, 111, 163, 184, 248,
    250, 258
theory and the enterprise perspective
    348-51
theory of the firm 51
Third World investment 106
Third World Multinationals 106-11
    characteristics 107-9
    geographic focus 109-11
    geographic origins 109
tied-houses 90
Tokyo 357
Toronto 160, 171
tourism 133
Townsville 172
transactional cities 357
transfer of technology 46
transfer pricing 52
Trinidad 244, 245, 253
Tunisia 250
Turkey 221
Turks and Caicos Islands 242

Uganda 244, 253
United Kingdom 19, 27, 29, 36, 54,
    57, 69, 89, 102, 115, 144, 147,
    150, 151, 216, 236, 245, 282-310
    Bradford 295
    Doncaster 295

East Anglia 286, 296, 297, 309
East Midlands 299, 309
employment performance 296
manufacturing heartland 295
Merseyside 304
North 291, 295, 299, 304, 309
Northern Ireland 288, 291, 295,
    299, 304, 307
North West 296, 297, 304, 309
private industry 291
regional job losses 291-7
Scotland 286, 297, 304, 308, 309
South East 286, 291, 295, 296,
    297, 299, 301, 307, 309, 331
South West 309, 312
sub-regional job losses 297-303
Wales 291, 295, 296, 297, 304,
    309
West Midlands 295, 296, 301
Yorkshire and Humberside 295,
    296, 304, 309
'unofficial levies' 140
urban-rural shift 303
USA 57, 69, 87, 102, 115, 144, 147,
    150, 151, 163, 196, 216, 274, 286
US corporate investment in the

Philippines 260-5
US-Japanese joint ventures 264

Vancouver 160, 171, 184
vehicle and component manufacturers
    288
vertical integration 8
Victoria 170, 184

West Africa 230, 234
Western Australia 170
West Germany 27, 36, 46, 116, 196,
    216, 219
West Indies 230
Windhoek 95
withdrawal of producer services 158
workforce size 30, 32
world cities 143, 146

Yate 330
yen, internationalisation of 196, 197,
    222, 223
Yogyakarta 133, 134

Zaire 250
Zambia 29, 91, 93, 95, 98
Zimbabwe 89, 98